THE FOURTH GENEVA
CONVENTION FOR CIVILIANS

THE FOURTH GENEVA CONVENTION FOR CIVILIANS

The History of International Humanitarian Law

Gilad Ben-Nun

I.B.TAURIS
LONDON • NEW YORK • OXFORD • NEW DELHI • SYDNEY

I.B. TAURIS
Bloomsbury Publishing Plc
50 Bedford Square, London, WC1B 3DP, UK
1385 Broadway, New York, NY 10018, USA
29 Earlsfort Terrace, Dublin 2, Ireland

BLOOMSBURY, I.B. TAURIS and the I.B. Tauris logo are trademarks of
Bloomsbury Publishing Plc

First published in Great Britain 2020
This paperback edition published in 2021

Copyright © Gilad Ben-Nun 2020

Cover design by Charlotte James
Cover image: Signing on Geneva Conventions of War © Bettmann / Getty Images

A catalogue record for this book is available from the British Library.

A catalog record for this book is available from the Library of Congress

ISBN: 978-1-8386-0430-1
PB: 978-0-7556-4620-3
eISBN: 978-1-8386-0432-5
ePDF: 978-1-8386-0431-8

Typeset by Deanta Global Publishing Services, Chennai, India

To find out more about our authors and books visit www.bloomsbury.com and
sign up for our newsletters.

To Moshe Ben-Nun (1948–1973) and Haim Ben-Nun – in loco parentis.

CONTENTS

ILLUSTRATIONS

ACKNOWLEDGEMENTS

The research presented in this book was made possible thanks to the financial and thematic support accorded to me by several institutions. The bulk of the work on this study was made possible thanks to a generous EU Marie Curie Individual Fellowship, executed between 2016 and 2018 at Verona University's Department for Public International Law. The awarding of a research project of this nature to a historian and his placing into the daily workings of a law faculty is hardly self-evident. I would like to thank the EU Commission's Horizon 2020 program for allowing and encouraging the methodological focus upon interdisciplinarity, which facilitated this study's emphasis upon the intertwined relationship between history and international law. An initial seed-funding fellowship at the German Historical Institute in Paris (2015), allowed for the preliminary examination of the Fourth Geneva Convention ('GC-IV') files deposited at the archives of the French Foreign Ministry ('Quai d'Orsay') in Paris – La Courneuve. The fellowship in Paris also allowed for my first foray into the ICRC archives in Geneva. A final stay in Leipzig, first at the Leibniz Campus – Eastern Europe Global Area (EEGA) and then at the Leibniz Institute GWZO – provided the time and space for the study's final stages of writing and editing.

Along the way, several people contributed considerably to the development and elaboration of this research. My first and most significant debt is to Professor Annalisa Ciampi from Verona University (former UN special rapporteur for the Freedom of Assembly). Beyond her generous sharing of her vast academic and intellectual knowledge of international law, humanitarian law and the law of armed conflict, I would like to thank Annalisa for her friendship, her precious advice and, especially, for all the support she has accorded me over the last three years of our cooperation.

I owe a second debt to Stefan Troebst at Leipzig University. A teacher-turned-friend, Stefan's encyclopaedic knowledge of Eastern European history and the history of modern international law was repetitively drawn upon by me all along this study. The exposure of the former Soviet bloc's vital role in the making of GC-IV along this study are in large part thanks to Stefan's facilitation and 'door opening' efforts at the Bulgarian National Archives in Sofia. Over the years, his insistence on the relevance (and need) of deep archival studies for the understanding of the historical development of modern international law and its meaning has exerted a considerable amount of influence on my own intellectual development. This is a good place to pay due tributes in this regard.

As with all historical studies of this sort, we historians are heavily dependent upon the help and cooperation of archivists in the archives we research. I probably owe my biggest debt in this regard to Varban Todorov – chief political archivist at the Bulgarian National Archives in Sofia. Varban's deep knowledge of Soviet history, with his even broader grasp of modern European history, was paramount for my understanding of the reasons behind the Soviet interests to participate and support GC-IV back in 1949. In Paris' La Courneuve archives, Anne Liskine and the archive's director Pascal Evan provided generous support in locating the French files so vital to the understanding of GC-IV's earlier drafting. At the ICRC archives in Geneva, Fabrizio Bensi – upon whose help and support so many of us historians writing about the ICRC rely – was his usual helpful self, sharing his knowledge generously, and providing ideas as to where to further search for relevant materials.

Other people who helped, advised, argued, supported and shared their ideas with me during this study include Pierre Hazan, Adam Skordos, Dietmar Mueller, Frank Hadler, Antje Zettler, Joachim Feldmann, Martina Keilbach, Judge Paulo Albuquerque (European Court for Human Rights), Luigi Condorelli, Diana Mishkova, Gabriella Monaco and Raphael Gross. My friend and research assistant David Bayer provided strong support and friendship along this way as well.

Looking back from the vantage point of a second monograph, I realize the impact which former teachers have had upon my thinking and my intellectual development. The academic rigour (and generous personal character) of my teachers, Avihu Zakai and the late Michael Heyd, at the Hebrew University's History Department and those of my teachers in Leipzig University's Global Studies structures, Matthias Middell, Ulf Engel and Stefan Troebst, still govern much of the manner in which I think, analyse and research. In my conduct with my students, I try to emulate their generous, open and hospitable qualities, in the hope of matching up to the high humane bar they have set.

Geoffrey Best – a beacon of knowledge and research on the history of modern international law passed away during the writing of this study. Though I never knew him, I – like all scholars of modern laws of war – owe him a considerable intellectual debt for his pioneering work in this field of study from the 1980s onwards.

Traveling to eleven archives around the world, and between Verona and Frankfurt am Main, has taken considerable time away from my family, Tamar, Razi and especially Keren. All three laboured tirelessly in favour of this study. I am deeply grateful for their help and assistance in its making. Finally, this book is dedicated to my late father Moshe (Maurice) Ben-Nun – a victim of war, and to my beloved uncle Lt. Col. Haim Ben-Nun who endured three full scale wars during his lifetime. Both would most certainly have agreed with its underlying conclusion as to the importance of reinvigorating the international stature and application of the Fourth Geneva Convention for Civilians for our day and age.

[Pursuant to the rules and regulation stipulated by the European Commission, the author hereby officially acknowledges and confirms that this book's research was funded through an *EU Horizon 2020 EU Marie Curie Individual Fellowship*

Grant Agreement #701275, executed at Verona University's Law Faculty, between September 2016 and August 2018. The author further acknowledges funding granted by the German Historical Institute in Paris (September–December 2015), the Leibniz Gemeinschaft's EEGA Science Campus at Leipzig University's Centre for Area Studies (September 2018–April 2019), and by the Leiniz Institute GWZO in Leipzig – who provided the final support, space and extra costs necessary for the completion and production of this manuscript.]

INTRODUCTION: 'A TREATY AFTER TRAUMA'

> The 'Geneva story' has scarcely so far been told except by lawyers to lawyers. … It can be told (and richly merits being told) more amply and historically.[1]

The miracle that was Geneva – August 1949

At 10.30 am on 1 August 1949, in a conference hall in Geneva, the 74-year-old French ambassador to the Geneva Convention's Conference of Plenipotentiaries requested the floor in order to say a few words. Turning to the Swiss Federal Counsellor Max Petitpierre, the ambassador congratulated the Swiss dignitary upon the occasion of his county's National Day. In his remarks, the Frenchman specifically emphasized the Swiss government's long-standing and heart-warming hospitality, which it had accorded the delegates over the past four months. He also stressed his gratitude to the conference's staff of translators and diplomatic administrators, who were hard at work on what should have been their national holiday. Applauded by the plenary, Petitpierre cordially thanked the French ambassador in turn for his warm words and stressed the Swiss government's sincere wish that the Conference of Plenipotentiaries would turn out to be a diplomatic success.[2] Upon receiving another round of applause, Petitpierre swiftly returned to the substantive discussion of articles and amendments – the usual daily routine of this international gathering.

Current readers of the Geneva Convention's *Final Record* might assume that this was little more than a cordial exchange of niceties between delegates within the routine context of a diplomatic conference. In fact, few statements within the *Final Record*'s four volumes and several thousands of pages were more laden

---

1. Geoffrey Best, *War and Law since 1945* (Oxford: Oxford University Press, 1994), p. 80.

2. *Final Record of the Diplomatic Conference of Geneva of 1949*, Berne: Federal Political Department, 1950 (hereinafter 'Final Record'). vol. 2-B, pp. 362–3, statements of Cahen-Salvador (France) and Petitpierre (president). For Cahen-Salvador's special emphasis on Switzerland's hospitality, see the *in extenso* stenograms of the deliberations of 1 August 1949's morning session. The *Final Record* succinctly summarized these comments and edited out some of them in its final book-bound printed version, published by the Swiss federal government in 1950.

with sub-textual meanings than this one. After all, just five years earlier, in the harsh winter of 1943–4, that same French ambassador, Georges Cahen-Salvador, along with his family, had fled Transport No. 62, which had departed the Drancy concentration camp north of Paris bound for Auschwitz. After a journey of some 500 kilometres southwards, they all arrived on the French–Swiss border at the Canton of Geneva. In late November 1943, the entire Cahen-Salvador family received *Genevois* asylum – their lives spared, in stark opposition to the fate of so many other Jews during the Second World War.

Now, a mere six years after receiving his *Genevois* asylum, Georges Cahen-Salvador – the chairman of the Fourth Geneva Convention for Civilians (GC-IV), here at this final Conference of Plenipotentiaries – would voice his gratitude. This was the man who had overseen the elaboration of GC-IV's very first draft at the 'Quai d'Orsay', diplomatic shorthand for the headquarters of the French Foreign Ministry, back in 1946–7 (as we will see in 'Omission 2'), the man who had served as GC-IV's chairperson during its elaboration at the 1948 XVII Red Cross Conference in Stockholm and the man who now chaired its final proceedings in Geneva in 1949.

As he stood to pay his tribute to Switzerland's 'spirit of brotherhood and of solidarity',[3] on whose behalf exactly was he speaking? Was it simply on account of all the country delegates present in that room during that early-August summer day?

Perhaps – and much more likely – he was speaking on his very own personal account: on behalf of his family and his children – and even his first grandchild, who had been born in Drancy in August 1943, and who had also been saved at that Franco–Swiss frontier in November 1943.

As Cahen-Salvador looked Max Petitpierre in the eye and thanked the Swiss federal counsellor for 'Switzerland's welcome', both men understood full well the sub-textual significance of the Jewish Frenchman's words. To be sure, all the other country delegates in the room that morning understood them just as well. In fact, during the final signing of the Geneva Conventions, celebrated ceremonially with full diplomatic decorum in December 1949, only two speeches were delivered in the name of all the country delegates present – one by Petitpierre, on behalf of Switzerland as the host, and one by Cahen-Salvador, who was accompanied on that occasion by the Italian ambassador.[4]

---

3. Final Record, Vol. 2-B, p. 362.

4. Israel State Archives (ISA) Foreign Ministry Files (MFA): ISA reference: ISA/ RG 93.38/1-31/MFA 10/ 19, Ministry of Foreign Affairs, Division of International Organizations, Files from the Israeli Delegation in Geneva, Memo No. 111, Re: Signature of the Geneva Conventions 1949, Geneva, 9 December 1949: 'According to the program fixed in advance, the only speeches were those of the President and – in the name of all the other dignitaries – of the delegate of France.'

The Fourth Geneva Convention for Civilians – a full
and comprehensive picture of its drafting history

In the entire history of modern international law, there exists only one set of treaties to which all United Nations (UN) member states have acceded, and which they have all signed and ratified – the Geneva Conventions of 1949.[5] Within these four conventions, it is the Fourth Geneva Convention for the Protection of Civilians that is seen today as a true crowning achievement of modern diplomacy post Second World War. Since the end of the Cold War, all international criminal tribunals – without exception – that have been set up by the international community to judge war crimes perpetrators, have relied on GC-IV's formulations for their statutes.[6] The 1998 Rome Statute of the International Criminal Court at The Hague (the ICC) actually begins its definition of war crimes with a reference to 'grave breaches of the Geneva Convention of 12 August 1949'.[7] If there should ever be a future international criminal tribunal to try the perpetrators of war crimes in today's Syria or Yemen, there is little doubt that its statutes would also depend on GC-IV's written letter.

With this almost primordial international legal stature, one would assume that over the course of the seventy years that have elapsed since its adoption, research concerning GC-IV would have yielded a full and comprehensive picture of its drafting history. Instead, and until now, research has hardly paid any attention at all to the treaty's drafters – to who these people actually were, and to how they perceived their work drafting this vital international humanitarian legal treaty. The current volume attempts to plug this research gap, and it will do so initially by highlighting several critical oversights in the prevailing scholarship (see 'Significant Historical Omissions in the Current GC-IV Literature').

To be sure, were the International Committee of the Red Cross (ICRC) to attempt to legislate GC-IV nowadays, there is virtually no chance that this treaty –

5. Frédéric Mégret, 'The Universality of the Geneva Conventions', in Andrew Clapham, Paola Gaeta and Marco Sassoli (eds.), *The 1949 Geneva Conventions: A Commentary* (Oxford: Oxford University Press, 2016), pp. 669–88.

6. Article 2 of the International Criminal Tribunal for the Former Yugoslavia (ICTY) states that this 'International Tribunal shall have the power to prosecute persons committing or ordering to be committed grave breaches of the Geneva Convention of 12 August 1949'. See the ICTY statute. Available at: http://www.icty.org/x/file/Legal%20Library/Statute/stat ute_sept09_en.pdf

Article 4 of the International Criminal Tribunal for Rwanda (ICTR), entitled 'Violations of Article 3 Common to the Geneva Conventions', states that the ICTR 'shall have the power to prosecute persons committing or ordering to be committed serious violations of Article 3 common to the Geneva Conventions of 12 August 1949'. See the ICTR statute. Available at: http://legal.un.org/avl/pdf/ha/ictr_EF.pdf.

7. The ICC's Rome Statute Article 8 paragraph 2. See the ICC Rome Statute. Available at: https://www.icc-cpi.int/nr/rdonlyres/ea9aeff7-5752-4f84-be94-0a655eb30e16/0/rome_ statute_english.pdf.

with its remarkable humanitarian pervasiveness – would be adopted by the world's current states; it simply would not see the light of day. Even under the remote eventuality that today's nation states could be brought to agree on some of its humanitarian principles, these would most probably be so deeply conditioned and qualified that no state, or war criminal, could have ever be held accountable for their deeds under its precepts.

Yet, what seems today diplomatically impossible in fact materialized between 1946 and 1949. Unqualified sentences such as Common Article 3's famous 'the following acts are and shall remain prohibited at any time and in any place whatsoever' were actually adopted by the majority of the world's states who were present at GC-IV's creation (Figure 1).

In contrast to virtually all the UN treaties from this period – which were, with the sole exception of the 1948 Genocide Convention, boycotted by the Soviets – the

Figure 1 Ambassador Georges Cahen-Salvador signing the Geneva Conventions for France, 12 August 1949. On the right, Swiss Federal Counsellor Max Petitpierre. © ICRC Photo Archives – Geneva 2018.

Figure 2 Opening ceremony of the Geneva Conference of Plenipotentiaries, 21 April 1949. Seated on the front row, third from the left: Rabbi Dr Georg Cohn, head of the Delegation for Denmark. © ICRC Photo Archives – Geneva 2018.

Soviet bloc actively participated in the treaty's making and, upon its conclusion, immediately acceded to its provisions. In fact (as we shall see in 'Omission 3'), without the Soviet bloc's active participation in GC-IV's most crucial drafting phase, at the 1949 Geneva Plenipotentiaries' Conference, the document would most probably not have been adopted – at the very least, not in its current, strongly worded form (Figure 2).

In hindsight, the treaty's final adoption in August 1949 – after three long years of tireless diplomatic drafting, countless clashes and existential moments, at which many thought this convention would never see the light of day – seems little short of miraculous.

One of GC-IV's most striking features, which has thus far been entirely overlooked by scholars, concerns the fact that several of its most influential drafters were Jews who had only recently survived the 1939–45 Nazi Holocaust. These included GC-IV's chairman, Georges Cahen-Salvador, who signed it on France's behalf, and Nissim Mevorah, the Civilian Convention's Bulgarian Soviet vice president, who had been spared the Holocaust's worst excesses and who oversaw its signing by the Soviet bloc countries.

They also included Georg Cohn, who, three decades earlier, had attempted to outlaw aggressive conquest as the first drafter of the non-recognition principle of territorial acquisition by force (later known as the 'Stimson Doctrine', after Henry L. Stimson, US secretary of state in the Hoover Administration, who finally instituted it). Rabbi Dr Cohn signed the convention on behalf of his native country, Denmark.

As a religious Jew, in October 1943, Cohn had also been forced to flee – leaving Denmark for asylum in neighbouring, neutral Sweden. All through GC-IV's various drafting stages, it was Cohn who headed a group of 'universalist' countries that argued in favour of the widest humanitarian protections available, at the expense of nation states' interests.

Publishing a book in 2019 about GC-IV, some seventy years after its conclusion, immediately invites the most perennial of questions: Does it matter at all? These days, with the blood of so many civilians being shed the world over and on a daily basis, what is the point of writing a history book about a convention that everybody (state and non-state actors alike) seems bent on breaching?

The short answer to these questions is that over the past seventy years – and especially when compared with the period from the Italian conquest of Ethiopia (then known as Abyssinia) in 1935, through the 1938 Japanese rape of Nanjing to the Nazi atrocities of the Second World War – GC-IV has, in fact, had an immense impact – especially on the life of civilians. Recent studies go so far as to convincingly demonstrate that even rebel groups are far more compliant with its tenets than we tend to assume.[8] When the UN deserted Rwanda during its 1994 genocide, the ICRC stayed on there. During those dark 100 days of genocide, it saved well over 65,000 people in that tiny East African republic. As we shall see, had it not been for Georges Cahen-Salvador and the World Jewish Congress delegate, Gerhart Riegner, in Stockholm in 1948, the ICRC would never have had the legal basis to intervene in genocidal situations in which a government annihilates its own nationals. Back in the late 1940s, it was the ICRC itself that was most opposed to this new responsibility that it now received from state parties. Forty-five years later, it assumed these responsibilities with an unbelievable degree of humanitarian heroism.

When weighing in the responses to the oft-voiced question 'Why have this treaty in the first place if no one abides by it?', it is worthwhile to recall the audiences to whom this question is being addressed. Rwandans, who were saved by the ICRC during their 1994 genocide habitually have a very different, and distinctly more affirmative, take on this question. West Bank Palestinians, who for the past half century have been occupied and oppressed by Israel, certainly have ample grounds to criticize GC-IV's continuing non-application in their regard. Yet confronted with the hypothetical question whether their condition would be better in a world devoid GC-IV, few (if any) would subscribe for this option. Once the issue is formulated thus, and posed to the societies most affected by GC-IV's breaches or outright non-application, the obvious answer as to its vital role immediately surfaces. Civilians who themselves have been impacted upon by war and armed conflict are usually the first to attest to the fact that the little help they did (and in the Palestinian case – still do) receive under their hard condition, often stemmed from

---

8. Hyeran Jo, *Compliant Rebels: Rebel Groups and International Law in World Politics* (Cambridge: Cambridge University Press, 2015), pp. 40–78; 110–22.

organizations and international legal procedures whose ontological foundation lie in GC-IV's text.

This book, then, comes to tell the story of the marvel of diplomacy known as GC-IV. It attempts to explain how this feat of diplomatic success came about by looking at the human protagonists who laboured for it and made it happen. In order to understand their thoughts and actions during this treaty's three-year drafting process, it retraces their biographies and attempts to understand how they themselves understood their own considerable diplomatic achievement in 1949.

The structure of this book

A considerable amount of attention has been dedicated over the years to GC-IV research in several disciplines: international law,[9] history,[10] international relations[11]

---

9. Geoffrey Best, *War and Law since 1945* (Oxford: Clarendon Press, 1994), pp. 80–179. Paul de la Pradelle, *La Conférence diplomatique et les nouvelles conventions de Genéve du 12 août 1949* (Paris: Editions Internationals, 1951) (hereinafter 'La Pradelle – La Conférence diplomatique'). Jean Pictet, *Commentary on the Geneva Convention Relative to the Protection of Civilian Persons in Time of War 12 August 1949*, Vol. IV (Geneva: ICRC, 1958) (hereinafter 'Pictet Commentary'). G. I. A. D. Draper, *The Red Cross Conventions* (London: Stevens & Sons Ltd., 1958). Hersch Lauterpacht (ed.), *Oppenheim's International Law*, Vol. I *Peace* (8th edn), Vol. II *Disputes War and Neutrality* (7th edn) (London: Longman Green & Co., 1955).

10. Monty Noam Penkower, 'The World Jewish Congress Confronts the International Red Cross during the Holocaust', *Jewish Social Studies*, vol. 41, no. 3/4 (Summer–Autumn 1979), pp. 229–56. Arieh Ben-Tov, *Das Rote Kreuz kam zu spät – Die Auseinandersetzung zwischen dem jüdischen Volk und dem internationalen Komitee vom Roten Kreuz im Zweiten Weltkrieg – Die Ereignisse in Ungarn* (Zurich: Amman Verlag, 1990). Geoffrey Best, *Humanity in Warfare: Modern History of the International Law of Armed Conflicts* (London: Routledge, 1983). Geoffrey Best, 'The Making of the 4th Geneva Conventions: The View from Whitehall', in Christophe Swinarski (ed.), *Studies and Essays on International Humanitarian Law and Red Cross Principles in Honour of Jean Pictet* (The Hague: Martinus Nijhoff, 1984), pp. 5–15. Amitzur Ilan, *Bernadotte in Palestine, 1948: A Study in Contemporary Humanitarian Knight-Errantry* (London: Macmillan & St. Antony's College, Oxford, 1989), pp. 49–55, 181–3. David Forsythe, *The Humanitarians: The International Committee of the Red Cross* (Cambridge: Cambridge University Press, 2005), pp. 49–60. Dominique-Debora Junod, *La Croix-Rouge en péril, 1945-1952. La stratégie du CICR, de la Seconde Guerre mondiale au conflit de Palestine – Eretz-Israël* (Lausanne: Payot, 1997). English translation: *The Imperilled Red Cross and the Palestine-Eretz Yisrael Conflict 1945-1952* (London: Paul Kegan and The Geneva Graduate Institute for International Studies, 2001) (hereinafter 'Junod Red Cross in Palestine'). Isabelle Vichniac, *Croix-Rouge, les stratèges de la bonne conscience: Enquete* (Paris: Alain Moreau, 1988).

11. Giovanni Mantilla, 'Forum Isolation: Social Opprobrium and the Origins of the International Law of Internal Conflict', *International Organization*, vol. 72, no. 2 (2018),

and political science.[12] A comprehensive drafting history that intertwines the legal making of the GC-IV legal substance into the biographical background of its drafters, as set against its distinct historical context, has thus far not been written. This book comes to address this gap. It does so by drawing attention to three aspects that, with the benefit of historical hindsight, seem among the most crucial to GC-IV's subsequent impacts. Correspondingly, each of its three parts focuses on one of these aspects. Notwithstanding the deliberate effort undertaken here to combine materials from various academic disciplines to tell this story, this study's first concentration, nevertheless, is on the GC-IV archival sources uncovered along its research, many of which were not available to earlier scholars.

Part One of the book looks at GC-IV's most fundamental principle, also enshrined in the now-famous Common Article 3 of all four Geneva Conventions – *Protection for All*. Nowadays, Common Article 3's basic provisions – which prohibit summary executions, hostage taking and torture and degrading treatment – are all considered an integral part of customary international law. They bind everyone, everywhere, with no exceptions. People in other types of conflicts, notably in International Armed Conflict – (IAC) (between two state parties), are eligible for higher levels of legal protection than that applicable to Non-International Armed Conflict – NIAC (within one state). Yet no argument can be made for Common Article 3's *non-applicability* – once an armed conflict has recognizably erupted. It is the minimum threshold and the bedrock minimum of protection for all people, which applies under all armed conflict circumstances.

Initially, however, this was certainly *not* everybody's intention. Rather, each party came to the drafting table with specific groups of people hitherto not protected, whom it wished the newly elaborated Geneva Convention for Civilians to now cover. Throughout GC-IV's three-year drafting process, the drafters gradually came to the understanding that they could not endlessly enumerate all the categories of people to be protected by the Civilian Convention, while defining those who ought to be excluded from its protective purview. The decision *not to enumerate anyone* – and, therefore, *to cover all* – was proposed by GC-IV's chairman, Georges Cahen-Salvador, in 1948 in Stockholm and was accepted there. It was he who also provided the French compromise solution at the 1949 Geneva Conference of Plenipotentiaries, when the diplomatic 'going got tough'. This finally

pp. 317–49. Giovanni Mantilla, 'The Origins and Evolution of the 1949 Geneva Conventions and the 1977 Additional Protocols', in Matthew Evangelista and Nina Tannenwald (eds.), *Do the Geneva Conventions Matter?* (Oxford: Oxford University Press, 2017), pp. 43–9, note 17–30. Giovanni Mantilla, 'Conforming Instrumentalists: Why the United States and the United Kingdom Joined the 1949 Geneva Conventions', *European Journal of International Law*, vol. 28, no. 2 (2017), pp. 483–511. Boyd van Dijk, 'Human Rights in War: On the Entangled Foundations of the 1949 Geneva Conventions', *American Journal of International Law*, vol. 112, no. 4 (2018), pp. 553–82.

12. Matthew Evangelista and Nina Tannenwald (eds.), *Do the Geneva Conventions Matter?* (Oxford: Oxford University Press, 2017).

saved Common Article 3 from being expunged from the Geneva Conventions text and allowed for its inclusion in the final document.

Part Two looks at what has arguably become one of GC-IV's most politically contentious aspects: its prohibition on settlements and colonization by conquerors who wish to transfer their native population into a territory that they have occupied militarily. Israel's settlements in Palestine, Turkey's conquest and repopulation of Northern Cyprus, Russia's illegal occupation of Eastern Ukraine and Crimea, Morocco's grip on Western Sahara and Armenia's actions in Nagorno-Karabakh are all examples of places where the 'inherent illegitimacy of occupation' has continued long beyond any international legal acceptability. As we shall see, Georg Cohn – the author of this prohibition (known formally as GC-IV's Article 49 paragraph 6) – inscribed it into the Civilian Convention's text in Stockholm almost single-handedly.

One important aspect currently absent from all accounts of GC-IV's making is the fact that the very same Rabbi, Dr George Cohn, was also the person who, back in 1922, had devised the principle of non-recognition of territorial acquisition by force – later known as the so-called Stimson Doctrine. All through the 1930s, Cohn would 'intellectually butt heads' with none other than the German jurist Carl Schmitt about what the former saw as the *a priori* non-legitimacy of conquest – and which Schmitt, of course, came to internationally substantiate in his Third Reich-era concept of *Grossraum*.[13] Seen in this light, then, GC-IV's prohibition on conquerors transferring their own population into their newly occupied territory should be understood in its larger legal context. For its drafter, Georg Cohn, it formed an integral part of the broader international prohibition on aggressive conquest, which began with the 1928 Briand-Kellogg Pact and which peaked fifteen years after Cohn's death, with the UN General Assembly's 1970 Declaration on Principles of International Law concerning Friendly Relations and Co-operation among States.[14] Aggressive conquest ought not to lead to a change of territorial title: when conquest occurs, the territory conquered is thus *occupied* –

13. Gilad Ben-Nun, 'Territorial Conquest: Its Prevalence, Demise, and Resurfacing: 1880s to the Present', *Connections: A Journal for Historians and Area Specialists*, 23 March 2019. Available at: www.connections.clio-online.net/article/id/artikel-4741.

14. *UN General Assembly Declaration on Principles of International Law concerning Friendly Relations and Cooperation among States in accordance with the Charter of the United Nations*, adopted 24 October 1970. UN. Doc. A/RES/25/2625. This Declaration repeats Cohn's principle of non-recognition of territorial acquisition by force as follows:

> The territory of a State shall not be the object of military occupation resulting from the use of force in contravention of the provisions of the Charter. The territory of a State shall not be the object of acquisition by another State resulting from the threat or use of force. No territorial acquisition resulting from the threat or use of force shall be recognized as legal. (Declaration's Point 1, paragraph 10)

The UN website is available at: http://www.un-documents.net/a25r2625.htm (accessed 26 January 2019).

precisely in order to block its international title from passing from the conquered to the conqueror.

Part Three looks at what has arguably been GC-IV's most painful handicap: states' attempts to routinely argue for its non-applicability. Remarkably, and in stark contrast to these often contemptible attempts by nation states, High Courts, both domestic (as in the United States and Israel) and international (the International Court of Justice – ICJ), have routinely and consistently held that GC-IV's provisions – and, especially, its Common Article 3 – always apply, in any place and to any person whatsoever. This high judicial consistency, both locally and internationally, has certainly *not* been demonstrated by these High Courts solely under legal 'laboratory conditions'. On the contrary, the judgement of the US Supreme Court in favour of Common Article 3's applicability after 9/11 and the Israeli Supreme Court's judgement in the midst of Israel's war and occupation of Lebanon in 1983 point precisely to its powerful effectiveness – notably in times of military stress and duress. The ICJ's own application of the Geneva Convention under a NIAC which pitted East against West during the Cold War in Nicaragua (*Nicaragua* vs. *United States* – 1986) is also surprising given that, back in 1949, the right of this very court to adjudicate over this treaty was mooted by its drafters. As we shall see in Chapter 8, the very same individual who removed the ICJ's prerogative to adjudicate over GC-IV in 1949 (Soviet delegate to the Geneva Conference of Plenipotentiaries Platon Morosov) would be the person to reinstall this right upon the World Court some forty years later – as he himself came to sit on its bench.

Chapter 1

BACKGROUND: SIGNIFICANT HISTORICAL OMISSIONS IN THE CURRENT GC-IV LITERATURE

Notwithstanding the advances in our understanding of the Civilian Convention's drafting and its historical circumstances, and despite Geoffrey Best's, Giovanni Mantilla's, Boyd van Dijk's and others' important contributions, several important omissions have been critically overlooked by all this previous scholarship, which requires highlighting at this early stage.[1] The remedying of these historical lacunae might also turn out to be of some importance for GC-IV's future legal interpretation, if and when legal scholars turn to debating questions concerning its drafters' true intentions for this treaty's provisions.[2] In this regard, one must recall

---

1. For Best's, Mantilla's and van Dijk's works see notes 9–12 in 'introduction'. Other important works include Cathrine Rey-Schyrr, *De Yalta à Dien Bien Phu: Histoire du Comité International de la Croix Rouge 1945-1955* (Genève: CICR 2007). Translated into English as: *From Yalta to Dien Bien Phu: History of the International Committee of the Red Cross 1945-1955* (Geneva: ICRC, 2017), pp. 209–51. William Hitchcock, 'Human Rights and the Laws of War: The Geneva Conventions of 1949', in Akira Iriye, Petra Goedde and William Hitchcock (eds.), *The Human Rights Revolution: An International History* (Oxford: Oxford University Press, 2012). Mark Lewis, *The Birth of the New Justice: The Internationalization of Crime and Punishment, 1919-1950* (Oxford: Oxford University Press, 2014), pp. 229–73. François Bugnion, 'Le Comité international de la Croix-Rouge et les Nations Unies de 1945 à nos jours: oppositions, complémentarités et partenariats', *Relations internationales*, no. 152 (2012/4), pp. 3–16.

2. One recent example of how a rift in the interpretation of international treaties can result in the difference between life and death concerns the question as to whether the non-refoulement principle of refugee protection applies on the high seas. The European Court for Human Rights' recent affirmative interpretation of non-refoulement's exterritorial applicability at sea has radically changed European policy in the Mediterranean, reversing the policy of 'push back' operations against seafaring asylum seekers and replacing it with search-and-rescue operations by European naval vessels. One can directly attribute the thousands of lives saved by these European navies to a change in the legal interpretation of the 1951 Refugee Convention due to this European Court ruling. The ruling was effected, to a large extent, thanks to the court's effort to ascertain the original intentions of the drafters

the considerable methodological divergence that exists between international jurists and historians. While the former are bound to view international treaties' *travaux préparatoires* (official records of the negotiation leading up to the final document) as secondary in importance to those treaties' textual reading,[3] a textual reading of any document divorced from its historical context and biographical reference to its drafters would be abhorrent to most (if not all) historians.[4] Thus, before delving into the book's three substantive parts, in the following pages I wish to briefly highlight six historical omissions – without whose explanation much of the reasoning behind the drafters' thinking might not be fully appreciated.

Omission 1: Jewish Holocaust-surviving delegates and the impact of the Second World War experiences on the GC-IV drafters

While much has been written about the ICRC and the Jewish Holocaust, the first important omission concerning GC-IV's drafting pertains to the fact that many of its key drafters were either Holocaust-surviving Jews or delegates who had experienced the Second World War's horrors in the most personal manner.[5] To

of the 1951 Refugee Convention concerning whether they would have assumed that non-refoulement's validity existed on land only, or rather in any place where a refugee was in plight – in stark contrast to the opinion of the US Supreme Court, which has maintained its textual interpretation of non-refoulement. See Gilad Ben-Nun, *Seeking Asylum in Israel: Refugees and the History of Migration Law* (London: I.B. Tauris, 2017), pp. 51–86.

3. Pursuant to common treaty-interpretation regulations as set out by the 1969 Vienna Convention on the Laws of Treaties Articles 31 and 33.

4. J. D. Mortenson, 'The Travaux of Travaux: Is the Vienna Convention Hostile to Drafting History?' *American Journal of International Law*, vol. 107, no. 4 (October 2013), pp. 780–822. Also see J. Klabbers, 'International Legal Histories: The Declining Importance of Travaux Préparatoires in Treaty Interpretation?' *Netherlands International Law Review*, vol. 50, no. 3 (December 2003), pp. 267–88.

5. Jean-Claude Favez, *Une Mission Impossible? Le CICR, les deportations et les camps de concentration nazis* (Lausanne: Editions Payot, 1988). Translated as: *The Red Cross and the Holocaust* (Cambridge: Cambridge University Press, 1998). Gerald Steinacher, *Nazis on the Run: How Hitler's Henchmen Fled Justice* (Oxford: Oxford University Press, 2011), Ch. 2: 'The Co-Responsibility of the International Red Cross', pp. 55–90. Gerald Steinacher, *Hakenkreuz und Rotes Kreuz: Eine humanitäre Organisation zwischen Holocaust und Flüchtlingsproblematik* (Innsbruck: Studien Verlag, 2013). Gerald Steinacher, *Humanitarians at War: The Red Cross in the Shadow of the Holocaust* (Oxford: Oxford University Press, 2017). In the current author's opinion, Kimberley Lowe's recent critiques of Steinacher are completely unmerited and probably have more to do with the often-ugly tendencies of younger upcoming scholars to carve out their own academic niche by downplaying the work of others. Steinacher's insistence on controversial ICRC president Carl Burckhardt's vile anti-Semitism, which subsequently surfaced in the guise of the committee's

date, none of the publications engaged with the treaty's drafting history has paid any attention to this important historical fact.

As previously mentioned, Georges Cahen-Salvador was the Civilian Convention's chairman both in 1948 in Stockholm and during the 1949 Geneva Conference of Plenipotentiaries. Back in 1940 and following the enactment of the *Statute Juif* in 1940, Cahen-Salvador was stripped of all his titles and dismissed from his presidency-section role at the Conseil d'état. The Cahen-Salvador family members were then incarcerated in the Drancy concentration camp. On the night of 20 November 1943, their names were included in Adolph Eichmann's deportation order of Transport No. 62 from Drancy to Auschwitz.[6] Thanks probably to the help of former colleagues who now served in the French Vichy government, Cahen-Salvador's train was stopped en route near Lerouville, where nineteen members of his family were taken off. After a subsequent journey of some 500 kilometres, they reached the Swiss border, where, on 23 November 1943, the entire family received its political asylum in Geneva.[7]

The Civilian Convention's vice chairman representing the Soviet bloc during the 1949 Geneva Conference of Plenipotentiaries – Nissim Mevorah, whose efforts largely facilitated the adoption of Common Article 3 there – survived the Holocaust by hiding in the Bulgarian capital, Sofia, throughout the war. Rabbi Dr Georg Cohn – the Danish delegate and leader of the 'universalist' states, who

non-intervention on behalf of European Jewry, in fact continued until the Holocaust-surviving delegates Cahen-Salvador, Gerhart Riegner and Georg Cohn – as states' delegates – simply put right the ICRC on its refusal to accept Common Article 3's all-encompassing nature (see Chapter 3, this volume). In the case of Article 49 paragraph 6 (the prohibition on the transfer of the occupier's own population into the occupied territory), as drafted by Georg Cohn in Stockholm, the ICRC yet again objected to the insertion of this text, which has subsequently turned out to be arguably GC-IV's most important contribution to current international affairs (see the Israeli occupation of Palestine, Turkey in Northern Cyprus, etc.). Lowe's comment that the ICRC was in the driving seat in 1949 in Geneva is factually wrong – the ICRC in fact debated, in the first place, if it should appear in Geneva at all. In short, subsequent historical scholarship (including the current volume) fully confirms virtually all of Steinacher's claims. Commentators and their commissioning editors (in this case, the well-respected German H-Net) should know better. For Lowe's flawed commentary, see Kimberly A. Lowe. Review of Steinacher, Gerald, *Humanitarians at War*. H-Diplo, H-Net Reviews. October 2017. Available at: http://www.h-net.org/reviews/showrev.php?id=49718.

6. Serge Klarsfeld, *La Shoah en France. Volume 3, Le calendrier de la persécution des Juifs de France. Tome 3, septembre 1942-août 1944* (Paris: Fayard, 2001), p. 1705.

7. See the official registry of persons who requested entry into the Canton of Geneva during the Second World War. Archive of the Canton of Geneva (*Archive d'état de Genève*), pp. 1–26 at 1. Available on the official online webpage of the Archive at: http://etat.geneve.ch/dt/SilverpeasWebFileServer/c.pdf?ComponentId=kmelia106&SourceFile=1249035575442.pdf&MimeType=application/pdf&Directory=Attachment/Images.

drafted the prohibition on colonization and settlements (Article 49 paragraph 6) and who successfully opposed the British motion for a non-limitation of the death penalty (Article 68) – escaped in a fishing boat across the Oresund Strait from Denmark to Sweden one night before Nazi SS (paramilitary *Schutzstaffel*) officers came to deport him and his entire family to the Theresienstadt ghetto (on Czech territory) on 2 October 1943.

In theory, one could make a bold claim that, granted these delegates' personal traumatic experiences merely four years prior to the Civilian Convention's signing, as they came to sit at the GC-IV drafting table they carried forward not their own ideas but rather those of their respective governments. This claim has a certain amount of truth to it. Yet the historical facts here attest to something much more fundamental: these delegates had been the ones to shape the humanitarian positions advocated for by their governments in the first place. France's nomination of Cahen-Salvador as its delegate in Stockholm and Geneva stemmed from his leadership of the entire effort to produce the draft Civilian Convention text, which France tabled at the ICRC's Government Experts' Conference in 1947. One would be hard pressed to brush off Cahen-Salvador's insistence (following a motion from the World Jewish Congress) that Common Article 3 cover all people including those targeted by their own governments, in a direct rebuff to the ICRC's official positions, as simply representing his government's position. In fact, Cahen-Salvador himself would explicitly mention his own *personal* Holocaust experiences as a key motivation for his positions throughout GC-IV's drafting (see Chapter 3).

As early as February 1948, six months prior to Stockholm, Nissim Mevorah was charged by the Bulgarian government with leading – on behalf of all Soviet bloc countries – a consolidated effort to articulate their positions vis-à-vis the proposed upcoming Civilian Convention text. As for Rabbi Dr Cohn, not only was he given a completely free hand by his government to fully articulate Danish positions concerning GC-IV prior to both Stockholm and Geneva but he was also tasked with the active coordination of his positions with those of the Nordic countries, Sweden and Norway, via close work with their delegates, whom he knew well – respectively, Torsten Gihl and Frede Castberg.

In addition, ample evidence points to similar impacts that the events of the Second World War had on other delegates present at GC-IV's various drafting tables. Speaking to the British Red Cross in 1957, the renowned jurist and scholar Colonel G. I. A. D. Draper explained the recent conflict's impacts on the realization of the Civilian Convention:

> This Civilian Convention was called into being by the civilized States of the community of nations as a direct result of the experience of the Second World War. ... In Auschwitz Concentration Camp alone 2 ½ million civilians died by gassing ... shooting, flogging, torture, hanging, starvation, typhus and tuberculosis. As the Commandant Hoess explained to me: 'if a prisoner should by any chance have escaped and should tell what occurred in the camp, nobody

would believe him.' He spoke the truth. ... Such a passage in man's affairs has cast a cloud of shame over all humanity that will not be removed for many a day.[8]

Draper was part of the British delegation to both Stockholm and Geneva, and would continue to advise the ICRC on a wide range of issues well into the 1960s.[9] The most remarkable feature of his statement, quoted above, concerns his *personal* experience of the ramifications of the Second World War, which echoed also in ICRC circles.[10] Draper did not just read about these events or overhear someone else referring to them; he *felt* them, first-hand, as the Auschwitz's commandant Rudolph Hoess had spoken specifically and directly to him.[11] This immediate, unbridled impact of the war facilitated the transfer of its horrors directly to GC-IV's drafting tables by its delegates who had witnessed it first-hand.

The acute and personal experiences of those delegates who represented member states in Geneva have been grossly overlooked by historians and international jurists alike. During the debate regarding GC-IV's Resolution 8 (see the so-called Mexican Resolution in 'Omission 4'), the Romanian delegate, Mrs Luca, provided a harrowing statement concerning her own experiences during the war:

I feel I must speak as one who has seen the ordeals suffered during the last war. My father, then sixty-two years old, and my two brothers with their families, were exterminated like hundreds of thousands of my fellow-countrymen. ... For three years, I witnessed the indescribable sufferings inflicted on the Soviet people in the zones occupied by the Germans. I still hear the cries of those women, of mothers maddened by grief in seeing their children killed by the machine-guns of aircraft at low altitude or exterminated in barbarous destructions which were not necessitated by any military exigency. I can see before my eyes sealed railway vans, thousands of men, women and children buried, half-living, in common

---

8. Michael A. Meyer and Hilaire McCoubrey, *Reflections on Law and Armed Conflicts: The Selected Works on the Laws of War by the late Professor Colonel G.I.A.D. Draper. OBE* (The Hague: Kluwer Law, 1998), p. 58.

9. For Draper's long-standing relationship with the ICRC well into the 1960s, see Chapter 9, n. 9.

10. *Pictet Commentary*, vol. 4, p. 5: 'In 1945 the work of revising the Conventions was overshadowed by the imperative necessity of extending their benefits to civilians. As President Max Huber so strikingly puts it, "War, as it becomes more and more total, annuls the differences which formerly existed between armies and civilian populations in regard to exposure to injury and danger."'

11. Draper served through the entire war in the British armed forces and was later part of the UK prosecution team at Nuremberg under Sir Maxwell Fyfe; he also served on the UK team assigned to the drafting of the new Geneva Conventions.

graves. Are so many innocent victims to be forgotten? Are they to be followed by others? Can we contemplate a new Auschwitz, Dachau, Buchenwald?[12]

This is a powerful statement by a country delegate, incorporated into the Geneva Conventions' *travaux préparatoires*. It demonstrates the intimate and specific knowledge of the atrocities of the Second World War, personally suffered by a delegate present at its drafting, and against which that delegate voted her country's drafting position vis-à-vis a specific resolution. This statement by the Romanian delegate, struck into the official record, certainly strengthens our reading of the Second World War's direct traumatic impacts which have their traces in GC-IV's wording. The 'carriers' so to speak of these experiences who brought the war's traces into GC-IV's text *were* the delegates themselves – Jews and non-Jews alike.

To be sure, not all delegates in Stockholm and Geneva appreciated the impact of the Second World War's horrors. To Sir Robert Craigie, the UK's head of delegation to the Geneva Plenipotentiaries Conference, the experiences of Denmark's Jewish delegate Georg Cohn were fraught with a 'somewhat exaggerated conception by the Danes of their suffering under German occupation', which rendered Cohn 'impervious either to reason or argument'.[13] (For a fuller account of the context for Craigie's remarks – Cohn's determined attempt to outlaw the death penalty – see Chapter 6.)

Considering that Cohn had left his house one day before Nazi SS officers knocked on his door with his deportation order to Theresienstadt, and that the fisherman who smuggled him and his children out of Denmark had been obliged to run the gauntlet of German naval patrol boats all night before he could arrive safely on the other side of the Oresund Strait in Sweden's safe haven, one wonders who exactly, given a choice between Craigie and Cohn, was truly 'impervious either to reason or argument'.[14] Britain's subsequent mass killing of civilians and combatants alike during its actions against uprisings in its colonies would seem rather to condone Cohn and condemn Craigie.[15]

12. *Final Record*, Vol. 2-B, p. 502, Statement of Mrs. Luca (Rumania) 34th Plenary session, 9 August 1949.

13. UK National Archives London – Kew, File # FO 369/ 4164, Sir Robert Craigie, Final Report from the Geneva Conference of Plenipotentiaries for the amendment of the New Geneva Conventions, November 1949, p. 7, §38.

14. On Cohn's family's escape from the Nazis and arrival in Sweden, see Emilie Cohn Roi, *Courtyards of Copenhagen: Georg Cohn in Quest of war Prevention – Seven Generations in Denmark* (Jerusalem: Rubin Mass Publishers 2003), pp. 136–42 [Hazerot Copenhagen: Georg Cohn Bemamaz Limnoa Milchama – Sheva Dorot Bedenemark– in Hebrew]. חצרות קופנהגן : גאורג כהן, במאמץ למנוע מלחמה שבעה דורות בדנמרק (ירושלים: ראובן מס תשס"ד – 2003). אמיליה כהן רואי.

15. See Chapter 9, this volume.

Much the same can be said of the ICRC's approach to the fact that the Jewish Holocaust-surviving delegates insisted on bringing their experiences to GC-IV's drafting table. Cahen-Salvador might well have seemed somewhat obstructive to the ICRC's Claude Pilloud (head of the committee's legal division) and Jean Pictet (director and later vice president of the ICRC) during the Conference of Plenipotentiaries and especially after it, as he praised France – with due cause, one ought to add – for its elaboration of GC-IV's first draft.[16] Yet neither Pilloud nor Pictet could have had the faintest idea of what Cahen-Salvador and his family had endured in the Drancy concentration camp as the ICRC's leadership procrastinated as to whether or not the organization should overstep its legal mandate for the sake

16. Much the same can be said about the ICRC delegates' attitude towards Cahen-Salvador in his capacity as French delegate and Committee III president. When reading Pilloud's reports and a letter from Pictet to the Swiss Foreign Ministry, one is immediately struck by the difference between their perceptions and that of the Holocaust-surviving Cahen-Salvador with regard to the Civilian Convention that the latter was forging with the ICRC delegates. Regarding Cahen-Salvador's personal, emotional involvement with the work at stake, Pilloud wrote that 'it is particularly due to Minister Cahen-Salvador, the President of Committee III, who took things very personally (*"il a eu une activité très personelle"*), at times in contrast to the ICRC's approach'.

See: Archives of the International Committee of the Red Cross (hereinafter 'AICRC), File # CR-254/ 1 bis, Les Conventions de Genève du 12 août 1949, 0–32, Doc. 1 bis, 'Confidentiel: CONFERENCE DIPLOMATIQUE: RAPPORT SPECIAL ETABLI PAR M.C. PILLOUD, Genève, 16 Septembre 1949' (hereinafter 'Pilloud Final Report') p. 6. In another passage, Pilloud mentions that 'faced with considerable French pressure, the election of M. Cahen Salvador as the president of Committee III was a regrettable choice from several perspectives: In certain cases, he cut ideas short, at times he disregarded the rules of procedure and showed a lack of patience with some of the speakers'; ibid., p. 12. After the signing of the Final Act, and certain media interviews in which Cahen-Salvador credited France (and himself) with the achievement of securing GC-IV, Jean Pictet was asked by ICRC president Paul Ruegger to communicate with the Swiss federal Foreign Ministry in order to enquire whether they, too, could put a word in to the press and newspapers, so as to 'square' the image projected by Cahen-Salvador of France as the leader behind the realization of the Civilian Convention; see: Archives of the International Committee of the Red Cross (hereinafter 'AICRC'), CR-254 – 1 Doc. # 39, letter from Jean Pictet to Roy Huzinker at the Press and Public Information department – Swiss Foreign Ministry, 24 October 1949. Factually, much of the credit taken by Cahen-Salvador – and France – was merited. As for his personal tones, these were already evident in his early interventions during the deliberations of the French interministerial committee back in 1946, concerning his proposed ICJ oversight clause (see Chapter 7, this volume). The rift between Jews like Cahen-Salvador and Denmark's George Cohn, who had experienced the Holocaust first-hand, and either Swiss delegates, who had sat safe and sound in their offices all through the Second World War, or British and American delegates, who had themselves never experienced the yoke of Nazi occupation on their home countries, was in all probability simply too wide to bridge.

of saving Jews such as him.[17] This would come to a head in 1948 in Stockholm, as the ICRC found itself overridden by Cahen-Salvador's insistence that Common Article 3 apply to all humans, including those targeted for harm or extermination by their own government, against the ICRC's own position that saw no merit in transgressing national domestic sovereignty (see Chapter 3). The dichotomy between those who had directly suffered under the yoke of German occupation, and those who had been spared, became the central separating barrier throughout GC-IV's drafting process.

Omission 2: The French draft – the Civilian Convention's very first state-endorsed blueprint

The second cardinal omission from current historical accounts of GC-IV's drafting concerns the French draft text that served as the fundamental basis of the treaty, first adopted by GC-IV's state parties in 1947. Many of the most vital elements of GC-IV as we know it today, and which were not thought of, nor incorporated into the 1934 Tokyo draft, first appeared in this French draft. Importantly, and contrary to the errors forwarded by van Dijk, Mantilla and others, GC-IV's first adopted draft was *not* prepared by the ICRC but rather was elaborated at the French Foreign Ministry ('Quai d'Orsay') during the second half of 1946 and the early months of 1947. It was this draft that was brought forth by the French delegation to the Government Experts' Conference convened by the ICRC in April of 1947 in Geneva. Against a parallel draft prepared by the American delegation at that venue – and even the ICRC's own 1934 Tokyo draft – the conference officially adopted the French text as its official working document and based all its deliberations on it.

This significant state of affairs concerning the French draft's predominance was repeatedly confirmed by Jean Pictet. He first referred to it in his seminal commentary to GC-IV, published in 1958.[18] Almost thirty years later, following his retirement, Pictet again reiterated his reference to this somewhat elusive French draft,[19] in remarks that echo those of Albert Clattenburg, the head of the US delegation to that conference, in the official bulletin of the US State Department back in 1947.[20]

17. On the meeting of the ICRC's leadership at the Hotel Metropole in Geneva to discuss whether or not to come to the aid of persecuted Jews in Europe in 1942 see: Favez, *The Red Cross and the Holocaust*, pp. 125–9.

18. *Pictet Commentary*, vol. IV, p. 8.

19. Jean Pictet, 'La formation du droit international humanitaire', *Revue International de la Croix Rouge*, no. 751 (January–February 1985), pp. 2–23, at 12.

20. Albert E. Clattenburg Jr., 'International Red Cross Meeting', *Department of State Bulletin*, (22 June 1947), pp. 1,205–7, at 1,206 (in the right-hand column). A copy of this report by Clattenburg can also be found at the Archives of the International Committee of the Red Cross (hereinafter 'AICRC') – CR- 211/ 1.

This draft was uncovered along this study at the French Foreign Ministry archives in Paris (declassified November 2015) – and a copy of it is available as Appendix 1. Notwithstanding its partial reliance on the ICRC's Civilian Convention draft text adopted in 1934 in Tokyo (the so-called Tokyo draft), as we shall see later, this French document departed rather radically from its Tokyo predecessor in several crucial respects. In order to fully appreciate the French draft's substantive departure from Tokyo, a few words about the ICRC's long-standing and continuous efforts in favour of a Civilian Convention merits further explanation here.

As van Dijk has importantly demonstrated, as early as 1920 the ICRC had begun its long push towards the adoption of a Geneva Convention for the Protection of civilians, having already observed the impacts of modern warfare on them during the First World War (1914–18). These efforts by the ICRC would continue virtually unabated until the adoption of an initial and rudimentary Civilian Convention text by the 1934 XVI International Red Cross Conference in Tokyo (the 'Tokyo draft').[21] Subsequently – with an absolute conviction in its humanitarian principles, and even before the end of the Second World War (as early as February 1945, in fact) – the ICRC was swift to 'pick up' on its 1934 Tokyo draft as it urged governments to prepare for an upcoming meeting in 1946 aimed at initially discussing the viability of adopting a Geneva Convention for Civilians.

Upon receipt of the ICRC's invitation to the 1946 preparatory meeting, France immediately stepped up to the task of drafting its textual version for the newly proposed Geneva Convention for Civilians, under a governmentally construed interministerial committee. This committee certainly did not start its work from scratch, as it already had before it the text of the 1934 Tokyo draft, which itself was an improvement on an agenda that the ICRC had already set out as early as 1925.[22]

The coordination of the committee was entrusted to Albert Lamarle – the director of the division of International Organizations at the Quai d'Orsay. A seasoned diplomat and veteran of the League of Nations with a vast experience in treaty-making, Lamarle would become the ICRC's key ally throughout the Civilian Convention's three-year drafting process. As with other international treaties of this period, the more general responsibility for the drafting of this new French version of the proposed Geneva Convention for Civilians was entrusted to the French Council of State (*Conseil d'état*). At its helm stood the renowned jurist René Cassin, who subsequently seconded its textual development to his direct subordinate, the president of the section for economy and labour laws at the

---

21. van Dijk, 'Human Rights in War: On the Entangled Foundations of the 1949 Geneva Conventions', pp. 559–66.

22. *XIIeme Conférence Internationale de la Croix Rouge, Genève 7 Octobre 1925, Annex au Rapport General, du Comitè International de la Croix Rouge, La Situation de Non Combattans Tombès au Pouvoir de l'ennemi*, a copy of which can be found in Danish Foreign Ministry Archives (hereinafter 'DFMA')– Copenhagen, Udenrigsministret, Gruppeordnede 1945–72, 6. U. 260. a/ BILAG – 3545,

Conseil – none other than Georges Cahen-Salvador.[23] Along with Cassin, Cahen-Salvador (who in 1946 was also nominated as the representative of the French Red Cross to the drafting process) worked closely with Pierre Mendès France, who, from 1945 onwards, served as the French ambassador to the UN Economic and Social Council (UN-ECOSOC).

That all three men at the Conseil d'état's helm – Cassin, Cahen-Salador and Mendès France – came to work together for the promotion of GC-IV's Civilian Convention was probably no coincidence. All three were like-minded humanitarians, who, each in his own way, came to play a major role in the application of humanitarianism in modern French society. Cassin began his engagement with the UN Human Rights Commission at roughly the same time as his Geneva Convention drafting involvement, and went on to work on the UN's Universal Declaration of Human Rights (1948) and the European Convention on Human Rights, for which he received the Nobel Peace Prize some twenty years later, in 1968.

Mendès France rose to become the prime minister of France in the early 1950s. In that role, he became the key instigator behind the dissolution of the French protectorates of Morocco and Tunisia. Mendes France resigned from the premiership in 1954 due to his conflicted views vis-à-vis those of most of his cabinet colleagues at the time, concerning France's occupation of Algeria and its atrocious conduct during the war there. As we shall see (Chapter 8), the connection of these three men with GC-IV's drafting becomes all the more interesting given the fact that France, along with the UK, refused to recognize this Convention's applicability to the wars that they conducted in their colonial dominions in the late 1950s and early 1960s. The fact that Mendès France resigned precisely because of his abhorrence at France's conduct at the beginning of the Algerian War of Independence cannot be dissociated from his earlier striving for the realization of GC-IV, the applicability of which was to be revoked in relation to Algeria.

The fact that all three leading bureaucrats in the French legal establishment responsible for the formulation of their country's drafted positions for the new and upcoming Geneva Convention for Civilians were Jews who experienced the consequences of the German occupation of France most certainly played a role in their outright humanitarian formulation of the French draft of the Civilian Convention text, which Lamarle brought with him to Geneva in 1947. As we shall see, Cahen-Salvador later formally attested to this on record. Notably, while Cassin and Mendes France accompanied Charles de Gaulle to London during the resistance leader's exile, Cahen-Salvador – who would chair GC-IV – was the only one of the three to directly experience the horrors of the Jewish Holocaust on French soil.

In addition, all three men most probably identified, in one way or another, with political views which one could regard as left-of-centre. Cassin was chosen

23. Cassin was the *Conseil d'état's* vice president (i.e. its effective head, as the role of its president – the prime minister of France – is largely ceremonial) from its reinstatement after the liberation of France in 1944 until 1960.

by the socialist premier Léon Blum to help create the United Nations Educational, Scientific and Cultural Organization (UNESCO) after the Second World War.[24] The socialist allegiance was most certainly true for Mendès France, who was officially one of the ardent leaders of this movement in France. And while we have no direct reference to Cahen-Salvador's personal political inclinations, his advocacy for fair worker's rights as the president of the section of labour and economy at the Conseil d'état points strongly towards moderately leftist socio-economic leanings of GC-IV's future president.[25]

Omission 3: The Soviet bloc's crucial role which enabled the creation of the Civilian Convention

Our third omission concerns the contribution of another significant actor – this time, the Soviet bloc. On 16 September 1949, one month after the signing of GC-IV's Final Act, Claude Pilloud, the head of the ICRC legal division, submitted his confidential report and legal annex concerning what had transpired during the entire 1949 April–August Conference of Plenipotentiaries to the ICRC presidency.[26] Its opening pages, devoted to a description of the political realities at the Plenipotentiaries' Conference, described each significant national delegation and evaluated the legal competencies of its delegates, the legal issues with which that country was concerned and its general positions – against or in favour of the humanitarian principles of the conventions as a whole. Concerning the Soviet delegation, Pilloud's words leave little space for interpretation:

> The delegation of the U.S.S.R merits some extended comments … we know that the delegation of the U.S.S.R took, in defence of the texts adopted by the Stockholm Conference, the most general humanitarian attitude, with the exception of certain points such as war criminals and protecting powers. This frequently resulted in the accord between this delegation and the ICRC, and I had the occasion of coordinating many times with one or the other of the Russian delegates, in order to reach the best result possible.
>
> That said, due to its lack of flexibility and at times even ignorance, the U.S.S.R. delegation did not always achieve its results, despite the certainly generous

24. French delegation to the UNESCO inauguration conference, 20 November–10 December 1946. See unesdoc.unesco.org/images/0011/001145/114580f.pdf (accessed 24 April 2017).

25. Alain Chatriot, 'Georges Cahen-Salvador, un réformateur social dans la haute administration française (1875-1963)', *Revue d'histoire de la protection sociale*, vol. 7, no. 1 (2014), pp. 103–28. Available at: www.cairn.info/revue-d-histoire-de-la-protection-sociale-2014-1-page-103.htm (accessed 24 April 2017).

26. AICRC, CR-254 – 1 bis, Document # 1: Confidentiel – 'Conference Diplomatique: Rapport Special Etabli Par M. C. Pilloud' (hereinafter 'Pilloud Final Report').

character of its proposals. ... Nevertheless, this delegation's role in the Conference was one of the most helpful ones, and *I dare not think what would have become of the 'Civilians' Convention had it not been for [the] presence of the Russian delegation* (*'j'ose à peine songer à ce que serait devnue la Convention "Civils" sans la presence de la delegation russe'*).[27] (Underline in the original, Italics added)

This account of the Soviet contribution in favour of the new Geneva Conventions' humanitarian precepts – written by one of the highest international legal authorities, and certainly the most impartial among them – is diametrically opposed to virtually all subsequent historical accounts concerning the Soviet involvement in GC-IV's making, as handed down by historians.

For instance, in 1994, Best wrote of 'meeting the Soviet bloc's well-contrived humanitarian offensive, which put the US and the UK on the defensive'.[28] In 2005, David Forsythe added that

to compound ICRC difficulties, most communist governments gave it little or no cooperation during the Cold War, seeing the organization – not entirely incorrectly – as a bourgeois extension of the liberal west. Soviet leaders initially suggested the U.S.S.R. might not show in meetings to further develop International Humanitarian Law, and Moscow's policy was to damage an ICRC that was closely linked to a hostile Swiss Confederation.[29]

In 2007, Catherine Rey-Schyrr – who published her study in and on behalf of the ICRC, and who had unparalleled access to the very archive from which Pillloud's aforementioned quote came – wrote that in the invitations to both Stockholm and the Conference of Plenipotentiaries 'no mention was made of the ICRC – even if it was anticipated it would attend on an expert capacity – from fear of providing the U.S.S.R. and the countries of the eastern bloc a pretext so as to eventually justify their absence from these events'.[30]

The central historical question here concerns the alleged Soviet absence from all GC-IV proceedings prior to the 1949 Geneva Conference of Plenipotentiaries, to which their representatives seemingly just 'showed up' – unexpectedly and unplanned.[31] However, the picture that emerges from an examination of the French and especially the Bulgarian Soviet archives tells a totally different story. In this picture, the Soviets were being both constantly informed and constantly encouraged by the French to attend and participate in GC-IV's various drafting stages from as early as December 1947. Furthermore, these French efforts were actively backed up by the United States, which at one stage even conditioned its

27. *Pilloud Final Report*, pp. 7–8.

28. Best, *War and Law*, p. 111.

29. Forsythe, *The Humanitarians*, p. 53. One should note that the footnote to this text refers to Best's *War and Law*, in the same pages as those quoted above.

30. Rey-Schyrr, *Histoire du Comité*, pp. 256–8.

31. That is certainly the image projected by Best in *War and Law*.

support for the revision of the Geneva Conventions on the ability to engage the Soviets and eventually get them on board.

As I explain at length in Chapter 3 – and based on the hitherto unpublished reports of the Civilian Convention's Soviet vice president Nissim Merorah deposited at the central communist archives of Bulgaria in Sofia – Best's, Forsythe's and Rey-Schyrr's accounts are fundamentally skewed. The Soviet bloc was well disposed towards, and in favour of, the reinvigorated humanitarian spirit that the ICRC brought to the early draft convention texts after the Government Experts' Conference of 1947 and were making all necessary preparations to actively participate in the 1948 Stockholm XVII Red Cross Conference. As we shall see, the Soviet decisions to boycott Stockholm and to attend Geneva in 1949 were both rather well merited when seen through Soviet eyes and given the twin realities of the Greek Civil War and the Berlin Blockade, both of which emergencies were raging at exactly that time.

By the time the Stockholm Conference opened, in fact, the Berlin Blockade (see 'Omission 4') was well under way. As discussed below, this heightening of East–West tensions had major consequences for GC-IV's drafting, and the blockade's lifting was directly related to the later success of the 1949 Conference of Plenipotentiaries. The Soviet representatives – who had been absent from the 1947 Geneva meeting, and were present as 'observers' and 'auditors' during Stockholm in 1948 – did not refrain from voicing their support for the French push in favour of extending humanitarian protections to *all* persons, including guerrilla combatants, which was to become Common Article 3, against the backdrop of the Greek Civil War (see 'Omission 5'). Given all these diplomatic efforts, and the positive Soviet reactions to them in February 1948, one cannot accept the historical picture of the Soviets simply 'showing up' to the April 1949 Conference of Plenipotentiaries over a year later, since it runs directly counter to ample and incontrovertible documented archival evidence.

Rather, the picture that emerges, and which the archival materials support, is that of a distant yet fully observant and clear-eyed Soviet Union, one that was engaged and constantly informed by multiple envoys in multiple international venues about developments in the conceptualization of the new Geneva Conventions. In this historical understanding, the Soviet participation in the 1949 Geneva Conference of Plenipotentiaries seems more like the culmination of a longer diplomatic fruition process that began with total hostility in April 1947, moved towards cautious yet open observation (*without* participation) during Stockholm in 1948, and which culminated in open participation and wholehearted support for GC-IV's humanitarian endeavour at the Plenipotentiaries' Conference of 1949.

Omission 4: The context of the Berlin Blockade and 'compromising under duress' – the imminence of the next war

Virtually all the authors who have written about GC-IV's historical development have taken care to mention the atrocities of the Second World War, the Nazi Holocaust and the Nuremberg and Tokyo war crimes trials as cardinal, contextual factors that influenced the thoughts and ideas of GC-IV's drafters. In addition, several important commentators (including Best and Forsythe) also referred to the Cold War context in which the drafters were operating, as well as the more general rise in East–West tensions between 1946 and 1949.

Nevertheless, all these authors, without exception, have omitted what was by far the central issue of the immediate period (1946–9) – one that had the utmost impact on the GC-IV's drafters – namely, the Berlin Blockade and the Allied Airlift that saved the western portion of that city, which became the largest logistical airlift effort in military history. The Soviet Union's attempt to starve West Berlin into submission and bring it under Soviet control began in June 1948, two months before the opening of the XVII Red Cross Conference in Stockholm. It ended just in time for the beginning of the Geneva Conference of Plenipotentiaries, which opened its doors on 12 April 1949. Most of the Soviet bloc nations actively boycotted the Stockholm Conference and refused to take part in its deliberations. In contrast, three weeks prior to the opening of the Geneva Conference of Plenipotentiaries the Soviets began easing off their ground blockade of West Berlin; they reopened road links to the besieged western part of the city, and recommenced cross-border rail connections between the Soviet- and Allied-controlled zones. Three weeks after this Soviet easing of restrictions on Berlin, their delegations arrived in Geneva – to the great surprise (and satisfaction) of all the other state parties.

Between June 1948 and April 1949, the Berlin Blockade was by far the most dangerous flashpoint for a possible military escalation between the two world powers anywhere on the planet. During the airlift, some 101 American and British airmen were killed in plane crashes and accidents, with aircraft landing at the rate of one per minute, day and night, including through the bitter 1948–9 Berlin winter. From a financial perspective, the operation ranked uppermost in both US and British military expenditure tallies for this period. But, most importantly, the blockade produced the conditions for a possible outbreak of war between the Soviet bloc and the Western powers on an almost daily basis. The single reason the Soviets did not obstruct the airlift, after they had totally blocked all land transport to West Berlin, was due to an explicit prohibition of the laws of war. Obstructing the Allied air traffic in any way would have amounted to a casus belli, and the Soviets knew this all too well. In fact, the next time such a similar scenario developed was in Korea in mid-1950, and this time matters did indeed descend into all-out war. In a subsequent paragraph of his report (first introduced in 'Omission 3'), Claude Pilloud explained this context further:

> The Conference was also influenced by the current political situation. It should be remembered that the Conference opened just a bit after an agreement and a relaxation of tensions ('*une détente*') thanks to the interventions on the question of the Berlin Blockade. It could well be that even the very presence of the U.S.S.R. delegation, [which] many did not expect to happen, probably did come about thanks to this political relaxation of tensions at this very stage.[32]

---

32. *Pilloud Final Report – Annex*, p. t, point 20 'political influences over the Conference'.

The impacts on the drafting process of the Berlin Blockade and the imminent prospect of the outbreak of another war resonate loudly through the Conference of Plenipotentiaries' *Final Record*. The last two days of the Geneva Conference (Tuesday, 9 August and Wednesday, 10 August 1949) were dedicated to discussions concerning proposed resolutions tabled by the various governments present – resolutions that all knew were devoid of any legal binding powers and were strictly declarative.[33] And it was during this declarative stage of the conference, when the Final Act was already past its last reading and endorsed, that some of the most sincere truisms concerning the underlying tensions and pressures affecting GC-IV's drafters were to be heard.

Tuesday, 9 August 1949 was almost entirely devoted to deliberations over declarative resolutions, tabled with the aim of sending a strong international message in favour of world peace, supplemented by moral objections to war and bellicose international behaviour. Resolution 8 – which supplements all four Geneva Conventions, and which forms an integral part thereof – reads:

> The Conference wishes to affirm before all nations: that, its work having been inspired solely by humanitarian aims, its earnest hope is that, in the future, Governments may never have to apply the Geneva Conventions for the Protection of War Victims; that its strongest desire is that the Powers, great and small, may always reach a friendly settlement of their differences through cooperation and understanding between nations, so that peace shall reign on earth for ever.[34]

To an occasional reader not conversant with its context, this resolution might sound somewhat naive – especially when one considers that it was written less than four

---

33. *Final Record*, vol. II- B, plenary meetings 34 (Tuesday 8 August 1949) and 35 (Wednesday, 9 August 1949), pp. 495–519. Available at: https://library.icrc.org/library/Default.aspx.

This is a methodological point that deserves attention. Historians and international lawyers differ in their approaches to non-binding resolutions, which are often inserted at the end of a treaty. To international lawyers, these resolutions mean little, precisely due to their non-binding status – and, hence, they are in many cases overlooked. To historians – who are interested in the *zeitgeist* during drafting, and the thoughts and considerations that were at work in the drafters' minds – such resolutions can prove invaluable, as they most often expose the true wishes and objectives that the drafters wanted to achieve by creating the treaty but that, for varied reasons (in many cases, political ones), were not attained. Yet when one wishes to search for the *intentions* of the drafters, these resolutions can often serve as a compass pointing to 'true north' in terms of the drafters' fundamental driving forces. In short, they deserve much more attention than they habitually receive in scholarship – especially legal scholarship. The ICJ's clear pitfall, as it totally disregarded GC-IV's extensive deliberations regarding the legal problems with regard to the use of nuclear weapons back in 1949, in its 1996 advisory opinion about this precise issue (discussed in 'Omission 5'), speaks for itself.

34. *Final Record*, vol. I, Resolution 8, p. 362.

years after the dropping of the atomic bombs on Hiroshima and Nagasaki, and the liberation of the Nazi death camps in Europe and the Japanese Prisoner of War (POW) camps in the Pacific. Yet a detailed reading of the deliberations that led to its eventual unanimous adoption exposes the psychological factors, chiefly of the imminent threat of all-out war, under which the treaty's drafters were operating, and which correspondingly triggered it.

The text of what was later to become Resolution 8 (also known simply as 'The Mexican Resolution') had its origins precisely in the extremely dangerous conditions that surrounded the Berlin Blockade and which were rightfully seen by both the West and the Soviet bloc as the most explosive theatre of operations worldwide, which could lead to an immediate outbreak of war. At the beginning of his presentation of the Mexican Resolution, Señor De Alba, the head of that country's delegation, reminded the delegates present of its origins:

> This proposal might be considered somewhat romantic, and perhaps more or less platonic. Nevertheless, the Paris Assembly [i.e. the 5th UN General Assembly, held in Paris between September and December 1948] showed the greatest interest in it. It was on the basis of this Mexican declaration that Mr. Evatt, the President of the Conference [i.e. the UN General Assembly – UNGA], and Mr. Trygve Lie, the Secretary General of the United Nations, launched their appeal to the Great Powers to endeavour to overcome the difficulties encountered within the United Nations Organisation and to find a favourable ground for the reconciliation of the existing divergences of opinion.[35]

De Alba here is referring to the long deliberations within the Fifth UNGA on the prospects of another world war. The appeal that he mentions was made by UN secretary general Lie so as to try and alleviate (sadly, to no avail) the highly volatile situation that had developed in Berlin precisely during this assembly. All the delegates present knew full well the risks and the imminent possibility of an outbreak of hostilities due to the Berlin Blockade. De Alba continued:

> When the time came to raise the blockade of Berlin, the Secretary General of the United Nations recalled in New York the Mexican proposal which had been adopted in Paris urging the Great Powers to settle their disputes within the framework of the United Nations. The meeting of the Foreign Ministers which took place two months ago in Paris may be regarded as a direct consequence of the unanimous desire expressed at the Conference for the preservation of the peace of the world.[36]

The point here is simple – yet its implications are considerable for a full understanding of GC-IV's circumstantial drafting conditions. The drafters were

---

35. *Final Record*, vol. 2 B, p. 510.
36. Ibid.

not only operating with the backdrop of past traumas affecting their judgement and the texts that they endorsed. They were also being heavily influenced by the acute and immediate threats of a new all-out war. One such threat had recently been averted following the lifting of the Berlin Blockade, yet to all the people in the drafting room the question was not '*if* another war *were* to come about' but rather '*when* the next war *will* come about'. This realization gives an entirely different flavour to the deliberations in Geneva, and to the compromises that were struck there. Compromising on a treaty due to the imminent threat of an upcoming conflict after one war had just recently been averted presents an entirely different context from negotiating a treaty in 'laboratory conditions' – in good faith, with hypothetical arguments being made for or against issues.

This point is crucial to understand the subsequent compromises made during the entire drafting process. Moreover, it is even more crucial in understanding to just how great an extent 'Geneva Law' was, in fact, a miracle of international law in the making. Never before had the world managed to secure a treaty to protect civilians. Never before had the world accepted an extension of protections even to non-state guerrilla movements (see 'Omission 6'). And never before had the world fully accepted that there were certain areas – that even in the midst of all-out war – were sacred and were not to be harmed in any manner: hospitals and other civilian medical facilities and humanitarian safe zones. The world had tried to secure such a treaty after the First World War – and failed. The ICRC had attempted to move forward on a Civilian Convention alongside the 1929 Convention on prisoners of war – and failed. It had tried to move forward on an adopted draft of a Civilian Convention in 1934 in Tokyo – and had failed there, too. When one bears all this in mind, the question that must surely be asked, from a historical point of view, is how it came to be that the ICRC's efforts in favour of civilians, which never materialized during the interwar period despite the ICRC's outstanding efforts back then, *did not* fail in 1949.

From a historical perspective, general circumstances that compel people's actions are widely appreciated; however, more than occasionally, one needs to examine the more specific, immediate circumstances of events in order to understand the direct contextual impacts that these have. The traumas of the Second World War were an undoubtedly important 'setting' in which the three years of GC-IV's drafting work unfolded, yet in all probability – as Pilloud testified – it was also thanks to *the immediate circumstances* of détente, between the Berlin Blockade and the Korean War, which provided the much-needed 'window of opportunity' for this particular treaty to come about.

Omission 5: The influence of the Greek Civil War on the elaboration of Common Article 3

Part of Common Article 3's initial framing was formulated at the French Foreign Ministry's interministerial committee, which oversaw the preparation of the French proposal for the Government Experts' Conference in Geneva in 1947.

Beyond the specificities of the French push for its eventual adoption (discussed in Chapter 3), the entire body of literature concerning Article 3 has overlooked the vitally important contextual impact that the Greek Civil War (1946–9) came to exert upon its drafting. While this conflict had its origins in the Nazi occupation of Greece, its most ferocious chapter took place between the 'Bloody December' of 1947 and September 1949, thus completely coinciding with GC-IV's drafting stages.[37]

What began as rivalry between Greek royalists and communists under Nazi occupation, metamorphosed into an all-out proxy war between the royalists, who were actively supported by the United Kingdom and the United States, and the communists, who received backing from the communist regimes of Tito's Yugoslavia, Bulgaria and Albania. The final stages of the war coincided almost to the month with the developments of the elaboration of GC-IV's texts, from August 1948 in Stockholm to August 1949 in Geneva. The Greek Civil War effectively ended with the final major offensive by royalist forces ('Operation Torch'), which ultimately crushed the communists in the north-west and north-east of the country, in September 1949.

For communists everywhere the developments in Greece felt very much like a reprise of the Spanish Civil War (1936–9). As in that previous struggle, to the Soviet bloc, it seemed as though the blood of communist fighters could be spilt 'free of charge' without any regard to humanitarian responsibilities.[38] As in Spain, the general expectation was that governmental forces captured by the communists should be legitimately entitled to the protections accorded to war prisoners. Yet these very same protections were being nakedly violated when it came to the captured communist forces. The 1929 Geneva Conventions in force simply did not apply to guerrilla fighters, separatists, armed resistance forces or forces opposed to the state. Back in 1936–7, any action undertaken by Marcel Junod – the ICRC delegate to the Spanish Civil War, and the man responsible for the ICRC's formidable actions in that conflict – simply had no international legal foundation.[39] This legal weakness ('*faiblesse*') had not escaped the attention of Junod or his republican and fascist interlocutors in Spain. The last-named were the first to sever ties and, as they began gaining the upper hand in that conflict, reneged on the ad hoc agreements for the benefit of prisoners that Junod had managed to secure.[40]

37. André Gerolymatos, *The International Civil War: Greece, 1943-1949* (New Haven: Yale University Press, 2016), pp. 99–178.

38. André Durand, *From Sarajevo to Hiroshima: History of the International Committee of the Red Cross*, Vol. 2 (Geneva: ICRC & Henry Dunant Institute, 1984), pp. 585–95.

39. See the ICRC webpage dedicated to Junod's actions during the Spanish Civil War, along with good images from the ICRC archives. Available at: www.icrc.org/eng/resources/documents/misc/5gkdsb.htm (accessed 28 April 2017).

40. Ibid.

Some eight years on, the Geneva Convention's *travaux préparatoires* were now dovetailing with yet another civil war, where again – in the absence of international legal coverage – *étatist* forces were legally hiding behind the absence of a Civilian Convention. They continued their grossly inhumane and atrocious actions against both the Greek civilian population and against enemy combatants in areas that supported the communists. As we shall see, it is exactly this repetitiveness of Spain, being played out all over again in Greece, which most bothered the Soviets. And it was at the Stockholm Conference in 1948 that the French delegate Lamarle alerted his Soviet observer interlocutors to the fact that after the experiences of the Second World War, France and many universalist countries had a high understanding for the Soviets' views.

Omission 6: The failed Soviet attempt to outlaw the use of nuclear weapons as a trigger for their nuclear test

With the exception of the deliberations concerning Common Article 3, no other single issue had taken up as much time at the Conference of Plenipotentiaries, nor had been as contentious, as the Soviet qualification on the usage of nuclear arms as inherently illegal under the terms of the new Geneva Convention for Civilians.[41] This issue is very much associated specifically with the upcoming Convention for Civilians, seeing as the ontological argument for banning the usage of such weapons was precisely the inability to distinguish between civilian and combatant, if and when such weapons were used.

From 6 July 1949 (the date of the first tabling of the Soviet amendment to illegalize nuclear weapons) until the closing 'stretch' prior to the signing of the Final Act (12 August 1949), the Soviet bloc continued relentlessly to try and impose a ban – even if only a declarative one – on the use of these weapons. In the course of those five weeks, Soviet delegates took the floor an unprecedented nine times with long speeches and motions in favour of this goal – yet, to no avail. The majority of member states present fell stringently in line behind the US–UK position, refusing to countenance voting to limit the use of such weapons.

Crucially, what is absent from all subsequent historical accounts of this episode is the contextual fact that just over two weeks after the signing of GC-IV's Final Act, on 29 August 1949, the Soviet Union conducted its very first nuclear test as it detonated an atomic bomb similar in size and impact to those dropped on the Japanese cities of Hiroshima and Nagasaki.[42]

41. Best, *War and Law*, pp. 111–14: Best provides all the references to the discussions at the 1949 Conference of Plenipotentiaries.

42. Alexander Peslyak, 'Building a Nuclear Deterrent for the Sake of Peace: On the 60th Anniversary of the First Soviet Atomic Test', in *Russian International News Agency (RIA Novosti)*, 31 August 2009. Available at: web.archive.org/web/20120310141609/http://en.rian.ru/analysis/20090831/155977682.html (accessed 24 April 2017).

One need not be a grand military strategist to understand that there is simply no earthly chance that the Soviets could have engineered a nuclear test from scratch within seventeen days of the signing of GC-IV's Final Act. Given the extensive preparations that the Soviet Union had undertaken long before it conducted this test (ostensibly to understand the impacts of the device that it was detonating) – including the construction of entire 'dummy' villages; an amassing of some 50 aircraft and dozens of armoured vehicles, some 1,500 heads of livestock and 30-metre-deep tunnels simulating underground rail facilities – the picture that emerges is of a Soviet delegation that came to the Geneva Conference of Plenipotentiaries in April 1949 with the nuclear option already well in hand. Thus, the idea that there was a clear and unequivocal connection between the failure to ban nuclear arms in GC-IV and the consequent decision of the Soviets to conduct their nuclear test, and ensure that the Americans knew about it, seems undeniable.

The idea that, at the time, the US military establishment was intoxicated with a feeling of unlimited military might has been well researched and historically proven beyond doubt.[43] The emerging American superpower was convinced that it was the only military force in possession of a nuclear bomb. There is also virtually no doubt that the reason behind the obstinate US refusal at the Geneva Conference to discuss any limitation on the use of nuclear weapons stemmed from an unequivocal conviction of this superiority and the military imbalance that the American negotiators falsely assumed they had over their Soviet interlocutors.

However, because the proceedings in Geneva were being followed by the world's press, the Anglo-Saxon countries could not simply rebuff the Soviet suggestion to ban nuclear weapons since this would have looked rather negative from a public-relations perspective. With harrowing images from Hiroshima and Nagasaki still very vivid in people's minds, to be seen opposing the blockage of such weapons would probably not have been stomached so well by Western and Eastern publics alike, a mere four years after the dropping of those thermonuclear devices over Japan. The Anglo-Saxon nations therefore opted to block the Soviet initiative on nuclear arms with two procedural arguments.

The first was purely process-oriented: the United States argued that had the Soviets desired to discuss the banning of nuclear arms, they ought to have tabled an amendment thereto at the beginning of the Conference of Plenipotentiaries in April 1949. The tabling of their motion 'so late in the day' (in July, some two months after the procedural due date) rendered it technically inadmissible. The second

---

43. William Burr, 'U.S. Intelligence and the Detection of the First Soviet Nuclear Test, September 1949', in George Washington University National Security Archive. Available at: nsarchive.gwu.edu/nukevault/ebb286/#4 (accessed 24 April 2017). On the US CIA's failure to detect the Soviet acquisition of a nuclear bomb and its move towards a nuclear test in the run-up to August 1949, see the CIA's own account: Donald P. Steury, 'How the CIA Missed Stalin's Bomb', Central Intelligence Agency (CIA) – Center for the Study of Intelligence. Available at: https://www.cia.gov/library/center-for-the-study-of-intelligence/csi-public ations/csi-studies/studies/vol49no1/html_files/stalins_bomb_3.html.

argument concerned the forum within which this matter was to be discussed. The Western Allied countries, wishing to block the issue from even being raised, stressed their view that the only forum in which such questions could be discussed – and, indeed, were being discussed at that very moment – was under the auspices of the UN's Atomic Energy Commission. Thus, from the perspective of the venue's nature, this issue lay wholly outside the purview of the Geneva Conventions on the laws of war – as these were being developed under the auspices of the ICRC.[44]

To be clear, Western countries were certainly not resorting to any tactics that the Soviets themselves had not employed during the Geneva Conference of Plenipotentiaries. The Soviets had, in fact, used the exact same type of procedural argumentation (that something lay outside ICRC purview and belonged properly to the UN) a mere week earlier on another issue – this time, concerning the Western countries' proposal to insert an ICJ dispute-settlement mechanism into all four Geneva Conventions, which the Soviets successfully scuppered.[45] As the Soviets were now getting a taste of their own medicine, the eloquent Australian ambassador Colonel Hodgson could not help but resort to a fitting Shakespearian quote against the chief Soviet delegate, Platon Morosov, who himself was well accustomed to abusing legal procedure in order to further his government's policy agendas:[46]

> This is what you call in my language being hoist with your own petard! On that question [i.e. the proposed idea of ICJ oversight], my Delegation agreed with the Soviet Union Delegation [i.e. that this ought not to be discussed]. We still stand by that. We think it is a correct statement of international law. ... This question [i.e. nuclear weapons] is one solely for the United Nations.[47]

44. Best, *War and Law*, p. 113.

45. See Chapter 7, this volume.

46. In his *Final Report*, under the heading of 'procedural nuisances', Pilloud noted that 'the fact that there were non-ending discussions and questions regarding procedure, has also to do, as I mentioned regarding other issues, with delegates which participate in one international conference after another, and who – without pertaining to any particular competences for that given conference's specific subjects, have on the other hand become perfect experts on issues of procedure, a subject which in turn they discuss extensively. In this regard, the delegates of the Soviet Union, especially Mister Morosov, are particularly distinguishable.' *Pilloud Final Report – Annex*, pp. d–e.

47. *Final Record, Fourth Geneva Convention for the Protection of Civilians in Armed Conflict* (12 August 1949), Conference of Plenipotentiaries, Statement of Hodgson (Australia) 34th Plenary session, 9 August 1949, vol. 2 B, p. 498. The reference to Shakespeare is, of course, to *Hamlet*, Act III Scene IV, where the messengers who are sent to kill the Danish prince on his English sea voyage are killed themselves. One must, however, concede that this specific metaphor employed by the Australian ambassador is particularly poignant as it refers to being thrust by an explosive weapon ('petard') in a diplomatic conference

One person who certainly saw things for what they were was the ICRC's own Claude Pilloud. Referring to the fact that the Western powers had resorted to procedural arguments to strike out the Soviet proposal to illegalize nuclear weapons, the ICRC's head jurist lamented:

> E. Abuse of the Procedure: ... My intention here is to cite particular cases in which it seemed to me that the procedure applied by the Conference was strictly wrong ('*nettement fausse*'). I mean first and foremost the discussion and the so-called 'atomic' resolution before Commission III [i.e. the Civilian Convention] ... a discussion began before Commission III ... to examine the 'competence of the Conference to recognize the resolution of the U.S.S.R ... the US delegation presented a motion of order which demanded that the Conference recognize its incompetence on this issue. The problem was precisely that this was the subject expressly chosen for that day's agenda, and the US delegation's request was in fact non-receivable – since it was the pre-ordered day's agenda. ... The only thing the US delegate achieved by raising this motion as a point of order, was to propose the closure of this discussion.'[48]

Pilloud was certainly in tune with real-life events. In the timespan that elapsed between the Plenipotentiaries' Conference adoption of the Geneva Conventions' Final Act (12 August 1949) and his report's date of publication (16 September that year), the Soviets had conducted their first nuclear test (29 August 1949). The ICRC archives leave no clue as to whether Pilloud knew of this test at the time he wrote his report. Be that as it may, on 22 September Pilloud must certainly have known just how correct he had been to raise this issue in his confidential final report on the diplomatic conference for the attention of his ICRC superiors. On that day, US president Harry S. Truman officially disclosed the fact that the Soviets had indeed conducted their first nuclear test – and that they now also had 'the bomb'.[49] One must admit that Pilloud's insights as to the negative impacts of the closure of the 'atomic' debate at the diplomatic conference some weeks earlier proved disturbingly prophetic, especially if one considers the rapid speed with which the nuclear arms race accelerated from 1950 onwards.

With these events set in train, one can now fully appreciate the importance of the historical omission of what transpired over the Soviet attempt to have the diplomatic conference adopt a resolution against the use of nuclear weapons. All the Soviets were asking for was a non-binding resolution that would *recommend*

---

whose aim it was to try and limit as much as possible the haphazard and indiscriminate use of explosives on civilians.

48. *Pilloud Final Report, Annex*, pp. f–g.

49. 'We have evidence that within recent weeks an atomic explosion occurred in the U.S.S.R', Statement of US president Harry Truman made on 23 September 1949, *Public Papers of the President of the United States: Harry S. Truman, 1949* (Washington, DC: GPO, 1964), p. 485.

that the Convention's state parties sign up to the 1925 Geneva Gas Protocol (which prohibited the use of chemical weapons – and to which, contrary to the Soviet Union, the United States had never acceded) and work towards a prohibition of the usage of atomic weapons.[50] But even that was too much for the Western powers to concede.

Beyond the historians' omission on this point lies the regrettable disregard by international jurists of this entire debate during the realization of GC-IV. On 8 July 1996, the ICJ handed down its advisory opinion concerning the 'Legality of the Threat or Use of Nuclear Weapons'.[51] While the court was split on whether use of these weapons would be illegal in any and all circumstances (even those in which a state was under existential threat), it did uphold the opinion that their use would be illegal under the precepts of international humanitarian law (Operational part E of the ICJ's advisory opinion) – via a narrow majority of seven judges against seven, with the Court's president casting the deciding vote as *primus inter pares*. A fair summary of the legal logic behind the court's conclusion that the use of nuclear arms contravened international humanitarian law by their intrinsic nature was provided by Judge Koroma. He concluded that these weapons,

> when used, are incapable of distinguishing between civilians and military personnel, and would result in the death of thousands if not millions of civilians, cause superfluous injury and unnecessary suffering to survivors, affect future generations, damage hospitals and contaminate the natural environment, food and drinking water with radioactivity, thereby depriving survivors of the means of survival, contrary to the Geneva Conventions of 1949 and 1977 Additional Protocol I thereto. It followed, therefore, that the use of such weapons would be unlawful.[52]

A reading of the more than 1,000 pages of the ICJ's concurring and dissenting opinions, procedural documents, press releases and summaries reveals a striking fact. In its entire deliberation process concerning the legality or otherwise of nuclear arms, the ICJ's judges did not refer even once to the deliberations held over this very same question within GC-IV's drafting process – that is, during the drafting of the very treaty upon which the ICJ was basing its conclusion

---

50. *Final Record, Fourth Geneva Convention for the Protection of Civilians in Armed Conflict* (12 August 1949), Conference of Plenipotentiaries, Statement of Vice President Mevorah (Bulgaria), 34th Plenary session, 9 August 1949, vol. 2 B, p. 500.

51. International Court of Justice, *Request for Advisory Opinion by the General Assembly of the United Nations concerning the Legality of the Threat or Use of Nuclear Weapons*, 8 July 1996. Available at: www.icj-cij.org/docket/files/95/10407.pdf (accessed 24 April 2017).

52. International Court of Justice, *LEGALITY OF THE THREAT OR USE OF NUCLEAR WEAPONS Advisory Opinion of 8 July 1996*, Summaries of Judgments, Advisory Opinions and Orders of the International Court of Justice, Dissenting opinion of Judge Koroma, p. 103. Available at: www.icj-cij.org/docket/files/95/7497.pdf (accessed 24 April 2017).

against their legality. This total disregard by the ICJ of the lengthy and important debates regarding the 'atomic question' (as it was then commonly referred to) during the 1949 Conference of Plenipotentiaries is poignantly symptomatic of the methodological and disciplinary 'divorce' between international lawyers and historians.

Not only did the ICJ judges not examine the several dozen pages in GC-IV's *Final Record* devoted to this issue, they also did not even care to consult Best's ground-breaking work, which would have provided them with a thorough summary of these debates and which had conveniently appeared in print in 1994, a mere two years before the ICJ's own deliberations on this issue.

The troubled ICRC post Second World War, and its admirable resurrection

The ICRC's problematic situation post Second World War – which, in contrast with the aforementioned omissions, has been well studied – is briefly explained here so as to complete the historical picture of GC-IV's drafting context. By 1946, with its 1944 Nobel Peace Prize now placing it firmly in the limelight, the ICRC was, paradoxically, experiencing probably its worst existential crisis in just over eighty years of its existence. Born in 1864 into a world in transition from empires to nation states, at a time that coincided with the birth of modern international law, the ICRC's legalism had emerged as one of its most salient character traits – and the one that brought the International Committee its influence and trustworthiness with national governments. The man who personified this legalistic ethos more than anyone else was ICRC president Max Huber.[53] Former two-term president of the first 'World Court' (the League of Nations' PCIJ), Huber was a scrupulous upholder of the rights of states in international law. In 1928, he turned down a further tenure at the PCIJ to take up the ICRC presidency. Faced with the ordeals of the Second World War – and true to his remarkable humanistic character – Huber worked tirelessly against the downward-spiralling moral debacle into which humanity was then descending.

In late 1946, as Huber sent out invitations to governments to attend the 1947 Geneva Government Experts' Conference, the ICRC had voted to replace him with its most controversial president – the ill-chosen Carl Burckhardt. With his royalist affinities, weakness for fascists and tacit anti-Semitism, Burckhardt was in all probability the worst candidate to head the ICRC after what had transpired during the Second World War. The organization itself was partially aware of this.[54]

---

53. Dietrich Schindler, 'Max Huber', *European Journal of International Law*, vol. 18, no. 1 (2007), pp. 81–95, at 93.

54. On Carl Burckhardt's tacit anti-Semitism, which proved highly problematic for the ICRC after the extent of anti-Jewish Nazi atrocities were revealed post Second World War, see Steinacher, *Hakenkreuz und Rotes Kreuz*, p. 29, n. 75–81. See also Rainer A. Blasius, 'Die wahre Erfindung ist so wahr wie der Traum: Der schweizerische Diplomat Carl Jacob

In 1948, after the Swiss diplomat's brief stint at its helm (he proved the shortest-serving ICRC president ever), the organization elected the remarkably able Paul Ruegger as its new chief.

Ruegger's foremost challenge lay in the acute need to repair the ICRC's deeply tarnished image in the eyes of the Western powers, due to its very problematic conduct vis-à-vis the Nazi Holocaust.[55] His second most important challenge was the need to mend the International Committee's relations with the Soviet bloc. From the Soviet point of view, the ICRC had stood idly by as the Nazi regime had obscenely and criminally mishandled Soviet war prisoners.[56] The Soviets, in fact, openly complained that the committee was providing warm shelter for Russian prisoners post-war, thus obstructing their return to the Soviet Union.[57] While the Soviets had similar concerns to those of their Western allies regarding the responsibilities of occupying military powers, they were also carrying with them a long history of diplomatic non-cooperation. During the interwar period, the Soviet Union had refused to take part in the League of Nations (until very late, in 1934, when the body was already internationally paralysed). Following the creation of the UN, the Soviet Union was virtually the only permanent member of the UN Security Council to continually use its veto power, exercising this prerogative no less than forty-nine times between 1946 and 1949, during the drafting of GC-IV.

Burckhardt als historische Quelle / Die Kontroverse um die Forschungsergebnisse Paul Stauffers', *Frankfurter Allgemeine Zeitung*, 2 June 1999, no. 125, p. 58.

55. Steinacher, *Hakenkreuz und Rotes Kreuz*, pp. 37–123; Steinacher, *Nazis on the Run*, Ch. 2: 'The Co- Responsibility of the International Red Cross', pp. 55–90. The standard work on this subject are Favez, *The Red Cross and the Holocaust*.

56. It should be remembered that when GC-IV's early drafting stages commenced in 1946, the Soviets were reeling from the experience of their soldiers being subject to mass summary executions by the Nazis all through the Second World War. Knowing full well that the Soviet Union had not bound itself to or signed the 1929 Third Geneva Convention for the Treatment of War Prisoners ('GC-III'), the Nazis went on to execute well over one million Soviet war prisoners – something that they were very careful *not* to undertake with American or British captured enemy soldiers. As Draper has noted, the Nazis were well aware of their opportunity to legally 'hide behind' this lack of signature of GC-III by the Soviets. While the latter rightfully perceived this as a criminal act – and, indeed, even brought Nazis who were responsible for this behaviour to trial for war crimes (as in the Kharkov Trials of 1943) – the international legal basis upon which the Soviets could operate was rather thin, given that the categories 'war crimes' and 'crimes against humanity' would only really come to the fore during the Nuremberg and Tokyo trials of 1946–7. And this was exactly when the Greek Civil war broke out, with the Soviets finding themselves yet again in a situation in which clear moral breaches were being committed against them, yet the legal apparatus that they would have wanted to invoke did not yet exist for their favour. See Meyer and McCoubrey, *Reflections on Law and Armed Conflicts: The Selected Works on the Laws of War by the late Professor Colonel G.I.A.D. Draper. OBE*, pp. 57–61.

57. Best, *War and Law*, pp. 84–5.

In 1946, during the ICRC's youth conference hosted by Swedish diplomat Folke Bernadotte and presided over by Prince Charles of Sweden, the French ambassador in Stockholm informed his foreign minister, Georges Bidault, that

> the Red Cross delegates from Eastern Europe, aside from Poland, had issued a violent political attack against their western counterparts, concerning future Red Cross plans. According to them the Red Cross, prior to its recent change of leadership, was directed by 'supporters of fascism' and 'murderers'. (*'suppôts du fascisme – assassins'*)[58]

It would take the French much effort to 'get the Soviets on board'. Yet their success in doing so, which materialized in April of 1949, was one of the key factors in bringing GC-IV to fruition.

GC-IV's drafting history revisited – the full historical picture

A thorough review of the circumstances surrounding the Fourth Geneva Convention's three-year drafting process yields a complex historical picture. Contextually, the emerging Cold War, the Berlin Blockade and its easing, and the Greek Civil War all contributed to an international sense of urgency to revise and revamp the laws of war. At the end of the day, on both sides of the Cold War, the recognition that ensuing conflicts were around the corner sank in. Before the ink had dried on the GC-IV text, the world was again engaged in a full-scale conflict – this time, on the Korean Peninsula. Behind all this lay the nuclear arms race, in which the Soviets somehow managed to close the technological gap on the United States and its Western allies. The failure of the Soviet attempt to outlaw the use of nuclear weapons amid the 1949 Plenipotentiaries' Conference did no more than prod the Soviets to test a nuclear weapon of their own. To this situation, one must add the developments concerning the ICRC. Its 'jumpstarting' of the drafting process launched the organization into the international political limelight at exactly the time that it found itself existentially most vulnerable. The drafting process in fact became the stage from which the Soviets could cast their accusations at the ICRC concerning its lack of conduct vis-à-vis Russian war prisoners during the recent world war.

One must also consider the organization's highly problematic conduct regarding the annihilation of Europe's Jews. This behaviour would be held against it all through the drafting process – especially by the World Jewish Congress.

---

58. FFMA, new archiving filing numbers, File # 76 CPCOM / Box 76 (old Nantes diplomatic archives reference Y – Internationale 76 Y- 23–4), Ambassador Jean Baelen to Prime Minister and Foreign Minister Georges Bidault '*Congress de la Croix Rouge de la Jeunesse*', 5 September 1946, received at the Secretariat of the Quai d'Orsay in Paris, 11 September 1946, p. 2.

The unveiling of the full extent of recent Nazi horrors at Nuremberg (1945–7) could not have boded well for the ICRC. Its excuses, legalistic or otherwise, for its inaction over the extermination of the Jews simply did not stand up after what the world had seen. To add insult to injury, the Red Cross movement had been responsible for issuing travel documents to the worst of the Nazi war criminals such as Adolf Eichmann, Josef Mengele and Klaus Barbie.[59] The US delegates, Albert Clattenburg and Ambassador Leyland Harrison were well aware of these actions, undertaken by the Italian Red Cross without the Geneva-based International Committee's knowledge (see Chapter 2's 'Stockholm's Human and Political Landscape'). It was they who alerted the International Committee to this situation, lest the Geneva-based body lose even more of its ebbing international credibility. On explicit instructions from US Secretary of State George Marshall, the ICRC was brought to order. Harrison, who would later head the US delegation to the 1949 Plenipotentiaries' Conference, was tasked with delivering the United States's harsh message. The International Committee quickly fell into line.[60]

The ICRC thus needed to muster all the international support that it could. With the UK's visceral antagonism towards the very idea of a Convention for Civilians, with the United States still undecided and with the Soviets scarred and tepid towards the ICRC due to its previous lack of action on their behalf, it was France that stepped to the fore and provided the ICRC with the unlimited diplomatic support that it so sorely needed. With its renowned diplomatic expertise, its seat on the UN Security Council, its experiences under Nazi occupation and its central political positioning between the Soviet and Western blocs, France emerged as the single most important *étatist* political force that provided unlimited backup to the ICRC. From its very first blueprint for the Civilian Convention in the Governments Experts' Conference (1947), through the soliciting of the Soviets in Stockholm (1948), and all through the 1949 Conference of Plenipotentiaries, France provided the heavyweight diplomatic 'backbone' that the vulnerable ICRC needed so badly. As the committee's Claude Pilloud wrote to his superiors after the signing of the Final Act,

> The <u>French Delegation</u> was rather similar in its composition to its predecessors in 1947 and in Stockholm. Within Commission III and within the mixed Commission [i.e. the Commission mandated to deal with Common Articles] this delegation provided a very significant securing support ('*un très grand secours*') for the ICRC experts. Very frequently, this delegation accepted to adopt as its own the amendments which we [i.e. the ICRC – Pilloud himself being the 'speaker'] wanted to see presented.[61]

59. Vichniac, *Croix-Rouge*, pp. 250–3; Steinacher, *Nazis on the Run*, pp. 21–3 and figures 6–17; Steinacher, *Hakenkreuz und Rotes Kreuz*, pp. 155–64.

60. Steinacher, *Humanitarians at War*, pp. 203–7.

61. *Pilloud Final Report*, p. 6 (underlining in the original). Archive of the International Committee of the Red Cross – Geneva (hereinafter 'AICRC'), File # CR-254/ 1, Les

This confidential statement by Pilloud is important in two respects. First, the ICRC was not a state party, and thus could not officially initiate or table drafting amendments to Articles. This role – according to Pilloud's testimony above – was carried forward by France on the ICRC's behalf. Pilloud's statement thus directly contradicts our historical understanding of what transpired at the Geneva Conference of Plenipotentiaries, since virtually all historians have until now been working under the assumption that the ICRC's views were carried forward – when needed by a state party – by the *Swiss delegation*, not by France. The fact that the ICRC turned 'very frequently' (*'très fréquentment'*) to the French to table the amendments that it could not propose as a Non-Governmental Organization (NGO) certainly defies this common understanding as to the supposedly symbiotic Swiss–ICRC relationship. In fact, when reading Pilloud's criticism of the positions of the Swiss delegation concerning Article 5, and its refusal to support the Soviet resolution on the prohibition of nuclear arms, one fully understands the tacit discords between the ICRC and the Swiss government in Bern.[62] With GC-IV, it was firstly France that had effectively become the ICRC's spokesperson for humanitarian causes – and only then the Swiss government.[63]

The second important aspect of Pilloud's statement regarding the French delegation concerns his reference to its absolute consistency and the continuity

Conventions de Genève du 12 aôut 1949, 0–32, Doc. 1 bis, Confidentiel: CONFERENCE DIPLOMATIQUE: RAPPORT SPECIAL ETABLI PAR M.C. PILLOUD, Genève, 16 Septembre 1949, p. 6.

62. 'I only regret to say that within the Drafting Group of Commission III, the Swiss delegate finally aligned himself with the Anglo-Saxon preview of restrictions to the application of the Convention for reasons of State-security [i.e. the Swiss endorsement of Article 5 of the Civilian Convention – GBN]. His alignment with the Anglo-Saxon position weakened those who up until then were opposed to it. In the same manner, as for my personal view, I regret that Switzerland did not abstain in the vote concerning the Conference competence to recognize the so-called "atomic" resolution.' *Pilloud Final Report*, p. 8.

63. On a more general note, one should add that during this period Swiss conservativism concerning international humanitarian treaties was certainly not restricted to the application of GC-IV. Zutter – the delegate referred to by Pilloud in the previous note, who sided with the positions expressed by the Anglo-Saxon delegations concerning GC-IV's controversial Article 5 – clung to his ultra-conservative positions some two years later, during the Conference of Plenipotentiaries of the 1951 Refugee Convention. There, he bitterly opposed the unbridled application of the non-refoulement principle, which put him in a stark minoritarian position vis-à-vis the majority of the other delegates who refused to limit or inhibit the scope of non-refoulement protection. See Gilad Ben-Nun, 'Non-Refoulement as a Qualifier of Nation-State Sovereignty: The Case of Mass Population Flows', *Comparativ. Zeitschrift für Globalgeschichte und Vergleichende Gesellschaftsforschung*, vol. 26, no. 3 (2017), pp. 111–14.

(including between its team members – Albert Lamarle and André Jacob) of its original policy lines as formulated early on in its 1947 draft Convention text.

With the benefit of hindsight, one could safely state that the Civilian Convention as we know it today, in its pervasive humanitarian form, would not have come about had it not been for France's unfailing support of the ICRC. This view, however, has thus far not featured sufficiently in the literature surrounding the making of the GC-IV. Much the same can be said of the Soviets' efforts to secure the Civilian Convention at the 1949 Plenipotentiaries' Conference. In order to obtain the full historical picture of GC-IV's drafting settings, one must now position the specific events that surrounded its time framing into it. These include the 'window of opportunity' and momentary détente after the lifting of the Berlin Blockade and the impact of the ongoing Greek Civil War.

Part One

PROTECTION FOR ALL: THE MAKING
OF COMMON ARTICLE 3

Who ought to come under the protective purview of international humanitarian law?

The immediate, and universally self-evident, answer of 'any human being' is invariably confronted with pressures to consider exceptions to this norm. Should humanitarian protections have been extended to *genocidaires* in Rwanda? Should ISIS fighters, who have exterminated Yazidi men en masse while mass-raping and sexually enslaving their women, enjoy the humane treatment that they have blatantly denied their harmless civilian victims? Practical and immediate dilemmas, for one, are not any less complicated. Under extreme situations, such as when a captured terrorist suspect has information about an explosive device just about to detonate (commonly referred to as the 'ticking bomb scenario'), can we torture that suspect so as to extract that information and perhaps save lives? Surely the harm and death prospectively to be caused as a result of the bomb's explosion must be weighed against the obvious infringement upon that detainee's rights once subjected to torture for the sake of that vital information's extraction. As the late Alistaire Horne observed, this dilemma was painfully perturbing to some French officials in their battle for Algiers back in 1957.[1] As Horne noted in his preface to the last edition of *A Savage War of Peace*, as late as 2001, other French officials 'unashamedly, indeed proudly, admitted to having tortured – in good cause'.[2]

International humanitarian law's answer to these dilemmas is single, solemn and unequivocal: summary executions of anyone are illegal; torture and degrading treatment – in any manner or form, under any circumstances whatsoever – is

---

1. Alistaire Horne, *A Savage War of Peace: Algeria 1954-1962*, 3rd edn (New York: New York Review of Books Classics, 2006), p. 19. In this preface to the 2006 edition of this classic work, Horne recalls the testament of the Prefect Teitgen of Algiers who was one of the French officials who refused to resort to torture. Confronted with the dilemma of terrible bomb that might go off and faced with a suspect who might know its whereabouts, Teitgen told Horne that he refused to allow this and 'I trembled the whole afternoon ... finally the bomb did not go off. Thank God I was right. Once you get into the torture business – you're lost.'

2. Horne, *A Savage War of Peace*, p. 18.

forbidden. The fundamental legal bedrock upon which these prohibitions are founded is Common Article 3 of the Geneva Conventions.

No other clause of the Geneva Conventions of 1949 has been subject to as much literature and legal debate as its Article 3 – common to all four conventions. Extending several fundamental humanitarian protections to NIACs, civil wars, guerrilla movements and even to terrorists, it has long been hailed as one of the greatest legal achievements of this convention.[3]

Yet its dictates have often proved difficult, not to say impossible, to accept: both for states and for armed non-state actors. Over the past seventy-odd years, and with the exception perhaps of Switzerland and a handful of Scandinavian countries, no liberal democracy has managed to fully live up to Common Article 3's humanitarian ideals. In turn, states have for the most part refrained from attempting to question the legal validity of its stipulations. Rather, in their attempt to circumvent the need to apply its protections 'at any time and in any place whatsoever', states have often striven to exclude *a priori* certain categories of people from its scope. As Part Three of this book demonstrates, the idea of rendering certain people 'beyond the pale' of Common Article 3's protective purview is anything but new. In fact, this tendency began almost as soon as the Geneva Conventions came into force. From the early 1950s onwards, both Britain and France revoked Common Article 3's application to their unfolding colonial insurgencies – from Malaya, through Algeria, to Cyprus and Kenya. One of the more recent examples of this tendency was undertaken by the George W. Bush administration as it falsely concluded that Al Qaeda and Taliban fighters lay outside its protective purview – having been tagged as terrorists. The US programme that condoned interrogators' torturing of these suspects in prisons, such as that at Guantanamo Bay, was the direct corollary of the US government's effort to argue for limits to Common Article 3's coverage. Subsequently, in *Hamdan vs. Rumsfeld*, the US Supreme Court concluded that the country's torture programme was illegal, thus opening the door for indictment of the people who administered it.[4]

Tellingly, the debate within the Bush administration as to whether Common Article 3 applied to Al Qaeda suspects did not centre on the convention as a whole but rather on the very specific question of whether Common Article 3 applied

---

3. In the language of the Convention: 'To this end the following acts are and shall remain prohibited at any time and in any place whatsoever:
  (a) violence to life and person, in particular murder of all kinds, mutilation, cruel treatment and torture;
  (b) taking of hostages;
  (c) outrages upon personal dignity, in particular humiliating and degrading treatment;
  (d) the passing of sentences and the carrying out of executions without previous judgment pronounced by a regularly constituted court, according all the judicial guarantees which are recognized as indispensable by civilized peoples.'
  4. Philippe Sands, *Torture Team: Rumsfeld's Memo and the Betrayal of American Values* (New York: Palgrave Macmillan, 2008), pp. 204–19.

in Guantanamo.[5] It is noteworthy that in 2002, the entity that ordered all other branches of the US executive *not* to apply Common Article 3 to Al Qaeda and Taliban suspects was President George W. Bush himself. Given the considerable divergences within and between the various arms of the US executive branch at that time, it should come as no surprise to learn that the debate needed to be settled by the highest executive authority – the president himself.

Controversies regarding Common Article 3 have habitually pitted nation states, who have pleaded its non-applicability, against human-rights NGOs and international organizations and media outlets, who have insisted on its applicability under all circumstances and towards all peoples. Legally, Common Article 3 serves as the lowest of thresholds, below which the Geneva Conventions do not actually apply, and above which they begin to bind both states and non-state actors by humanitarian strictures.

Chapter 2 charts the initial ideas for protection that emerged at the conferences in Geneva (1947) and Stockholm (1948), and addresses the thorny dilemma of 'state consent'. Chapter 2 explores the 'universalist revolution' that took place in Stockholm, which succeeded in extending protections to all civilians, including those nationals who are being targeted by their own proper government, within the recognized territorial boundaries of their state. Chapter 3 records the 'final act' in this particular legal drama, in which the cooperation of the entire Soviet bloc was assured.

5. Sands, *Torture Team*, p. 189.

Chapter 2

INITIAL IDEAS FOR CIVILIAN PROTECTION: THE DILEMMA OF STATE CONSENT

Resistance combatants, civilians targeted by their
own government and all prisoners of war

As explained in the Introduction to this volume, GC-IV's first full textual draft, which would come to serve as the blueprint for the Geneva Convention we know today, was initially developed under the watchful eyes of Georges Cahen-Salvador and Albert Lamarle at the Quai d'Orsay. From July 1946, as France established its interministerial committee for the development of the Civilian Convention, the ministry's staff worked tirelessly to sharpen the draft of this French text – right up to the opening of the Government Experts' Conference in Geneva, at which Lamarle presented it in April 1947.

As early as July 1945, with the Second World War barely over in Europe, and still raging in the Pacific, the French Council of Ministers had begun considering the need to revise the Geneva Conventions of 1929.[1] That same month, the

---

1. French Foreign Ministry Archives (hereinafter FFMA), La Courneuve Paris, File 768 – SUP/ 160, Gouvernement Provisoire de la République Francaise: Ministère des Prisonniers de Guerre, Déportés et Réfugiés. Révision de la Convention de Genève, 9 July 1945, Ref. PL / AB (M. Lamarle – written in pencil over the printed stencil). See also in the same file: Decision of the French Council of ministers (10 July 1945) to create the interministerial committee for the revision of the Geneva Conventions, signed 7 August 1945. On the ICRC memorandum sent by Max Huber to all heads of National Red Cross Societies declaring the beginning of the Geneva Conventions' revision process see Rey-Schyrr, *From Yalta to Dien Bien Phu*, pp. 212–14. It is worth noting here that within the French documents, there is absolutely no mention of the massacre of Sétif, which took place just two months earlier. This is not surprising, as France saw events in Algeria as a totally internal affair – viewing the North African country, with its three *départements* of state, as an integral part of France (as opposed to the protectorates of Morocco and Tunisia) – and thus regarding them as domestic police actions that had virtually nothing to do with the IRC Conventions. On this approach by France see: Raphaëlle Branche,'The French Army and the Geneva Conventions during the Algerian War of Independence and After', in Matthew Evangelista and Nina

ministers decreed the creation of the aforementioned interministerial committee – composed of civil servants, advisers and external legal counsel – which would be tasked with drawing up the French official position concerning their revisions.[2] The creation of the French interministerial committee coincided with the 1946 preliminary conference of Red Cross National Societies, which met in Geneva between 26 July and 3 August that year.[3] Its participants included a wide range of both governmental and non-governmental representatives. The French government was represented by delegates from the Ministry of War Veterans, the Quai d'Orsay, a member of the army's general staff, the surgeon general and the ministries of welfare and education. Complementing these governmental delegates were representatives of French associations of people affected during the Second World War under the German occupation of France. These bodies included two separate national associations of deported and incarcerated members of the French Résistance, and the national federation of French forced-labour workers. Both these groups were being led by a gifted female jurist Ms André Jacob.

The most important task that lay before the French interministerial committee that summer was drafting its own version of a Red Cross Convention for the Protection of Civilians. The committee was certainly not starting from scratch; it had before it the draft Civilian Convention text elaborated during the International Conference of Red Cross and Red Crescent societies in Tokyo in 1934, which itself was an improvement on an agenda that the ICRC had already set as early as 1925.[4]

The coordination of the interministerial committee was entrusted to Albert Lamarle – division director for International Organizations at the Quai d'Orsay. Towards the end of 1946, probably around October, the committee had already managed to elaborate a preliminary concept paper for the textual development of its version of the Civilian Convention.[5] While certainly influenced by harsh

Tannenwald (eds.), *Do the Geneva Conventions Matter?* (Oxford: Oxford University Press, 2017), p. 161.

2. French Foreign Ministry Archives (hereinafter 'FFMA') – La Courneuve Paris, File # 768 – SUP/ 160, *Dossiers: Création d'une commission interministérielle chargée d'étudier les modifications des Conventions de Genève*, letter from French Red Cross President Sice to Foreign Minister Georges Bidault 11 June 1946.

3. *Report on the Work of the Preliminary Conference of National Red Cross Societies for the Study of the Conventions and of Various Problems Relative to the Red Cross Geneva, July 26-August 3, 1946*, ICRC, Geneva, January 1947. Available off the website of the ICRC Library at: https://library.icrc.org/library/default.aspx

4. *XIIeme Conférence Internationale de la Croix Rouge, Genève 7 Octobre 1925, Annex au Rapport General, du Comitè International de la Croix Rouge, La Situation de Non Combattants Tombès au Pouvoir de l'ennemi*, a copy of which can be found in Danish Foreign Ministry Archives (hereinafter 'DFMA') – Copenhagen, Udenrigsministret, Gruppeordnede 1945–72, 6. U. 260. a/ BILAG – 3545.

5. FFMA, File # 768-SUP / 160 bis, *Rapport sur la nécessité d'élaborer un projrct de convention internationale pour la protection de la population civile en temps de guerre, et*

French experiences under recent German occupation, the authors were well aware that they needed to strike a balance between the rights of the occupied and those of the occupying forces – if only because France herself was now officially a military occupier in Germany:

> There should be a general effort on behalf of all committee members and especially by us – members of the federation of deported and incarcerated members of the *Résistance* who have been impacted by the unequal fight against the atrocious German occupation … to look at the other side (*'passer de l'autre coté de la baricade'*), and avoid seeing the problem as one of a 'Resistant' on the one hand and an Occupying Power on the other. We must not forget that today, France is an Occupying Power, and the Convention Project is an international, or rather – a humanitarian one.[6]

Accordingly, Jacob and her associates wished to provide for the possibility of protection for combatants from a civilian population who took up arms in resistance against an occupier. On the other hand, their draft needed also to accommodate the fact that large portions of any civilian population would either *not* take part in hostilities or do so passively. The recent French experience, whereby only a small majority of the population actively resisted the German occupier (granted that a majority of French people might well have sympathized with the resistance) meant that the new convention text had to accommodate this majority of people *before* catering for the new category of legitimate resistance fighters, which Jacob and her associates wished to somehow bring under the new convention's purview. While the 1934 Tokyo draft certainly provided a sound framework for civilian population who did not take part in hostilities, it did not include any provision whatsoever for resistance fighters.[7]

The solution for which Jacob opted was simple and straightforward. The basis for her draft convention text was indeed the Tokyo draft, but its pages were split in the middle with a dotted line (see Appendix 1). The parts of the pages above the dotted line included the Tokyo draft text of 1934's proposed Civilian Convention; those parts beneath the dotted line included the additional text that the French

---

sur les principes qui doivent presider a sa redaction, FEDERATION NATIONALE DES DEPORTES ET INTERNES DE LA RESISTANCE (no date). Given the rudimentary nature of this document and the fact that the first full draft of the French Civilian Convention text already existed by February 1947, and given that most sessions of the internministerial committee really took shape after the summer break of July–August 1946, my best guess is that this concept paper was probably drawn up around October 1946. Its language is very reminiscent of the statements made by the forced-labour federation's representatives Jacques Duhamel and Pierre Hemery within the transcripts *process verbaux* of the interministrerial committee at this time.

6. Ibid., p. 2.

7. See the text of the Tokyo draft. Available at: https://ihl-databases.icrc.org/ihl/INTRO/ 320?OpenDocument

interministerial committee wished to add to the Tokyo draft. As an additional stipulation to Article 1 of the latter text, an annexed rule of the convention stipulated the following:

> The laws, rights, and duties of war apply not only to armies, but also to militia and volunteer corps fulfilling the following conditions:
>
> 1. To be commanded by a person responsible for his subordinates;
> 2. To have a fixed distinctive emblem recognizable at a distance;
> 3. To carry arms openly; and
> 4. To conduct their operations in accordance with the laws and customs of war.
>
> In countries where militia or volunteer corps constitute the army, or form part of it, they are included under the denomination 'army'.[8]

In addition to this new text in Article 1, Jacob and her associates also added two new Articles (2 and 3), which further widened the defence accorded to irregular combatants and militias. While the Tokyo draft's Article 2 had been concerned solely with civilians wishing to leave an occupied territory, the new French equivalent raised the possibility of that same civilian population deciding to rise up in an armed struggle against the incoming occupier:

> Article 2: The inhabitants of a territory which has not been occupied, who, on the approach of the enemy, spontaneously take up arms to resist the invading troops without having had time to organize themselves in accordance with Article 1, shall be regarded as belligerents if they carry arms openly and if they respect the laws and customs of war.[9]

The second annexed Article that Jacob and her associates added to the text (Article 3) was perhaps the most far reaching, as it effectively nullified the distinction between the occupied population and combatants as such: it conferred upon *all fighters* – those within fighting outfits carrying arms (so, 'combatants'), and those outside of the definition of 'combatants' – the rights of prisoners of war (as per the 1929 Geneva Conventions):

> Article 3: The armed forces of the belligerent parties may consist of combatants and non-combatants. In the case of capture by the enemy, both have a right to be treated as prisoners of war.[10]

---

8. *Jacob's 1ˢᵗ Civilian Convention Draft*, p. 2. Available at: https://ihl-databases.icrc.org/applic/ihl/ihl.nsf/ART/195-200011?OpenDocument

9. Ibid. Available at: https://ihl-databases.icrc.org/applic/ihl/ihl.nsf/ART/195-200012?OpenDocument

10. Ibid., pp. 2–3. Available at: https://ihl-databases.icrc.org/applic/ihl/ihl.nsf/ART/195-200013?OpenDocument

Thus, France in effect opted to incorporate the first three Articles of the annexed regulations for war on land of the 1907 Hague Conventions (the so-called Hague regulations), which described the conduct that armed occupying forces were to abide by vis-à-vis the civilian population of any other country that they invaded. These included the stipulations for recognizing lawful combatants (command structure, emblem, open carriage of arms, etc.), the regulations governing an uprising of a civilian population being invaded (*levé en masse*), and the granting of POW status to lawful militia and resistance fighters within that zone of occupation.[11]

To contemporary readers, this might seem a strange conflation of the laws of the so-called IAC between recognized states as opposed to the so-called NIAC which takes place *within* one given state, between its different warring parties, given that the French team referred to all resistance fighters, both those *within* the territory being invaded (as in Nazi-occupied France during the Second World War) and those targeted by their own government in-country (as happened to the French Résistance fighters who were targeted in France by 'their own' French Vichy regime). In short, the whole point that the French legal team wanted to stress here was what France saw as the inalienable rights of resistance fighters, combatants and civilians – wherever they were geographically, and to provide them with a basic set of legal protections vis-à-vis the authorities targeting them – wherever and whomever they might be.

Back in 1946, The Hague Regulations were, in fact, the only legally existing international norms that said anything about the protection of civilians in times of war. Thus, the French legal team's idea was simple and straightforward: to take these existing rules and apply them 'across the board' to all civilians, in all cases and under all circumstances – thus bringing them all under the new Civilian Convention's protective purview. It is worth noting here that this idea, of the protection to be afforded to all resistance fighters and all civilians, was also endorsed in full by the military representative within the interministerial committee – Colonel Rousenne, who signed off on its final version as elaborated by Jacob and Lamarle.[12]

---

11. FFMA, File # 768-SUP / 160 bis, Davinroy, Duhamel, Hemery, Jacob, Mechbert, 'Commission Interministrielle Chargee d l'étude des Additions et Modifications a Apporter aux Conventions de Genève du 27 Juillet 1929: Sous-Commission pour l'Elaboration du project de la Convention Relatif a la Protection des Civils en Temps de Guerre', Projet de Convention Internationale pour la Protection des Civils en Temps de Guerre (1947).

12. FFMA, new archiving filing numbers, File # 768 SUP/ 160-bis. Révision des conventions de Genève. At the end of this file are deposited the private papers of Colonel Rousenne, bound by a paper written in red. The file contains an exchange of several handwritten notes between Lamarle and Rousenne – written in personal, informal and friendly language – indicating their long-time acquaintance. 'Interministerial commission for the revision of the Geneva Convention of 1929, Drafting Committee of the Text to be Approved by the Commission, drafted by: JACOB, CHAYET, PERRIN'. This draft convention text has eighteen pages (not numbered) and is full of handwritten corrections

Despite this, as we shall see, Lamarle faced several obstacles at Geneva, and the idea of extending protection to civilian nationals targeted by their own government would require the emphatic contribution of the World Jewish Congress even to get it onto the agenda.

Lamarle's failed attempt to convince the Geneva Government Experts' Conference of April 1947

While the draft convention text as elaborated by Jacob went through several changes, the wording of the first three Articles annexed to the Tokyo draft, as Jacob and her colleagues from the resistance had authored them, remained unchanged.[13] And it was this draft, with the wording of these Articles 1, 2 and 3 upfront, that Albert Lamarle brought with him to Geneva on 14 April 1947 to the Government Experts' Conference.[14] However, the reception to these French ideas in Geneva, both from the other governments present and from the ICRC itself, was lukewarm to say the least – with the Anglo-Saxon governments (the United Kingdom, the United States and Commonwealth countries such as Australia, South Africa, Canada and New Zealand) being outright hostile to them.

Upon arrival at the Government Experts' Conference in Geneva in April 1947, the plenary elected a sub-commission mandated to deal with the issue of 'Partisans', and it was within this working group that Lamarle's three new Articles came up for discussion.[15] On the conference' second day, Lamarle reported to Paris that

> the articles concerning the internment of civilians were first discussed this morning … the president of the sub-commission, the vice president, the rapporteur and the staff of the ICRC, and another designated member, began their work with the French project [i.e. Jacob's draft brought forward by Lamarle] as their basis for discussion.[16]

in turquoise fountain-pen ink over the printed black-and-white text, which was written by Colonel Rousenne.

13. The most notable being in its dispositions towards execution of the convention and the insertion of an ICJ dispute-settlement mechanism in Articles 29 and 30.

14. For the ICRC record of this Conference, see: International Committee of the Red Cross, *Report on the Work of the Conference of Government Experts for the Study of the Conventions for the Protection of War Victims* (Geneva, 14–26 April 1947). Available off the website of the ICRC Library at: https://library.icrc.org/library/docs/CDDH/CEG_1947/CEG_1947_TRAV_RAP_ENG_03.pdf.

15. INTERNATIONAL COMMITTEE OF THE RED CROSS, *Report on the Work of the Conference of Government Experts for the Study of the Conventions for the Protection of War Victims* (Geneva, 14–26 April 1947), pp. 107–10.

16. FFMA, File # 768-SUP / 159, TELEGRAMME A L'ARRIVEE, GENEVE le 15 Avril 1947, recu par expres le 17 Avril à 16 heures, Conference preliminaire en vue de la

The next day, as intensive discussions within this working group began taking shape, Lamarle experienced in full force the Anglo-Saxon opposition to his views:

> The sub-committee charged with studying the problem of the protection of 'internal combatants' (*'combattants de l'intérieur'*) resumed its work this morning. In response to the arguments of the British and American delegations, who beyond everything are fearful of diminishing the security of occupying forces, the French delegation stressed the risk of the conflict carrying forward a far more violent and terrorizing character in the case where the 'partisans' were to feel less protected. Our interlocutors admitted that this, in effect, was an important element, yet as they underlined, there is equally a considerable risk in the other direction.
>
> Recognizing that the 'internal war' (*'guerre de l'intérieur'*) could take an even more violent form in future conflicts, the British delegate said that our ideas 'might be timely within ten or twenty years' but that, for the moment, an occupying power must do all in within its powers to stop and pre-empt attacks which are perpetrated and executed on behalf of clandestine forces. I replied that it would be regrettable to wait for yet another conflict, which would entail even more cruel developments, so as to recognize the absolute necessity for the codification of these new aspects of war.[17]

The next day saw much success for Lamarle's efforts on behalf of the Civilian Convention: it was during this session that Article 21 of the French draft, which prohibited a whole series of actions by occupying forces, was incorporated into the newly elaborated proposed Civilian Convention text. Several of these actions had not featured in the 1934 Tokyo draft, but had in fact been perpetrated by German occupying forces during the Second World War:

> The workings of Commission No. 3 (Protection of Civilians) is progressing fast. The Tokyo project is serving as the textual basis for discussion, and its Titles I, II, and III have already been examined by a subcommittee, in which the French delegation is participating and which shall be finally submitted to the plenary. The interventions of the French delegation, inspired by our project [i.e. the Jacob draft], have positively influenced the debate on many points. Particularly, the dispositions of Article 21 of our project (taking of hostages, arrests etc.) have

revision et de l'extension des conventions de Geneve de Juillet 1929, N. 30 , de la part de M. LAMARLE.

17. FFMA, File # 768-SUP / 159, TELEGRAMME A L'ARRIVEE, GENEVE le 16 Avril 1947, recu par avion le 17 Avril à 16 heures, 'Conference preliminaire en vue de la revision et de l'extension des conventions de Geneve de Juillet 1929, N. 34, de la part de M. LAMARLE'. Note that the term *combattants de l'intérieur* is also a Second World War term, and was very specifically referred to with regard to both French Resistance fighters and the resistance against the Nazis in Greece.

been all largely retained. The clause of this same article of ours, which prohibits the deportations of individuals and collectives outside of their country of residence finally prevailed in the Committee, after long discussions in which our delegates were required to defend our positions vigorously ... difficulties have appeared due to the British and American delegations concerning the status of 'partisans', given the eventuality that these countries might occupy foreign territories in the future.[18]

Despite such positive steps, by the end of the Government Experts' Conference it had become clear to the French representatives that their idea of extending the Geneva Convention's protections to all combatants, including those falling under the technical terms 'partisans' or 'internal combatants', was not going to be easily accepted by most states. In one of his last reports from the conference, Lamarle wrote to French foreign minister Georges Bidault,

> *Application of the Convention*: the tendency which is prevailing here is to avoid as much as possible the issue of the convention's scope of application, colonial rules, civil wars, etc. This here is with all regards a delicate problem because of its legal aspects and the discussions centred around the legality or illegality of these or those authorities.[19]

Lamarle's message was quite clear: these were merely preliminary stages in the drafting of an important international treaty and, as with all diplomatic endeavours, time and patience were going to be required for it to come to fruition. Yet this cause was by no means lost. On the contrary, the French were ready to carry on pushing for the further extension of protections of the Geneva Conventions to resistance fighters and internal combatants – in civil wars – and, understandably given their recent history, once a territory had been occupied by a foreign force.

---

18. FFMA, File # 768-SUP / 159, TELEGRAMME A L'ARRIVEE, GENEVE le 17 Avril 1947, recu par avion le 19 Avril à 16 heures, 'Conference preliminaire en vue de la revision et de l'extension des conventions de Geneve de Juillet 1929, N. 40, de la part de M. LAMARLE. The wording of the French draft convention's Article 21 read: The High Contracting Parties shall not take any measure, against a collective or individual inhabitants of an occupied country, which is contrary to their integrity and human dignity. Any measure of discrimination dictated and motivated by national, racial, confessional, cultural or political grounds shall be rigorously excluded. The condemnation of any person whose individual responsibility has not been judicially proven is prohibited. Measures such as the taking of hostages and their summary execution, deportations, collective punishments ('*les amendes collectives*'), the destruction of villages and towns are all prohibited.

19. FFMA, File # 768-SUP / 160, Lamarle à le ministere des affaires étrangeres, *projet de convention pour la protection des populations civils en temps de guerre*, 22 avril 1947, no. 453, receipt stamp – foreign ministry secretariat – 24 April 1947. p. 3 (last paragraph before the fountain pen signature).

World Jewish Congress efforts to extend protection to civilian nationals targeted by their own government

Another body intimately involved in the passing of Common Article 3 was the World Jewish Congress (WJC). At the heart of this involvement lay an attempt by the Congress to prompt the ICRC to incorporate a strong prohibition on state governments killing and abusing their own nationals – not only in newly acquired militarily occupied territories outside of that states' native and internationally recognized borders but also within the legal boundaries of the state itself. The WJC's ideas resulted directly from the experience of anti-Jewish atrocities, both within Germany and beyond Germany's officially recognized borders under Hans Frank's 'General Government' in Poland, where the majority of Nazi extermination camps (Auschwitz, Treblinka and the like) had in fact been established.

However, the story of the involvement of the WJC – and, more specifically, its Geneva-based representative Gerhart Riegner – in Common Article 3's early drafting stages is intimately connected to the Red Cross's problematic conduct vis-à-vis the extermination of the Jews of Europe during the Second World War. The complex relations between the WJC and the ICRC during the Second World War have been well researched by Jean-Claude Favez and Gerald Steinacher.[20] The WJC, with Riegner at its helm, had repeatedly attempted to exert pressure on the ICRC to apply legal protections to Jewish victims, in a continuous manner, from 1942 until the very end of the war.[21]

From the outbreak of hostilities, the WJC understood full well that the only way to persuade the ICRC to intervene on behalf of Jewish victims was to convince the organization of the international legality of such an intervention. The WJC's legal efforts in this field were spearheaded in Geneva by Riegner, who had a PhD in International Law and was a former pupil of the well-known jurist Hans Kelsen. In 1942, it was the former who, in his prescient 'Riegner Telegram', first alerted the WJC's leadership to the fact that Nazi Germany had officially embarked on its mission to annihilate the entire Jewish population of Europe ('The Final Solution'). Riegner reported to his superiors in WJC New York, President Nahum Goldman and the leading international lawyer (and founder of the WJC's Institute for Jewish Affairs) Dr Jacob Robinson.[22] By the 1940s, Robinson had over thirty years' experience in the highest echelons of international legal circles and treaty-making

20. Favez, *The Red Cross and the Holocaust*, pp. 126–30. Steinacher, *Humanitarians at War*, pp. 42–8.

21. Gerhart Riegner, *Never Despair: Sixty Years in the Service of the Jewish People and of Human Rights* (Chicago: Ivan R. Dee & The US Holocaust Memorial, 2006), pp. 35–164.

22. Egle Bendikatè and Dirk Roland Haupt (eds.), *The Life, Times and Work of Jokūbas Robinzonas – Jacob Robinson* (Sankt Augustin: Academia Verlag, 2015).

at the League of Nations, and was one of the world's foremost experts on minority rights.[23]

In March 1945, the WJC obtained information from its network of informants in Europe that the Nazi authorities had decided to separate Jewish war prisoners of the Allied armies (including Britain and the United States), who enjoyed full ICRC legal protection as war prisoners under GC-III of 1929, from the rest of their fellow captured POWs.[24] In a cable from 7 March 1945, WJC New York headquarters urged Riegner to take up this issue urgently with the ICRC:

> Informed that Germans segregating Polish-Jewish war prisoners in special ghettoes closed in barbed wire. Great danger extermination possibly involving Jewish war prisoners. Other nationalities taking up this matter with American British Russian authorities Please communicate immediately with IRC [International Red Cross] urge their strongest intervention with German authorities in view of unprecedented violation of international law rules of warfare and cable back results.[25]

The WJC's concerns were well founded. By January 1945, the US General Command had already issued orders whereby American G.I.s with Jewish surnames were explicitly commanded to destroy their dog tags and refrain from demonstrating any signs of their Jewish faith if captured. In one episode of exemplary courage, on 25 January 1945, Master Sergeant Roddie Edmonds refused to disclose who of the 1,000 American captive soldiers with him at the Ziegenhain POW camp in Germany were Jews. Threatened at gunpoint by the German commanding officer to disclose the names of Jewish American G.I.s, Edmonds replied, 'We all are Jews.' On the insistence of the German officer, and under threat of execution, Edmonds provided him solely with his name, rank and serial number as required by the 1929 GC-III and stressed that should he be executed the German officer would be subject to trial for committing a war crime, in a conflict that Germany was clearly going to lose within a few months. The German officer stood down, and Edmonds managed to save the lives of some 200 Jewish American soldiers that day.[26]

---

23. Gil Rubin, 'The End of Minority Rights: Jacob Robinson and the Jewish Question in World War II', in *Simon Dubnow Institute Yearbook 2012* (Göttingen: Vandenhoeck & Ruprecht Verlage, 2012), pp. 55–72.

24. Favez, *The Red Cross and the Holocaust*, p. 127.

25. World Jewish Archives at the Hebrew Union College Cincinnati (hereinafter 'WJCA'), File # 11 Box H 324, Switzerland, Red Cross, 1942-1947, Cable from Arieh Tartakower to Gerhart Riegner, 7 March 1945.

26. Sargent Edmonds was posthumously recognized as a 'Righteous Amongst the Gentiles' by the Israeli Holocaust Memorial Yad Vashem. See: Julia Hirschfeld Davis, 'Saying "We all are Jews" Obama honours American's Life-saving efforts during the holocaust', *The New York Times*, 27 January 2016.

Nevertheless, the ICRC saw no reason to alter its long-standing policy of non-intervention vis-à-vis the Nazis targeting Jewish POWs – even when the organization had a clear and unequivocal legal mandate to do so, as per GC-III. In his reply to the WJC dated 16 May 1945 (one week *after* the official German capitulation), ICRC president Carl Burckhardt had the audacity to reply to Rieger's request for ICRC as follows:

Concerning the 'separation' of Jewish war prisoners, Article 4 of the Convention does not provide sufficient legal groundings to open an official proceeding which has chances of success, without enquiring upon the motivations of this action prior to countering its unforeseen and eventually prejudicial effects. ... These motivations on the part of the German authorities have remained unanswered. ... The separation of prisoners does not seem to us to constitute, in and of itself, and infraction of the Geneva Convention's dispositions, and cannot be confounded with treatments which are essential for conditions of life ... we understand that the separation of Jewish prisoners of war could consist, and justly so, of legitimate apprehensions. Yet legitimate as these apprehensions are, they do not provide the proof of fraudulent malicious intentions.[27]

When faced with the discrepancy between events as they actually unfolded and the words and ideas often uttered by historical figures, historians engaged with materials from the Holocaust are often brought up short by such occurrences – in which the subject of their enquiry displays such intellectual dishonesty that the historian is rendered speechless. This happened to Saul Friedlander in 1960, during his interview with the former German admiral Karl Dönitz, who swore to Friedlander that he knew nothing of the Nazi extermination of the Jews during the Second World War (Dönitz being the immediate German head of state after Hitler's suicide in May 1945).[28] For Bettina Stangneth, it was the discovery of Eichmann's full interviews with Wilhelm Sassen, in which he took pride in the administration of the Final Solution: 'If 10.3 million of these enemies had been killed', he declared, then 'we would have fulfilled our duty.'[29] This stands in direct contrast to Hannah Arendt's portrayal of this sworn Nazi as a mere human accident

27. World Jewish Archives at the Hebrew Union College Cincinnati (hereinafter 'WJCA'), File # 11 Box H 324, Switzerland, Red Cross, 1942–7, Letter from Jacob Burckhardt to Gerhart Riegner 16 May 1945, with adjacent answer memorandum dated 24 May 1945, signed by J. de Trax, director of the Division for Prisoners of War. All underlining in the ICRC original document.

28. Hans Riebsamen, 'Saul Friedländer: Einer der großen Gelehrten' ins *Frankfurter Allgemeine Zeitung*, 2 Dezember 2012.

29. Bettina Stangneth, *Eichmann before Jerusalem: The Unexamined Life of a Mass Murderer* (New York: Alfred Knopf, 2014), p. 304. See also: Jennifer Schuessler, 'Book Portrays Eichmann as Evil, but Not Banal', *The New York Times Book Section*, 2 September 2014.

of a person succumbing to the machinery of evil in her renowned account of the Eichmann trial.[30]

A similar bewilderment and confusion struck the current author when faced with the ICRC's official response to Riegner, quoted above. To state, after the capitulation of Germany and the full disclosure of Nazi atrocities, that German motivations in separating Jewish POWs from their Allied comrades could not have predetermined their intended fate (extermination) constituted the crudest form of intellectual dishonesty on the part of ICRC. Burckhardt's reply to Riegner was dated 24 May 1945, a good forty days after British armed forces had liberated Bergen-Belsen concentration camp (15 April 1945), with all the gruelling images that emanated from there and which were certainly well known to all the armed forces involved and to the Red Cross.

The example of Bergen-Belsen is pertinent here, for it was there, in the German territory of Lower Saxony, that the precise procedure of separation of Jewish (and Soviet) POWs was undertaken by the SS once it had seized control of the POW camps from the then-disintegrating Wehrmacht back in December 1944. Most of the deaths of some 50,000 Russian and Jewish POWs there took place in what was known as 'the Special Camp' (*Sonderauflage*), a separate facility in which conditions were deliberately made worse so as to do away with as many inmates as possible given that concentration camps on German soil (with the single exception of Dachau) did not have the gas-chamber and crematorium facilities with which the extermination camps in Polish territory were equipped. To argue at the end of May 1945 that the separating out of Jewish POWs was, in and of itself, not an illegal action according to Article 4 of the Third Geneva Convention could not be interpreted as anything other than a naked attempt at self-exoneration, coupled with the ultimate betrayal of the principles that the ICRC proclaimed it followed. With President Burckhardt's well-known previous Nazi sympathies, and now with proof of the ICRC's inaction as POWs were separated and then killed en masse, it is little wonder that the WJC came to harbour long-standing suspicions of the ICRC. Thus, in the upcoming Geneva Conventions, the first category of people on whose behalf the WJC was going to fight were future prisoners of war.[31]

Yet POWs were actually only a secondary group whose protection required the WJC's special priority and attention. For at the end of the day, war prisoners at least enjoyed the fact that an IRC Convention (GC-III) had already been achieved

---

30. On Arendt's clear intellectual dishonesty regarding Eichmann, within the more general perspective of the justification of war crime tribunals from Nuremberg (1946) through the Jerusalem Eichmann trial (1961) to the post-Cold War International Criminal Tribunals for the Former Yugoslavia and Rwanda (ICTY/ICTR), see Gilad Ben-Nun, 'The Victor's Justice Dilemma: Public Imagery and Cultural Transfer from Nuremberg to The Hague', *POLEMOS: Journal of Law, Literature and Culture*, vol. 13, no. 1 (Spring 2019).

31. WJCA, File # 12 box H324, 18 April 1947, Memorandum addressed to Gerhart Riegner from Leon Kubowitzki, along with the draft revisions for 1929 Geneva Convention Concerning Treatment of Prisoners of War.

and signed in 1929 for their benefit. Civilians, on the other hand, could claim no such recourse to any international treaty. Thus, the WJC's foremost priority lay in convincing the ICRC (and the world at large) that the groups most in need of protection were civilian nationals of a country whose own regime was bent on their targeting and destruction. The problem of genocide was certainly not new, although the term had only relatively recently been coined – by Raphael Lemkin who also partially authored the Genocide Convention, which was being negotiated at roughly the same time as the deliberations over GC-IV began to take shape.[32]

Riegner and his colleagues at the WJC understood full well that the more international legal conventions provided clauses of protection against the targeting of a particular group by its own national government, the broader would be the international legal space within which one could act in favour of persecuted and decimated populations. Previously, during the 1915 Armenian genocide, when nationalist Young Turks had driven the Armenians to the point of annihilation, they did so without officially infringing any international agreement or treaty. As Juliusz Makarevicz, Raphael Lemkin's law professor at the University of Lviv (Lemberg to its Austro-Hungarian citizens), explained to him, as long as the Turks were carrying out their atrocities on their own national soil, they could kill Armenians as a farmer kills his entire flock of vermin-stricken chickens. National sovereignty was all but sacred, even when its wielders exterminated their own subjects.[33] This needed to change in the post-Holocaust world. At the very least, it was imperative that the ICRC – as the 'caretaker' of humanity – be granted the legal bedrock upon which it could justifiably argue against governments who were playing the national-sovereignty card, and thus banking on their supposed immunity and the protection of their domestic realms.

The first word concerning the beginning of the Geneva Conventions' review process reached Riegner in July 1946. Given the troubled relationship between the WJC and the ICRC, and the latter's problematic conduct during the recent war, tensions between the two organizations were bound to surface. They first came to a head at a conference held by the ICRC leadership one month prior to the Government Experts' Conference of April 1947. At this preliminary meeting, the International Committee wished to garner inputs from leaders of religious and faith-based institutions involved in the massive relief efforts undertaken across Europe during and immediately after the Second World War. The meeting's terms of reference specifically centred on securing the religious needs of POWs, based on the experiences of that previous conflict. These inputs would then be incorporated into the ICRC's and governments' considerations concerning the

---

32. Philippe Sands, *East West Street: On the Origins of Genocide and Crimes against Humanity* (New York: Weidenfeld and Nicolson, 2016), pp. 137–89. Lewis, *The Birth of the New Justice*, pp. 181–228.

33. Gilad Ben-Nun, 'The Expansion of International Space: UNHCR's Establishment of Its Executive Committee ("ExCom")', *Refugee Survey Quarterly*, vol. 36, no. 3 (2017), pp. 1–19 at 17–18. Sands, *East West Street*, p. 148.

Geneva Conventions' revisions. Important institutions that were invited to and took part in this preliminary gathering included the YMCA federation, Pax Romana, the World Council of Churches, the International Bureau of Education, Catholic Relief and the WJC. The ICRC was well represented by President Max Huber and Vice Presidents Martin Bodmer and Ernest Gloor, along with other officials.[34]

Given that this March meeting's agenda was set solely on a narrow and technical rethinking of the religious aspects not sufficiently covered in the 1929 POW Convention, Riegner duly concentrated his motions on the two problems that most perturbed the WJC concerning POWs during wartime – namely, their separation from other, non-Jewish, prisoners and their subsequent summary execution and cremation by the Nazis so as to do away with any evidence of their killing. Riegner's demand for a future prohibition on cremation was swiftly accepted by all the other participants, and was almost immediately positively endorsed by the ICRC:

> In view of the abuses made in this respect [i.e. the cremation of dead war prisoners], especially through the mass cremation of prisoners so as to make disappear the traces of war crimes, the representative of the WJC very strongly supported the proposal to forbid or at least to restrict such cremations in the future. Consequently, it was agreed that in the future, cremations would not be allowed, except for hygienic or religious reasons.[35]

Article 120 of today's GC-III for the protection of war prisoners – which prohibits cremation on exactly the grounds mentioned above, and which stipulates the orderly issuance of death certificates – is the direct textual descendent of Riegner's intervention in March 1947.[36]

34. WJCA, File # 10 Box D 106, International red cross Conferences 1946–8, original filing under WJC 265, note 1947, Gerhart Riegner to the directorate of the WJC: THE REVISION OF THE CONVENTIONS ON PRISONERS OF WAR AND CIVILIAN INTERNEES: 8-page Report on a Conference in Geneva, March 1947 (hereinafter *Riegner March 1947 Report*).

35. *Riegner March 1947 Report*, p. 2 point 1 at the bottom.

36. *Pictet Commentary*, vol. 3, p. 567, n. 1. Pictet writes that 'the provisions concerning cremation were first proposed during the preparatory work on the First Convention, at the meeting of experts in March 1947, and were later endorsed by all subsequent conferences of experts', while mentioning in a footnote that 'this meeting, which was convened in Geneva by the International Committee of the Red Cross, was attended by representatives of the various associations assisting prisoners of war'. Any reference to Riegner and the WJC's involvement here, based on the story of what had happened to Jewish war prisoners during the Second World War, was swiftly omitted from Pictet's record. See the electronic databased version of Pictet's commentary. Available at: https://ihl-databases.icrc.org/appl ic/ihl/ihl.nsf/1a13044f3bbb5b8ec12563fb0066f226/f43b90f23b62371bc12563cd00429183.

Riegner's second point – that of ensuring that prisoners of war should not be separated on the bases of ethnicity or race, as per the experiences of Jewish combatants within the various Allied armies during the Second World War – was also adopted and was inserted into GC-III's proposed revised text. It subsequently made its way into that Convention's Article 22 paragraph 3, which states that 'prisoners of war … shall not be separated from prisoners of war belonging to the armed forces with which they were serving at the time of their capture'.[37] The final 'stretch' in the insertion of this provision, as we know it today, was undertaken due to a UK amendment at the 1949 Conference of Plenipotentiaries.[38]

So much for issues concerning POWs – yet for Riegner, the 'big issue' of protecting civilians from their own government remained unanswered. And while the March 1947 meeting's agenda was limited to technical matters concerning war prisoners, Riegner decided that it was a suitable forum to begin raising this most painful issue. Accordingly, on 4 March, he 'dropped a diplomatic bomb' at the ICRC's feet:[39] the newly proposed Civilian Convention ought to protect *all civilians* – both those of an occupied territory being invaded by a foreign power and those nationals of a government bent on harming its own.

This debate was not going to be an easy one – and certainly not with the ICRC's Huber at its helm. Indeed, Huber's reply to Riegner's motion, which opted to discuss self-targeted civilians, left little room for debate:

The ICRC would not be permitted by states concerned to intervene in favour of their own nationals in time of peace or war. This problem would have to be dealt with by the Human Rights Commission of the UN. The ICRC could only act in places where inter-state reciprocity was granted and the protection of nationals of the persecuting state was a typical example where this was not the case.[40]

37. *Pictet Commentary,* vol. 3, p. 185, referring to the debates at the 1947 Government Experts' Conference on this issue. The record of the Government experts' conference of April 1947 explicitly makes reference to the fact that the stipulations of the 1929 Convention, which allowed detaining powers to separate war prisoners, 'had given rise to abuses, and duly noted the recommendation made by the meeting of religious Associations, convened in March by the ICRC'. Here again, any reference to Riegner's and the WJC's explicit pursuit of this issue, based on what had happened to Jewish war prisoners during the Second World War, was omitted. See: *Report on the Work of the Conference of Government Experts for the Study of the Conventions for the Protection of War Victims* (Geneva, 14–26 April 1947), p. 131. Available off the website of the Library of Congress at: https://www.loc.gov/rr/frd/Military_Law/pdf/RC_report-1947.pdf.

38. *Pictet Commentary,* vol. 3, p. 185, n. 2, referring to the deliberations of the drafting committee of GC-III on 5 July 1949. See *Final Record,* vol. 2-A, p. 347.

39. Penkower, 'The World Jewish Congress Confronts the International Red Cross during the Holocaust', pp. 229–56 at 248.

40. *Riegner March 1947 Report,* p. 5 third paragraph.

Huber was, of course, merely stating the obvious for any international lawyer. International law was based on state consent. The internal affairs of a state were its own concern, and no matter how painful this was the ICRC could not meddle in the affairs of those states – even when they were exterminating their own subjects. The internal realm of states was reserved exclusively for their policing, and the newly adopted UN Charter, in its Article 2, said exactly that outright. When compared with the League of Nations, the UN in fact represented a retrograde step in the empowerment of international and national non-state actors and NGOs in their attempts to quell and qualify nation-state powers. Granted its *sui generis* nature, the ICRC was itself one such non-state actor.[41]

Yet when Riegner tabled his motion, he was not only talking to the ICRC. The room also contained nation states' delegates, and it was to them that the WJC delegate really addressed his remarks. If he could win the hearts of state delegates (and their respective governments), then the ICRC would be left with little choice but to follow suit. How states would react to these ideas, even how they would view them, was still relatively unknown in 1947. The next forum in which such ideas could be discussed would be the XVII Red Cross Conference in Stockholm – the first such gathering since Tokyo 1934 and the end of the Second World War. Riegner was already gearing up for it, and the dilemma of state consent was moving closer to resolution.

41. Mark Mazower, *No Enchanted Palace: The UN and the end of Empire* (Princeton: Princeton University Press, 2009), p. 148.

Chapter 3

STOCKHOLM'S UNIVERSALIST REVOLUTION: PROTECTIONS TO ALL CIVILIANS

No civilian in conflict beyond the pale of Common Article 3 – August 1948

By the end of the Governments Experts' Conference, two things had become clear to the WJC. On the one hand, Riegner's recommendations concerning the treatment of POWs would be endorsed wholeheartedly by the ICRC. On the other hand, his ideas for the newly proposed Civilian Convention would be vehemently opposed by that body. As the French delegate, Albert Lamarle, observed in 1947, even the seemingly clear-cut case of the French Résistance's struggle during the Second World War and the occupied French civilian population who legitimately supported them, and who were executed en masse by German occupation forces, could not easily be brought under the new Civilian Convention's purview due to the UK's imperviousness on the issue. If application of the newly proposed Civilian Convention was already being heavily contested concerning the rights of resistance movements' combatants and guerrilla fighters in an occupied country, then its application to a country's own nationals within its legitimately recognized borders was seen as taking not one but several steps too far. To be sure, this was hardly the fault of the ICRC. States would simply not accept interference in their internal affairs.

Yet for Riegner and the WJC, after the recent annihilation of European Jewry, the idea of the Civilian Convention *not* being applicable to cases of a state targeting its own nationals was anathema. By 1948, the WJC had launched a full-blown media and public relations campaign targeting US senators and congressmen, the US Red Cross, and the US State Department in an effort to influence Americans to extend the Civilian Convention's *ratione personae* so as to also cover civilians being targeted by their own government.[1]

Yet the ICRC would not budge. Its proposed text for the new Civilian Convention, which the delegates arriving in Stockholm received, stated that

> in all cases of armed conflict which are not of an international character, especially cases of civil war, colonial conflicts, or wars of religion, which may

1. Penkower, *The World Jewish Congress Confronts the International Red Cross*, p. 249.

occur in the territory of one or more of the High Contracting Parties, the implementing of the principles of the present Convention shall be obligatory on each of the adversaries.[2]

Asked by Riegner if and how this proposed Article protected civilians targeted by the own regime, Claude Pilloud, the director of the ICRC's legal division, bluntly reiterated, 'The Convention was not intended to protect civilians from their own proper government.'[3] By the end of the Stockholm Conference, however, it was clear to all parties (and, not least, to the ICRC itself) that the textual version finally adopted did explicitly and formally cover *all* humans in conflict – including those targeted by their own government. The fact that this text largely survived the Stockholm Conference intact, and was endorsed by the member-state voting plenary, is the most remarkable aspect of the evolution of Common Article 3 at the drafting stage.

How did this remarkable turnaround come about?
The answer to this question is not at all obvious: one must remember that this is arguably the most universal Article in the most important international humanitarian law convention passed post Second World War. Common Article 3 was *the* most far-reaching article in terms of its international consequences, and indeed *the* most sovereignty-qualifying article of the entire GC-IV.

One crucial component that might perhaps help to explain the 'humanitarian miracle' lies in the character, nature and biography of the people who were 'around the drafting table' as this Article was being textually hammered out. The radical change that Common Article 3 underwent in Stockholm concerning the protection of civilians targeted by their own government relied heavily on the human network and the array of actors' interests, political positions and players who were present at the drafting table in the Swedish capital that summer in 1948. To understand Stockholm's considerable contribution to Common Article 3's making, one must first turn to the people in the room, to who they were and to their interpersonal connections.

Stockholm's human and political landscape – and the 'Swedes of Palestine'

In his thorough study of the ICRC in the immediate aftermath of the Second World War and the Nazi Holocaust, Gerald Steinacher masterfully portrayed the array of different interests that had come to prevail in the two-year build-up to the XVII

---

2. XVIIth INTERNATIONAL RED CROSS CONFERENCE (STOCKHOLM, AUGUST 1948) DRAFT REVISED OR NEW CONVENTIONS FOR THE PROTECTION OF WAR VICTIMS, Geneva May 1948, p. 153 (hereinafter *Civilian Convention Text BEFORE Stockholm*).
3. See full quote and context in p. 82, n. 35.

1948 Stockholm Red Cross Conference.[4] In brief, in the run-up to Stockholm the picture of the ICRC is one of an organization existentially challenged on multiple fronts. By the end of the war, the organization was financially almost bankrupt and relied heavily on foreign contributions – primarily from the US-based American Red Cross. To add to its financial difficulties, the International Committee's reputation had become deeply tarnished, both in the eyes of the WJC thanks to its Holocaust record and equally so in the eyes of the Truman administration. The latter issue was due to the scandalous assistance that its Italian subsidiary in Rome and Genoa had forwarded to Nazi war criminals in their flight from Allied justice to Latin America, aided by the issuing of Red Cross travel certificates.[5]

In its strategic efforts to address these challenges, the ICRC first undertook to reshuffle its entire cadre of directors. It swiftly relieved the heavily tainted Carl Burckhardt of his presidency and bestowed the position on Paul Ruegger, a fierce human-rights defender, in his stead. Alongside Ruegger, the younger ICRC guard included Frédéric Siordet (born 1899), who became the focal point for the revision of the Prisoners of War Convention (GC-III) and who would later become ICRC vice president for several terms between 1951 and 1979. Claude Pilloud (born 1913), who played a similar role for the Civilian Convention's revision, would become the director of the ICRC's legal division. Roger Gallopin (born 1911) had already, in 1946, assumed the role of ICRC chief of operations. Yet above all other people within this ICRC younger guard, there stood Jean Pictet (Figure 3).

Born in 1914 into one of the most illustrious *Genevois* aristocratic families, Pictet had joined the ICRC's legal department in 1937 after briefly working as a private-sector lawyer in Geneva and Vienna during the mid-1930s. All through the Second World War, as Pictet served as President Huber's right-hand man, he came to experience first-hand the humanly difficult and legally complex conditions that the International Committee had routinely to confront.

Pictet also bore witness to Huber's deeply legalistic approach to the ICRC's work – an approach that now, during the late 1940s, was being heavily criticized not only by Jewish organizations, as we have seen in Chapter 2, but also by the Soviets, as we shall see in Chapter 3. The fact that Jews exterminated during the Holocaust were nationals of governments that had decided to kill their own citizenry – and therefore fell outside the protective purview of any international treaty – was a valid *legal* argument for the ICRC's non-intervention on their behalf until the very last stages of the war. Yet it was exactly this *legalistic* approach by Huber that was now threatening to bring the entire roof down on the International Committee's own head.

Much the same could be said for Soviet hostility to the ICRC. It was true that the Soviet Union had never signed the 1929 Prisoners of War Geneva Conventions.

4. Steinacher, *Humanitarians at War*, pp. 112–90.

5. Gerlad Steinacher, *Nazis on the Run: How Hitler's Henchmen Fled Justice* (Oxford: Oxford University Press, 2011), pp. 232–41.

Figure 3 The ICRC legal delegation at the 1949 Geneva Conference of Plenipotentiaries. From left at the front desk, with the ICRC name in front of him, Professor Carry (law professor at the University of Geneva and senior legal advisor to the ICRC), Frédéric Siordet, Roger Gallopin and Claude Pilloud (in the black suit, sitting on the right). On the left-hand side of the picture, behind Professor Carry, is seated Georges Cahen-Salvador (president of Committee III for the development of the Civilian Convention), and at the left-hand side, behind the name-sign of France, is Albert Lamarle. © ICRC Photo Archives – Geneva 2018.

So, when Huber maintained his legally watertight but politically narrow approach of not confronting the Nazi regime on its atrocious treatment of Soviet POWs, he was sacrificing his moral high ground so as to secure his legal front. As Huber's right-hand man, Pictet witnessed with alarm the consequences of this stringent legalism on the committee's part and its apparent divorce from fundamental humanitarian considerations.

Pictet's answer to this conundrum was to fundamentally transform the entire international legal landscape into the form in which it is known today. Rather than limiting the ICRC's actions by virtue of its legalism, Pictet's idea was, conversely, to widen this legalism – almost *ad inifinitum*. The aristocratic *Genevois* lawyer understood that if the legal definitions could be so broadened that no human being would be beyond their provisions, then the problem of states fending off the ICRC on account of the Conventions' alleged non-coverage of certain groups of people would be resolved – once and for all. It is within this context that one must understand Pictet's unwavering drive to extend the protections of the Geneva Conventions beyond the narrow definitions of 'International Conflicts' into 'Conflicts of a Non-International character' – that is, taking it into the territory of what became the Geneva Convention's Common Article 3. As Nobel Peace Prize laureate Sean McBride (himself the delegate of Ireland to the GC-IV's *travaux préparatoires*) explained,

> Jean Pictet played an important role in helping to find a solution that would extend the protection of the *Geneva Conventions* to internal conflicts of non-international character ... it was largely due to Jean Pictet's efforts that that the now famous Article 3 of the four Geneva Conventions was finally accepted and incorporated in each of the four Geneva Conventions. It is this Article that provides that in conflicts of a non-international character the parties must observe a number of essential humanitarian principles. It is indeed the provisions of this Article 3 which have been invoked on many, occasions since 1949.[6]

To be sure, Pictet's more 'activist' approach was not entirely shared by the ICRC's more conservative elements. Following the Stockholm Conference, Pierre Mendès France (French ambassador to UN-ECOSOC) wrote to Foreign Minister Robert Schuman about Pictet's challenges:

> our delegate Lamarle took the advantage of his stay in Geneva to discuss with the directors of the ICRC's legal department Messieurs Pictet and Pilloud the preparation of the Stockholm Conference and specifically the essential problems posed by the project to revise the Geneva Conventions ... it must be considered that the opinions of Monsieur Pictet ... are perhaps not identical [to] those of all the members of the ICRC ... as he belongs to one of those patrician families of Geneva wherein the traditions of the fight for independence are still rather lively.[7]

Both in his successes with Common Article 3 and in his failures (as in the fruitless attempt to introduce an ICJ judicial dispute-settlement mechanism into all four Geneva Conventions), Jean Pictet was consistently looking to 'go beyond the legalities' and widen as far as possible the humanitarian protection afforded by the Geneva Conventions.[8]

---

6. Sean McBride, 'The Legality of Weapons for Societal Destruction', in C. Swinarski (ed.), *Studies and Essays on International Humanitarian Law and Red Cross Principles in Honour of Jean Pictet* (Leiden: Martinus Nijhoff Publishers, 1984), pp. 401–9, at 403.

7. FFMA – Paris – La Courneuve, new archiving filing numbers, File # 372 QO / Box 13 (old Nantes diplomatic archives reference S.3.15), Pierre Mendes France to Foreign Minister Schuman, *Project of revision and Extension of the Geneva Conventions*, memorandum dated 2 August 1948 [so *prior* to the Stockholm Conference], p. 5.

8. This notion would eventually bring him to question the very idea of 'just war' theory, stressing the danger of attributing justice to some combatants while excluding others beyond the pale of protection. See Jean Pictet, 'The Laws and Customs of Armed Conflicts', *Review of the International Commission of Jurists* (March 1969), p. 25.

While this idea of 'going beyond the legalities' had its origins in events surrounding the Spanish Civil War, the first time that the ICRC really pushed forward its humanitarian agenda 'full throttle' without a firm international legal basis for its securement work in favour of civilians was in Palestine in 1948. Previously – in Ethiopia (1935) and under Marcel Junod's shuttle mediation during the Spanish Civil War (1936–9) – the International Committee's field delegates had often exercised a 'healthy distance' from their ICRC headquarters. The civilian-securement actions for Greece during the Second World War, for example, fell largely under the patrimony of the Swedish Red Cross – not the ICRC. The committee's relief efforts in Palestine, however, were mandated, headed and unequivocally supported from the very top of the ICRC. These efforts included multiple missions by President Ruegger in person to Jerusalem with shuttle mediations to Tel Aviv, and large logistical efforts in favour of now-uprooted Palestinian refugees long before the UN began its own relief efforts, which eventually triggered the creation of UNRWA, the United Nations Relief and Works Agency for Palestine Refugees in the Near East.[9]

The fact that Ruegger's actions in Palestine coincided with GC-IV's textual development in the run-up to the Stockholm Conference was not entirely coincidental. Beyond its Soviet challengers, its internal generational shift, its financial crisis and its recovery from the damage created by Burckhardt's tenure, the International Committee faced stern in-house criticism from members of the League of Red Cross and Red Crescent Societies – heralded primarily by the Swedish Red Cross, with Folke Bernadotte at its helm.[10] One must bear in mind that beyond Palestine's strict humanitarian needs, the ICRC had a vested interest in contributing to a solution to the Palestinian crisis, which had captured international political attention from the outbreak of hostilities there following UNGA Resolution 181 (adopted on 29 November 1947) recommending the partition of that territory into two neighbouring states.

In his July 1948 visit to war-torn Jerusalem, ICRC president Ruegger discussed with his Swedish Red Cross counterpart, Folke Bernadotte (also the UN chief mediator in Palestine), the agenda for the upcoming Stockholm Conference.[11] Over cups of cardamom-spiced Arabic coffee in the courtyard of the American Colony Hotel, along the frontlines of an already-partitioned holy city, Ruegger and Bernadotte agreed that the first place where 'Red Cross Safe Zones' would formally

9. Junod, *Red Cross in Palestine*, pp. 253–68. On the controversies surrounding of Junod's account, see Forsythe, *The Humanitarians*, p. 55, n. 7.

10. Best, *War and Law*, pp. 86–7. Also see Steinacher, *Hakenkreuz und Rotes Kreuz*, pp. 91–100.

11. See the ICRC report on its activities in Palestine, published in July 1948 – *La Comité international de la Croix Rouge en Palestine* – a copy of which was sent to all ICRC-engaged governments, and which can be found both at FFMA, 76 COM-S.3.15, 'Droit de Guerre', and in the Danish National Archives (DNA – Rigsarkivet), Udenrigsministriet 0002, Gruppeordende 1945–72 - 3545, 6U 260.a/BILAG.

be tested would be Palestine. Known at the time simply as 'Geneva Zones', these Red Cross-demarcated areas were to be respected by all belligerents, who were instructed to spare them from indiscriminate bombings – thus enabling civilian populations to flee there.

Ruegger successfully negotiated with Jerusalem's warring parties two such 'Red Cross' safety zones, one near the UN's headquarters around the former British High Commissioner's Palace and the other around the King David Hotel. In tandem with this humanitarian success, Ruegger thus theoretically formulated and legally defined the idea of Red Cross zones for civilians in armed conflict. The first international document that carried this idea into the fray of international diplomacy was Stockholm's draft for GC-IV, under its Annex 1.[12] Neither the 1934 Tokyo draft nor the initial 1946 Red Cross Societies meeting – nor, indeed, the 1947 government experts' draft – purported to contain anything even remotely resembling this Annex on safety zones.

A year later, at the 1949 Geneva Plenipotentiaries Conference, Annex 1 would serve as the basis for the Civilian Convention's well-known Article 14.[13] The breaking of the sanctity of safety zones (as in Srebrenica and Goražde in Bosnia and Herzegovina in 1995) would ultimately be criminalized by the ICTY. Yet the birth of safety zones, as a legally defined category that pertains to specific geographical demarcations, had its true origins in the ICRC's actions in Jerusalem in July 1948. As the ICRC explained in 1952,

> Neutralized Zones of Jerusalem: It was during the conflict in Palestine in 1948 that, for the first time, refuge areas were organized under the control of the International Committee. ... The Jerusalem Safety Zones were one of the Committee's most striking successes in Palestine, and an experiment of the highest interest. ... The experience was of the greatest importance for discussions at the XVIIth International Red Cross Conference in Stockholm, 1948, and later at the 1949 Diplomatic Conference, on the revised drafts of the Geneva Conventions which contained new Articles dealing with the creation of Hospital and Safety Zones and Localities. The example of Jerusalem led to a new development in the Fourth (Civilian) Convention-Neutralized Zones which can be set up temporarily, and in the actual fighting area.[14]

It would take well over a year, from the Jerusalem of 1948 to the Geneva of the Plenipotentiaries' Conference of 1949, but this idea would eventually make it into 'the legal rule book' as an integral part of GC-IV.

---

12. *Final Record*, vol. 1, pp. 141–2. Draft Convention for the Protection of Civilian Persons in Time of War (Draft as approved by the XVIIth International Red Cross Conference), ANNEX 1: Draft Agreement Relating to Hospital and Safety Zones and Localities.

13. This Article is identical with the Sick and Wounded Convention's (GC-I's) Article 23.

14. *International Review of the Red Cross*, vol. 5, No. V Supplement, May 1952, pp. 131–44.

Ruegger might not have had any general official legal international basis to work from as he proposed his 'Geneva Zones' idea in 1948 Jerusalem. He did, however, have a very *specific* international legal basis to depend on as he undertook to create the Red Cross Neutral Zones in Jerusalem. When the UNGA formally adopted the partitioning of Palestine, under UNGA Resolution 181 of 29 November 1947, that resolution officially designated Jerusalem as an international condominium to be administered by the UN. UNGA Resolution 181 was based on the work of the United Nations Special Committee for Palestine (UNSCOP), which, following Britain's return of the troubled Palestine file to UN hands, was commissioned by the UNGA to study the 'problem' of Palestine and to devise proposals for its resolution. The person in charge of the 'Jerusalem file' under UNSCOP – who would go on to work in Palestine for Folke Bernadotte, the UN mediator there – was Paul Mohn. In 1947, based on his experience as the former president of the Swedish Red Cross's Commission of Securement for Greece back in 1942, Mohn had elaborated, on his own accord, one of the first draft versions for the upcoming Civilian Convention, which was presented at the 1947 Government Experts' Conference in Geneva that year. This proposal was later disseminated on behalf of the International League of Red Cross and Red Crescent Societies to all National Societies worldwide[15] (Figure 4).

At the same time, in 1947, Mohn was now working for 'The Swedes of Palestine' (see below) in UNSCOP. Being charged with the internationalization of Jerusalem in preparation for the upcoming UN partition plan, Mohn coordinated this UN concept of an international and neutral Jerusalem with Ruegger's idea of Red Cross neutralized zones during heightened violent conflict. For Mohn, who had been a senior Red Cross official and was now a high-ranking UN official, the amalgamation of these two neutralities – of the UN and of the Red Cross type – made total sense. From late 1947 onwards, it even achieved international legal recognition, being adopted by the UN Geneva Assembly in UNGA Resolution 181. Probably between March and August 1947 (before Ruegger began his efforts in Jerusalem, and prior to the Stockholm Conference), Mohn had already drawn up, in pencil on transparent sketch paper, Jerusalem's initial boundaries – to be eventually adopted as the neutralized UN Condominium future boundaries, for Sandstrom's UNSCOP committee report[16] (Figure 5).

15. FFMA, File # 768-SUP / 160, *President of the French Red Cross to French Foreign Minister* (written on French Red Cross letterhead) *Paris 2 September 1947*, Ref. P/AK/sj 11.450, receipt stamp of Foreign Ministry secretariat, 4 September 1947.

16. While the map has no date, based on its demographics (so before the outbreak of hostilities and the departure of Palestinian refugees from Jerusalem, and the fall of the Old City's Jewish quarter in 1948) the most probable date of this sketch would be between March and August 1947. Mohn even cared to mention the future international condominium's demographic composition (visible at the bottom-right corner of his sketch) of 115,000 'non-Jews' and some 100,000 Jews.

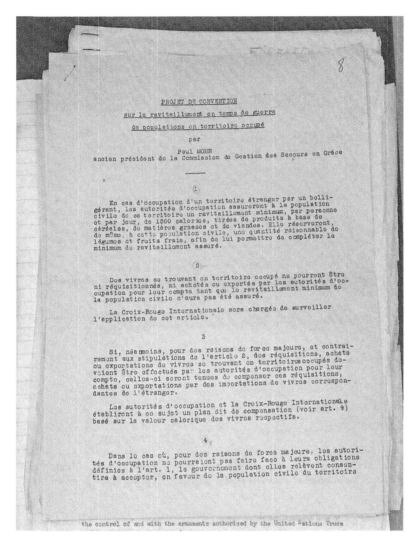

Figure 4 Project for the securement of livelihoods of populations in occupied territories during times of war, by Paul Mohn: former president of the Securement Commission for Greece, April 1947. Archive of the Carolina Redivivia Library – Uppsala Sweden, Manuscript and Private Collections section – deposited private archive of the late Paul Mohn, File # 22.

By July 1948, heavy fighting had already broken out in Palestine, and Ruegger was becoming deeply involved in efforts to secure neutralized zones for civilians in Jerusalem. With the frontlines of both combatant sides now hardened, Rueggger requested that Mohn propose a possible sketch for a full neutralized Red Cross zone across Jerusalem. The idea of increasing neutral zones to cover entire cities, and even whole countries, was not new: similar concepts, which had originated in Switzerland, were being promoted by the Swiss federal counsellor Emil Anderegg,

Figure 5 Archive of the Carolina Redivivia Library – Uppsala Sweden, Manuscript and Private Collections section – deposited private archive of the late Paul Mohn, File # 23, Maps of Paul Mohn's files. © Carolina Rediviva Library Uppsala, Photo by Gilad Ben-Nun.

who had long been toying intellectually with such proposals.[17] Mohn's application of this idea of a widened neutralized zone in Jerusalem soon found its spatial interpretation in the following map that he produced for Ruegger (Figure 6).

Using a tourist map of Jerusalem, Mohn sketched the area (seen in Figure 6 between the two red lines) that would be designated as part of the proposed neutralized zone.

In an adjacent map, he explicitly wrote the following neutral designation (Figure 7).

Paul Mohn was not working in limbo. In fact, he was part of a small group of Swedish diplomats who would play a crucial role in Middle Eastern politics from the mid-1940s until after 1967: these were 'the Swedes of Palestine'. In understanding

17. Junod, *The Imperilled Red Cross and the Palestine-Eretz Yisrael Conflict 1945-1952*, pp. 157–9.

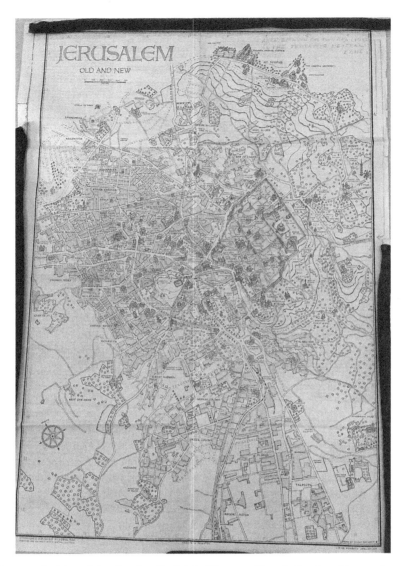

Figure 6 Archive of the Carolina Redivivia Library – Uppsala Sweden, Manuscript and Private Collections section – deposited private archive of the late Paul Mohn, File # 23, Maps of Paul Mohn's files.

the personalities behind Stockholm's success, one must also examine the intricate web of personal connections, roles, biographical intricacies and overlaps between the different Swedish delegates at the conference – many of whom shouldered simultaneous international roles in Palestine at the time.

At the helm of the Red Cross's Legal Commission in Stockholm stood the Swedish Supreme Court Judge Emil Sandström. A recognized international legal authority, and since 1946 a member of The Hague's Permanent Court of Arbitration,

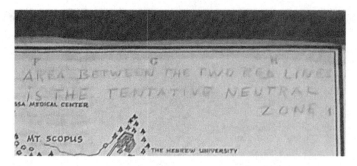

Figure 7 Archive of the Carolina Redivivia Library – Uppsala Sweden, Manuscript and Private Collections section – deposited private archive of the late Paul Mohn, File # 23, Maps of Paul Mohn's files (detail). Mohn's caption, written in red chinograph crayon, reads, 'AREA BETWEEN THE TWO RED LINES IS THE TENTATIVE NEUTRAL ZONE'.

Sandström had recently completed his tenure as the chairman of UNSCOP, which in 1947 recommended to the UNGA the partition of Palestine (Figure 8).

Folke Bernadotte, the chairman of the Swedish Red Cross who opened the ICRC Stockholm Conference in August 1948, was simultaneously mandated as the first ever UN Special Representative of the Secretary General in Palestine, a role that he had been given three months earlier. Bernadotte was in fact charged by the UN Security Council with the execution of the UN's partition plan for Palestine, which his colleague Sandström had brought into being.

As the senior figure in the Swedish Red Cross, who took over its chairmanship three weeks after the Stockholm Conference's closure due to Bernadotte's assassination in Jerusalem, Sandström was no stranger to the problems associated with the protection of civilians during wartime. Between 1943 and 1945, he had chaired the Red Cross Swedish-backed rescue Commission for Greece, taking over this role from Paul Mohn. This body had been established during the Second World War, under Sweden's neutral auspices in accord with both Nazi Germany and the Allies, to provide food and humanitarian aid to the Greek civilian population under occupation by the Nazis. To this end, Sweden sent tonnes of food and supplies to Greece from 1942 until the end of the war, using Swedish shipping vessels that carried its neutral flag on the high seas and which cruised along mutually recognized international shipping routes that were secured from naval and submarine attacks thanks to Swedish neutrality. Sandström's experience in Greece just three years before Stockholm formed only a small fraction of the overall impacts which that conflict would exert on GC-IV's wording; however, Greece, more than any other conflict theatre, would shape Common Article 3's final text.

Mohn, Sandström and Bernadotte were all intimately related. In 1942, Mohn had been commissioned to take up the presidency of the Greek Rescue Commission, to which he was then engaged by his native government of Sweden. When the Swedish government decided to take on board the effort of saving the Greek populace from starvation and death under the Nazi yoke, Sandström, being

Figure 8 Judge Sandström (centre) – president of the 1952 XVIII Red Cross Conference in Toronto. From right to left: Roger Gallopin (ICRC Chief of Operations), Judge Emil Sandström (chairman of the Federation of Red Cross and Red Crescent Societies and correspondingly chairman of the Toronto Conference), Frédéric Siordet (ICRC director), Paul Ruegger (ICRC president) and the young Jean Pictet (at that stage already ICRC director general), August 1952. © ICRC Photo Archives – Geneva 2018.

of a much higher public and political stature, was sent in to replace Mohn in Athens. In 1947, as Sandström received his mandate as the chairman of UNSCOP, he immediately called on Mohn to join him as his right-hand man, charging him with drawing up what would later become the actual partition plan for Palestine[18] (Figure 9).

18. Ofer Aderet, 'the quite Swedish Zionist who partitioned Palestine has become a bit less mysterious', in *Haaretz*, 24 November 2017 (in Hebrew).

Figure 9 The decommissioning of the Greek Rescue Commission – June 1945. Front row, standing second from the left: Judge Emil Sandström, September 1945. © ICRC Photo Archives – Geneva 2018.

The second document discussed at Stockhom, which was intimately related to Mohn's draft convention text and was explicitly formulated as its counter-project, was the draft Civilian Convention text tabled by the delegate of the Greek Red Cross to Stockholm (over a year after Mohn's draft proposal) and the former (and future) Greek foreign minister, Michal Pesmazoglou.[19] At Stockholm, Pesmazoglou would preside over Sub-commission I of the legal commission, charged with the elaboration of changes to GC-I (the Convention for the Sick and Wounded).

The contextual importance of Mohn's, Pesmazoglou's and Judge Emil Sandström's efforts in recognizing the impact of the Greek Civil War on the realization of GC-IV are important here, since both Mohn's and Pesmazoglou's drafts were the result of their direct involvement in rescue operations in Greece over the preceding seven years. Sweden's Mohn and Sandström worked closely on an almost daily basis with Pesmazoglou – their key interlocutor at the Greek Red Cross. Heinrik Beer – the Swedish Red Cross's secretary – likened Pesmazoglou's extensive legal expertise to that of Georges Cahen-Salvador, the elected president of

19. FFMA, File # 768-SUP / 160, *Contre-Project pour la la ravitaillement des populations civilis en cas d'occupation militaire en temps de guerre* Par: S.E. Monsieur Michel Pesmazoglou-Ancien Ministre, Avocat, Conseil de la Croix Rouge Hellénique. The text clearly speaks in the past tense about 'the project by the respectable Paul Mohn, tabled during the last red Cross gathering', which implies that this document was tabled at Stockholm in August 1948.

Commission III (in charge of drafting the Civilian Convention) both in Stockholm and at the 1949 Geneva Conference of Plenipotentiaries.[20]

The WJC's draft changes to Stockholm's proposed GC-IV text

In addition to its laborious advocacy campaign for amendments to the Stockholm's text on NIACs, as detailed in Chapter 2, and in its official consultative stature, the WJC also took on the formulation of the legal positions and draft proposals that it wished to table at Stockholm for the consideration of the participating states and national Red Cross societies (Figure 10).

The lead on this effort was entrusted to the WJC's legal department in New York, headed by Dr Jacob Robinson; his brother Dr Nehemiah Robinson (who wrote the first legal commentaries on the 1948 Genocide Convention, the 1951 Refugee Convention and the 1954 Convention on Statelessness); and the former Jewish-German judge Dr Gerhart Jacoby.[21]

A survey of the WJC's ideas for the new Civilian Convention shows a clear evolution of thinking, from an initial resentful attitude towards the ICRC in 1947 towards wholehearted support, by 1948, of the ICRC's vision in the drafting of the new Civilian Convention.[22] Nevertheless, with regard to the newly proposed

20. Henrik Beer, 'Jean Pictet and the National Societies', in Christophe Swinarski (ed.), *Studies and Essays on International Humanitarian Law and Red Cross Principles in Honour of Jean Pictet* (The Hague: Martinus Nijhoff, 1984), pp. 855–9, at 856. Beer's high opinion of Pesmazoglou's extensive legal expertise was echoed at the Conference of Plenipotentiaries when the president of the convention was required to assemble a politically balanced party of five international legal experts to consider issues concerning rules of procedure. Pesmazoglou was chosen alongside the US, USSR, Finnish and Norwegian delegates, most of whom were professors of international law. See *Final Record*, vol. 2 A, p. 29. Later in the Geneva Conference, Pesmazoglou was unanimously elected as the Rapporteur of Commission II (Prisoners of War Convention), yet had to return to Greece in May 1949 due to the further escalation of the conflict there, upon which his role as rapporteur was taken over by the Swedish delegate, Söderblom; *Final Record*, vol. 2 A, p. 235, n. 1. Pesmazoglou's crowded task list at the Conference, in all probability due to his remarkable legal experience, was explicitly referred to by both the UK and the USSR delegation heads; *Final Record*, vol. 2 A, p. 483.

21. On Jacoby see his obituary published by the Jewish Telegraphic Agency 22 August 1960. Available at: http://pdfs.jta.org/1960/1960-08-22_160.pdf.

22. The full evolution of the WJC positions, from hostility towards the ICRC towards a positive view of the organization, can be observed in the draft texts which Jacob Robinson and Jacoby formulated for Riegner to represent in Geneva and Stockholm. This included a 'toning down' of the WJC' diplomatic language by Jacob Robinson. In the final WJC Memorandum, submitted for the consideration of governments and Red Cross National Societies, the WJC explicitly acknowledges the efforts of Commission III of the 1947

Figure 10 Count Folke Bernadotte – president of the Stockholm Conference, discussing the Conference's preparations with Henrik Beer, secretary of the Swedish Red Cross, August 1948. © ICRC Photo Archives – Geneva 2018.

Civilian Convention's non-application to civilian nationals being targeted by their own government, the WJC still harboured deep concerns:

> Unchanged remained also the principle which has for us the utmost importance, namely that no protection is given to the subjects of a belligerent state. Thus, if Turkey should decide to exterminate the rest of her Armenian population, if Syria, Egypt, Iraq, Lebanon start massacring all Jews who live within their borders and are their subjects – the Red Cross won't be able to stir a finger in order to help them.[23]

Correspondingly, in his instructions for Stockholm, Gerhart Riegner received explicit guidelines from Jacob Robinson to push for the inclusion of nationals

Government Experts' Conference and the subsequent far-reaching changes that went into the proposed ICRC Civilian Convention draft for Stockholm: 'The efforts made by Commission III in the draft and in the annexes attached to it are highly appreciated by the World Jewish Congress and find its fullhearted support. The suggestions coincide to a high degree with the claims and requests which the World Jewish Congress considers indispensable on the basis of the tragic experiences of the last World War.' See WJCA, File # 3, Box # C 100, World Jewish Congress, proposals - civilians 21 April 1948.

23. WJCA, File # 10 Box D 106, International Red Cross Conferences 1946-1948, original filing under WJC 265, note 1947, Gavronsky to Jacoby, 8 June 1948, 3rd paragraph from the top.

being targeted by their own government within the draft text of what would become Common Article 3.

So much for the positions of the WJC. Yet at the end of the day, the WJC, respectable and important as it was, was no more than an accredited NGO advocating for what it saw as an important issue. It held no voting powers at the XVII Red Cross Conference; was neither a national society nor a member state; and, with all due respect to Jewish suffering during the recent Holocaust, was by no means an unbiased organization. It was the staunchest supporter of Israel, which at that very moment was engaged in a battle for its very existence against five invading Arab armies in parallel with the flight en masse of Palestinian refugees from Palestine – now being openly cared for by the ICRC delegations in that region. While the reference to the plight of the Jews of the Arab world in the above-quoted memorandum was not without merit given the now-open legislation by the Arab League in favour of expelling all Jews in its member states and confiscating their assets, the WJC could certainly not be seen as a neutral NGO merely advocating universal humanitarianism.[24]

It was, however, seen as an important 'player' on the international scene, by the 'Swedes of Palestine' and, specifically, by Folke Bernadotte – the chairman and declared leader of the Stockholm Conference.[25] A read through Bernadotte's papers, deposited at the Swedish National Archives in Stockholm, confirms that he both received the WJC memorandum for Stockholm and was in direct contact with its main representative in Stockholm, Hillel Storch, regarding Riegner's upcoming representation of the WJC's behalf in Stockholm.[26] Storch and Bernadotte had been very well acquainted since the latter's rescue operation to save Danish Jews during the well-known 'White Buses' operation of April 1945.[27] As a result of direct negotiation with SS head Heinrich Himmler at the time, Bernadotte had managed to secure the rescue of several thousand Jews from the collapsing Nazi Reich

24. WJCA, File # 10 Box D 106, International Red Cross Conferences 1946–8, original filing under WJC 265, 30 December 1947, Translation of Arab League Legislation against Jews in the League's Arab member-state countries, REP: SDW: bog. 1056.

25. For a broader view of the complex relations between Bernadotte's assassination in Palestine and his remarkable rescue of Jews from Nazi Germany merely three years beforehand, see Donald Macintyre, 'Israel's Forgotten Hero: The Assassination of Count Bernadotte – and the Death of Peace', in *The Independent*, 17 September 2008.

26. Swedish National Archives ('Riksarkivet') Stockholm, File # UD 1920 ARS Dossier system, HP 908, inner file: Grupp 12, X, file marked 'Palestina 1948 September 22'

27. On Bernadotte's and Storch's personal connections during this effort, see Agneta Greayer and Sonja Sjöstrand, *The White Buses: The Swedish Red Cross Rescue action in Germany during the Second World War* (Stockholm: Publication of the Swedish Red Cross, 2000), p. 8. Also published in David Cesarani and Paul A. Levine (eds.), *Bystanders to the Holocaust: A Re-evaluation* (London: Frank Cass, 2000), pp. 237–68.

in the face of Eichmann's adamant demands to continue exterminating them.[28] Bernadotte's last personal file from Palestine prior to his assassination, deposited at the Swedish Archives, also includes Storch's appeal to him as chairperson of the IRC Conference to work towards the protection of Jews in Arab countries (most notably Syria, Iraq, Yemen and Libya), who were already coming under fierce attack due to events in 1948 Palestine.[29]

An examination of the private archive of Paul Mohn, the second most senior figure of the 'Swedes in Palestine', confirms Mohn's receipt of the WJC memorandum for Stockholm as well as its material concerning dangers to the Jews in the Arab world.[30] The same archive boxes also contain a copy of Mohn's very own draft plan for the Red Cross Civilian Convention text of GC-IV (discussed above) and his charts for the Jerusalem Red Cross Safety Zone, which he himself drew up at the request of both Bernadotte and Ruegger in July 1948 as the former's chief aid responsible for Jerusalem. These plans for Red Cross Safety Zones thus went hand in hand with UNSCOP's partition plans for Jerusalem, which Mohn of all people was responsible for, in the run-up to the UN's endorsement of Sandström's final recommendation for partition under UN General Assembly Resolution 181.[31]

Between Mohn's work on the Red Cross zone in Jerusalem, Bernadotte's chairmanship of the Red Cross Conference in Stockholm and his connections to the entire Jewish–Palestine issue (which dated back to his efforts during the Nazi Holocaust in Europe), Sandström's close work with both men since 1943 in Greece and Mohn's work for Sandström in UNSCOP and, later, as Bernadotte's chief diplomatic aid in Jerusalem, there can simply be no doubt that the WJC's views concerning the newly envisaged Civilian Convention were going to receive a fair hearing in Stockholm.

28. On Bernadotte's work to save Jews towards the very end of the Second World War in last-minute negotiations with Himmler, see Sune Perrson, 'Folke Bernadotte and the White Buses', *Journal of Holocaust Education*, vol. 9, no. 2–3 (2000), pp. 237–68.

29. Swedish National Archives ('Riksarkivet') Stockholm, File # UD 1920 ARS Dossier system, HP 908, inner file: Grupp 12, X, file marked 'Palestina 1948 September 22', Memorandum of *The Nation* on King Farouk of Egypt's collaboration with the Nazis and the Mufti of Jerusalem. This memorandum was also submitted to the United Nations Economic and Social Council (James Malik) in June 1948, just prior to the Stockholm Red Cross Conference.

30. Paul Mohn Private Archive, Uppsala University Library Carolina Rediviva, Manuscripts and Special Collections Section, Paul Mohn Boxes 22–23.

31. Elad Ben-Dror, *Ralph Bunche and the Arab-Israeli Conflict: Mediation and the UN 1947–1949* (New York: Routledge, 2015), pp. 11–32. See also interview with Ben-Dror, in which he confirms Mohn's drawing of the UNGA Resolution 181 partition line based upon his diary entry, deposited in Mohn's papers at the Uppsala University Library Carolina Rediviva.

Cahen-Salvador's drafting genius and the final securement of Common Article 3's protective purview over civilians targeted by their own governments

Remarkable as it sounds, to date none of the historical descriptions of the making of Common Article 3 has paid any attention to the fact that at the outset of the 1948 XVII Red Cross Conference in Stockholm the official understanding of state parties, National Red Cross and Red Crescent Societies and, most importantly, the ICRC itself was that the newly envisaged Civilian Convention was *not* intended to include civilians targeted by their own government under its protective purview.[32] By the end of Stockholm Conference, however, the understanding of all parties was the diametrically opposite: the new Civilian Convention would indeed also apply to governments targeting their own subjects. This humanitarian achievement was first and foremost due to France's actions in favour of this inclusion – specifically, to Georges Cahen-Salvador's drafting ingenuity.

The WJC's cause of extending the convention's applicability to self-targeted civilians was equally important for France. Yet contrary to the Congress, which was merely an NGO with advisory powers, France was one of the new Civilian Convention's initiators, and the ICRC's biggest supporter. In the run-up to the Stockholm Conference, the highest echelons of the French establishment had already taken the decision that they were going to press forward on this issue.

On 16 August 1948, one week prior to the Stockholm Conference's opening ceremony, Pierre Mendes France, the French ambassador to UN-ECOSOC sent a long report to Foreign Minister Robert Schuman (Figure 11).

Following up on a meeting between Cahen-Salvador's subordinate, Albert Lamarle, and Raphael Lemkin, Mendes France took the time to share with Schuman the reasoning that would need to be applied to extend the protections already accorded in the drafts to resistance fighters to all civilians – including those targeted by their own government.

---

32. *La Pradelle – La Conférence diplomatique* makes no mention of any significant evolution of Common Article 3 in Stockholm. Pictet, in his commentary, also makes no reference to any debates concerning civilians targeted by their own government in Stockholm with regard to Common Article 3's application. See *Pictet Commentary*, p. 30. This critical historical lacuna unfortunately applies also to the new ICRC 2016 commentaries. See *New 2016 ICRC Commentaries on the 4th Geneva Convention*, paragraph 373, footnote 47. The only thing stated here is that 'the deletion of the examples of armed conflicts not of an international character contained in the ICRC draft ("especially cases of civil war, colonial conflicts, or wars of religion") was ultimately guided by the view that too much detail risked weakening the provision because it was impossible to foresee all future circumstances and because the armed conflict character of a situation was independent of its motives'. Not a single word about genocide-targeted victims. Available at: https://ihl-databases.icrc.org/applic/ihl/ihl.nsf/Comment.xsp?action=openDocument&documentId=59F6CDFA4907 36C1C1257F7D004BA0EC#47_B.

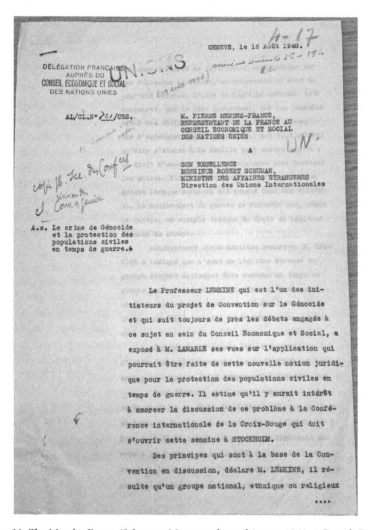

Figure 11 The Mendes France/Schuman Memorandum of August 1948. © French Foreign Ministry Archive La Courneuve. Photo by Gilad Ben-Nun.

Lemkin was a well-respected international lawyer, who had coined the term 'genocide' and who was coming close to securing his lifelong goal in the form of the UN Genocide Convention, which was then approaching its very last stages of endorsement.[33] Mendes France well understood the conflation of terms – for instance, between a minority's 'mutiny' and its 'legitimate resort to self-defence' – once governments with genocidal or ethnic-cleansing aspirations became bent on

33. Lewis, *The Birth of the New Justice*, pp. 181–228 See also: Philippe Sands, *East West Street: On the Origins of Genocide and Crimes against Humanity* (London: Weidenfeld and Nicolson, 2016), pp. 137–89.

the destruction of whole sections of their populace. Explaining to Foreign Minister Schuman the complexities of the overlap between the protection already accorded in the newly envisaged Civilian Convention to resistance fighters and the need to extend this to civilians targeted by their own government, Mendes France wrote,

> Professor Lemkin, who is one of the initiators of the project for a convention against Genocide, and who is following the debates of ECOSOC closely, shared with Monsieur Lamarle his views on the application which this new juridical notion [i.e. the idea of Genocide] has for the protection of civilian populations in times of war. He estimates that there is an interest in engaging in a discussion on this problem at the international Red Cross conference in Stockholm. The principles at the base of the Genocide Convention affirm that a national group, ethnic or religious, [which] is threatened by systematic destruction by an occupying power, would be in a situation of legitimate defence. The idea of legitimate defence is already well established on the individual level by different legislations in different countries, and ought to be extended. Presently, this right concerns one's immediate family. … It ought to be equally applicable to a group once that group's existence is under threat. The uprising of the Ghetto of WARSAW is, even before the principle is laid down ('*avant la lettre*'), a typical example of such a legitimate right of defence.[34]

To current readers, Lemkin's conflation between genocide committed within a country where a government was killing its own nationals (so German Jews in say Dachau concentration in Bavaria prior to 1939), and genocide committed by a foreign power who had invaded a foreign sovereign country (as in the case with the Warsaw Ghetto mentioned earlier) might seem odd. Given the clear distinction we make today between NIAC (so the case in country as within Germany) and IAC (so the case of the Warsaw Ghetto), Lemkin's explicit reference to 'an occupying power' – which exists only in IAC – would as point to his reference to IAC. Yet, here, one must be careful of not committing the methodological error of historical anachronism. The NIAC and IAC categories only come into force after August 1949, once GC-IV had been endorsed. Before this date, neither the NIAC nor the IAC had any ontological legal meaning, since no treaty was ever internationally legislated – which included these categories. What is most important to take from Mendes France's passage is Lemkin's focus on the category of civilians being targeted by their own proper governments. These were hitherto prior to Stockholm never been considered as being eligible for international protection, since this would have been (and still is today!) tantamount to the breach of a state's sovereignty. The issue of the need to protect civilians anywhere, including from their own government if need be, is the crux of the matter here (Figure 12).

---

34. FFMA, File # 768-SUP / 159 t.e.r., AL/ CL.No. /21/CES, *Pierre Mendes-France à Robert Schuman: Le crime de Génocide et la protection des populations civilise en temps de guerre*, Delegation Francaise Aupres du Conseil Economique et Social des Nations Unies, Genève le 16 Août 1948, pp. 1–2 (hereinafter '*Mendes-France- Schuman Stockholm Memorandum*').

Mendes France thus communicated this policy line to the French delegation in Stockholm. There, his arguments could scarcely have fallen on more attentive ears than those of his Holocaust-surviving head of delegation and *Conseiler d'Etat*, Georges Cahen-Salvador. By now, Cahen-Salvador was also the unanimously elected chairman of Sub-Commission III of the Red Cross Legal Commission in Stockholm – the very body in charge of drafting the text of the newly envisaged Civilian Convention. The general Red Cross Legal Commission (Cahen-Salvador's direct superior in Stockholm) was being chaired by Judge Emil Sandström. The Greek delegate Michel Pesmazoglou (Sandström's old friend from the Swedish Rescue Commission for Greece) was elected the chairman of Sub-Commission I and charged with drafting the Sick and Wounded Convention (GC-I). Sandström left little room for manoeuvre: all the subcommittee chairmen under him were long-standing close associates whom he knew well. The 'ducks were now all lined up correctly' for the Geneva Conventions' rewording process to unfold.

The division of labour between the various sub-commissions and the plenary was quite straightforward. Each sub-commission discussed and debated its draft convention text. Points that were agreed upon would be brought before the plenary for final endorsement. Points of contestation would be worked over at the sub-commissions and, in the absence of agreement, would be shared with the plenary for resolution. The text of Common Article 3, then still known as Common Article 2's 4th paragraph, was worked over within both Sub-Commission I (Sick and Wounded Convention) under Pesmazoglou and Sub-Commission II (Prisoners of War Convention, GC-III) headed by the US Generals Paul and Starr. At this stage, it was already envisaged that the provisions concerning NIAC would be inserted, in one way or another, as common articles into all four Geneva Conventions.

Almost immediately – during the first week at Stockholm, in Sub-commission III's session of 21 August – the issue of whether the new Civilian Convention would apply to genocides and civilians targeted by their own government came to a head. Following the adoption of a Norwegian proposal to also include within its purview the case of civilians incarcerated in their own country during a civil war, Chairman Cahen-Salvador gave the floor to WJC delegate Gerhart Riegner. He proposed inserting paragraph 4 of Article 2 of the POW Convention into the Civilian Convention text, thus extending the protections for civilians to officially also cover nationals targeted by their own government. This was exactly what Max Huber had refused to undertake back in 1947. Taking the floor directly after Riegner, Claude Pilloud, the director of the ICRC's legal division, starkly intervened against this motion:

> (Mr. Pilloud – ICRC): responded that the objective of the Convention *was not* to protect civilians from their own government ('*la Convention n'a pas pour objet dé protéger les civils contre leur propre Gouvernement*).[35]

35. *Stockholm XVII Red Cross Conference, Debates of the Sub-Commissions of the Legal Commission, afternoon session of Saturday 21*[st] *August 1948*, p. 50. Emphasis added.

With the question of the Civilian Convention's application remaining unresolved within Sub-commission III, the issue was now destined to resurface in the legal commission's plenary – this time, under Judge Sandström's chairmanship.[36] This debate, on whether to include under the Civilian Convention's protective purview people targeted by their own government, was left until the very last day of the legal commission's deliberations – Friday 27 August 1948. As Judge Sandström opened the debate that morning, he bestowed the first right to speak on the WJC observer Riegner, who stated that he

> would like to draw attention to internal conflicts *within* a country ... for example the scenes which took place in 1938 in Germany where the State's armed forces literally annihilated ('*écrasé*') thousands of civilians, and burnt their houses and their places of worship. ... We [i.e. the WJC] believe this case should also be covered. ... We have undoubtedly been opposed on account of the argument that this Convention is not intended to protect people against their own proper government.[37] (Figure 12)

Throughout the Stockholm Conference, debates surrounding the application of the Civilian Convention to situations of NIAC revolved around the question of which cases ought to be covered by this clause – exemplified in the terms 'civil wars, colonial conflicts, or wars of religion'. Riegner wished to add another category to the cases mentioned, to also include genocides. Yet when President Sandström turned to hear the ideas of Georges Cahen-Salvador, the chairman of the Civilian Convention's drafting committee, the debate took a striking turn.

Applying a methodologically opposed approach to that of Riegner, Cahen-Salvador opted to *reduce* Article 2's wording and restrict it to its bare minimum of general principle. Rather than trying to hopelessly cover the infinite array of possible cases that might one day arise, Cahen-Salvador stated,

> I fully understand the preoccupations of the previous speaker [i.e. Riegner] and completely identify myself with them ('*Je m'y associe pleinement*'). And yet, I believe that within an international convention such as ours, the more we try to be precise, the more we weaken its dominating principle. I would therefore opt to restrict the wording to the bare general minimum *covering all cases*, and solely

---

Available from the website of the ICRC Library at: https://library.icrc.org/library/docs/DOC/11670.pdf.

36. *Stockholm XVII Red Cross Conference, Debates of the Legal Commission, morning session of Friday 27*[th] *August 1948, discussions of Article 2*, pp. 36–7. Available off the website of the ICRC Library at: https://library.icrc.org/library/docs/DOC/18382.pdf

37. Ibid.

Figure 12 World Jewish Congress delegate Gerhart Riegner (second from left) correcting drafts at the Stockholm XVII Red Cross Conference August 1948. © ICRC Photo Archives – Geneva 2018.

maintaining the words 'international war or civil war'. ... In short, I believe we have an interest in leaving the text as brief and simple as possible.[38]

With President Sandström now firmly behind his line of argumentation, Cahen-Salvador thus sealed the debate:

> The more our legal formulations are imperative, clear, precise, and non-detailed, the higher our chances to achieve our goals. It is impossible, within a legal text, to preview all the circumstances which could come about in the future ... I worry, lest our text remains a dead letter, and hope it is rapidly and completely adopted by governments. The more we complicate it, the more we preclude the possibility of obtaining its unanimous endorsement. It is under this preoccupation that I demand to maintain the text as it is ... and strike out ... the words 'especially in cases of civil war, colonial conflicts, wars of religion'. Let us leave nothing but the general formula, which incorporates (*'qui englobe'*) *all possible cases, including those we at the moment cannot envisage.*[39]

38. Ibid., p. 40; emphasis added.
39. Ibid., p. 43; emphasis added.

And so it came about that the final text concerning NIAC, adopted by the Stockholm Conference, came to read:

> In all cases of armed conflict not of an international character which may occur in the territory of one or more of the High Contracting Parties, each of the Parties to the conflict shall be bound to implement the provisions of the present Convention.[40]

The wording here was anything but accidental. As the article opted to use the geographical scope of 'in the territory of one or more of the High Contracting Parties', it explicitly made itself applicable also *within* country, to cases of a government targeting its own. Cabling Jacob Robinson at WJC headquarters in New York, Gerhart Riegner rejoiced at the fact that, thanks to the sole maintenance of the general formula of paragraph 4 of Common Article 2, victims targeted by their own government would now be covered by the newly proposed Civilian Convention:

> Legal committee of the seventeenth International Red Cross Conference presided by Judge Sandstroem Ex-UNSCOP Palestinian enquiry passed important change to Article TWO of proposed convention treatment of civilians time of war removing limitation of it being operative solely quote in civil wars colonial conflicts and wars of religion unquote, and calling for obligatory implementation of the convention quote in all cases of armed conflicts which are not of an international character unquote thus giving principal convention clause wider possibilities of application specially point of view of Jews and other minorities incapable of warlike resistance stop.[41]

Stockholm's universalist revolution had materialized. No person would be beyond the pale of Common Article 3's most basic humanitarian tenets.

---

40. *Revised and new Draft Conventions for the protection of war victims: texts approved and amended by the XVIIth international Red Cross Conference*, Geneva October 1948, p. 114. Footnote 2 on the same page laconically states that 'the words "especially cases of civil war, colonial conflicts or wars of religion" have been deleted'. Available off the website of the ICRC Library at: https://library.icrc.org/library/docs/CDDH/CI_1948/CI_1948_PROJET _ENG_04.pdf.

41. WJCA, File # 10 Box D 106, International Red Cross Conferences 1946–8, original filing under WJC 265, RCA D 136 telegram, 30 August 1948 Stockholm 165/ 161, signed BAUM.

Chapter 4

THE FINAL ACT: THE SOVIETS COME
ON BOARD – GENEVA 1949

'I dare not think what would have become of the "Civilian" Convention'

The remaining stages of the story of how protection for all was enshrined into the Geneva Conventions, especially within Common Article 3, during the 1949 Geneva Conference of Plenipotentiaries have been amply and thoroughly told by Best, Mantilla and recently by van Dijk.[1] In brief, the idea of extending the Geneva Conventions' protection to all combatants and civilians saw two failed attempts within the textual battles over the wording of what was then still Common Article 2, with the United Kingdom and the United States, attempting to limit its scope, ranged against the Soviet, Scandinavian and BENELUX countries, who opted for its expansion.[2] Wishing to break the impasse, Georges Cahen-Salvador and Albert Lamarle orchestrated yet another feat of what Geoffrey Best has termed as a 'genius of French intervention'.[3] They put forward the idea of creating a new common article that would cover all internal wars and NIACs, and which would include a rudimentary set of basic protections applicable to all people no matter who or where they were. These protections – which now outlawed torture, summary killings, degrading treatment and the taking of hostages – were also non-derogable. The new Common Article 3 also stipulated the administration of fundamental due legal processes and, equally importantly, secured the ICRC's role and official right to intervene on behalf of victims. It was this French proposal, as embraced by the majority of the delegates in Geneva, that saved Common Article 3 from being 'gutted' by the United Kingdom and the United States and enabled its insertion into the conventions as we know them today.

1. See notes 9–12 in 'Introduction'.

2. Best, *War and Law since 1945*, pp. 94–179. Anthony Cullen, *The Concept of Non-International Armed Conflict in International Humanitarian Law* (Cambridge: Cambridge University Press, 2010), pp. 25–49. Mantilla, 'The Origins and Evolution of the 1949 Geneva Conventions and the 1977 Additional Protocols', pp. 43–9, n. 17–30.

3. Best, *War and Law since 1945*, pp. 168–78 at 174.

Few delegations were as forcefully committed to the idea of a basic protection for all civilians as that of the Soviet Union, spearheaded by its gifted diplomat (and, years later, two-term judge at the ICJ) Platon Morosov.[4] In his confidential report to his ICRC superiors, Claude Pilloud alluded to the vital role played by the Soviets in securing the Civilian Convention's text, clearly stating that 'he dare not think what would have become of the "Civilian" Convention had it not been for the presence of the Russian delegation'.[5]

So, in the end, it was the Soviets who diplomatically saved Common Article 3 from being gutted. How did it come about that they, of all people, suddenly became so pro-humanitarian in 1949? Was it all just one great Soviet propaganda stunt – or were there also some deep and serious humanitarian concerns at the heart of their efforts in Geneva? In short, were the Soviets bringing to the drafting table fundamental considerations hitherto not sufficiently represented there in the light of their previous absences in 1947 and 1948 – and, if so, what exactly were those considerations?

Historical scholarship has, for the most part, viewed the Soviet bloc's participation in the drafting of GC-IV at the 1949 Conference of Plenipotentiaries as part of a broader, Machiavellian 'peace offensive'.[6] The bloc's representatives were absent, so runs this narrative, from all of GC-IV's proceedings prior to 1949, and decided to 'show up' in Geneva – unexpected and unannounced – at the very last moment.

As we have seen in 'Omission 2' of the Introduction, Geoffrey Best wrote of 'the Soviet bloc's well-contrived humanitarian offensive, which put the US and the UK on the defensive',[7] David Forsythe observed that 'Moscow's policy was to damage an ICRC that was closely linked to a hostile Swiss Confederation'[8] and Catherine Rey-Schyrr wrote that the invitations to both the Stockholm Conference and the Conference of Plenipotentiaries were sent without any explicit mention of the ICRC 'for fear of giving the Soviet Union and the Eastern European countries an excuse not to attend'.[9]

At the end of the day, according to this line of argument, the Soviets were devoid of true humanitarian intentions and never really cared about the development of international humanitarian law under the new Geneva Conventions in the first place. Their participation in the drafting of GC-IV, along with their unequivocal support for the Stockholm draft's textual version of Common Article 3, was nothing more than a propaganda stunt. This was aimed at unmasking the cynicism of Western countries such as the UK, which fought to reduce the conventions'

4. Anthony Cullen, *The Concept of Non-International Armed Conflict*, pp. 45–6.

5. *Pilloud Final Report*, pp. 7–8. See also above n. 41.

6. Best, *War and Law since 1945*, pp. 107–14.

7. Ibid., p. 111.

8. Forsythe, *The Humanitarians*, p. 53. One should note that the footnote to this text refers to Best's *War and Law since 1945*, in the same pages as are quoted above.

9. Rey-Schyrr, *From Yalta to Dien Bien Phu*, p. 225.

protective standards so as to legally enable its unabated targeting of communist combatants, from Greece to Malaya, as the end of British colonial rule unfolded.

In contrast to this theory of Soviet Machiavellianism, sources from the French, ICRC and Bulgarian archives quoted later in the chapter tell a very different story. As Pilloud explained to his ICRC leadership,

> many times, I found myself in need of rallying behind the views of the U.S.S.R. against those of the Anglo-Saxons. We know that under the current political conditions such a position by the ICRC [i.e. that it aligns itself with the Soviet bloc and not with the position of Western allies] is sometimes hard to understand.[10]

What is one to make of this discrepancy between historical scholarship and the clear, unbridled and, most importantly, non-partisan testimony from the ICRC's archives?

To answer this question, we first need to delve into the web of wartime experiences that the Soviets brought with them to the drafting table in Geneva in 1949 so as to see what manner of understandings these were, which might have contributed to their enhanced humanitarian approach there.

France and the Soviets' traumatic experiences which brought them to GC-IV's drafting table before Stockholm

The decade since 2010 has seen a considerable step forward in our historical understanding of the Soviet experience under Nazi occupation, from 1940 to 1945, in what Timothy Snyder and Mark Levene have respectively termed 'the Bloodlands' and the 'European Rimlands' – the 1,000-mile stretch of territory between Western Poland and the St Petersburg–Kursk line west of Moscow, plus the Balkans from the Black Sea to Italy and from Slovakia down to southern mainland Greece and Crete.[11]

The picture that has emerged from Snyder's and Levene's recent studies on what transpired in these territories is truly horrific.[12] Out of some fifty million casualties of the Second World War, roughly half perished solely within the Soviet sphere of influence.[13] Sadly, in the world prior to GC-IV, most of these victims did not enjoy any recourse to the legal protections offered by the three existing Geneva Conventions.

---

10. *Pilloud Final Report – Annex*, pp. N-O, point 4, 'Friends and Adversaries'.

11. Timothy Snyder, *Blood Lands: Europe Between Hitler and Stalin* (London: Penguin, 2010). Mark Levene, *The Crisis of Genocide: Vol 2: Annihilation – The European Rimlands 1939- 1953*, Oxford: Oxford University Press, 2013.

12. Ibid.

13. For these casualty figures see Ronald Grigor Suny, *The Cambridge History of Russia Vol. III- the 20th Century* (Cambridge: Cambridge University Press, 2006), pp. 225–8.

The example of Belarus (then Belorussia) is a case in point. Of its over 9 million inhabitants in May 1941, prior to the German invasion of the Soviet Union (Operation Barbarossa), 1.6 million civilians were directly killed by the Germans – primarily due to a deliberate policy of their starvation, instigated thanks to the 'intentional refusal on the Wehrmacht's part to give *available* food to them'.[14] Another 700,000, as Soviet war prisoners, were executed by the Nazis, who grotesquely argued that their 'blood was free' since the Soviet Union had not signed up to the 1929 POW Geneva Convention. In addition, 500,000 Jewish Belarusians were exterminated as part of the Nazis' 'Final Solution' to Europe's 'Jewish Question'; being civilians, they did not come under the ICRC's purview without a Red Cross Civilian Convention in force. A further 320,000 Belarusians, counted as partisan 'enemy combatants' (most of whom were, in fact, unarmed civilians), were also killed. Finally, an estimated two million Belarusians were deported as slave labour to Germany and Western Poland, with an additional one million fleeing east to the Russian-controlled areas of the Soviet Union. As Snyder has noted, 'By the end of the war, half of the population of Belarus had either been killed or moved. This cannot be said of any other country'.[15]

Now let us try to apply the Geneva Conventions that were in place in 1941 to the aforementioned categories. With all the civilians unprotected, either from killing or from deportation outside of the occupied territory, and with the 700,000 Russian POWs also not covered since the Soviet Union had not signed the Third Geneva Convention of 1929, virtually no single person in Belarus could have claimed any sort of legal protection as per the existing Red Cross Conventions of 1941. In a world in which humanitarian law had more exceptions to its precepts than categories of people that it actually covered, and in which half a country's population could be decimated, we could certainly concede that the Soviets' suspicions of the ICRC's rigid and restrictive legal reading of its own conventions were well merited. Add to this the Soviets' awareness of people like Carl Burckhardt, with his latent anti-Semitism and problematic tacit acceptance of the Nazis, and we can sympathize with their view of the Red Cross as 'supporters of fascism' and 'murderers' (*'suppôts du fascisme – assassins'*) as expressed in the French ambassador to Stockholm's report cited in the Introduction.

By the end of the 1947 Geneva Government Experts' Conference, the international challenges that lay ahead – and which would hinder the adoption of the newly envisaged Geneva Conventions in their more pervasive humanitarian form – were all too obvious to France. In his dispatches from the Government Experts' Conference, Lamarle could not hide the fact that the British delegation saw French ideas for the extension of the protections of the Geneva Conventions to civil wars and 'partisans' as 'perhaps applicable in 20 years'. From a French point of view, this showed a blatant disregard for the ordeal endured by the country's resistance during the war years. Indeed, French negative feelings towards this British downplaying of their Second World War experience under Nazi occupation

---

14. Snyder, *Blood Lands*, p. 251. Levene, *Annihilation: The European Rimlands Vol. 2*, p. 240. Italics in the original.

15. Snyder, *Blood Lands*, p. 251.

reverberated loudly through the corridors of the Quai d'Orsay. The Anglo-Saxon countries, which had largely avoided the experience of Nazi occupation, were not going to suddenly perform a *volte-face* and identify with this cause, no matter that it was championed by France and supported by virtually all the countries that had suffered such an experience – including Europe's Low Countries and the Scandinavian nations to the north.

Yet there was another group of countries that could identify wholeheartedly with the French position. These were the members of the Soviet bloc, with the Soviet Union at their helm. The idea that a post-World War II convention revising the laws of war yet excluding from its signatories the continent's entire Eastern bloc would be tantamount to an international 'dead letter' was so obvious as to lie in the realm of platitude. The meaningful revisions planned for the Geneva Conventions, and the realization of French ambitions for Common Article 3, were dependent on Soviet participation in the drafting process – and the sooner the better.

The greatest hurdle needing to overcome in this regard concerned the visceral hostility that the Soviets harboured towards the ICRC, and which now became directly apparent to French diplomats.[16] The Soviets' open hostility towards the International Committee was down to the Russian perception that it had stood idly by as the Nazi regime obscenely and criminally mishandled Russian war prisoners, and – as we have seen in the Introduction – the Soviets now openly accused the ICRC of providing warm shelter for post-war Russian prisoners, thereby deliberately obstructing their return to the Soviet sphere.

From May 1947 onwards, therefore, a full French diplomatic *démarche* was set in motion – with the country's ambassadors in Washington, London, Brussels and Moscow all 'on board' in trying to engage with the Soviets. The particular technical diplomatic avenue chosen was engagement with the Soviet Red Cross rather than directly with the Soviet government.[17]

In a letter from Geneva to French foreign minister Georges Bidault, Lamarle reported on his extensive discussions with the ICRC about the need to engage with the Soviet Union and build a strategy that would counter Soviet accusations against the committee. In his concluding report to Bidault from the 1947 gathering, Lamarle informed his foreign minister that the president of the Belgian Red Cross, speaking on behalf of all the National Societies, had officially pleaded with the French government to take up the task of engaging the Soviet Union so as to have them on board by the time delegations gathered for the Stockholm Conference the following year.[18]

---

16. FFMA, File 768-SUP / 160, Albert Lamarle Telegram No.44, *Conférence préliminaire pour la revision des Conventions de Genève: Abstention de l'U.S.S.R.*, Geneva 21 April 1947, received in Paris 23 April 1947.

17. FFMA, File 768-SUP / 160, Albert Lamarle Telegram No.44, Conférence préliminaire pour la revision des Conventions de Genève: Abstention de l'U.S.S.R., Geneva 21 April 1947, received in Paris 23 April 1947.

18. FFMA, File 768-SUP / 159, Note: Prochaines Conférences en vue de la revision des Conventions de Genève, Paris 24 May 1947, p. 4.

Between April 1947 and January 1948, there were multiple communications between the French ambassadors in London, Washington and Brussels, who discussed with their national interlocutors in those capitals the need to engage the Soviets.[19] What became clear at this early stage was that the best course of action would be to engage the senior representatives of the Soviet Red Cross societies and see if they could bring the Soviets to the table. These efforts were coordinated by Dr Pierre Depage – the Belgian Red Cross president, and a sworn Belgian communist with well-known and long-standing ties in Moscow.[20] In November 1947, Foreign Minister Bidaut reported to the French ambassador in London that

> it was not until recently, during a regional conference of Red Cross Societies in Belgrade, that Dr. Depage managed to meet with the representative of the Soviet Red Cross Alliances … Mr. Petrovski. He, according to our ambassador in Brussels, seemed rather evasive during the discussions with Dr. Depage. He gave the impression of being torn, between his desire for more humanitarianism in a war to come, and the need to cooperate with the national Red Cross societies of the UK, the US, Sweden and the Lower Countries, which were showing hostile sentiments towards the U.S.S.R. The incidents which transpired during the Belgrade conference, and the harsh criticism of the Red Cross societies of the Eastern countries, against those mentioned above, certainly contributed to Mr. Petrovski's heightened hesitation.[21]

In late February 1948, the Soviet government officially informed the French ambassador in Moscow that it viewed favourably the review of the Geneva Conventions, in accordance with the commonly accepted practice of submitting proposed texts first to a conference of Red Cross societies – in this case, scheduled for the coming August in Stockholm – and later to be presented and worked over by an international conference of state parties.[22] Much of this is confirmed from the sources at the Bulgarian national archives.[23]

---

19. FFMA, File 768-SUP / 160, File: *USSR: Abstentions*, marked as a separate file in blue pencil within this archive carton.

20. Steinacher, *Humanitarians at War*, p. 198.

21. FFMA, File 768-SUP / 159, Le Ministre des Affaires Etrangeres a M. l'Ambassadeur a Londres, Révision et extention des Conventions de Genève de 27 juillet 1929, No. 4070 UN, 10 November 1947.

22. FFMA, File 768-SUP / 160, File: USSR: *Abstentions, Telegram No. 358, 22 February 1948 at 15:15 hours*, received 22 February 1948 at 22: 30 hours, official, receipt stamp 24 February 1948. This file at the French Foreign Ministry archives is a full folder of well over fifty documents and French inter-embassy communiques solely concerned with getting the Soviets 'on board' in the drafting of GC-IV, between April 1947 and August 1948.

23. Bulgarian National State Archives (hereinafter '*BNSA*'), Fund # 1481, batch 1, File 1040 'Bulgarian Red Cross Correspondence: 1947-1952'.

From November 1947 until after the official opening of the Stockholm Conference in mid-August 1948, an extensive exchange of policy-related letters took place between the Bulgarian, Czechoslovakian, Yugoslav and Hungarian National Red Cross Societies.[24] In preparation for the Stockholm Conference, the Bulgarian joint Foreign Ministry and National Red Cross representative prepared an extensive memorandum, written in French, which was sent to the Swedish Red Cross in Stockholm, detailing in full the positions that Bulgaria and the *rest of the Eastern bloc* would advocate at Stockholm vis-à-vis the newly proposed Civilian Convention and its novel idea of protecting internal combatants:

> The modification which we have proposed to bring into the Conventions mentioned in this memorandum, as well as into the project to establish a Convention for the conditions and protections of civilians in times of war, could possibly answer many points of aspiration of certain European countries [i.e. France]. These new dispositions which we propose, should, amongst other things, assure better protections for the rights of civilian populations and partisans, which under current prescriptions concerning 'internal combatants' have proven to be insufficient by the developments of warfare which have outrun these existing provisions. It would seem important, not least for them [i.e. for civilians and internal combatants], that the envisaged Conferences could benefit from the experiences which these countries have acquired during the last conflict.[25]

The ending of this Bulgarian four-page preparatory memorandum for Stockholm speaks for itself: 'We repeat: the revision of the Geneva Conventions and their extension to civilians are the most important issue of the Conference in Stockholm.'[26]

From Stockholm to the Geneva Plenipotentiaries' Conference: The Greek Civil War and the Soviet Securement of Common Article 3

The Stockholm Conference was scheduled to open on 20 August 1948. Citing their protest at the invitation extended to the National Red Cross Society of

---

24. Ibid. See memorandum from the Czechoslovakian government to the Bulgarian government to coordinate positions vis-à-vis the Stockholm Conference (Doc. # 40, 7 February 1948), from several Eastern bloc governments including the Hungarian government (Doc. # 62, 29 May 1948), the Yugoslav government (Doc. 112), the Soviet Union (Doc. 105).

25. Ibid. Memorandum of the Popular Republic of Bulgaria to the Red Cross Conference in Stockholm, 12 June 1948, Doc. 70–1, last paragraph. The full memorandum can be found in Doc. 87–90 in the same file.

26. Ibid., p. 4 (Doc. 90); Italics added.

Franco's fascist Spain, the Bulgarian government informed the Swedish Red Cross secretariat that its Red Cross delegation would not attend.[27] In an orchestrated top-down manner, the Hungarian, Yugoslav and Czechoslovakian Red Cross Societies followed suit. The Soviets would send only a delegation of so-called observers to the scheduled meeting of the Federation of Red Cross and Red Crescent Societies that would take place in tandem with the ICRC's Geneva Conventions' drafting session, but would appropriately refrain from taking part in deliberations over their upcoming revision. Given their ample preparation for the Stockholm Conference, as clearly demonstrated by the in-depth Bulgarian studies of the ICRC draft convention texts, which had arrived in Sofia in May 1948, one is bound to wonder at this last-minute refusal to attend. The answer to this conundrum lies in understanding the revulsion engulfing the Eastern bloc – and especially the Balkan republics of Bulgaria, Albania and Yugoslavia – at the sight of the wholesale murder of communist resistance fighters taking place exactly at that very moment in the neighbouring Greek Civil War.

From the perspective of the Eastern bloc, while the ink had barely dried on the newly proposed Civilian Convention text – along with its ground-breaking Article 2, which extended protections to exactly the kind of resistance fighters represented by the Greek communists – the resistance fighters were being executed en masse, in part by British military personal deployed to Greece and supported by the United States. By mid-1947, the British had lost some 2,000 of their troops in the fighting in Greece – which also incidentally served as the first theatre of operations in which the United States employed its well-known (and ruthlessly anti-communist) Truman Doctrine, which had as its stated purpose the countering of Soviet geopolitical expansion.[28] To add insult to injury, the Spanish fascists – predecessors of the Greek royalist–fascist executioners – who had carried out many similar actions and had duly been cast out of international gatherings, were now being rehabilitated and invited to events associated with – of all things – universal humanitarian causes. Understandably, this was all too much for the Eastern bloc to stomach.

And this, in fact, was (almost verbatim) what the president of the Soviet Red Cross wrote to Count Bernadotte on 15 August 1948. In his letter, Dr Cholodkoff, the president of the alliance of Soviet Red Cross and Red Crescent Societies, explains,

> Having received the preliminary materials in preparation for the XVII Red Cross Conference, the directorship of the Soviet Red Cross and red crescent could not find it possible to attend this gathering for the following reasons. The second

27. Ibid., letter from Peter Poplateff, extraordinary envoy and plenipotentiary minister of the Popular Republic of Bulgaria, to Henrik Beer, secretary general of the Swedish Red Cross, 19 August 1948, Doc. 103.

28. Amikam Nachmani, 'Civil War and Foreign Intervention in Greece: 1946-49', *Journal of Contemporary History*, vol. 25, no. 4 (October 1990), pp. 489–522 at 500.

world war had demonstrated the fascist governments (Germany, Italy, Japan) do not observe the Geneva Conventions. As is well known, cruelties hitherto unknown in human history were committed in the POW camps and in camps for civilians in these countries. The ICRC, upon whom it is incumbent, according to the statutes, to safeguard the rigorous observation of these conventions, knew of these cruelties, yet shut its eyes in face of these cruelties and did not take any measures to counter these violations of the conventions by these countries.

Thus far in his letter, Cholodkoff was explicitly referring to the discrepancy between the legalistic positions taken by the ICRC and the realities on the ground as they had unfolded. The latter – as we have seen – were at their very worst in exactly those Soviet zones occupied by the Germans, such as Belorussia, Ukraine and Poland. Yet Cholodkoff was referring to not merely the infringements that had taken place in the past but also those being perpetrated at the same time as his lines were being written:

> And even after the war, the ICRC has not protested even one single time against the crimes of the monarchist-fascists in Greece, nor against the wholesale bloodletting in Indonesia and Vietnam … amongst the invitees we also find the Spanish government of Franco, who was condemned by world public opinion of all the democratic countries, indeed also expressed by the resolution of the UN General Assembly of 12 December 1946.[29]

What exactly was there to misunderstand here?

The very same communists who had fought and died en masse against the Nazis in Greece, and against the Japanese royalists in Malaya, were now being murdered by British armed forces in both countries. And yet again, the ICRC appeared subservient to its policy of non-interference in cases where its legal mandate was not unequivocally and wholly accepted by all parties. To rub salt into the wound, after all the woes that fascism had brought upon the world, its last remnants (in the shape of representatives of Franco's Spain) were now being rehabilitated into the community of nations. It looked for all the world as if the atrocities and mass graves of the Spanish Civil War – the very same conflict that the venerable ICRC delegate Marcel Junod had attempted to ameliorate but had been shamefully cast aside by those very fascists – had never occurred.

Thus, on the one hand, to say that the Soviets had ample and justifiable reasons for boycotting Stockholm would be an understatement. On the other hand, the ICRC for its part simply, and overtly, had no legal ground whatsoever to work from in caring for Greek resistance fighters and civilians in virtually all the conflicts Cholodkoff cared to mention above. Absent any legal basis to work from, and given Western governments' clear resistance against any ICRC humanitarian

---

29. FFMA, File 768-SUP / 159 ter, Stockholm Files, Letter of Cholodkoff to Bernadotte, 15 August 1948.

intervention in Greece, under these legal constraints – what exactly was the ICRC supposed to do?

Reflecting on these Soviet sentiments during the Stockholm Conference, Albert Lamarle telegrammed French foreign minister Robert Schuman to report on his unofficial 'corridor discussions' with senior Soviet officials. Three high-ranking Soviet Red Cross delegates had arrived, as promised, as official 'observers' to the gathering of members of the International Federation of Red Cross and Red Crescent Societies that was taking place in parallel to the ICRC's Geneva Conventions' drafting session at the same venue. Following his renewed motion to incorporate The Hague regulation clauses into Common Article 3's final Stockholm draft (previously rejected – as seen in Chapter 1 – during the 1947 Government Experts' Conference), Lamarle reported on how the Soviets saw this French motion:

> A few hours ago, I had a conversation with the senior figure of the three 'auditors' from the Soviet Alliance of Red Cross and red Crescent Societies. The Soviet delegate completely understood and identified with this French motion [i.e. in favour of a broad wording of Common Article 3 so as to protect resistance fighters]. He stated that: 'the International Committee of the Red Cross ought, in the case of a civil war as *is currently underway in Greece*, to proceed with enquires, once one side has accused the other of committing atrocities. Had we participated in this Conference and proposed such an enquiry capacity, we would have received objections that our proposal was not part of the agenda, and we would have been defeated by an overwhelming majority which would have come up against us.' I told my interlocutor that if the Soviet Red Cross desired to raise this or that issue, that was all the more reason for them to participate in the Conference, and that contrary to his belief, the result of such a vote was most certainly not predetermined. Following his affirmation that 'the International Committee of the Red Cross should speak more of peace and less of war', I underscored the resolutions which were adopted in Stockholm exactly to that end regarding the role of the ICRC with regard to international comprehension [i.e. of further dissemination of international humanitarian law principles]. The Soviet 'auditor' expressed his desire to discuss with me again towards the end of the Conference.[30] (Italics added)

Lamarle finalized his report to Schuman by quoting the concluding words of his Soviet interlocutor:

> In essence he said: 'the Governments could, if they wanted, envisage Conventions for war time, yet the role of Red Cross societies is a concrete humanitarian one, and not a juridical-legal one.'

---

30. FFMA, File 768-SUP / 159 bis, Telegram No. 391, *ABSENCE DE L'U.S.S.R. A LA CONFERENCE DE LA CROIX ROUGE, Par M. LAMARLE, Stockholm 28 August 1948*, received 30 August 1948 12h.

Therein lay the Greek Civil War's crucial contextual impact upon Common Article 3's drafting, and for that matter upon GC-IV's drafting writ large. Only now did the Soviets come around to fully digest the legal conundrums, and constraints under which the ICRC was operating. And thanks to Lamarle's clarification, its excruciating legal bind was now clear to the Soviets. The substantive impact of this Soviet realization would come to the fore some ten months later at the Geneva Conference of Plenipotentiaries, where the Soviet bloc stood firmly behind the ICRC's calling to secure its legal right to intervene on behalf of civilians in non-international and international armed conflicts. The endorsement of Clause 2 of Common Article 3, which exactly secures this right for the ICRC to intervene, should be associated directly with the above-mentioned passage by Lamarle – and the effects of the Greek Civil War.

Nissim Mevorah, Common Article 3 as the 'Mini-Convention' and the lost preamble's replacement with Cahen-Salvador's Article 32

Lamarle's telegram, written two days before the close of the Stockholm Conference, is instructive. It refutes outright the received historical wisdom that the Soviets simply 'showed up' at the Geneva Conference of Plenipotentiaries some eight months later, following the relaxation of their grip on West Berlin during the city's blockade, in April 1949. As discussed earlier, French advances and attempts to bring the Soviets on board for the project of the new Geneva Convention for Civilians had, in fact, already begun in mid-1947 with secret back-channel approaches. These bore fruit in the Soviet decision to work towards Stockholm – already taken by February 1948, some six months prior to that gathering's commencement. With the benefit of hindsight, the Soviet decision not to come to Stockholm after all should be seen for what it was: a temporary halt of the general Soviet effort in favour of the Geneva Conventions. This effort eventually came to fruition at the 1949 Geneva Conference of Plenipotentiaries.

In his final report on the Conference of Plenipotentiaries, concerning the preparedness of the Soviet delegation, Claude Pilloud noted that

> all the principal Convention texts [i.e. the Stockholm drafts] were translated into Russian, and within several weeks already prior to the conference these delegates became very well prepared. It is due to this, that afterwards, the formal instructions provided to this delegation were to safeguard firmly the texts adopted in Stockholm with only a few amendments. ... It is certain that [the Soviets'] total lack of knowledge of the official languages of the Conference, and their corresponding necessity to always speak via translation rendered their situation amongst the delegations ever more difficult.[31]

---

31. *Pilloud Final Report*, p. 7.

Moscow was well aware of its linguistic, and probably also technical, inferiority to the Western Allied delegations in Geneva. The most acute juncture at which such structural disadvantages might come to the fore was in the choice for the vice chairmanship of the newly elaborated Civilian Convention, under Georges Cahen-Salvador's presidency. With a clear view of having someone diplomatically and linguistically competent to represent them, the Soviets proposed, and all parties unanimously accepted, that the Civilian Convention's vice chairmanship for the Eastern bloc be entrusted to the Bulgarian delegate – Dr Nissim Mevorah. In his final report, Pilloud alluded to Vice Chairman Mevorah's vital role in bridging gaps between East and West:

> The delegations of eastern Europe followed scrupulously the positions forwarded by the delegation of the U.S.S.R. The most active delegate of these countries, and certainly the most intelligent, was Monsieur Mevorah, the leader of the Bulgarian delegation, who tried repeatedly on many occasions, and very tactfully, to find good solutions and compromises.[32]

Mevorah was credited for his ability to break diplomatic impasses notwithstanding his firm adherence to a Soviet world view. In the annex to his final report, Pilloud clearly identifies Mevorah as a 'friend' of the ICRC, with whom special contacts and an ongoing relationship ought to be cultivated at the International Committee's headquarters in Geneva.[33] Who, then, was Mevorah – and how did he, of all people, arrive at the conference's vice chairmanship?[34]

Born 1881 in Sofia into a family of Sephardic Jews exiled in the sixteenth century, who had received asylum in the Ottoman Empire, Nissim Mevorah studied law in the Bulgarian capital and then completed his doctorate in law at the University of Geneva in 1914.[35] While in Geneva, as he developed a strong affinity towards Marxism, Mevorah befriended Vladimir Illich Lenin, who had fled there in 1905 following the failed Communist Revolution in Tsarist Russia that year.[36] Returning to his homeland, in 1920, Mevorah became one of the three founding fathers of the Bulgarian Communist Party.

---

32. Ibid., p. 10.

33. Ibid., Annex, p. O.

34. For a full biographical sctech of Nissim Mevorah's life see: Petko Dobčev, 'Prof. d-r Nisim Mevorach. Biografičen očerk' [Prof. Dr Nisim Mevorach – biographical entry] in: *Evrejski imena v bălgarskata juridičeska nauka*, Sofija 2006, pp. 80–90. [in Bulgarian].

35. Nissim Mevorah, 'De la Formation des contrats, doctrine et jurisprudence françaises considérées au point de vue des théories modernes' *thèse de doctorat*, Lausanne: E. Toso & Cie. 1914. A copy of this thesis can be consulted at the Bibliothéque Nationale de France François Mitterrand, ref. 8- THETA GEN DR-80.

36. Barouh Mevorah, 'Proffessor Nissim Mevorah's Bulgarian-Jewish Way of Life', *East-European Quarterly*, vol. 19, no. 1 (March 1985), pp. 75–80 at 76.

Being married to a Gentile, Mevorah, along with his family, was spared the fate of much of the rest of Bulgarian Jewry, who during the Second World War were deported from their homes into work-camps – albeit graciously saved from the grimmer destiny awaiting European Jewry as a whole, in part thanks to the efforts of the Bulgarian Orthodox Church in Sofia.[37] Hiding out in the capital throughout the war, Mevorah organized clandestine actions in favour of Jews and persecuted Bulgarian communists along with his son, the well-known poet Valerie Petrov (who, years later, was considered for the Nobel Prize in literature), who was an active member of the Bulgarian anti-Nazi underground there.[38] Thus, like many of GC-IV's prime movers, Mevorah was a Holocaust-surviving Jew who knew personally, and all too well, what it meant being a civilian targeted by his own government – as had in fact happened to 7,762 Bulgarian-Macedonian Jews, who were deported and murdered in Auschwitz, with just over 200 of them surviving the Holocaust.[39]

Being a senior figure in Bulgaria's post-World War II communist regime, and after a stint as a judge in the post-war trials of Bulgarian fascists, in 1947, Mevorah assumed his country's second-highest diplomatic commission, as its ambassador to Washington, presenting his credentials to President Truman later that year.[40] With this background in mind, the reasons behind Soviet leader Joseph Stalin's decision to appoint Mevorah as the Soviet bloc's vice chairman in Geneva become clearer. A gifted jurist with an excellent command of French and English, a communist-bloc ambassador to the United States well acquainted with Washington's corridors of power and yet a long-standing sworn communist, Mevorah could provide the Soviet bloc with the diplomatic clout and credibility that it sorely needed in Geneva.

Yet there was one more element in his background that helps to explain his vital role in Geneva in 1949. Mevorah was also an expert on Greece, who spoke Greek and who knew well the atrocities committed by Bulgarian fascists in Greece's northern territories during the Second World War, under its Bulgarian occupation there. Three years later, in 1952, Mevorah would help to chair the first session of the Bulgarian–Greek Reparations Commission, which was charged with determining the rate of compensation due to Greece from his homeland for the wartime damages that the latter had caused. In 1965 – three years before his death, and upon this commission's successful conclusion – Mevorah was invited to the

37. Ibid., p. 76.

38. Author's interview with Ana Hadzimisheva, Nissim Mevorah's great-granddaughter, held in the bookshop ('Nissim's') that still bears her great-grandfather's name (and portrait). Sofia, 30 May 2017. See also: Mevorah, *Nissim Mevorah's Bulgarian-Jewish Life*, p. 76.

39. Stefan Troebst, 'Macedonian Historiography on the Holocaust in Macedonia under Bulgarian Occupation', in Stefan Troebst (ed.), *Zwischen Arktis, Adria und Armenien: Das östliche Europa und seine Ränder Aufsätze, Essays und Vorträge 1983-2016* (Köln & Wien: Böhlau Verlag, 2017), p. 406, n. 1.

40. Mevorah, *Nissim Mevorah's Bulgarian-Jewish Life*, p. 77.

Figure 13 The Bulgarian Delegation to the Greece-Bulgaria Reparations Commission 1952 – Nissim Mevorah as head of the delegation sitting at the centre table fifth from left. ©Bulgarian National Archives – Sofia. Photo by Gilad Ben-Nun.

Source: Bulgarian National Archives, Fund 1578, # 1, 66.

Figure 14 The reopening of the Bulgarian Embassy in Athens in 1965, after decades of hostilities – Mevorah is on the right. ©Bulgarian National Archives – Sofia. Photo by Gilad Ben-Nun.

Source: Bulgarian National Archives, Fund 1578, # 1, 66.

reopening of Bulgaria's embassy in Athens, several decades after its closure during the late interwar period (Figures 13–15).

As the Bulgarian ambassador to Washington in 1947 – and with his long-standing ties to Moscow, dating back to his friendship with Lenin in Geneva – Mevorah saw first-hand how heightened Cold War suspicions could turn deadly – as was the case with Greece's civil war and Truman's inauguration of his eponymous doctrine in March 1947, just as Mevorah started his US ambassadorial tenure.

With the UK's military withdrawal from Greece, and falsely believing that Stalin sought to support the Greek communists, US president Truman launched

Figure 15 Caricature of Nissim Mevorah in 1951, commissioned by the Bulgarian government commemorating commendable Bulgarian politicians and jurists. ©Bulgarian National Archives – Sofia. Photo by Gilad Ben-Nun.

Source: Bulgarian National Archives, Fund 893 K, # 1, 17.

a massive arms and financial support package to Greece (and Turkey). He thus strengthened royalist and proto-fascist elements in both those countries, which would – partly as a result thereof – each descend into military-juntas some two decades later. In fact, as the US State Department subsequently acknowledged, not only did Stalin 'deliberately refrain from providing any support to the Greek Communists' but he also 'had forced Yugoslav Prime Minister Josip Tito to follow suit, much to the detriment of Soviet-Yugoslav relations'.[41] Yet in 1947 Washington, confronting US officials with the facts – that is, that the Soviets were *not* supporting Greek communists, as per the terms of the 1943 Tehran Declaration – was futile. The Americans had their opinions. If in 1946, Ho Chi Minh could bend over backwards and commit himself to the Atlantic Charter, truly wishing for US friendship but to no avail, then Washington ambassadors such as Mevorah stood no chance whatever of swaying their US counterparts away from their misconceived perceptions concerning Greece.[42]

Thus in 1947, as the ICRC was taking its earliest steps towards GC-IV's drafting at the Geneva Governments Experts' Conference, Mevorah watched from the sidelines as the United States mistakenly inflamed the Greek Civil War with more arms and support for the royalists. Meanwhile, back in Sofia, and thanks to his long-standing acquaintances in Geneva, since his university days there, he was now tasked with coordinating all the material (in French) that began arriving from the ICRC to Bulgaria in preparation for the Stockholm Conference.[43]

All the Red Cross files at the Bulgarian National Archive were handled by Mevorah. He himself wrote the memorandum of the Bulgarian Red Cross, drafted in French and sent to the ICRC in Geneva dated 12 June 1948 (so, eight weeks prior to the opening of Stockholm), in which Bulgaria officially communicated to the ICRC that it would participate in Stockholm.[44] In the event, Mevorah did not make

41. See the US government's official entry 'The Truman Doctrine – 1947' in *US State Department- Office of the Historian*. Available at: https://history.state.gov/milestones/1945-1952/truman-doctrine

42. On the tragic US misreading of the Vietnamese struggle for independence, on Ho Chi Minh's true desire for American friendship and on his repeated (and unanswered) telegrams to Truman – all of which, years later, resulted in the US involvement in Vietnam, costing the lives of over 3 million Vietnamese and over 50,000 Americans – see the Pulitzer-Prize-winning account by Fredrik Logevall, *Embers of War: The Fall of an Empire and the Making of America's Vietnam* (New York: Random House, 2014), pp. 92–122. For a sharp yet concise presentation of the same, see James M. Lindsay, 'Remembering Ho Chi Minh's 1945 Declaration of Vietnam's Independence', *Council on Foreign Relations Blog*, 2 September 2016. Available at: https://www.cfr.org/blog/remembering-ho-chi-minhs-1945-declaration-vietnams-independence.

43. Bulgarian National Archives Sofia, Files of the Bulgarian Red Cross, Fund No. 1481, # 1, 1040.

44. Bulgarian National Archives Sofia, Files of the Bulgarian Red Cross, Fund No. 1481, # 1, 1040, Doc. # 70. MEMORANDUM (in French), handwritten red pen marks on the top right corner indicating the date 12.vi. 1948.

it to the Swedish capital in 1948. Yet at the GC-IV's final and most crucial drafting stage, during the 1949 Geneva Conference of Plenipotentiaries, the Bulgarian communist would grow to become by far the most indispensable delegate within the entire Soviet bloc, with whom diplomatic compromises could be struck.

Mevorah's special stature in Western eyes was confirmed from the start as Georges Cahen-Salvador himself explicitly requested his nomination as vice chairman of Committee III, charged with elaborating the Civilian Convention in Geneva. As the plenary early on (25 April 1949) graciously (and unanimously) confirmed Cahen-Salvador's chairmanship, it heeded the old man's request and followed suit with Mevorah's unanimous confirmation as well.[45] From then on, Mevorah acted as Cahen-Salvador's right-hand man in a manner that would certainly have been familiar to the old French Conseiller d'État. In all, Mevorah chaired four sessions of the roughly fifty that Committee III undertook, each time being explicitly bestowed with the chairmanship by Cahen-Salvador.[46] The latter also charged him with acting as chief rapporteur in the specific drafting committees for no less than eleven articles of the entire Civilian Convention.[47]

At times, when one reads Mevorah's statements, especially when he was required to assume Cahen-Salvador's own duties upon his absence as chairman, one gets the feeling that he actually tried to emulate the dictums of the *éminence grise* himself. With the United Kingdom and the United States serving as military occupiers in both Germany and Japan, the last thing that those Allied countries desired was an international convention that would coerce them to provide more food and supplies than they were already doing to their occupied German and Japanese civilian populations. Being charged with the Articles that dealt with these very aspects, Mevorah

> warned the Committee against accepting amendments which, like that of the United States of America, tended to weaken the Stockholm wording ... such as 'within the means available to it', 'if possible' or 'shall endeavour' would weaken to a regrettable extent the scope of the provisions under discussion.[48]

45. *Final Record*, vol. 2- A, p. 619.

46. Mevorah chaired sessions 3, 7, 9 and 39. See, respectively, *Final Record*, pp. 625, 636, 641, 754.

47. Mevorah served as chief rapporteur for all the articles concerning the securing of conditions for civilians in occupied territories and the responsibilities of occupying powers (today's Articles 55–60; originally, Articles 49–54), including food supplies, hygiene and public health, spiritual assistance and relief. For Cahen-Salvador's charging of Mevorah with drafting these articles, see *Final Record*, vol. 2-A, p. 669. For Mevorah's reposts to Cahen-Salvador and the plenary with the results of his party's drafting work, all of which was unanimously accepted by the plenary, see *Final Record*, vol. 2-A, pp. 752–3. In addition, Mevorah was charged by Cahen-Salvador with heading the drafting of all the Articles concerning Chapter V of today's text (Articles 136–141). See *Final Record*, vol. 2-A, pp. 791–2.

48. *Final Record*, vol. 2-A, p. 669.

Mevorah had just flown in from Washington in early 1949 back to Europe. He knew all too well the English-language British Common Law tendency to qualify any sentence in favour of force majeure.[49] He was certainly not in the mood for the British or American type of insertions that would allow states 'off the hook' with regard to their responsibilities to occupied civilians. Following his experiences in occupied France (a situation that, with the exception of Britain's tiny Channel Islands, was alien to US or UK wartime experience), his choice of words could just as well have been those adopted by Cahen-Salvador himself.

The other side of Mevorah's work consisted of bridging the gap with the Soviet bloc. In terms of its own modest size – representing a small and, in 1949, financially impoverished population – Bulgaria could not afford to send more than two delegates to Geneva.[50] Mevorah might not always have been in total agreement with his Russian counterparts but nevertheless, in virtually all cases, Bulgaria scrupulously followed suit – as did the other sixteen delegations of the Soviet bloc – once the USSR delegation put down any amendment to any Article. Bulgaria, in fact, hardly tabled any amendments of its own during GC-IV's entire drafting process. Instead, Mevorah's primary task was to find ways to reach out to, convince and persuade Western delegations of the merits of the multiple amendments that the Soviet Union under Platon Morosov's leadership – saw fit to table. Be it on the issue of Soviet POWs wishing not to return to the Soviet Union or on the failed Soviet resolution calling for a general ban on the use of nuclear weapons (as outlined in 'Omission 5' of Chapter 1), Mevorah often proved a better and more eloquent speaker than Morosov did.[51]

Yet there was one instance in which one feels that it was Mevorah who influenced Moscow rather than the other way around. This was on the Soviet bloc's securing of Article 32 in today's GC-IV. No other Article in the Civilian Convention drew as much of its text and thematic thrust from the Nazi Holocaust as this one did. It states that

the High Contracting Parties specifically agree that each of them is prohibited from taking any measure of such a character as to cause the physical suffering *or extermination* of protected persons at their hands. This prohibition applies not only to murder, torture, corporal punishment, mutilation and *medical or*

49. See Mevorah's own quote on this principle in British Common Law, as he chastised the United States: 'Obviously, to quote a maxim of common law, "no one is bound to do the impossible"; but that adage referred to absolute impossibility.' *Final Record*, vol. 2- A, p. 619.

50. Statement by Mevorah, 7th plenary meeting, Wednesday, 25 May 1949, *Final Record*, vol. 2-A, p. 40.

51. On the issue of POWs, see Best, *War and Law since 1945*, p. 138. For Mevorah's scathing diplomatic dressing-down of the United States and the United Kingdom over their reluctance to call for a ban on nuclear weapons, in stark contrast to any logical vision towards the limitation of war and its horrendous consequences a mere four years after Hiroshima and Nagasaki, see *Final Record,* vol. 2-B, p. 499.

scientific experiments not necessitated by the medical treatment of a protected person, but also to any other measures of brutality whether applied by civilian or military agents.[52]

Any reader conversant with the Holocaust's history of will immediately recognize what this Article is about – namely, the Nazis' extermination of European Jewry and many other people such as the Sinti and Roma, four million Poles, Russians, Ukrainians and others. As is clear from Article 32's reference to 'protected persons' the crimes enlisted in it precisely because they were not internationally legally criminalized beforehand with regard to the conduct of military occupiers. At the end of the day, Germany chose to commit most of these crimes *not* on its native soil but rather in occupied Poland, where all the Nazi extermination camps were established. The clear reference to Joseph Mengele's medical experiments in Auschwitz's notorious Block Number 10 is virtually self-explanatory in this context. In his final report to Bulgarian foreign minister Vladimir Poptomov, at the end of the Geneva Plenipotentiaries' Conference, Mevorah explained where and how Article 32 (then still known as Article 29-A) had been born:

> Article 29-A represents a great gain for us and the U.S.S.R. The Mexican and then the French delegate [i.e. Cahen-Salvador] stated that this article is the moral justification of the conference before the peoples of the world, especially after the removal of the preamble. This text explicitly prohibits 'any measures causing physical suffering or the extermination of the protected persons'. … The Anglo-Americans led a long fight against this text, but we prevailed and it remained in the convention.[53]

Article 29-A was, in actual fact, Cahen-Salvador's brainchild. Initially intended to appear upfront in GC-IV's preamble, once it became clear (after week-long discussions) that no agreement could be struck concerning this preamble's text, Cahen-Salvador – in association with the Mexican delegation – proposed the basis for this text, which was later modified thanks to a Soviet amendment tabled by Morosov.[54]

The intimate relationship between Article 32 and Common Article 3 was explained by none other than Cahen-Salvador himself. In a lengthy speech delivered one week before the Geneva Plenipotentiaries Conference's closing ceremony, the 'old man' explained the reasoning behind his fundamental push

52. Text of GC-IV's Article 32 (Italics added), available at the ICRC's website: https://ihl-databases.icrc.org/applic/ihl/ihl.nsf/9861b8c2f0e83ed3c1256403003fb8c5/0146c998773b1496c12563cd0051bc2f.

53. Bulgarian National Archives – Sofia, Fund 1481, OII1, 851, Diplomatic New Conventions, Nissim Mevorah Final Report to Bulgarian Foreign Minister Vladimir Poptomov, 10 August 1949, p. 13 (Doc. # 124). Translation from Bulgarian by Martin Petrov.

54. For Morosov's final touches to Article 32's text, see *Final Record*, vol. 2-B, p. 645.

in favour of it. He began by lamenting the failure to secure a preamble for GC-IV, stressing its importance and – not least – his *personal* experience, which had driven him to support the preamble, and now Article 32 in its stead:

> Article 29A, together with Article 31, is all that actually remains of the ill-fated Preamble. ... This Preamble was intended to proclaim those humanitarian principles ... as well as a summary of the preliminary provisions, and of the essential measures embodied in our Convention for the prevention of the atrocities ... *which many of us have experienced.*[55] (Italics added)

And now Cahen-Salvador reached his cardinal point: the lost preamble was meant to encapsulate the most fundamental principles of the entire Civilian Convention. Articles 32, 33 and 34 had now become the true heart of it all – the very heart that had also evolved into Common Article 3:

> It is essential that these Articles [i.e. Articles 32, 33 and 34] express the whole contents of the Preamble now ... reproduced in an Article which [unfortunately] relates exclusively and completely to civil war 'in the case of armed conflict not of an international character occurring in the territory of one of the High Contracting Parties, each Party to the conflict shall be bound to apply, as a minimum, the following provisions' [i.e. today's Common Article 3].
> The acts prohibited at all times and in all places ... are then quoted; ... 'violence to life and person, in particular murder of all kinds, mutilation, cruel treatment and torture'; secondly, 'taking of hostages'; thirdly, 'outrages upon personal dignity, in particular humiliating and degrading treatment'; and lastly sentences passed and executions carried out without previous judgment.[56]

In conclusion, Cahen-Salvador reminded the delegates that Article 32 was

> the essential substance of the minimum humanitarian safeguards to which the persons whom we intend to protect are entitled, *even though they do not enjoy the benefit of all the provisions of the Convention.*[57] (Italics added)

To summarize, Article 32, along with Article 33 (prohibition of pillage, reprisals and collective punishments) and Article 34 (prohibition of hostage taking), is little more than a reiteration of Common Article 3's principles – yet now extended to all humans in war, as opposed to Common Article 3's exclusivity to people under NIACs. GC-IV's drafters failed to arrive at an agreed preamble for the same reason that the entire Civilian Convention almost collapsed on account of Common

---

55. Statement by Cahen-Salvador, 3 August 1949, 26th plenary session of the convention for the Protection of Civilians, *Final Record*, vol. 2-B, p. 409.

56. Ibid.

57. Ibid.

Article 3 – namely, GC-IV's scope of application. The United Kingdom and the United States were bent on creating a piecemeal convention, applying different prerogatives to different categories of people. To them, guerrilla fighters could under no circumstances enjoy the same rights as sovereign-government soldiers. The Soviets and the Nordics – as harbingers of universalism, as seen in the previous chapter – wished for an all-encompassing convention that would be applicable to all people, under all circumstances, in all places.

GC-IV's most basic dilemma was whether it would be truly universal at its core or whether, already contained within its definitions, it would seek to differentiate between peoples. To address Geoffrey Best's perplexity as to why the preamble failed to materialize, it was the aforementioned fundamental schism that prevented it from being accepted by both sides in Geneva.[58] In lieu of its lost universality, given the compromise inherent in Common Article 3's limitation of rights (as opposed to the *entire* convention's applicability to people under IAC), came Articles 32–34. In them, Cahen-Salvador and Morosov attempted to reinvigorate GC-IV's universalism.

Over the years, Common Article 3 has been referred to as 'a convention in the miniature', alluding to the prevailing view of its provisions as GC-IV's absolute essence while securing the inalienable right of all people to be spared from the acts that it unconditionally prohibits. Ironically, the term 'mini-convention' was not meant as a compliment to the endorsement of Common Article 3 as a humanitarian achievement but rather as a derogatory reference to its fundamental conciliatory idea. Coined by the Soviet delegate Morosov,[59] the term 'a convention in the miniature' signalled for the Soviets the inability of the Plenipotentiaries' Conference to accept 'the broadest humanitarian measures contained in the Convention', which the Soviets officially tabled as a proposal for the entire conference to adopt.[60] In short, the Soviets were proposing the application of *all* the provisions of the Geneva Conventions *in their entirety* to situations of NIACs. Morozov's derogatory tone was addressed to the Plenipotentiaries Conference's decision to opt for what he saw as a meagre half-measure, which in his eyes did not go remotely far enough in terms of its substantive protective measures.

58. Best, *War and Law since 1945*, p. 106: 'The missing preamble was one of the two big events of the Convention making process to which the Conventions themselves offer no clue.' Without access to Soviet archives back in 1994 when he wrote his book, Best could not understand why the preamble never materialized. He therefore ascribed Article 32 simply to the attempt of the drafters to 'distance themselves from excessive Second World War practices' – see: Best, *War and Law since 1945*, p. 1126.

59. *Final Record*, vol. 2 B, p. 98 at the bottom, statement by Morosov (USSR), 37th meeting of the special committee of the committee for common articles ('joint committee), Friday 8 July 1949, 10.00 am.

60. *Final Record*, vol. 2 B, p. 35, Seventh Report drawn up by the Special Committee Application of the conventions to armed conflict not of an international character, 11th meeting of the Joint Committee, Tuesday 19 July 1949, 10.00 am.

GC-IV's universal application – or lack thereof, as per the UK and US positions – was one of the two most contentious obstacles that needed to be overcome in order to secure the Civilian Convention's successful conclusion. Paradoxically, the other issue – the banning of nuclear weapons – proved to be the less alarming of the two in terms of its diplomatic potential to derail the entire Plenipotentiaries' Conference. After all – as 'Omission 5' of the Introduction makes plain – the Soviets already 'had the bomb', and they were bent on detonating it in their first nuclear test should a ban on such weapons not be secured at Geneva.

Mevorah probably had no knowledge that the Soviets had this nuclear 'ace up their sleeve'. To continue the analogy, the United States and the Soviet Union virtually 'held all the cards' on this matter anyway, so there was little that the Bulgarian diplomat could do about the nuclear issue. However, he was all too aware of the other make-or-break issue's alarmingly destructive diplomatic potential – and few people were better positioned to help in the controversy surrounding GC-IV's universal application. Cahen-Salvador had put forward Mevorah's inspired Common Article 3 compromise, which essentially amounted to universalism with limits, and the latter was probably the 'mover and shaker' who brought the Soviets to accept this arrangement and back down from their extreme position of threatening to wreck the entire conference over the issue. Between the Soviets' rigidity and Cahen-Salvador's conciliatory spirit, therefore, Mevorah was certainly leaning towards his fellow Holocaust-surviving chairman.

A close reading of the documents certainly points to the possibility that Mevorah and Cahen-Salvador cooperated and jointly moved to draw the Russians away from 'blowing up' the conference. Certainly, Mevorah's two earlier dispatches from Geneva to the then Bulgarian foreign minister, Vasil Kolarov, demonstrate a much higher degree of anxiety than his final communication to Kolarov's successor, Vladimir Poptomov, following Kolarov's appointment as the prime minister in July 1949, in the midst of the Plenipotentiaries Conference.[61]

But perhaps more important was the debate at the Plenipotentiaries' Conference on Cahen-Salvador's Article 29-A. Being accorded solely observer status to the 1949 Conference, Poland could not (and did not) actively participate in any of its debates. Nevertheless, on one single occasion, during the debate on Article 29-A, Chairman Cahen-Salvador extraordinarily requested that the plenary accord the Polish observer the right to address the conference. In his speech in favour of Article 29-A, the Polish observer undertook to support the Soviet Union in its

61. For Mevorah's first dispatch from the Geneva Plenipotentiaries Conference, see Bulgarian National Archives – Sofia, Fund 1481, OΠ1, 851, Diplomatic New Conventions, Nissim Mevorah Report to Bulgarian Foreign Minister Vasil Kolarov, 5 June 1949 (Doc. # 88 – Doc. # 111). For Mevorah's first dispatch from the Geneva Plenipotentiaries Conference, see Bulgarian National Archives – Sofia, Fund 1481, OΠ1, 851, Diplomatic New Conventions, Nissim Mevorah Report to Bulgarian Foreign Minister Vasil Kolarov, 20 July 1949 (Doc. # 150– Doc. # 153 – dispatch incomplete).

efforts to arrive at a wording of this article that would allow it to vote in its favour, just before Mevorah's own statement to that exact effect:

> Mr. KALINA (Poland) said that out of six million Polish citizens who had lost their lives in the last war, the majority had been victims of systematic measures of extermination. Members of the Conference could hardly conceive the methods followed by those responsible. It was on those grounds that the general wording proposed by the Soviet Delegation was in his view preferable to that of the Drafting Committee.[62]

We should stress here again that this was the only statement that Poland made during the entire Conference of Plenipotentiaries. With Stalin's harsh grip on the country during those years, and his indictment of Władysław Gomułka's government just a few months earlier, the appearance of a Polish delegate in favour of a Soviet position could have been thought unlikely. As the Soviet bloc's vice chairman of the Civilian Convention, there can be virtually no doubt that Mevorah single-handedly secured this sole appearance by Poland – in favour of the Soviet wording for Article 29-A.

In his final report to Bulgarian foreign minister Poptomov, at the end of the Geneva Plenipotentiaries' Conference, Nissim Mevorah laconically captured this Soviet universalist spirit, which eventually prevailed in the making of Common Article 3:

> Evaluation of the conventions: The conventions produced can be characterised in short as an attempt at humanising war. They are dominated by the principles of the Red Cross, strengthened by the bitter experience of the barbaric outbursts of the Germans during the past world war. They now encompass humane treatment of prisoners of war, the outlawing of taking hostages, the outlawing of torture, the outlawing of genocide, the outlawing of forced labour; the protection of the Red Cross emblem in any territory or on any vehicle, the protection of the civilian population, and especially of children, women, and the elderly; the rule of law in war and the prohibition of retroactive laws, the limitation upon the administration of the death penalty, the outlawing of collective punishment, outlawing reprisals, regular humanitarian protection, the contact with protecting countries and powers, the right to correspondence, to receiving aid and so forth.[63]

---

62. Statement of the Polish observer Kalina, 13th meeting of Committee III (Civilians), Wednesday, 15 June 1949, *Final Record*, vol. 2-A, p. 718.

63. Bulgarian National Archives – Sofia, Fund 1481, ОП1, 851, Diplomatic New Conventions, Nissim Mevorah Final Report to Bulgarian Foreign Minister Vladimir Poptomov, 10 August 1949, p. 10 (Doc. # 121). Translation from Bulgarian by Martin Petrov.

This is how Mevorah, the vice chairman of the Civilian Convention, understood the new Geneva Conventions – and especially the Convention for Civilians, which in 1949 he had laboured so hard to draft.

The historical picture, then, of how a 'humanitarian miracle' such as Common Article 3 came to be adopted in Geneva is actually quite clear. Whereas both at the 1947 Government Experts' Conference and in 1948 in Stockholm, 'the humanitarians' were in a minority led by France and Denmark, the coming on board of the Soviet Union with no less than seventeen extra states at the Geneva Conference of Plenipotentiaries fundamentally changed the electoral landscape in the 1949 Geneva voting plenary, as opposed to previous state gatherings. With the pendulum shifting sharply back to the centre now that the Soviets and their allies were at the drafting table, and away from the previous pro-occupier (US–UK) 'electoral colleges' in Geneva 1947 and Stockholm 1948, the final acceptance of Common Article 3 as a set of basic humanitarian provisions on which all could agree – albeit without the entire conventions' stipulations being applicable, as a good compromise and as the negotiation's basic common ground – makes complete sense.

None of the communist nations that had suffered the appalling casualty numbers quoted by Snyder and Levene had been represented – either at the 1947 Geneva Governments Experts' Conference or at the 1948 XVII Red Cross Conference in Stockholm. Put simply, no Western European power (France included) could have had the remotest idea of what the harshest realities of the Second World War had been like for these 'Bloodlands' – the very essence of what the new Geneva Conventions were trying to ensure never happened again.

The most fundamental attribute shared by Cahen-Salvador and Mevorah was their unabating desire for a universal and all-encompassing purview for the Civilian Convention, based on their *personal* experiences as drafters who had also been Holocaust survivors a mere four years prior to GC-IV's making. Consequently, in their eyes, no human being ought to have been beyond GC-IV's protective pale.

Be it through the ICRC's insistence that the Civilian Convention *not* cover people under genocide targeted by their own government or via the UK's refusal to admit that guerrilla fighters were just as human as colonial occupation forces (and certainly more morally justified), the greatest danger posed to the Civilian Convention was the loss of its universalism. The UK's view, which would have sliced the Geneva Conventions into an endless list of human categories and then cherry-picked the people who might benefit from its protections, would have resulted in a never-ending rota of legal pretexts for *who not* to apply the Geneva Conventions to. Had this position prevailed, people like Gerhart Riegner would have been left 'hung out to dry' yet again, and there probably would not have been a Civilian Convention at all – since the Soviets would not have been able to stomach it. With communist guerrillas fighting their way forward – from Greece to Malaya, to Indonesia and Indochina – piecemeal legal categories and humanitarian conventions as full of holes as a Swiss cheese were substantively worthless in Soviet eyes. Universalism – as enshrined in Common Article 3 and in GC-IV's Articles 32–4 – was the only remedy to the past occurrences of the Second World War. It was also the correct remedy for the upcoming traumatic realties of decolonization – which, at this historical juncture, lay just around the corner.

Part Two

THE INHERENT ILLEGITIMACY OF OCCUPATION: ARTICLES 49 AND 68

Prohibition of population transfers and restrictions on the administration of the death penalty

Why is prolonged military occupation so inherently wrong in our eyes? To the average reader, the answer to this question seems quite obvious. In a world in which all people are regarded as being equal, and all ought to enjoy their right to self-determination, the condition whereby one human group forcefully controls another within a territory legally deemed and broadly conceived as indigenously belonging to that oppressed group seems morally repulsive. Despite our current familiarity with such problematic situations on a global scale, however, the very idea that a territory can be in a limbo-like state of 'military occupation' – that is, neither belonging to its conqueror nor granted to the occupied people in it – is, in and of itself, a novelty in human history. In the history of the laws of nations, it is little more than a century old.

The crux of the matter lies in the nature of military conquest – which, in contrast, is a phenomenon as old as humanity itself. From time immemorial up until the second half of the nineteenth century, the ultimate result of a territory's military conquest, once the conquered party had been completely subjugated and had ceased to exercise any resistance (*debellatio*),[1] was the transfer of its ownership to the conqueror. In his 1951 course at The Hague Academy of International Law, in the aftermath of the Second World War, the renowned international jurist Hans Wehberg explained conquest in pre-modern international law as follows:

> Under classical international law, it was generally estimated that the simple occupation of a foreign territory permitted its annexation ... once the enemy had been completely defeated, as in a *debellatio*, and once the conqueror managed to appropriate the territory in its entirety ... the law of conquest was applicable

---

1. The legal term for the end of a conflict caused by the complete destruction of a hostile state.

pure and simple.[2] In the classical law of the *jus publicum europaeum*,[3] war and conquest were inseparable.

Demonstrating the power of this concept of conquest, Wehberg went on to quote none other than Max Huber, the *ICRC president and two-term president of the League of Nations' Permanent Court of International Justice.* As late as 1898, the scrupulously legalistic Huber emphatically and unequivocally maintained that territorial conquest corresponded to the transfer of sovereign title to the territory conquered.[4] A mere half century later, however, Huber's understanding that under State Succession (the title of his famous book) conquest would facilitate the transfer of sovereignty and ownership of the conquered territory to its aggressor was rendered anathema by most of the world's states and by the majority of international legal scholars. The new UN Charter explicitly prohibited any war of aggression, which the Nuremberg trials considered a harsh crime alongside war crimes and crimes against humanity.[5] By the late 1950s, and certainly by the 1960s, occupation came to be regarded, in the recent words of legal academic Eyal Benvenisti, as 'a state of exception for international law' – that is, as an anomaly to the norm.[6] The normal state of international affairs sees a state governing its own territory and the people in it. Occupation, as in 'the effective control of a power over a territory to which that power has no sovereign title, without the volition of the sovereign of that territory', no longer transferred that territory's sovereign title to its conqueror.[7]

Benvenisti's above-quoted definition stands in diametric opposition to Huber's understanding of conquest in international affairs. For Huber, reflecting international law in 1898, the probable corollary of a war of conquest and *debellatio* was a territory's transfer of ownership. Under Benvenisti's definition, which reflects international law in 2012, the necessitated corollary of a war of conquest *cannot* result in that territory's transfer of title to the conqueror.

The story of this radical shift in international legal thinking – overturning the norms of some 5,000 years of human history, during which conquest precipitated

---

2. Hans Wehberg, 'L'interdiction du recours à la force: le principe et les problèmes qui se posent', in *Collected Courses of The Hague Academy of International Law ('Recueil des Cours')*, The Hague Academy of International Law, vol. 78, no. 1 (1951), pp. 6–120 at 87.

3. European public law.

4. Max Huber, *Die Staatensuccession: Volkerrechtliche und Staatsrechtliche Praxis Im XIX Jahrhundert* (Leipzig, 1898), p. 20 quoted in Wehberg, *L'interdiction du recours à la force*, p. 88.

5. Benjamin B. Ferencz, 'A Nuremberg Legacy: The Crime of Aggression', in *Washington University Global Studies Law Review*, vol. 15, no. 4 (2016), pp. 555–60 at 556.

6. Eyal Benvenisti, *The International Law of Occupation*, 2nd edn (Oxford University Press, 2012), p. vii.

7. Ibid., p. 3.

territorial acquisition – has been well surveyed elsewhere.[8] Broadly speaking, the historical narrative of this shift goes as follows. From the middle of the nineteenth century onwards, a steady march that favoured the rights of peoples, coupled with growing limitations on the repellent uses to which warfare had been put, came to the fore. One catalyst for this 'historical march forward' was technological advancement in the means of military destruction, which suddenly enabled the wholesale automated killing of millions of people on an unprecedented scale and with unheard-of speed and lethality. The other catalyst came in the form of the growing notion of sovereignty belonging to peoples who inhabit a land indigenous to them. The end of the First World War and the creation of the League of Nations, along with the birth of a host of new states based on the idea of peoples' self-determination, became pivotal in the rise of the notion of a territory 'occupied' rather than conquered.[9] The rise to prominence of the Red Cross (established in 1864), and its central idea of instilling humanity into the inevitability of warfare, also filtered into this process. The almost linear ascent of international humanitarian treaty-making also conformed to this narrative – from the first Geneva Convention (1864) to the third (1929) for War Prisoners, along with the Hague Conventions for War on Land (1899–1907), the successful banning of chemical and biological weapons following the experiences of the First World War under the terms of the 1925 Geneva Gas Protocol, through to the Geneva Convention for Civilians (1949) and, later, its Additional Protocols (1977).[10]

The *conditio* sine qua non for this historical march forward was what Sharon Korman has termed as 'the demise of the right of conquest'.[11] In a recent study, Oona Hathaway and Scott Shapiro have argued in favour of the vital role played by the 1928 Briand-Kellogg Pact for the outlawing of war in the construction of the UN Charter and the world's international legal order post-1945.[12] To them, 1928 was the year in which this forward march in the demise of conquest and the reduction of aggression in international affairs really took off. From there on, so goes the theory, it was plain sailing towards the reduction of aggressive wars for territorial conquest.

However, this historical-march-forward narrative, which relates the demise of conquest as a linear historical procession from the 1920s onwards, is, in fact,

---

8. Geoffrey Best, *Humanity in Warfare: The Modern History of the International Law of Armed Conflicts* (London: Methuen, University Paperbacks, 1983). Benvenisti, *The International Law of Occupation*, Ch. 2–7, pp. 20–202.

9. Erez Manela, *The Wilsonian Moment: Self-Determination and the International Origins of Anticolonial Nationalism* (Oxford: Oxford University Press, 2007).

10. Best, *Humanity in Warfare*, pp. 129–330. On the relative success of the 1925 Geneva Gas Protocol, see Best, *War and Law Since 1945*, pp. 306–7.

11. Sharon Korman, *The Right of Conquest: The Acquisition of Territory by Force in International Law and Practice* (Oxford: Oxford University Press, 1996), pp. 133–301.

12. Oona Hathaway and Scott Shapiro, *The Internationalists: How a Radical Plan to Outlaw War Remade the World* (New York: Simon and Schuster, 2017).

highly flawed. It tragically overlooks the existence of the most serious political and ideological alternative contender to the demise of conquest from the mid-1920s until 1945. This is perpetual military occupation – better known by its Latin term, used by Carl Schmitt, who elaborated it as *Occupatio Bellica*. The late 1920s and, especially, the 1930s saw a period of contest between two opposing world views rather than being simply dominated by one ideological stratum, as in the demise of conquest. Japan's occupation of Manchuria; Italy's violent seizure of Libya and Ethiopia; Germany's reconquest and militarization of the Rhineland, forceful *Anschluss* of Austria, violent seizure of the Sudetenland and occupation of Bohemia and Moravia – none of these *Occupatio Bellica* was executed in an ideological vacuum. Rather, they were policy corollaries of the ideological nemesis of the demise of conquest – namely, Carl Schmitt's *Grossraum* theory.

Moreover, and perhaps more forcefully even *after* 1945 and the adoption of the UN Charter, the demise of conquest was certainly not the only 'ideological game in town'. Internationally legitimized perpetual occupation – and even full conquest, with the transferal of territorial title – was seen as genuine alternatives to the demise of conquest in several places. Not only had *debellatio* not perished but it was also explicitly relied upon by the most eminent of legal luminaries, Hans Kelsen, of all people – the mentor, as we saw in Chapter 1, of WJC delegate Gerhart Riegner – unapologetically justified the massive post-war territorial annexations of Silesia, Pomerania and Königsberg to Poland and the Soviet Union on account of Germany's alleged non-existence as a state – thus rendering irrelevant its stance vis-à-vis these changes to its territory now that it ceased to exist as a legitimate state subject to international legal laws and norms.[13] Post-1945, the United States would have no problem in securing for itself an area of some 3 million square miles filled

---

13. In 1944, Hans Kelsen who had already fled to the United States, and who was working as a research associate in Berkeley, was called on by the US government to begin work on the legal regimes that were to come once the imminent Allied victory over Germany materialized. Kelsen concluded that since Germany would cease to exist as a state and would no longer be a recognized subject of international law and norms, the Allies were no longer bound by The Hague Convention's regulations towards it and could basically dispose of its territories as they pleased – as per the concept of *debellatio*. See Hans Kelsen, 'The International Legal Status of Germany to Be Established Immediately upon Termination of the War', in *American Journal of International Law*, vol. 38, no. 4 (October 1944), pp. 689–94, at 692. See also Hans Kesen, 'The Legal Status of Germany According to the Declaration of Berlin', in *American Journal of International Law*, vol. 39, no. 3 (July 1945), pp. 518–26 at 519. For a sharp (and well-merited) critique of Kelsen's view, see Christian Tomuschat, 'Prohibition on Settlements', in Andrew Clapham, Paola Gaeta and Marco Sassoli (eds.), *The 1949 Geneva Conventions: A Commentary* (Oxford: Oxford University Press, 2016), p. 1554, n. 5 and 7. For the full contextualization of Kelsen's arguments, and the extent to which his *political* views on Nazi Germany's defeat became entangled with the *legal* views that he expressed (not least, thanks to his personal experiences of persecution by the Nazis), see Thomas Olechowski, 'Kelsens Debellatio-These. Rechtshistorische und

with some 700 islands in the Pacific Ocean (the US Trust territory of the Pacific Islands) under its 'strategic trusteeship' there. In 2019, at the time of writing, the United States still controls the islands of Tinian and Rota, whose inhabitants do not enjoy any democratically elected political delegated representation in Washington. The island of Guam, which also came under US control thanks to conquest post-1945, has since become an integral part of US territory, with one delegate in the US Congress in Washington.

The narrative problem of the demise-of-conquest theory becomes glaringly obvious when its adherents are confronted with the realities of the Second World War. Confronted with Carl Schmitt's parallel narrative – which justified extremely violent means of oppression against civilian populations who opposed their *Occupatio Bellica* by Japan, Italy and Germany – they have resorted to explaining the complete debacle of humanitarian norms between 1930 and 1945 as nothing more than an unfortunate 'historical blip'.[14] The Second World War is thus seen as a phase in which humanitarian laws limiting armed conflict were simply suspended – no more. This time period – which saw the ascendance of 'Hitler's Empire' in Europe, the Japanese conquest of Manchuria and later of East Asia, and the Italian conquest of Libya and Ethiopia – is seen as the paradigmatic period of international legal *exception*. Before it, we had the linear march forward of international humanitarian law; after it, the march of international law resumed unabated; in between lay fifteen years of limbo. Benvenisti framed this historical narrative of the 1930–45 international legal limbo as follows:

> The occupations during WWII signify a new phase in the law of occupation … characterized not by the occupants' adaptation of the 1907 Hague law to modern exigencies, but rather by most occupants' disregard of this law. Ultimately, this phase culminates with the Introduction of the 1949 Geneva Convention Relative to the Protection of Civilian Persons in Time of War [GC-IV], which reformulated several aspects of the law of occupation in response to the experience of the recent war.[15]

In short, we had the development of the laws of occupation from the mid-nineteenth century, which were first codified in 1907 via the Hague Conventions; these were disregarded – that is, 'put on hold' – during the Second World War; and then came the Fourth Geneva Convention for Civilians to merely reformulate some aspects of what had already been achieved before this 'historical blip' – from which point, we have carried on forward ever since.

rechtstheoretische Überlegungen zur Kontinuität von Staaten', in Clemens Jabloner (ed.), *Gedenkschrift Robert Walter* (Wien: Manz Verlag, 2013), pp. 531–52.

14. Korman, *The Right of Conquest*. See especially Part II: The Demise of the Right of Conquest in the 20th Century, pp. 133–248.

15. Benvenisti, *The International Law of Occupation*, p. 131.

In order to understand the reasons behind much of GC-IV's drafting, one must first come to grips with the ideological contest that was taking place amid the highest echelons of international legal thinking from 1930 until 1950 concerning the very nature of military conquest. On the 'universalist' side of this ideological divide stood the thinkers Walther Schücking, Hans Wehberg and Georg Cohn. They all advocated the international-sanctioned limitation of war. On the other side of this clash stood the two figures who embodied, more than any others, the will to return to a world in which military conquest led to territorial entitlement: Carl Schmitt and Werner Best. This ideological contest would carry on all through the 1930s. In it, ideology would also mix with personal circumstances, as the observant Jewish Cohn would be personally persecuted by Werner Best, Hitler's plenipotentiary in Denmark and the executor of Schmitt's fanatical ideology. In the aftermath of the Second World War, Cohn would be the leading champion of the rights of occupied peoples in GC-IV's *travaux préparatoires* – both at Stockholm and, especially, at the 1949 Geneva Conference of Plenipotentiaries.

In order to understand Georg Cohn's positions in the drafting of GC-IV Article 49 as he took on the fight to illegalize any population transfers, either out of an occupied territory (as in the deportations of Europe's Jews to Poland) or into a newly conquered territory (Germans into Western Poland and Denmark), we must first understand the contest that took place during the 1930s between the aforementioned universalists and advocates of conquest.

Chapter 5 delves into this contest and examines the birth of the non-recognition doctrine for the acquisition of territory by force (the so-called Stimson Doctrine), whose true initiator was Georg Cohn. It explains Carl Schmitt's elaboration of his famous *Grossraum* theory as the most vitriolic opposition to Cohn's elaboration of non-recognition. Chapter 6 examines Cohn's single-handed legislation in Stockholm of paragraph 6 of Article 49, which prohibits the transfer of any part of an occupant's population into a conquered territory. Finally, Chapter 7 explores Cohn's crusade against the legalization of the death penalty in occupied territories (Article 68), which the United Kingdom and the United States vehemently advocated at the Geneva Plenipotentiaries' Conference of 1949.

Chapter 5

CONQUEST CONTESTED: GEORG COHN, CARL SCHMITT AND NON-RECOGNITION

The most Utopian idea of them all

The notion of a territory under occupation, without the legal possibility of full transfer of its sovereign title to its conqueror, has first and foremost to do with the delegitimization of wars of aggression in international relations. Hans Wehberg summed up this idea as follows:

> The moment we had ceased to consider war as a legitimate means of national politics, we had struck a mortal blow upon the entire institution of territorial annexation.[1]

Wehberg's words, written in 1951 just a few months after GC-IV came into force (21 October 1950), signify the endnote in an international movement to limit wars of aggression, which began almost half a century earlier with the Hague Conventions (1899 to 1907). Written after the unconditional surrenders of Germany, Italy and Japan, with the ramifications of their disastrous territorial-expansionist ideologies now plainly obvious to everyone, Wehberg's argument against the legality of annexation and in favour of the complete illegalization of conquest seemed tautologous. With the UN Charter (Article 2, paragraph 4) now firmly on his side, outlawing wars of aggression and the use of force in international relations had evolved to become the substantive bedrock underpinning the new international world order post-1945.[2]

Yet interestingly enough, had Wehberg proposed that very same argument little more than a decade earlier, he would probably have been dismissed as a delusional utopian by 'realist' thinkers such as E. H. Carr:

---

1. Wehberg, *L'interdiction du recours à la force*, p. 88.
2. Article 2.4 of the UN Charter states that all UN member states 'shall refrain in their international relations from the threat or use of force against the territorial integrity or political independence of any state, or in any other manner inconsistent with the Purposes of the United Nations'.

There is, among many people interested in international affairs, a strong inclination to treat law as something independent of, and ethically superior to, politics. ... In theories of international law, utopia tends to predominate over reality to an extent unparalleled in other branches of jurisprudence. Moreover, this tendency is greatest at periods when anarchy is most prevalent in the practice of nations ... since 1919, natural law has resumed its sway, and theories of international law have become more markedly utopian than at any previous time.[3]

Carr wrote these words in August 1939, just one month before Hitler's invasion of Poland and the outbreak of the Second World War in September that year. As a sworn British communist, Carr was an ardent opponent of fascist territorial-expansionist ideologies, and as strong a believer in the cause of world peace as Wehberg was. And yet, few critics of the global movement in favour of international law's omnipotent ability to solve all disputes during the interwar period were as harshly critical as Carr was at that time. His scathing critique of people such as Hersch Lauterpacht, whose *Function of Law in the International Community* garnered almost biblical adherence from internationalists, placed Carr firmly at the helm of the 'realist' camp, which sought to avoid the supremacy of international law over power politics.[4]

Carr's seminal study in international relations was read by many as a requiem for notions such as 'the moral force of law', the 'rule of law' and the maintenance of 'international law and order'.[5] He was advocating a balance between realist power politics and international law, and in 1939 no international action was more representative of power politics than forceful conquest and subsequent territorial annexation. The Japanese grip on Manchuria (1931); the Italian takeover of Libya and Ethiopia (1935); and the Nazi *Anschluss* of Austria (1938), followed by the Sudetenland (1939) and, finally, Bohemia and Moravia (1939) were all forceful military occupation-turned-annexations whose reasoning emanated from a world view premised upon the international legitimacy of conquest. Faced with this deluge of seemingly permanent military occupations and their implicit acceptance by most international powers (Britain and France officially reinstated diplomatic relations with Italy *after* its invasion of Ethiopia), by 1939, international law – and the League of Nations as its chief custodian – was clearly 'on the ropes', awaiting its 'knock-out blow' so to speak.

The fundamental ideas behind the League of Nations' Covenant had been a direct result of the heightened sense of urgency to act against the aggressive

---

3. E. H. Carr, *The Twenty Years' Crisis 1919-1939: An Introduction to the Study of International Relations* (London: Harper, 1939), p. 174.

4. Hersch Lauterpacht, *The Function of Law in the International Community* (Oxford: Oxford University Press, 1933). See Carr's bitter critique of Lauterpacht's positions in Carr, *The Twenty Years' Crisis 1919-1939*, p. 195, n. 1 and p. 207.

5. Carr, *The Twenty Years' Crisis 1919-1939*, p. 170.

militarist ethos prevailing in the run-up to the First World War. With the architects of the League being predominantly British – under the leadership of intellectuals like H. G. Wells and Gilbert Murray, and statesmen such as Lords Cecil and Grey – the tone set by this process was, first and foremost, an anti-German one. As early as 1914, Wells had framed the outbreak of the First World War as a universal effort led by the British against German aggression, in an effort to wage a *War that Will End War* (to cite the title of his collection of articles of that year). He proposed the realization of Immanuel Kant's long-standing call for a form of League of Nations (the Prussian philosopher's actual phrase had been 'a league of peace'), which, by February 1919, had become fully elaborated along with its covenant, its council and its assembly.[6]

Looking back from the perspective of 1939, all of this seemed to Carr to be far too utopian.[7] Of all the League's aspirations, the outlawing of wars of aggression for the sake of territorial aggrandizement, as evident in the covenant's Article 10 was perhaps the most utopian idea of them all.[8] Article 16 of the covenant, which automatically activated the obligation by all the League's members to take immediate action against aggressors, was, in fact, the ground upon which the US Congress long abstained from joining the League of Nations. The United States also abstained from joining the latest war for the sake of safeguarding its neutrality in international affairs.[9] Indeed, the one issue that most perturbed the League vis-à-vis its relations with the United States was precisely the latter's neutrality in international affairs.

6. H. G. Wells, *The War That Will End War* (London: Palmer, 1914). H. G. Wells, *The Idea of a League of Nations* (Boston: The Atlantic Monthly Press, 1919). Viscount Grey et al., *The League of Nations* (Oxford: Oxford University Press, 1919) (February).

7. Martyn Housden, *The League of Nations and the Organization of Peace* (Abingdon: Routledge, 2012), pp. 8–11, 'Super-State, Commonwealth, Utopia'.

8. Article 10 of the League's Covenant stated that 'the Members of the League undertake to respect and preserve as against external aggression the territorial integrity and existing political independence of all Members of the League. In case of any such aggression or in case of any threat or danger of such aggression the Council shall advise upon the means by which this obligation shall be fulfilled.' For the League's Covenant, see its text on the website of Yale University's Law School. Available at: http://avalon.law.yale.edu/20th_century/leagc ov.asp#art16.

9. In the United States, the resistance of the Republican Party to Article 10 and its sense of collective security under the League's Covenant was most forcefully voiced by Senator Henry Cabot Lodge, the chairman of the Senate Foreign Relations Committee. President Wilson's understanding that any amendment to Article 10 would deal a mortal blow to the entire idea of the League led him eventually to give up on attempts to have the United States join the new world organization. See Charles Laderman, 'The United States and the League of Nations', *Oxford University's Research Encyclopaedia for American History*, notes 20–2. Available at: http://americanhistory.oxfordre.com/view/10.1093/acrefore/978019932917 5.001.0001/acrefore-9780199329175-e-314#acrefore-9780199329175-e-314-note-22.

The problem with neutrality

Few issues were as contested during the run-up to the First World War, and especially after it, as the notion of international neutrality. From the mid-nineteenth century onwards, as the system of Western military alliances gradually built up, countries such as Belgium, Luxembourg, Switzerland, Denmark, Sweden and, most notably, the United States came to embrace a position of neutrality within this sphere of growing reciprocal international animosities. The official act that triggered the entry of the UK and France into the First World War was the German invasion of Luxembourg and Belgium, both of which were avowedly neutral countries. By invading and occupying these nations, Germany not only triggered the British and French declarations of war but also enshrined its image in the minds of other states as the epitome of bellicosity, prepared for the sake of its military objectives to subject other neutral European countries that had done it no harm to the painful experience of military occupation.

The US neutrality, which translated into that country's decision to refrain from engaging in what was seen as an internal European struggle an ocean away, was certainly not viewed favourably by the UK or France. Not until 1917, with the uncovering of the 'Zimmerman Telegram', which pointed firmly to Germany's plans to destabilize the Western hemisphere in its planned military cooperation with Mexico, and its active targeting of American commercial shipping vessels in the Atlantic, did the United States join the French–UK alliance, thus finally breaking the war's stalemate.[10]

Georg Cohn invents the non-recognition principle

The obvious problem with traditional neutrality was its passivity in international affairs. Neutral countries, so the theory ran, stood by while atrocious things were taking place; as long as 'they and theirs' were not affected, they did nothing. Furthermore, even when they did want to act, during times of war or heightened international tensions, there were precious few measures that they could resort to without immediately losing their neutrality in the eyes of one (or both) of the belligerents concerned. It was this 'logical straitjacket', which implicitly associated neutrality with passiveness and international inaction, that the Danish international jurist Dr Georg Cohn resolved to tackle.

Born in 1887 in Germany's Frankfurt am Main, Georg (Aryeh) Cohn moved with his family at a young age to his maternal grandparents' home in Copenhagen in 1896. Growing up in a deeply religious family that formed part of the congregation of the 'Father of Jewish neo-orthodoxy', Rabbi Samson Raphael Hirsch, the young Georg received a Talmudic education alongside his attendance of the Slomanns

10. Barbara Tuchman, *The Zimmermann Telegram: America Enters the War 1917–1918* (London: Penguin, 1985).

Skole – the most distinguished *gymnasium* in the Danish capital. Following his graduation in law and philosophy from the University of Copenhagen, earning that august institution's gold medal for his graduation thesis, Cohn enlisted to compete for an opening at the country's foreign ministry. In December 1913, Danish foreign minister Erik Scavenius (who would, many years later, become the head of the country's transitional administration under the Nazis) officially enlisted Cohn into the Foreign Ministry as a legal expert specializing in public international law.[11]

In August 1914, at the outbreak of the First World War, Cohn, who was still an apprentice at the Danish Foreign Ministry (and barely nine months on the job), found himself in the midst of national efforts to remain neutral and keep Denmark out of the chain of interstate wars and hostilities that was engulfing Europe. Since the end of the Second Schleswig War of 1864 and the Danish defeat at the hands of Prussian minister president Otto von Bismarck, who subsequently annexed the entire duchy of Schleswig (known to the Danes as 'South Jutland'), Denmark had taken a strategic decision never again to confront German military might. With the occupation of the neutral states of Belgium and Luxembourg, Cohn, as the sole Danish expert on the international laws of war and neutrality, was charged with the monumental task of keeping Denmark neutral, and out of the war – all at the tender age of twenty-seven.[12] At the end of the war, in 1919, Christian X, the king of Denmark, bestowed on Cohn one of the highest decorations of the Danish kingdom (Ridder of the Dannebrog Order) for his successful accomplishment in safeguarding Danish neutrality throughout that conflict. In 1920, Cohn joined Denmark's delegation to the first assembly of the League of Nations, and that same year was nominated as the head of the Department for international organizations at the Danish Foreign Ministry.

---

11. See Georg Cohn's family biography as recorded by his daughter in Hebrew: Emilie Cohn Roi, *Courtyards of Copenhagen: Georg Cohn in Quest of War Prevention – Seven Generations in Denmark* (Jerusalem: Rubin Mass Publishers, 2003 – in Hebrew), pp. 136–42 [*Hazerot Copenhagen: Georg Cohn Bemamaz Limnoa Milchama – Sheva Dorot Bedenemark*]; חצרות קופנהגן : גאורג כהן, במאמץ למנוע מלחמה שבעה דורות בדנמרק,(ירושלים:ראובן מס תשס"ד – 2003). אמיליה כהן רואי pp. 86–7 [in Hebrew. All translations from the Hebrew by the author].

12. In an interview that he gave many years later, in 1937, Georg Cohn reminisced, 'when I entered the foreign ministry as a young apprentice – it was mainly due to my scientific academic curiosity to understand better the issues of international law, on which I was writing at the time, and which I wished to better understand. A short while later the war broke out. The Germans invaded Belgium, and then began the hard times for Denmark, [which] was neighbouring the roaring thunder of the guns. We were a very small group of people at the foreign ministry, and I was charged first and foremost, as the expert on international law and the laws of neutrality, to bear the largest share of the brunt in terms of the daily work. This was a very strenuous and hectic period, when we worked day and night, for the entire four full years of the war'. Cohn Roi, *Courtyards of Copenhagen: Georg Cohn- In Quest of War Prevention*, p. 87.

The experiences of the First World War compelled Cohn to deal with a wide array of issues associated with the laws of war, neutrality and conquest. He became an expert on the Hague Conventions of 1907, specifically with regard to the economic neutrality of civilian shipping routes. This included issues as diverse as maritime explosive anti-ship mines and the blocking of seaports, instances in which British and German military vessels ran aground in Danish territorial waters (with their crews respectively being detained by Denmark as POWs until the war's end) and the rights of inspection of Danish commercial sea vessels. In addition, the war years gave Cohn his first chance at working directly both with the Red Cross – both at the national level with Danish, British and German Red Cross societies and at the international sphere – with the Geneva-based ICRC. Between 1915 and 1918, Denmark provided hospitalization services to wounded soldiers from both Germany and the UK, who were medically treated according to the best care available in Danish hospital facilities. It also was during these years that Cohn was directly engaged, for the first time in his professional career, with the Geneva Conventions.

One of the most important aspects of his work during this time concerned the nature of military occupation – in his case, concerning the region of North Jutland. Following the signing of the Versailles Treaty, this territory held a plebiscite and consequently returned to Danish sovereignty after some fifty-six years under German military rule. The return of North Jutland confronted Cohn with his first experiences of post-occupation legal repercussions. As Benvenisti has pertinently noted, the fact that a territory was legally or illegally occupied does not absolve the legitimate sovereign, at that occupation's end, from dealing practically with the legal impacts of the actions taken by the occupier when it was still in charge of that occupied territory.[13] Thus, in 1920, Cohn found himself chairing the subcommittee concerned with the pension rights of the bureaucrats of North Jutland from the region's German-speaking minority, who had suddenly come under Danish rule after working their entire lives as civil servants for the German occupation administration there.[14]

As he undertook to keep his beloved Denmark neutral and out of harm's way, the task of securing and maintaining Denmark's neutrality nevertheless frustrated Cohn greatly. An ideological pacifist at heart, he found himself hard pressed to accept the passivity of traditional neutrality when confronted with the horrendous consequences of modern warfare. Influenced to large degree by Sigmund Freud's new discoveries in human psychology, Cohn began to regard war, and especially wars of aggression, as a human disease – a pathology and a psychological *malaise*, whose onset was similar in its consequences to that of the bubonic plague that had struck Europe during the seventeenth century.[15]

---

13. Benvenisti, *The International Law of Occupation*, Ch. 11, pp. 302–3, n. 9–13.

14. Cohn Roi, *Courtyards of Copenhagen: Georg Cohn- In Quest of War Prevention*, p. 89.

15. Georg Cohn, 'War in Its Pathological, Psychological and Sociological Aspects', in Georg Cohn (ed.), *Neo-Neutrality* (New York: Colombia University Press, 1939), pp. 262–81.

To a pacifist advocate of neutrality such as Cohn, the greatest conundrum and logical discrepancy lay in extracting the 'classical' doctrine of neutrality from its passiveness in the face of warfare – especially given its new technological ethos. Articles 10 and 16 of the League of Nations' Covenant, which ultimately condoned the use of force (i.e. 'war') against aggressors, were based, in his view, on a logical oxymoron. If war was the ultimate pathological evil behaviour of humans, how could one pathology be justified to stop the very same and equally dangerous pathology from the other side? Yet the alternative of simply sitting back and passively watching as the world brought itself to destruction, as per the prevailing tenets of the policy of neutrality, seemed to Cohn equally morally unfathomable and morally irresponsible.

The answer lay not in everybody resorting to the use of force, but rather in the neutrals taking an active role in world affairs for the sake of war prevention. This new spirit of activity on behalf of neutral powers, which Cohn rightfully associated with Swiss humanitarianism and the principles of the International Red Cross movement, translated into his new concept of 'neo-neutrality'. The more that active neutral states could become harbingers of peace by refusing to resort to the use of force while abandoning the sidelines in order to actively join in the 'play' of international affairs on the side of peace in the international arena, the more power their pro-peace messages would carry.

Grossly oversimplified, war could be divided in its most rudimentary forms into two types: *defensive* and *offensive* military campaigns. Even neutral states (such as Switzerland, Sweden or Denmark) had armed forces to protect their recognized territories from invasion. Thus, the problem arose not in the actual existence of armed forces per se, but rather in what these armed forces were tasked with. Obviously, the biggest problem with war lay first and foremost in its aggressive employment for the sake of territorial aggrandizement.

Yet if prospective conquerors could be permanently deprived of the fruits of their conquest, then their incentives for wars of aggression for the sake of territorial enlargement would be significantly curtailed. A general ban on the international recognition of such conquests might be a significant step towards such a deprivation – Cohn postulated. The challenge was how to make such non-recognition a binding universal principle of international law. With this idea in mind, in 1922, Cohn drafted, and convinced the Danish government to circulate among all the League of Nations' members and those of the Pan-American Union of states,[16] a draft proposal for the non-recognition of the acquisition of territory by force.[17] Cohn's text, which for the first time framed what would later become the famous principle of non-recognition, read as follows:

16. The regional organization comprising the states of the Western hemisphere, renamed after 1947 as the Organization of American States (OAS).

17. Cohn, *Neo-Neutrality*, p. 109, n. 146.

In the future, territorial acquisitions in Europe shall not be lawful if resulting from war, conquest or the conclusion of a peace treaty. Any agreement or arrangement made contrary to this principle shall be null and void and will not be recognized by the High Contracting Parties.[18]

It is worth noting here that all the subsequent sources (without exception) concerning the concept of non-recognition trace its origins back to this text from 1922 as drafted by Georg Cohn on the Danish government's behalf.[19] Five years later, in 1927, the Pan-American Union opted for a similar draft resolution in its codification of Pan-American international law (project number 30).[20] Roughly a decade later, US secretary of state Henry Stimson built upon Cohn's work to elaborate his famous declaration concerning the United States's non-recognition of Japan's illegal conquest of Manchuria, and later concerning Italy's violent conquest of Ethiopia.[21] It would take a further half century, until 1970, before the world would accept the doctrine of non-recognition as a binding principle in international affairs, buttressed by sanctions emanating from its wide acceptance in international law.[22]

The years from 1922 until the outbreak of the Second World War saw Georg Cohn rise to become one of the most distinguished international jurists of his age. In 1925, he represented Denmark at the Assembly of the League of Nations in tandem with his membership of the Danish–Swiss Arbitration Committee. In 1929, Cohn was nominated as a judge of the Permanent Court of Arbitration (PCA) in

---

18. Ibid.

19. Wehberg, *L'interdiction du recours à la force*, p. 91. Robert Langer, *Seizure of Territory: The Stimson Doctrine and Related principles in Legal Theory and Diplomatic Practice* (Princeton: Princeton University Press, 1947), p. 47. Philip Jessup, 'Harvard Research in International Law – Draft Convention on the Rights and Duties of States in case of Aggression', *American Journal of International Law* (*'AJIL'*), vol. 33 (1939), Special Supplement p. 892. All subsequent sources such as Benvenisti, *The International Law of Occupation* (p. 140, n. 41) quote the Jessup Draft Convention in *AJIL*, unfortunately failing to mention to true origins of the doctrine.

20. Cohn, *Neo-Neutrality*, pp. 106–11.

21. Wehberg, *L'interdiction du recours à la force*, pp. 94–7.

22. UNGA Res. 2625, 24 October 1970, *Declaration on Principles of International Law concerning Friendly Relations and Co-operation among States in accordance with the Charter of the United Nations*, Article 1 (11): 'The territory of a State shall not be the object of acquisition by another State resulting from the threat or use of force. No territorial acquisition resulting from the threat or use of force shall be recognized as legal.' Available at: http://www.un-documents.net/a25r2625.htm. On the *jus* cogens status of the doctrine of non-recognition, see Benvenisti, *The International Law of Occupation*, p. 142, n. 51 quoting James Crawford.

The Hague.[23] In 1930, the United States and Poland jointly nominated him as the president of their joint arbitration committee. Upon the signing of the arbitration treaty between the two countries, Cohn received one of the highest Polish state awards in recognition of his contribution to the successful culmination of this diplomatic endeavour. In 1932, regarding Norway's claims to Greenland, Cohn spearheaded the Danish defence team before the PCIJ's bench where he ultimately prevailed, securing full Danish sovereignty over that territory.[24] In 1939, Cohn was chosen to deliver the summer semester lectures at the Academy of International Law at The Hague.[25]

During these years, between Cohn's initial elaboration of non-recognition and the outbreak of the Second World War, two subsequent international developments helped to further cement his anti-war efforts in the international arena. The first of those developments was the aforementioned Briand-Kellogg Pact. Signed in 1928 by most states – including the United States (which as mentioned earlier had never even joined the League of Nations) – this pact generally outlawed wars of aggression. In their recent study of the Kellogg Pact Hathaway and Shapiro have convincingly demonstrated the long-standing importance of this international agreement and its direct consequential corollary as in the prohibition of international aggression, which ultimately made it into the UN Charter.[26] The brainchild of US secretary of state Frank Kellogg and French foreign minister Aristide Briand, the pact was also designed as a way of reintegrating the United States into the League of Nations' system of collective security, albeit without its official membership. In Paris, the two people who worked directly under Briand in framing the pact's textual terms were none other than René Cassin and Georges Cahen-Salvador[27] (Figure 16).

23. 'Jew Named to Permanent Arbitration Court at Hague', *Jewish Telegraphic Agency* (JTA), 3 June 1929. Available at www.jta.org/1929/06/03/archive/jew-named-to-perman ent-arbitration-court-at-hague (accessed 27 December 2016).

24. Cohn Roi, *Courtyards of Copenhagen: Georg Cohn- In Quest of War Prevention*, pp. 176–7.

25. Georg Cohn, 'La théorie de la responsabilité internationale' dans *Recueil des cours de l'Académie de Droit International de la Haye,* vol. 68 (1939), pp. 207–312 [*Collected Courses of The Hague Academy of International Law*].

26. Hathaway and Shapiro, *The Internationalists*, pp. 101–351.

27. The French team behind Foreign Minister Briand included, aside from Cassin and Cahen-Salvador, renowned diplomats such as René Massigli (the architect of the League of Nations' Disarmament Conference in 1931), André François-Poncet (ambassador to Germany, and later French Commissioner in Occupied Germany from 1945 until 1955) and Pierre Laval – later prime minister and French foreign secretary. All can be observed in a Figure 4.2, a picture taken in 1931 of the French Delegation to the 11th Assembly of the League of Nations in 1931. Available at: https://www.gettyimages.de/detail/nachrichten foto/picture-taken-in-1931-of-the-french-delegation-nachrichtenfoto/868960654#picture -taken-in-1931-of-the-french-delegation-attending-the-11th-of-picture-id868960654.

Figure 16 The French Delegation to the League of Nations in 1931. Seated at the centre – French foreign minister Aristide Briand. Standing second from the left – René Cassin. Standing on the far-right is Georges Cahen-Salvador. © Getty Images.

While many of the Briand-Kellogg Pact's principles eventually made it into the UN Charter, back in 1929 the idea of an international legal prohibition on wars of aggression was rather novel.[28] Yet what the Briand-Kellogg Pact did not discuss was military occupation. In his study of the pact commissioned by the Carnegie Endowment, which became the standard reference text regarding its interpretation, Hans Wehberg – who relied heavily on Georg Cohn's interpretation

28. The growing academic controversy surrounding the effectiveness (or the lack thereof) of the Briand-Kellogg Pact is beyond the scope of this study. For the opinion supporting the pact's relevance and its impact on future international developments, see Hathaway and Shapiro, *The Internationalists: How a Radical Plan to Outlaw War Remade the World*, especially pp. 309–51. For a balanced, authoritative (and positive) approach to Hatahway and Shapiro's work, see Mark Mazower's extended review of their book in *The Guardian's* (16 December 2017) historical book section. Available at: https://www.theguard ian.com/books/2017/dec/16/the-internationalists-review-plan-outlaw-war. For a scathing (and wholly unjustified!) critique, see Stephen Walt's negative review of the book: 'There's Still No Reason to Think the Kellogg-Briand Pact Accomplished Anything', *Foreign Policy Magazine*, 29 September 2017. Available at: https://foreignpolicy.com/2017/09/29/theres-s till-no-reason-to-think-the-kellogg-briand-pact-accomplished-anything.

of it – explicitly quoted the latter's lamentation over this deficiency. At the end of the day, as both Wehberg and Cohn noted, the pact *did not* outlaw, but rather unfortunately permitted, military occupation.[29]

A second, and somewhat less known (albeit equally important) international instrument that incorporated Cohn's non-recognition doctrine was the Saavedra Lamas Treaty of 1933,[30] better known as the Inter-American Anti-war Treaty of Non-aggression and Conciliation.[31] Signed as part of the efforts on behalf of American states to regulate their conduct in the Western hemisphere according to international legal principles, the Saavedra Lamas Treaty fundamentally altered the manner in which Latin American states engaged with one another. Intimately connected to the Montevideo Conference held that same year, it provided the first firm legal basis to all subsequent anti-war treaties in the Western hemisphere. The 1948 American Treaty on Pacific Settlement ('The Treaty of Bogota') and the 1967 Treaty for the Prohibition of Nuclear Weapons in Latin America and the Caribbean ('The Treaty of Tlatelolco' – the first regional instrument to prohibit nuclear weapons) both explicitly drew their origins from Saavedra Lamas.[32] Article 2 of this treaty read as follows:

> The High Contracting Parties declare [that] territorial questions must not be settled by violence, and that they will not recognize any territorial arrangement

29. Hans Wehberg, *The Outlawry of War* (Washington, DC: The Carnegie Endowment for International Peace, 1931). The book is a significant extension to the winter semester course that Wehberg gave at The Hague Academy of International Law. See Hans Wehberg, 'Le problème de la mise de la guerre hors la loi' dans *Recueil des cours de l'Académie de Droit International de la Haye*, vol. 24 (1928), pp. 147–306 [*Collected Courses of The Hague Academy of International Law*]. In the chapter concerning the Kellogg–Briand Pact (pp. 63–93), the pages concerning the interpretation of the pact in detail are mostly based on and quoted from Cohn's extensive article of 1929: Georg Cohn, 'Kellogg-Vertrag und Völkerrecht', *Zeitschrift Für Völkerrecht*, vol. 15 (Breslau, 1929). See Wehberg, *The Outlawry of War*, pp. 82–90, p. 82, n. 1, p. 83, n. 3, p. 85, n. 1, p. 86, n. 4, p. 87, n. 4, pp. 87–90 carry full descriptions in the main body of the text of Cohn's open disagreements with the British delegate Sir Cecil Hurst, during the 10th Assembly of the League of Nations, concerning Britain's request to extend the possibilities of military actions on the League's behalf, based upon Articles 10 and 16 of the Covenant.

30. The brainchild of Carlos Saavedra Lamas, Argentinian minister of foreign affairs at the time the treaty was concluded.

31. See: Hugo Caminos, 'The Saavedra Lamas Treaty (1933)', in *Max Planck Encyclopaedia of Public International Law* (Oxford: Oxford University Press). Available at: http://opil.ouplaw.com/view/10.1093/law:epil/9780199231690/law-9780199231690-e77?prd=OPIL#.

32. Davis Robinson, 'The Treaty of Tlatelolco and the United States: A Latin American Nuclear Free Zone', *American Journal of International Law*, vol. 64, no. 2 (1970), pp. 282–309.

which is not obtained by pacific means, nor the validity of the occupation or acquisition of territories that may be brought about by force of arms.[33]

In the accompanying materials, which Argentinian foreign minister Carlos Saavedra Lamas sent to all the member states of the Pan-American Union in 1933, he explicitly and exclusively quoted Georg Cohn's Danish proposal of 1922 and his other studies as the singular sources behind the treaty that now bore his (Saavedra Lamas's) name. In 1936, upon Saavedra Lamas's receipt of the Nobel Peace Prize for this accomplishment, the *Danish Daily* newspaper *Ekstra Bladet* celebrated the Nobel laureate's reference to Cohn's work, referring to him as 'the Father of the Saavedra-Lamas Treaty' (Figure 17).

In his 1939 book *Neo-Neutrality*, Cohn crystalized his view on how to reconcile the passiveness of neutrality with his ambition of being proactive in the hindrance and prohibition of war.[34] Prefaced by the well-known US international jurist (and later ICJ judge) Philip Jessup, the over-400-page monograph expounded a coherent vision for the policy choices that confronted neutral states in their efforts to preserve the newly born multilateral system, in an engaged manner, through their support for the economic side-lining and punishment by sanction of states who acted aggressively in world affairs. Significant parts of the book were dedicated to a study of the failure of the League of Nations' economic sanctions against Italy, following its violent conquest and annexation of Ethiopia.[35] By the end of the book, Cohn could only lament the implicit recognition of Italy's aggression, which, rather than being punished by the League's members, was largely condoned by them. This, in turn, had torpedoed the League's entire international stature and had eventually led to its demise – so argued Cohn.[36] By 1939 then, aggression, in the form of violent conquest and subsequent incorporation into the aggressor state's territorial apparatus, was back on the international agenda as a legitimate policy tool of state conduct – notwithstanding the partial and inconsistent non-recognition of such conquests, as with Stimson on Manchuria.

From 'conquest' to 'occupation': The imperial-fascists strike back

Georg Cohn's vision for a world relieved of state aggression, which, as we have seen earlier, he set out to orchestrate through the workings of international legal

---

33. See the text of the treaty off the website of Yale University's Law school. Available at: http://avalon.law.yale.edu/20th_century/intam01.asp#art2.

34. Cohn, *Neo-Neutrality*, translated into English by Keller and Jensen (New York: Columbia University Press, 1939) with a foreword by Philip C. Jessup (himself an ICJ judge from 1961 until 1970) – reviewed very positively by Francis Deák in *The University of Chicago Law Review*, vol. 7, no. 2 (February 1940), pp. 403–5, and by Malbone W. Graham, *California Law Review*, vol. 28, no. 4 (May 1940), p. 537.

35. Cohn, *Neu-Neutrality*, pp. 98–130, 239–50 (failure of the sanctions).

36. Ibid., p. 170.

Figure 17 Cover page of the *Danish Daily* newspaper *Ekstra Bladet* from 25 November 1936, with the picture of Georg Cohn. © Ekstra Bladet 2018.

Source: The caption reads: 'A DANISH BASIS FOR THE ARGENTINAIN PEACE PRIZE: The father of the Lamas Treaty is Dr Georg Cohn. As the Argentinian foreign minister Dr. Saavedra Lamas received the Nobel Peace Prize, it is worth remembering that this unique South American treaty is based on draft proposals and legal research whose origins are Danish. THE PROPOSAL OF DR. COHN. The principle of non-recognition of territories achieved by conquest was first clarified by the department director at the foreign ministry Dr. Georg Cohn, in a 1922 draft which was sent of behalf of the Danish government to all other governments. The US later adopted this principle, which it termed as "the Stimson Doctrine", and which has been applied by the League of Nations in the Sino-Japanese conflict in Manchuria, as it is currently being used as the basis for the positions of the League's member states against Italy's conquest of Abyssinia. RECOGNIZED BY ARGENTINA. It is noteworthy that Argentina recognizes this [i.e. Cohn's single-handed elaboration of non-recognition] and in the supplementary materials sent to the different governments, Dr. Cohn's research was explicitly mentioned as the sole source of this doctrine, without mention of any other scholar or previous reference works.'

instruments outlawing war, such as non-recognition and the Briand-Kellogg Pact, was all well and good. The only problem was that all through the 1920s and the 1930s, the reality of international relations on the world stage was diametrically opposed to Cohn's expounded views. Internationally, the acquisition of territory by force did not cease. It merely dressed itself in a different ontological garb.

To begin with, there were the conquests by France and Great Britain during the First World War of parts of the failing Ottoman Empire. Rather than being reversed, or genuinely turned over to the indigenous peoples living in these so-called 'liberated' areas, both Great Powers opted to hold on to their new acquisitions. Therefore, with the help of the League of Nations' Mandate system, the First World War's victors, who were now the official sovereigns of the British Mandates from Iraq to the Mediterranean and the French Mandates from inland Syria to the coast of the Levant, vastly increased their territorial holdings. The intellectual dishonesty of the League's mandate system, and the fact that these international directives were little more than a thin disguise for continued territorial control (albeit with a more palatable and internationally accepted legal form of words), was clear to most 1920s and 1930s contemporaries. As Susan Pedersen has convincingly demonstrated, the majority of policy makers, mandate holders and the subjugated peoples within these areas shared a rather crude understanding of the facts. Mandates were nothing more than an international legal veneer, which came to facilitate territorial conquests while providing them with a mantle of international legality and political legitimacy.[37]

Under the new international realties of the League of Nations, diplomatic 'good form' was now considered to be encapsulated in a shift from *conquest* to *occupation*. If as late as 1911, American intellectuals were still speaking in terms of 'state succession' in international law, by the early 1920s this vocabulary had morphed into the notion of *occupation*.[38] Yet the practice was all but the same – acquisition of territory by force for the sake of a state's aggrandizement. What changed, however, was the rhetoric: this now accommodated a degree of temporariness implicit in the concept of *occupation*, behind the guise of which territorial acquisition could continue unabated. Perceptive international lawyers were quick to detect this glaring gap between the old international practice and its new rhetoric – and none more so then Carl Schmitt!

Schmitt witnessed first-hand the vile implications of these discrepancies between reality and rhetoric, with regard to the new concept of occupation and its facilitating of territorial appropriation under the guise of international law. Under the terms of the Treaty of Versailles, the German Rhineland was to remain demilitarized and initially occupied by French, Belgian and British armed forces. Should Germany fail to pay its insurmountable debts, as deliberately imposed on it in the Versailles Treaty, France and Belgium were openly permitted to seize

---

37. Susan Pedersen, *The Guardians: The League of Nations and the Crisis of Empire* (Oxford: Oxford University Press, 2015), pp. 17–81.

38. Amos S. Hershey, 'The Succession of States', *The American Journal of International Law*, vol. 5, no. 2 (April 1911), pp. 285–97.

further German territory so as to extract their outstanding debts directly from the revenues that these newly occupied lands would generate. While Marshall Ferdinand Foch, the French military commander of the Rhineland, was initially inclined to respect the rights of German subjects under his occupation, as soon as the natural frictions between military administrators and the occupied civilian population began to take their toll, the French military swiftly changed its conduct towards the German civilians of the Rhineland, substituting their initially good-willed military administration with harshly oppressive military subjugation practices.[39]

As a native of the Rhineland, Schmitt witnessed first-hand the consequences of 'occupation' as per the new vocabulary. Yet even more than the occupation of the Rhineland, it was the French and Belgian invasion and extremely violent occupation of the Ruhr – Germany's industrial heartland that so perturbed Schmitt. From winter 1923 to August 1925, and in response to Germany's inability to continue its reparation payments under the Versailles Treaty, the French and Belgian governments invaded and militarily occupied the Ruhr and exported its mined iron ore directly to their countries. Much more than economy, the main ideological driving force behind this violent occupation was national vengeance, as France and Belgium 'lawfully claimed the pound of flesh nearest to the German heart thus feeding their revenge' in the Shakespearean sense of this term for Germany's violent occupation of their countries just a few years earlier. Resorting to the same tactics used by the Germans in their occupation of Belgium, Belgian and French occupation forces abducted and executed hostages without trial, used human shields, undertook mass expulsions of workers and civil servants who were deprived of their assets (all without trial), and administered their own regular share of atrocities such as torture and summary executions.[40]

Lecturing on 14 April 1925 (so *before* he could have known that the French–Belgian occupation of the Ruhr would soon end, in August that year), Schmitt, in his habitual analytical manner, framed the base characteristics of the new legal concept of *occupation* adhered to by the League of Nations and the entire international community:

> Modern imperialism has developed new methods of domination and exploitation (mandates, protectorates, lease and intervention treaties) that avoid open political annexation. Transferring these methods to European peoples of culture would be no less an injustice than direct oppression by way of political annexation.[41]

39. Ernst Fraenkel, *Military Occupation and the Rule of Law: Occupation Government in the Rhineland 1918-1923* (Oxford: Oxford University Press, 1944), p. 7.

40. William Rasch, 'Anger Management: Carl Schmitt in 1925 and the Occupation of the Rhineland', *The new Centennial Review*, vol. 8, no. 1 (2008), pp. 57–79 at 65.

41. Rasch, *Anger Management: Carl Schmitt and the Occupation of the Rhineland*, p. 67. Schmitt's overt distinction between 'European peoples of culture' and other people under

As Martti Koskanniemi has recently noted, for Schmitt 'internationalization', as in the application of international law to a certain world problem, was a term whose usage had come about in the specific context of the Rhineland question.[42] It was little more than a polite way of saying that international questions would be settled by those international *military* powers (France, the United Kingdom, the United States, etc.) who were able to decide where and when to apply the measure, and what it would mean in each case. International law was thus not about objective adjudication, but rather about providing power politics with a false, crude and intellectually dishonest mantle of 'objectivized' legalism. For Schmitt, the signature of the Briand-Kellogg Pact merely denoted a shift in definitions, not in international practice. With an agreement to outlaw war signed, the central distinction was no longer the old historical one between war and peace, but rather that between permanent and temporary territorial occupations. Conquest was now left to those powers who decided 'what is a passing, and what is a permanent – occupation'.[43]

It is important to stress once more the ideological context here. While Georg Cohn, Walther Schücking, Hans Wehberg and their pacifist friends were positing ideas for the outlawing of war through international instruments such as non-recognition, the atrocious realities of occupation were playing out the world over. From the Rhineland and the Ruhr, through Africa and the Middle East, to the newly awarded Australian mandates in Papua New Guinea and the Cook Islands, permanent occupations – sanctioned and legalized under international law – had supplanted conquest as the preferable international legal procedure for land appropriation. The Middle East, partitioned as it was between France and Britain under Sykes–Picot,[44] and West Africa were territories that were not being merely *administered* but rather were having their land *sold outright* – with ownership and title being passed, in the latter case, to white settlers in both Cameroon and Nigeria.[45] In the Middle East, between oil-rich Iraq and the oil refineries of Haifa

occupation around the world yet outside the European hemisphere would help him later to justify Germany's occupation of 'the others' – in this case, of the lands of Slavic people in Central and Eastern Europe.

42. Martti Konskenniemi, 'Carl Schmitt and International Law', in Jens Meierhenrich and Oliver Simons (eds.), *The Oxford Handbook of Carl Schmitt* (Oxford: Oxford University Press, 2016), pp. 592–611.

43. Ibid., p. 600.

44. The Sykes–Picot Agreement, officially known as the Asia Minor Agreement, was a secret 1916 accord between the UK and France, which defined their mutually agreed spheres of influence in the Middle East.

45. On the selling of land to white settlers in the former German colonies (now League of Nations' mandates) of Cameroon, Togo and Tanganyika, and the tacit acceptance by the League's Mandate Commission of this neo-colonial practice, see Pedersen, *The Guardians*, pp. 138–40. For François Georges-Picot's role in the carving up of both the Middle East and Cameroon, alongside his British counterpart Mark Sykes, see James Barr, *A Line in the*

and Sidon, the British Petroleum Company (the ancestor of today's BP) received *ownership* of its H2 and H3 transmission stations along Sykes–Picot's partitioning lines between the French and British Mandates of Syria and Iraq–Transjordan.[46]

As is clear from the quote earlier, as early as 1925, Schmitt had already grasped this new twist of international law, as its disingenuous use of the term 'occupation' became abundantly clear in his eyes. And roughly around the same time as the sealing of the Briand-Kellogg Pact, from 1928 onwards, the German jurist began to consolidate his thoughts vis-à-vis this new and indefinite character of occupation – now openly and shamelessly sanctioned by the League of Nations. Schmitt thus began to contemplate what this would entail for the new emerging world order.[47]

With the ink on the Briand-Kellogg Pact barely dry, the conceptual resurgence of conquest was back on the world stage – this time in East Asia. In September 1931, Japan invaded Manchuria. Wishing to avoid the League of Nations' economic sanctions, Japan resorted to 'the innovative idea of a puppet state' with a 'fictitious indigenous government', which was supervised by Japanese consultants, and the assurance of Japanese interests through a 'bilateral agreement'.[48] While Wehberg and Cohn probably viewed Stimson's non-recognition of the Japanese occupation of Manchuria positively, many of their contemporaries – including Carl Schmitt, of course – saw Stimson's declaration as nothing more than an exercise in American intellectual hypocrisy. Ever since the 1898 Spanish–American War, the United States had claimed sovereignty over the Philippine islands – the first full US overseas holding beyond the territorial scope of North America.[49] By 1935, merely three years after Japan had instilled its puppet regime in Manchuria, the United States did much the same in the Philippines, with the presidential election of Manuel Quezon. African and Middle Eastern realities of occupation were not

Sand: The Anglo-French Struggle for the Middle East 1914-1948 (New York: Norton Books, 2011), pp. 15–31.

46. For BP's ownership of its oil pipeline until the 1950s and the British–American-instigated coup d'état against Iranian prime minister Mohammad Mosaddegh, who opted to nationalize and repatriate the land rights that were granted during the League of Nations period to Britain on the oil pipeline, see Robert Fisk, *The Great War for Civilization: The Conquest of the Middle East* (New York: Harper Perennial, 2006), p. 115. For British Petroleum's role in the region, from its acquisition of petrol rights in Iran and Iraq during the very same year that the Kellogg–Briand Pact was signed (1928), see James H. Bamberg, *The History of the British Petroleum Company: Vol. 2 – The Anglo-Iranian Years 1928-1954* (Cambridge: Cambridge University Press, 1994), pp. 11–61.

47. Gary L. Ulmen, Translator's introduction to Carl Schmitt, *The Nomos of the Earth in the International Law of the Jus Publicum Europaeum* (New York: Telos Press, 2006), p. 19.

48. Benvenisti, *The International Law of Occupation*, p. 132. This modus operandi of erecting puppet governments in occupied territories would continue unabated to this day, as is evident in Turkey's continued occupation of Northern Cyprus.

49. Salah D. Hassan, 'Never-Ending Occupations', *The New Centennial Review*, vol. 8, no. 1 (Spring 2008), pp. 1–17 at 3.

so different to Asian ones. In 1935, Italy invaded Ethiopia, and while the League's economic sanctions did little to affect Italian policies, both Britain and France, in turn, came to eventually accept Italy's occupation and officially recognize it. By 1938, both countries had restored their diplomatic ties with fascist Italy under Benito Mussolini.

'Grossraum theory' – Carl Schmitt's aggressive conquest answer to non-recognition and the Briand-Kellogg Pact

By the mid-1930s, and in tandem with his active membership in the Nazi regime, Schmitt gradually built up the legal-political thinking that would later form the ideological bedrock for the Nazi occupation of Europe. This was his *Grossraum* theory. In essence, what the German jurist proposed was a splitting of the world into geo-regional spheres of control, which would be governed by different world powers according to linguistic and cultural hegemonic qualities. The powers heading these 'great-spaces' (the literal translation of *Grossräume* in the plural) would be polities that adhered to their own distinct geopolitical vision, which in turn would translate into their overbearing linguistic–cultural posture which they would then forcefully apply 'top down' on all other peoples, cultures and countries within their respective *Grossräume*.

Schmitt's first official exposition of his *Grossraum* theory took place on 1 April 1939, a mere two weeks after the annexation of Bohemia and Moravia.[50] The sequence of dates and events, and the venue that he chose for his lecture, all carry ample significance here. The venue was, of all places, the law faculty at the University of Kiel – the very same faculty and institute for public international law that Walther Schücking and Hans Wehberg had established back in 1926. Schmitt's lecture also took place after three forceful German annexations of territories that came about without war or armed conflict: the *Anschluss* of Austria (12 March 1938), the annexation of the Czechoslovakian Sudetenland (1 October 1938) and the recent forceful acquisition of Bohemia and Moravia (15 March 1939). In Schmitt's eyes, Nazi Germany's conduct was qualitatively no different to that of Japan in Manchuria, Italy in Ethiopia or, for that matter, the United States in the Philippines across the Pacific. The world was progressively being divided into hemispheric *Grossräume*: Japan in Asia (under the slogan 'Asia for the Asiatic peoples'); the Western hemisphere under US hegemony (thanks to the Monroe Doctrine); Central Asia under Russian (Slavic) rule and Great Britain, as the world's maritime empire, was charged with the control (and order) of the world's high seas.

Within this somewhat schematic partitioning of the world, Europe seemed to Schmitt to be the natural German *Grossraum*. In his eyes, Germany was

---

50. Joseph J. Bendersky, *Carl Schmitt: Theorist for the Reich* (Princeton: Princeton University Press, 1983), p. 257.

merely executing the same policy as everybody else. Hitler himself argued that the very first example of a *Grossraum* was, in fact, the Americas under the US Monroe Doctrine and its prohibition on European intervention in this Western hemisphere: 'We Germans support a similar doctrine for Europe – and above all for the territory and interests of the Greater German Reich.'[51]

Much has been written recently regarding Schmitt's *Grossraum* theory as the predecessor to the unimaginable atrocities undertaken by Nazi Germany in the areas that it occupied under its *Grossraum* before and during the Second World War.[52] Nevertheless, virtually all the contemporary authors who have studied Schmitt's *Grossraum* concept have failed to recognize one simple fact, of which, back in the late 1930s, Schmitt himself was all too well aware: military occupation *was legally compatible and was wholeheartedly allowed for* under the terms of the Briand-Kellogg Pact.

Notwithstanding their lamentations, even stern pacifists such as Wehberg and Cohn had to concede that under the international law of the 1930s military occupation, whether 'pacific' or 'warlike', was indeed fully acceptable under Article 2 of the pact.[53] Towards the end of his Carnegie Endowment commentary on the Briand-Kellogg Pact, Wehberg expounded his wish that occupation would also – in the future – be prohibited.[54] Yet in 1931 – and aside from the Rhineland, which now enjoyed the prohibition of occupation thanks to German foreign minister Gustav Stresemann's drafting brilliance over Article 2 of the 1925 Treaty of Locarno – that was no more than wishful thinking.[55]

---

51. Ibid., p. 258.

52. Mathias Schmoeckel, *Die Großraumtheorie: Ein Beitrag zur Geschichte der Volkerrechtswissenschaft im Dritten Reich, insbesondere der Kriegszeit* (Berlin: Duncker & Humblot, 1994). See also the edited volume by Rüdiger Voigt, *Großraum-Denken Carl Schmitts Kategorie der Großraumordnung* (Stuttgart: Steiner Verlag, 2008), pp. 185–206 (contribution by Oliver Eberl), pp. 207–20 (contribution by Daniel Hildebrand). For a good overview of Schmitt's entire spatial conceptual framework, see Oliver Simons, 'Carl Schmitt's Spatial Rhetoric', in Jens Meierhenrich and Oliver Simons (eds.), *The Oxford Handbook of Carl Schmitt* (Oxford: Oxford University Press, 2016), pp. 776–802.

53. Wehberg, *The Outlawry of War*, pp. 84–5: 'Let us now examine which wars are proscribed by the Kellogg Pact. In order to answer this question, we must take the point of view that, in accordance with Article 1 of the Kellogg Pact, only "war" is proscribed, but not the military occupation of foreign territory, nor other reprisals of a military nature.' Georg Cohn, quoted by Wehberg (*The Outlawry of War*, p. 85, n. 1) arrives as the exact same conclusion. See: Cohn, 'Kellogg-Vertrag und Völkerrecht', p. 174.

54. Wehberg, *The Outlawry of War*, pp. 99–100 § 2. 'The Peaceful Occupation of Foreign Territory'.

55. Following the skirmishes that took place in and around the occupied Rhineland, it was hardly a surprise that the 1925 Treaty of Locarno would be preoccupied with this region. Yet tellingly, the implicit understanding enshrined into the Locarno Treaty against the legality of military occupation or invasions was not extended to Eastern Europe,

Schmitt never expressed his opinions on how exactly his *Grossraum* theory ought to be operationalized, nor did he ever refer to the harsh methods of violence towards civilians within occupied territories that would be required so as to 'pacify' conquered civilians into submission before his putative hegemon. Nevertheless, by April 1939, as Schmitt delivered his Kiel lecture, the horrifying implications of the *Grossraum* doctrine were all too obvious. The behaviour of the Italians in Ethiopia, including the wholesale deployment of chemical weapons against civilians in 1935 as part of that country's failed attempt to subjugate the population, and the atrocious rape of Nanking by the Japanese in 1937 were merely logical consequences of this fanatical ideology.[56] To state that the effectuation of *Grossraum* demanded the forceful subjugation of the peoples within its realm would be an understatement.

It is at this juncture that the point about military occupation being legally acceptable under the Briand-Kellogg Pact becomes so crucial, as it provided tacit licence and a legal shield for occupiers from international reprimand as they unabatingly targeted civilian populations under their control. For Schmitt, who had personally experienced these realities in the Rhineland during the mid-1920s, this was nothing new. The concept of merely rendering war illegal, as per the ideas of Briand-Kellogg Pact, seemed anathema to him. As he succinctly put it,

> It is not only possible, but often even necessary to recognize wars, feuds, reprisals, and applications of force of various kinds as a means of effecting changes. However, these methods and procedures are bracketed; they do not jeopardize the comprehensive spatial order as a whole. War does not disturb this order.[57]

War, in the Clausewitzian sense, was a necessary extension of state affairs. For Schmitt, the point was not to outlaw it but to try and 'reign it in'. Once the world had decided to legally outlaw war as a legitimate tool in international affairs, actors were bound to accept that. Internationalists such as Hersch Lauterpacht, Georges

---

notwithstanding the ample motions of Poland in the League of Nations' 8th Assembly (1927), where the newly born East-Central European countries tried hard (and failed) to enact an 'East Locarno Pact' that would apply to Germany's eastern front. As it turned out, the storm that would engulf Eastern Europe under the Nazi and Soviet occupations merely a decade later read like a Chekhovian alarm of 'gun seen on stage in the first Act which would fire in the third', when one thinks of this deliberate precluding of Eastern Europe from the international legal protection against military occupation. On the attempt by Poland to enact an 'East Locarno Pact', see Wehberg, *The Outlawry of War,* pp. 42–6.

56. Iris Chang, *The Rape of Nanking: The Forgotten Holocaust of World War II* (New York: Basic Books, 1997). On the Red Cross experience during the Italian occupation of Ethiopia, see Rainer Baudendistel, *Between Bombs and Good Intentions: The International Committee of the Red Cross (ICRC) and the Italo-Ethiopian War, 1935-1936* (New York: Berghahn Books, 2006).

57. Carl Schmitt, *The Nomos of the Earth,* p. 186.

Scelle and Arnold McNair got their way, and Schmitt was going to accept that too. Yet what Schmitt did stress – and pertinently, one might add – was the fact that by outlawing war these internationalists were unleashing consequences for the international order, as well as for occupied people, the scope of which they simply could not envisage.[58] If war was outlawed, and occupation was allowed, then the simple solution would be to transfer the realm of forceful territorial changes from war to indefinite occupations. The *Grossraum* theory did just that; and, what's more, it was legal – even in the eyes of Schmitt's staunchest adversaries. Its victims would be the occupied civilians.

Werner Best's execution of the Grossraum doctrine in Germany, France and Denmark

The most problematic aspect of the forceful application of *Grossraum*, 'top down', on the people to be subjugated under it boiled down to one essential question: How would the hegemon deal with the existence of inherently unwanted people within their *Grossraum*?

For his part, Carl Schmitt was not inclined to provide any concrete answer to this question. Faithful to his renowned tendency for ambiguity, Schmitt maintained a healthy intellectual distance from any (and all) operational aspects of his *Grossraum* brainchild. Indeed, it was this very ambiguity that saved him from war crimes prosecution in Nuremberg just after the war.[59] As the prudent jurist refrained from discussing any operational aspects of his theory, that task was taken up by the technically capable and fanatical Nazi official, Werner Best.[60]

From an early age, Best was personally acquainted with the realities of military occupation, having grown up in the post-World War I French-occupied Rhineland between Darmstadt and Mainz. In his early years as a student, Best actively organized many vigilante actions against the French occupation forces – both in the Rhineland and, especially, during the French–Belgian occupation of the Ruhr (1923–4), including time spent in a French-run prison for these actions. Best excelled in his legal studies, earning his doctorate in law from Heidelberg University in 1927, and, after a successful clerkship and the tough German bar-association examination (*Stattsexamen*), was nominated as a junior judge to the lower court of the State of Hessen at the young age of twenty-six.[61]

Being a stern believer in a harsh form of German nationalism, and in contrast to Schmitt's opportunistic grounds for Nazi membership, Best joined the Nazi

58. Ulmen, Translator's introduction to Carl Schmitt, *The Nomos of the Earth*, pp. 21–2.

59. Bendersky, *Carl Schmitt: Theorist for the Reich*, pp. 264–73.

60. Ulrich Herbert, *Best. Biographische Studien über Radikalismus, Weltanschauung und Vernunft 1903–1989*, 3rd edn (Bonn: J.H. Dietz Verlag, 1996).

61. Leni Yahil, *Test of Democracy, The Rescue of Danish Jewry in World War II* (Jerusalem: The Magness Press of the Hebrew University, 1966), p. 281 [in Hebrew].

apparatus early on in 1930. A fervent believer in the biological *völkisch* aspect of the Nazi creed, Best enlisted in the SS in 1931 and rose through its ranks thanks to a combination of his sharp analytical skills, his keen sense of ambition and a special talent for the unscrupulous execution of lethal violence. In 1934, he served as a key orchestrator of the killing of Ernst Röhm, co-founder of the SA *Sturmabteilung*, and his supporters during the 1934 Nazi 'Night of the Long Knives' (also known as the 'Röhm Purge'). Promoted for his actions by Hitler and Himmler, Best then entered the innermost circle of the SS, becoming its chief legal ideologist and its third highest-ranking official – second only to Reinhard Heidrich, the 'Reich-Protector' of Bohemia and Moravia, and, ultimately, Himmler himself.[62] Reminiscing in hindsight, Adolf Eichmann recalled Best as 'the GESTAPO's architect' and 'the one who set things into legal formations'.[63] It was Best who, in 1935, provided Heidrich and Himmler with the legal arguments to support the SS takeover of the German state: he coined the legal terminology for administrative protective detention (*Schutzhaft*), which was clearly outside, and in breach of, Germany's constitutional criminal legal framework at the time.[64]

From the late 1930s onwards, Best acquired extensive operational experience in the mass removal of people whom the Nazis considered 'unfit to dwell' within the German *Grossraum*. In 1938, he headed the SS operation for the rounding up and deportation of all Polish Jews, residing as foreign nationals in Germany, and their disposal at the Polish border.[65] A year later, Best was charged with the establishment of the SS death squads (*Einsatzgruppen*) that first swept through Poland in 1939–40, cementing the German grip on this occupied land with wholesale executions, and with overall responsibility for the deportation and removal of the Jews towards extermination camps in the East.

In June 1940, Best was promoted further to the level of ministerial director. He became the chief civilian administrator of the German occupation of France, operating out of Paris. In 1941, he took on several extensive missions across 'Hitler's Empire' in an attempt to generate a structured and comprehensive approach to all areas that by that time had already come under German Nazi rule.[66] In a series of well-thought-out articles, from late 1941 until July 1942, Best sought to operationalize the various modalities of Nazi occupation while building a suitable typology for the different Nazi approaches towards the different peoples now subjugated within their *Grossraum*.

In essence, Werner Best envisaged four types of administrative setups, ascending in their degree of local subjugation of the populations under control, across the

62. Herbert, *Best: Biographische Studien über Radikalismus*, p. 144.

63. Yahil, *Test of Democracy, The Rescue of Danish Jewry in World War II*, p. 282.

64. Ibid.

65. Alina Bothe, '*Polenaktion*' – *The Persecution of Jews with Polish citizenship in Germany from 1938 until the end of WWII*, lecture delivered at 2nd International Conference of the Sugihara House, Kaunas, Lithuania, 24 May 2018.

66. Mark Mazower, *Hitler's Empire* (New York: Allen Lane, 2006), pp. 223–56.

divergent regions now held by Nazi Germany. Denmark was to be subjected to the most lenient form of German military rule – namely, 'informal' administration. In this case, the Danish government and all its agencies would remain in place and would be merely 'directed' by the German plenipotentiary there. France (where Best was currently serving), Belgium and the Netherlands were to be subjected to 'supervisory' administration. Here, German officials would work through the national civil services in a more 'top down' manner, preserving these national entities and their local staff yet directing them much more firmly than in the informal Danish case. The Protectorate of Bohemia and Moravia would be subjected to Best's third type – 'ruling' occupation. In this category, the Germans would take on a full reshaping of what was left of the entire national bureaucracy and remain permanently cautious of impending threats to Germany's rule. Poland would be subjected to the highest and most cruel form of subjugation – namely, 'colonial' administration (type 4). Here, as in Hans Frank's 'General Government', the 'inferior civilizational level of the inhabitants required the occupiers to take up the burden of government themselves', reducing the local population to the minimum levels of tasking for the sake of 'order and health'.[67]

Best's typology of occupations is crucial to our understanding of the clash between the opposing views concerning occupation that would later surface during GC-IV's drafting. In concurrence with Schmitt's vision of *Machtrecht* ('power law'), Best continued directly from where Schmitt left off, identifying the different *Grossräume* with the nations that controlled them as hegemons. From this stemmed Best's logical equation between *Grossraumordnung* ('the order of great spaces') and what he termed *Volksordnung* ('the order of peoples'):

> In the *Volksordnung*, the stronger peoples forcefully coerce and impose their will over and upon the weaker peoples.[68]

In short, *Grossraumordnung* unequivocally necessitated violent forceful subjugation.[69] As Mark Mazower has noted, Best's superiors, Heidrich and Himmler, utterly despised the need to heed legal considerations in their subjugation of East-Central Europe. In fact, both men probably built up a mild contempt for Best himself – precisely because of the latter's conviction and belief in the validity of legal systems, which triggered his insistence on the need for the German occupational apparatus to remain within a *legal* boundary of sorts, albeit one premised upon *Machtrecht* principles.[70]

Best's modality of occupation was premised on the need to avoid the coercive elements implicit in the harsh subjugation of occupied peoples as far as possible.

67. Ibid., p. 235. Mazower's interpretation here is based upon Herbert, *Best: Biographische Studien über Radikalismus*, pp. 290–2.

68. Yahil, *Test of Democracy, The Rescue of Danish Jewry in World War II*, p. 282.

69. Herbert, *Best: Biographische Studien über Radikalismus*, p. 284.

70. Mazower, *Hitler's Empire*, p. 237.

The more the peoples within the German *Grossraum* managed their own affairs, with the minimal amount of resources deployed for their management by the German Reich, the longer the German control of its *Grossraum* could continue. Drawing largely on classical sources, with his examples dating back to the Roman Empire, Best envisaged the possibility of a *Pax Germanica* à la *Pax Romana*, with an embedded parallel between the Nazi conquests and the Roman military superiority over smaller nations and patron–client relationships that had facilitated the Roman *Herrenvolk*'s long-lasting governance over the multitude of peoples existent in the Roman sphere of control during the *Pax Romana*'s almost 200-year duration.[71]

In October 1942, Werner Best reached the zenith of his Nazi professional career: he was nominated by Hitler to the post of Germany's Reich Plenipotentiary in Copenhagen. Denmark would become the place where he would attempt to implement his vision of 'a self-limiting and restrained approach to occupation' within the German *Grossraum*.[72] Once in Denmark, Best set out to deal with what he saw as the two most problematic issues facing the successful administration of *Grossraum* – namely (a) the taking and summary execution of hostages as reprisals for the killing of German staff in occupied Europe and (b) the forced mass movement of populations, either in deportation *away* from the German *Grossraum* (the Jews) or in the transplanting of Germans into newly colonized areas. It is here, in reference to these two issues that one ought to understand the impact of Best's policy choices on GC-IV's drafters (first among them, Georg Cohn) in their later elaboration of that convention's Articles 49 and 68 (see the following two chapters).

The issue of hostage execution was certainly not foreign to Best, seeing as he was one of the chief architects of SS *Einsatzgruppen* activities during the German conquest of Poland from September 1939 to May 1940.[73] Nevertheless, a crucial turning point in this regard occurred on 16 September 1941. Following the German invasion of the Soviet Union in June that year, and with civilian and guerrilla resistance actions against German military personal on the rise, Hitler issued his infamous '1–100' order. It decreed, as Germany's official reprisal strategy, the requested killing of one hundred hostages for every German soldier killed by resistance fighters in all German-occupied areas.[74]

71. Best, July article. For an overview of the classical Roman notions of patron–client relations, see Ernst Badian, *Foreign Clientelae: 264-70 B.C* (Oxford: Clarendon Press, 1958). See also its sequel for the period of the Roman Principate: Ernst Badian, *Roman Imperialism in the Late Republic*, 2nd edn (Ithaca: Cornell University Press, 1968).

72. Mazower, *Hitler's Empire*, p. 237.

73. On Best's deep involvement in the creation of the *Einsatzgruppen* and their employment in during the conquest of Poland, see Herbert, *Best: Biographische Studien über Radikalismus*, pp. 234–40.

74. Research on the '1–100' order and German reprisals against hostages have been well researched and are beyond the scope of this study. Among the path-breaking studies

From his Parisian vantage point at the time, Best wholeheartedly opposed to what he saw as the adoption of 'Polish methods' and their ill-advised implementation in Western-European France. His objection rested primarily on ideological–racial and *völkisch* grounds.[75] In his view, the importation into France of methods adopted by German occupation forces in Poland effectively meant treating 'Aryan' (or rather, semi-Aryan) races such as the French in the same manner as Slavic *Untermensch* (subhuman) races such as the Poles. By September 1941, Best was already well advanced in the codification of his four types of occupational regimes within the German *Grossraum*. Applying the aforementioned order for the summary execution of hostages across Hitler's Empire in its entirety meant that the senior command in Berlin did not bother to make the distinction, so vital in Best's eyes, between the different types of occupation that he elaborated. This was also true for his new posting – Denmark.

From 1943 onwards, Best fought unceasingly against Berlin's actions in Denmark, be it in the mass deportation of Danish police officers to Buchenwald (2,235 deported, of whom 117 died in that concentration camp) or the application of the '1–100' hostage execution order there.[76] Best's position here, and his meticulous documentation of it, partially served as the grounds for his dismissal and partial acquittance during the de-Nazification trials after the Second World War.[77]

In the same manner as with the issue of hostage taking and execution, Best's approach to the transferal of populations into and out of the German-occupied areas stemmed first and foremost from his *Grossraum* vision. Consistent with his view as to the incompatibility of Jews with the German *Grossraum*, Best consistently strove for their total removal from his territorial spheres of control. In 1938, it was he who was primarily responsible for the deportation of Polish Jews to the Polish–German border some months prior to the German invasion of Poland in September 1939. Once in Paris, Best took the lead in the orchestration of the roundup and incarceration of the Jews of France, and later played a major role in

on this issue was Christopher Browning's 1983 study of the German reprisals in Serbia, which set the stage for his well-known refutation of the then-held dichotomy between the actions of the German Wehrmacht and the SS, which – almost a decade later, in 1992 – Browning famously substantiated in his celebrated monograph *Ordinary Men: Reserve Police Battalion 101 and the Final Solution in Poland*, New York: Harper Perennial, 1992. See Christopher Browning, 'Wehrmacht Reprisal Policy and the Mass Murder of Jews in Serbia', *Militärgeschichtliche Mitteilungen,* vol. 33, no. 1 (1983), pp. 31–47. For a good recent overview of the German military's reprisal policies and execution of hostages, see Ben Shepherd, *Hitler's Soldiers: The German Army in the Third Reich* (New Haven: Yale University Press, 2016), pp. 190–297.

75. Herbert, *Best: Biographische Studien über Radikalismus*, p. 303.

76. Ibid., pp. 392–4, and see also p. 394, n. 203.

77. Herbert, *Best: Biographische Studien über Radikalismus*, pp. 403–32.

their deportation to the extermination camps in the East.[78] Once in Denmark, he continued his push towards the removal of the Jews and, as in Paris, here too he worked in close coordination with Adolf Eichmann – the central figure in charge of the implementing the 'Final Solution' on the Jews within the German Reich.[79]

The consolidated effort by the Danish people and their rescue of Danish Jewry almost in its entirety during the Second World War is well documented.[80] As the senior Danish diplomat Bo Lidegaard has recently explained the most crucial period in this rescue comprised the fourteen or so days between the issuance of the SS deportation decree on Hitler's explicit orders of 16 September 1943 and the final relocation of those Jews to Sweden between 29 September and 1 October – the date set for their final deportation.[81] Adolph Eichmann – who arrived in Copenhagen in early September following the resignation of the Danish government and the house arrest of King Christian X on 29 August 1943, and who was infuriated by this failure of his deportation policy for the Jews – partially blamed Werner Best for this SS failure.[82]

Georg Cohn, Werner Best, Carl Schmitt and the final unfolding of Grossraum

Werner Best was well acquainted with Georg Cohn's long-standing international stature and his association with the attempts to illegalize conquest under

78. On Best's role in the legal stripping of French Jews of their rights (*Entrechtung*) following his reuse of the legal measure of arrests according to national-security interests (a measure first legally concocted by Best for internal use in Germany back in 1934), see Ulrich, *Best*, 258–65. On his primary role as the central strategic planner of the deportation of both foreign-national Jews in France (from Poland, Czechoslovakia and so on – some 150,000 of whom had come to reside in Paris since the mid-1930s) and, later, of French Jewish citizens, including Georges Cahen-Salvador's family, see the sub-chapter 'From incarceration to deportation' (*Von der Internierung zur Deportation*) in Ulrich, *Best*, pp. 309–14.

79. On Best's coordination of the deportation of the Jews of France on 4 March 1942, see Herbert, *Best: Biographische Studien über Radikalismus*, p. 317, n. 186. On his coordination with Eichmann for the deportation of the Jews of Denmark, based on Eichmann's telegram to Best on 16 September 1943, see Herbert, *Best: Biographische Studien über Radikalismus*, p. 366, n. 122.

80. Leni Yahil, *The Rescue of Danish Jewry* (New York: Jewish Publication Society, 1984). See also: Leo Goldberger (ed.), *The Rescue of the Danish Jews: Moral Courage under Stress* (New York: New York University Press, 1987).

81. Bo Lidegaard, *Countrymen: The Untold Story of How Denmark's Jews Escaped the Nazis, of the Courage of Their Fellow Danes – and of the Extraordinary Role of the SS* (New York: Alfred Knopf, 2013), pp. 16–127.

82. Cohn Roi, *Seven Generations in Denmark*, p. 132. See also: Herbert, *Best: Biographische Studien über Radikalismus*, pp. 366–73.

international law. Entries in the diaries of the long-serving Danish foreign minister, Peter Munch, confirm Best's personal interest in the fate of his Jewish nemesis, Cohn. On 28 August 1942, Munch wrote that 'the Germans have inquired over Cohn's roles in the Foreign Ministry'.[83] From that day onwards, and on the explicit recommendation of his old friend Nils Svenningsen (director of the Danish Foreign Ministry), Cohn maintained an increasingly low profile, reducing as much as possible his presence at the Foreign Ministry buildings that were now overseen by Best's SS subordinates. Cohn and his family also left Copenhagen for their summer house in Rungsted, some 40 kilometres to the north, so as to avoid daily contact with the German occupation authorities in the capital.

At noon on Thursday, 30 September 1943, Tito Wessel – the Danish ambassador to Chile, and Georg Cohn's lifelong faithful friend – arrived abruptly at Cohn's summer house in Rungsted. Wessel informed Cohn that deportation orders for him and his entire family had now been formally issued. Within hours, German troops and SS personnel were instructed to arrive at Cohn's residence to implement his deportation to Theresienstadt. Wessel insisted that the Cohn family leave the house instantly and go into hiding. They packed and left immediately and were hidden at Havreholm Palace – the noble family residence of the Janssen family. Three days later, the Cohn family's departure was organized by the Danish Underground. On the night of Rosh Hashana (the religious Jewish New Year) at 02.00 am, 2 October 1943, the Cohn family boarded a fishing boat that transported them over to Sweden's Helsingborg harbour with the help and knowledge of the local Danish police force.[84] On 17 October 1943, the entry in former foreign minister Peter Munch's diary read:

> Regarding special cases of deportation of senior Danish-Jewish officials that the Scavenius government was specifically concerned about, Werner Best had discussed their status with Nils Svenningsen. Einar Cohn – the Chief Danish economist received an extraordinary permit to leave the country for Sweden. Concerning Georg Cohn – he and his entire family had escaped the country without a permit and had crossed over [i.e. to Sweden].[85]

By the end of 1943, the conceptual victory of the advocates of *Grossraum* – Carl Schmitt and Werner Best, who each favoured the legalization of conquest – seemed to have been sealed. In the ideological clash between Georg Cohn's non-recognition of the acquisition of territory by force and Schmitt's and Best's juridical–ideological rejoinder in the form of their *Grossraum* theories, the latter pair seemed to have had the last word.

83. P. Munch, *Erindringer: 1870- 1947* (Copenhagen: Nyt Nordisk Forlag, 1967), Vol. VII, p. 333.

84. Cohn Roi, *Seven Generations in Denmark*, pp. 137–9.

85. P. Munch, *Erindringer: 1870- 1947*, vol. VIII, p. 232. Also quoted in Cohn Roi, *Seven Generations in Denmark*, pp. 140–1, n. 44.

This ideological clash also bore truly personal traits. In 1939, Carl Schmitt decided to deliver the very first public presentation of his *Grossraum* theory at the University of Kiel's law faculty. This was, as outlined above, the very faculty and very same institute for public international law that his ideological opponents Walther Schücking and Hans Wehberg had established in 1926. Its signal ideology was multilateralism and the Pacific Settlement of disputes. Schücking and Wehberg were the great German universalist pacifists who had fought hardest against the bellicose nature of German, Japanese and Italian fascist expansionist theories at the League of Nations.

As the Nazis came to power in 1933, they immediately terminated Schücking's term as the German judge at the Permanent Court of International Justice in The Hague. In parallel, Hitler ordered the removal of Schücking from his academic position at Kiel. Schmitt's decision to deliver his *Grossraum* speech in the German Baltic city thus carried a clear and overt message. His pro-war approach to international law, and his ideological–legal justification for the acquisition of territory by force, had prevailed over Schücking's and Wehberg's universalist voices. Walther Schücking died in 1935, heartbroken, in exile in The Hague. Hans Wehberg chose Geneva as his exile of preference. Schmitt decided to deliver his *Grossraum* speech in Kiel in order to ideologically spit on Schücking's grave.

Werner Best's personal persecution of Georg Cohn ran parallel to Schmitt's ideological desecration of Schücking's international legal legacy. For two decades, from 1922 until his exile in 1943, Georg Cohn was the key proponent, alongside Schücking and Wehberg, of the illegitimacy of the use of force in international affairs. In his fanatical *völkisch* version of *Grossraum*, Werner Best opted to answer Cohn in kind. If Cohn refused to accept conquest, then Denmark was now an integral part of the German *Grossraum*. As a Jew, under Best's ideology, Cohn had no place in this German *Grossraum*. His removal, and that of his entire Jewish kin, was a categorical necessity in Best's *völkisch* take on Schmitt's *Grossraum* ideology. People such as Cohn, who argued forcefully against the use of force, would be removed from that *Grossraum* – by force. In a literal echo of the German term *Machtrecht*, might had become right.

Chapter 6

COHN'S DRAFTING OF THE PROHIBITION ON SETTLEMENTS – ARTICLE 49 PARAGRAPH 6

From conquest to colonization

Researchers who examine GC-IV's history correctly cite the horrors of the Nazi occupation of Europe as the foundational experience that shaped this treaty's drafting. In Jean Pictet's 660-page commentary on the Civilian Convention, the term 'Second World War' appears some 220 times throughout this seminal work. The delegates who sat down to draft GC-IV did not merely elaborate this convention's Articles in a general sense. Instead, in many instances, GC-IV's drafters deliberately articulated its Articles in order to counter specific experiences from the Second World War – some of which they personally had experienced. As we have seen in Part One, this was precisely the case with Georges Cahn Salvador and Gerhart Riegner in their joint drafting of Common Article 3. Much the same can be said of Georg Cohn's drafting of GC-IV's Article 49 paragraph 6 which prohibits the construction of settlements and colonization of a territory conquered by a military occupier.

As demonstrated in Chapter 5, Cohn began his campaign to render conquest illegal under international law in 1922 with efforts to endorse non-recognition as the legal nemesis of territorial conquest. His drafting of Article 49 paragraph 6 of GC-IV was thus a direct logical corollary of that position – now famously known as the 'Stimson Doctrine'. Added into GC-IV's text during the 1948 Red Cross Conference in Stockholm, Article 49 paragraph 6, which prohibits military conquerors from transferring their own population into territories that they have conquered, was designed to forestall conquest's most gruesome effect – namely, its metamorphosis into a permanent non-ending military occupation, which would eventually morph into outright annexation.

This prohibition on population transfer into a subjugated territory by its conqueror, which survived the 1949 Geneva Plenipotentiaries Conference intact, is the one relied upon today by international-community organs – such as the UN Security Council, the ICJ, the Council of Europe and the African Union – in their struggle against modern-day colonization. Recent examples of states that have occupied land through conquest so as to later colonize it with their own nationals include Morocco's occupation of Western Sahara; Turkey's invasion, occupation and colonization of Northern Cyprus; and, most well-known, Israel's occupation of the Palestinian territories bracketed between the 'West Bank' of the Jordan River and the 1949 Israel–Jordan armistice line ('The Green Line').[1] Russia's 2014 invasion, occupation and, finally, annexation of the Crimean Peninsula and its control of Eastern Ukraine is the most recent example of this type of state conduct.

Of all these cases of occupation-turned-annexation, none has given rise to more acute international controversy – and jurisprudence – than Israel's conquest of the Palestinian territories in 1967 and its subsequent construction of settlements there. At the heart of Israel's claim to the Palestinian territories lies its argument that the 'West Bank' is not an *occupied* territory but rather a *disputed* one. Had Jordan lawfully owned the West Bank and been granted sovereign title over this area by the international community, so argue the Israelis, only then would their actions have amounted to an occupation under the terms of GC-IV. However, Israel had in fact – so claim jurists Yehuda Bloom and Meir Shamgar and, lately, Justice Edmond Levy and Allen Baker – forcefully seized this territory from a Jordan that, in itself, had no legal title to it. Jordan, they argue, seized this territory at the British Mandate's moment of termination in 1948 and had subsequently never received recognition for this 'land-grab' from the international community. Hence, in their eyes, Israel's conquest of the 'West Bank' renders this territory not occupied but, rather, disputed.

The fact that Israel conquered the West Bank as a result of Jordanian aggression against it, which manifested itself in Jordan's invasion of pre-1967 Israel, buttressed by Jordan's declaration of war against it, is historically not disputed. There is simply no question as to the fact that Israel came to conquer the West Bank as a result of a war it did not start, under which it was the state being attacked, and from which its reaction in self-defence yielded at the end of the day the Jordanian loss of the West Bank due to Israel's military superiority.

Nevertheless, Israel's settlement policy in the West Bank violates international law in the crudest of manners – not because of the status of the *territory*, but rather – because of what this conquest does to this territory's indigenous population – the Palestinian people. For Georg Cohn who drafted GC-IV's prohibition on settlements as is spelled out in Article 49 paragraph 6, this prohibition had first and foremost to do with the well-being and rights of the local conquered civilians, irrespective of who started which war and why.

Grossraum's aftermath: Potsdam, Nuremberg, the Genocide Convention and GC-IV

The conquests of the Second World War, and the subjugation of conquered civilian populations, were certainly not a new historical phenomenon. Yet the *Grossraum* vision of conquest, as adopted by the Nazis, was nevertheless novel. The idea that there were certain racially undesired peoples (e.g. Jews, Roma and

---

1. Tomuschat, 'Prohibition on Settlements', pp. 1551–73.

Sinti, etc.) whose existence within the *Grossraum* could simply not be tolerated, and which necessitated their deportation and removal beyond that *Grossraum's* pale, was certainly a new idea. Throughout human history, multiple populations have been deported and exiled. Nevertheless, it was not until the dovetailing of fanatical modern racial theories with the desire for territorial conquest (as in Best's version of *Grossraum*) that deportations became synonymous with conquest. In 1907, when The Hague Regulations were adopted, conquest did not yet imply a racial desire for the removal of peoples. Commenting on Article 49's relationship with Nazi ideological developments, and the absence of such thinking during the drafting of the Hague Conventions (1899–1907), Jean Pictet observed that

> The Hague Regulations do not refer to the question of deportation; this was probably because the practice of deporting persons was regarded at the beginning of this century [i.e. the twentieth century] as having fallen into abeyance [i.e. a state of temporary disuse or suspension].[2]

Far from having fallen into abeyance, however, the forcible uprooting of whole population groups from their long-standing places of residence became one of the most notable aspects of the Second World War.[3] Even *after* that conflict, German legal advisers whose opinions were sought by the ICRC, for the sake of GC-IV's future elaboration, stressed Pictet's above-quoted understanding of the 1907 Hague Conventions.[4] Odd as it might sound, under international law before and during the Second World War, deportations as such – without the added component of the desire to utilize them for ethnic eradication – were simply, internationally, not prohibited. The chief author of these German legal opinions to the ICRC, Conrad Roediger, most certainly did not voice these legal opinions out of any affinity with the Nazi cause.[5] In fact, Roediger was one of the few German jurists who tried to confront the Nazi state apparatus about its anti-Jewish actions. Correspondingly – and following post-war West German chancellor Konrad Adenauer's German 'reset', enshrined in the 1949 West German Constitution – Roediger swiftly found himself on the bench of the highest court in the land: the German Federal Constitutional Court located in the southwestern city of Karlsruhe, from September 1951 until his retirement in 1956.[6]

---

2. *Pictet Commentary*, p. 279.

3. While estimates as to how many people were actually uprooted during the Second World War vary, most scholars agree that it certainly exceeded thirty million persons – an overwhelming majority of whom were displaced between Europe and the Urals. See Joseph Schechtman, *European Population Transfers: 1939-1945* (New York: Oxford University Press, 1946).

4. Lewis, *The Birth of the New Justice*, pp. 248–9.

5. Ibid., pp. 248–9, n. 82–3.

6. German Federal Foreign Ministry Archives ('*Auswärtiges Amt-Archiv*') Berlin, located at the central offices of German Foreign Ministry – Gendarmenmarkt (and *not*

All in all, the international community's reaction to mass population uprooting was, at best, chequered. While at Nuremberg the Allies did indeed prosecute Nazi war criminals on account of their involvement in deportations (primarily, but not solely, of the Jews of Europe), other international forums proved much more ambivalent about forced population displacement. The UN Charter fell silent concerning deportations; they were, in fact, regarded as necessary – and had been agreed upon by the Allies at the Potsdam Conference of 1945. From the latter part of that year onwards, and provided they were carried out in an 'orderly fashion', the expulsions of some twelve million Germans from Eastern Europe into the new entities of both East and West Germany took place – in large part in retaliation for the uprooting of populations undertaken by Nazis between 1939 and 1945.[7] Correspondingly, the drafting efforts undertaken by Raphael Lemkin in favour of the Genocide Convention, which was eventually signed in December 1948, also witnessed the *removal* of references to deportation despite its having been an interrelated component of virtually all genocides.[8] In a post-war Europe being ethnically reshaped for the future, visions for the demographic re-engineering of the continent were tacitly accepted by the world's Great Powers as a legitimate means of settling past scores concerning unwanted ethnic minorities.

Remarkably, and in stark contrast to the Genocide Convention (1948), GC-IV's language (1949) is blunt, clear and incontrovertible: deportations are not only illegal under GC-IV's terms, they are also considered among the worst offences punishable under its 'Grave Breeches' clause, Article 147. Perhaps even more remarkable is the fact that this harsh prohibition against population deportation was *not* the result of the events of the Second World War; *this prohibition already existed within the Civilian Convention's earliest Tokyo draft of 1934* (so prior to Nazi crimes committed between 1939 and 1945).[9] That the ICRC was so far in front of virtually all other organs of the international community in its understanding of

---

at the Central German Archives in Berlin-Lichterfelde), Nachlass: Roediger, Conrad. See also file # 1380, Band 118, Genfer Konferenz Rotes Kreuz – Politisches Archiv Auswärtigen Amts.

7. Matthew Frank, *Expelling the Germans: British Opinion and Post-1945 Population Transfer in Context* (Oxford: Oxford University Press, 2008).

8. On the removal of the prohibitions against deportation in the earlier drafts of the Genocide Convention, see material under the sub-heading 'Deportation and genocide: The missed opportunity' in Vincent Chetail's 'Is There any Blood on My Hands? Deportation as a Crime of International Law', *Leiden Journal of International Law*, vol. 29, no. 3 (2016), p. 919, n. 9–10.

9. *Draft International Convention on the Condition and Protection of Civilians of enemy nationality who are on territory belonging to or occupied by a belligerent. Tokyo, 1934*, Article 19 paragraph 6: 'Deportations outside the territory of the occupied State are forbidden, unless they are evacuations intended, on account of the extension of military operations, to ensure the security of the inhabitants.' Available at: https://ihl-databases.icrc.org/ihl/INTRO/320?OpenDocument.

the acute and critical nature of population deportation certainly merits further research, which is, unfortunately, beyond the scope of the present volume.

Notwithstanding this prescient appearance, the initial wording of the anti-deportation clause in GC-IV's earliest textual version – prepared by the ICRC for the Governments Experts meeting of April 1947 – saw a considerable 'ratcheting up' of the rhetoric concerning deportations, when compared to that of the 1934 Tokyo draft.[10] At the XVII Red Cross Conference in Stockholm, the text against deportations was further strengthened. Prohibitions were firmly put in place concerning family separations and both group and individual deportations, as well as an advanced need of notification of the occupied territory's protective power in case of an evacuation on humanitarian grounds. Finally, it was at Stockholm that the prohibition on the transfer of the occupiers' own population into a newly conquered territory was added into Article 49's text – in its sixth paragraph.[11]

The manner in which the international community reacted to the ethno-demographic consequences of Nazi actions in the aftermath of 1945, at the level of both Great Powers and international institutions (the UN's organs, the ICRC and the like), share one crucial feature. They were all (in one way or another) construed as an answer to the consequences arising from the application of Schmitt's and Best's *Grossraum* visions. The stipulations of Potsdam in 1945 were initially meant to serve as a reversal of the demographic changes instituted by the Nazis over the preceding six years. By 1948, as the Genocide Convention was being drafted, many central-European thinkers and policy makers (most notably, Czechoslovak president Edvard Beneš) had shifted their sights away from a simple reversal of *Grossraum*'s consequences towards active punishment of the Germans. This was coupled with a deliberate effort to do away with the existence of German minorities in East-Central Europe 'once and for all' and, in Stalin's own words, to 'give them the feeling of what it was like to be under the rule of others'. This changing of the German *Grossraum*'s hegemon also meant that its *Herrenvolk* would now bear the brunt of the defeat of Schmitt's and Best's ideologies.[12]

10. The wording drawn up by the 1947 Government Experts meeting stated that 'individual or collective deportations or transfers, carried out under physical or moral constraint, to places outside occupied territories, *and for whatever motives*, are prohibited. This prohibition applies to all persons in the said territories'; Italics added. See: *Report on the Work of the Conference of Government Experts for the Study of the Conventions for the Protection of War Victims*, Geneva, ICRC 14–26 April 1947, p. 288.

11. *Revised and new Draft Conventions for the protection of war victims: Texts approved and amended by the XVIIth international Red Cross Conference*, Geneva, October 1948, pp. 127–8.

12. Matthew Frank, *Making Minorities History: Population Transfer in 20th Century Europe* (Oxford: Oxford University Press, 2017), p. 274, n. 33.

The post-war continuation of 'occupy-annex-deport'

The central pillar of *Grossraum*'s translation into actual policy was the entrenching of conquest via the deportation of populations from forcefully occupied territory, which was later officially and declaratively annexed. While this Nazi logic of 'occupy-annex-deport' was executed across the entirety of Hitler's Empire during the Second World War, it had, in fact, already begun before the official opening of international hostilities – in the *Anschluss* (annexation) of Austria and the immediate deportation of the Jews from that territory. By 1947, as GC-IV's earlier drafts were being worked over by the ICRC and France (as we saw in Chapter 1), non-recognition, particularly of unilateral annexation as the legal manner in which states consolidated control over their captured bounty of forcefully seized territory had become one of the declared cornerstones of the new UN Charter (Article 2 paragraph 4). Correspondingly, *Grossraum*'s authors, Schmitt and Best, and its central tenets of 'occupy, annex, and deport the ethnically unwanted' had by now made it onto the Nuremberg charge sheet. The inescapable relationship between forceful territorial acquisition and ethnic cleansing had been fully exposed – and was now prosecutable. Little wonder, then, that for GC-IV's drafters the mere need to refer to the now-delegitimized term 'annexation' in their own convention's text posed a problem.

In its first version of the Civilian Convention, therefore, the ICRC used the term 'alleged annexation'. Wishing to forcefully repudiate even the slightest possibility that occupations which morphed into annexations could ever be legally valid, the International Committee qualified it with the adjective 'alleged', signalling the intention that, in fact, forceful annexation could *never* be rendered legal in international eyes. The only reason the ICRC even opted to include the word 'annexation' in its proposed Geneva Convention text in the first place was in order to explicitly prohibit states from taking harmful actions against civilians under its guise. If annexation – even 'alleged' annexation – was explicitly illegitimate, then its unilateral declaration by any state could not in any way alter the rights and privileges of civilians within the territory just conquered. This prohibition against any derogation of the conquered population's rights was so important to GC-IV's drafters that it even merited the use of a term that they abhorred – annexation. Article 2 of the text finally adopted by the 1947 Governments Experts' Conference, which in itself already included a further strengthening of the ICRC proposed text against annexation, was unequivocally clear:

> No measures taken by the occupying Power with regard to an occupied country, such as alleged total or partial annexation of territory, changes in institutions or government, and so forth, can deprive the civilian population of the rights and protection guaranteed under the present Convention.[13]

---

13. *Report on the Work of the Conference of Government Experts*, p. 274. In its own remarks on this text, the ICRC explicitly acknowledged that its text was weaker than the one

Talk concerning the illegitimacy of conquest, the inviolability of rights and the illegality of annexation as an accepted measure in the conduct between states after the adoption of the 1945 UN Charter was all good and well. Yet one should not forget the actual historical context here: between 1946 and 1949, not only was annexation still being widely practised, it was, in fact, the Allied powers' preferred manner of international conduct as they reshaped the world's post-war map. British prime minister Winston Churchill and US president Franklin D. Roosevelt might have claimed in the Atlantic Charter that they 'seek no aggrandizement, territorial or other', but these words were regarded as 'obstacles to outright annexations that would have to be (and were) circumvented.'[14] At the end of the day, neither Churchill nor Stalin, nor Roosevelt and Truman, held their annexation desires at bay. At Potsdam, Stalin secured the Soviet annexation of Königsberg (today's Kaliningrad enclave) to compensate for Russia's perennial lack of a warm-water naval port that was not a prisoner of the 'Black sea jail' controlled by the Turkish-held Bosporus and Dardanelles straits. The Soviet Union would also extend west up to the 1920 Curzon Line, annexing roughly a third of Poland's pre-World War II territory.

On Churchill's insistence, and in return for its lost territories in the east, the Allies annexed to Poland areas of both Silesia and Pomerania up to the Oder–Neisse line, including the German city of Danzig (today's Gdansk). These had been among the most vehemently contested areas during the interwar period with regard to mixed minorities' rights. In North East Asia, the Soviet Union annexed the Sakhalin Peninsula and the Kurile Islands from Japan.

The United States, for its part, secured for itself an area of some 3 million square miles filled with some 700 islands in the Pacific Ocean (the US Trust territory of the Pacific Islands), which, while not officially annexed to the United States, was subsumed under the term 'strategic trusteeship'. This was a 'concept invented by and for the United States and was meant as a compromise between the general principles of the Atlantic Charter, which excluded annexation, and the particular security requirements of the United States, which required exclusive rights to territory conquered from the enemy.'[15] The UN officially signed off on this US modality for territorial annexation in 1947, at the same time as GC-IV's drafters were sitting down to forcefully repudiate annexation's conceptual legitimacy.

Yet despite legitimized annexations the world over, the wording of the Stockholm draft agreed upon in 1948 was even more unequivocally against that practice than what was agreed upon in Geneva a year earlier. At Stockholm, the delegates completely struck out the words 'alleged annexation' from the GC-IV draft and spoke solely of the inviolability of the rights of civilians once they had

finally adopted by the country delegates, who came out more forcefully against annexation at this 1947 meeting.

14. Korman, *The Right of Conquest*, p. 165.

15. Ibid., p. 163.

been conquered, 'in any case or in any manner whatsoever'.[16] The very recent international reality where annexations were still common, as in the cases of the territories of Sakhalin, Pomerania or the Pacific island of Saipan belonged to the past. Stockholm's delegates were looking to draft a convention for the future.

Stockholm's efforts at strengthening Article 47's anti-annexation text was further bolstered by a structural change that the drafters adopted there, which proved to be critically significant for the refutation of *Grossraum*'s 'occupy-annex-deport' logic. In the 1947 governments experts' text, the prohibition on annexation and the inviolability of rights was a general one, applicable to the convention as a whole, and was intended to appear upfront as its Article 2. In contrast, under the text that emerged from Stockholm annexation was now directly related to deportation, as enshrined in the opening Article of the proposed convention's Section III concerning an occupier's conduct in their occupied territories.[17] This intimate and intricate connection between both prohibitions, on annexation and on deportation, which entered into the Stockholm text in 1948 remained intact all through into the Final Act as we know it today.

Georg Cohn drafts the prohibition on settlements and conquest-based colonization: The insertion of Article 49's paragraph 6 at Stockholm

In their work, GC-IV's drafters sought to formulate the new Civilian Convention's terms so as to directly challenge each of *Grossraum*'s three componential elements. By the time of the Stockholm Conference, GC-IV's Article 47 which stressed the inviolability of the local population's rights irrespective of conquest, which derived its inviolability from the non-recognition of forceful territorial appropriation as per Georg Cohn's framing of this principle back in 1922, was already firmly in place. *Grossraum*'s occupation-turned annexation component was thus answered. The prohibition on deportation (today's Article 49 – back then still Article 45), which had existed within the Civilian Convention since its earliest 1934 Tokyo draft, was now also already well in place so as to counter *Grossraum*'s deportation component.

Yet *Grossraum* had one other fourth component which neither Schmitt nor Best stressed, but which was practiced and applied by the Nazis throughout their empire between 1939 and 1945: the resettlement and repopulation of their forcefully vacated territories with fresh German colonizer populations. In order to 'tie the knot' and provide a comprehensive answer to this extra element of Nazi colonization dictum for the sake of future generations, GC-IV's drafters still needed to come up with a textual answer to this last policy component of

---

16. See Article 43 in: *Revised and new Draft Conventions for the protection of war victims: Texts approved and amended by the XVIIth international Red Cross Conference,* Geneva, October 1948, p. 127.

17. Ibid.

Grossraum – the resettlement of populations of the conquering power within its new forcefully conquered territory.

The drafting of today's Article 49 paragraph 6 of GC-IV (then, still Article 45) took place during the deliberations of the Stockholm Conference's legal commission over the proposed revised drafts of the Civilian Convention – on Sub-commission III's second day of discussions, under Georges Cahen-Salvador's chairmanship. This was the very same forum in which the elaboration of the text for the future Common Article 3 had – as we saw in Part One – taken place between Gerhart Riegner and the chairman. During the morning session of Tuesday, 24 August 1948, as discussions commenced on the proposed Article 45, which stipulated a prohibition on the deportation of civilians outside of their own territory, the chairman opened the session with Georg Cohn's statement. Without further delay, Cohn tabled his amendment, which would add to Article 45 the following clause:

> The occupying power is prohibited from deporting or transferring a part of its own population, or the population of any other territory which it occupies into a territory which it occupies.[18]

In his verbal explanatory remarks to this proposed text, Cohn added that the sole purpose of his amendment was 'to protect the population of an occupied state from the invasion of other peoples'.[19] In the customary manner, as per any proposed amendment by a country delegate, Chairman Cahen-Salvador then gave the floor to the ICRC's legal-division director, Claude Pilloud, so as to receive the organization's views on the text just proposed. In a similar manner to his negative approach concerning Riegner's proposal that Common Article 3 cover civilians targeted by their own government (see Chapter 3), Pilloud also took a negative stance with regard to this new text:

> Mr. Pilloud (ICRC): believed that this [i.e. the demand that an occupier refrain from transferring their population into the territory that they had conquered] belonged to the responsibilities of the occupying power, towards which the ICRC can have no resort. We [i.e. the ICRC] should look more to protect those civilians expelled from a country.[20]

As with Common Article 3, here too the ICRC was sticking to its rigid legalistic approach, designed to minimize the organization's exposure to any situation that might bring it into contention or conflict with occupying state parties. Following the International Committee's scepticism, Cahen-Salvador called on the well-

---

18. *Stockholm XVII Red Cross Conference, Debates of the Sub-Commissions of the Legal Commission, afternoon session of Saturday 21ˢᵗ August 1948*, pp. 61–2. Available from the website of the ICRC Library at: https://library.icrc.org/library/docs/DOC/11670.pdf.

19. Ibid., p. 62.

20. Ibid.

respected Norwegian delegate, Frede Castberg, to express his government's positions vis-à-vis Cohn's new amendment. Casteberg did not mince his words:

> The Norwegian government commends Monsieur Cohn's proposal, because it considers that this new paragraph shall protect the nationals of an occupied country against an invasion of persons coming from other territories, who will require feeding etc.[21]

At the suggestion of Sweden (Denmark's and Norway's drafting ally), Sub-commission III turned over Cohn's proposed text to a drafting committee to be reconsidered. Once this text was fully ready for distribution, it would be returned to that sub-commission's members for their review. During the next day's reading of Cohn's proposed text, and after some editorial revisions, the final text adopted by Sub-commission III, and later by the plenary, is the very same text that we know today from Article 49 paragraph 6:

> The Occupying Power shall not deport or transfer parts of its own civilian population into the territory it occupies.[22]

A reader not fully conversant with the diplomatic intricacies of the Stockholm Conference might assume that the aforementioned debate, within Sub-commission III of the Red Cross's legal commission, was little more than an abstract exchange of different legal opinions between delegates. On the one side stood Denmark under Cohn's leadership, supported by the Nordic countries (Norway, Sweden) and the United States, in contrast to the ICRC's more sceptical approach as represented by Pilloud. Canada, which supported the ICRC's scepticism, in fact abstained during the final vote on this amendment by Cohn, stressing that 'the Convention's objective is not to indicate to states how they ought to conduct their warfare'.[23] This Canadian view probably mirrored almost to the letter the International Committee's own position on this point. The truth is, however, that politics and personal biographies determined the course of this debate every bit as much as legal opinions did. A brief contextualization, with the benefit of documents from the Swedish Royal Archives, provides a very different viewpoint on the debate that transpired within that conference room in Stockholm during those summer days of August 1948.

In the first place, there was the premediated and long-standing tri-patriate coordination of positions between all three Nordic countries – Denmark, Sweden and Norway – that were present at the Stockholm drafting table. The Swedish files concerning GC-IV's entire drafting process, from 1947 all the way through to the 1949 Geneva Conference of Plenipotentiaries, are full of direct correspondence

---

21. Ibid.
22. Ibid., p. 78. Session of Wednesday, 25 August at 2.30 pm.
23. Ibid., p. 78. Statement by Wershof (Canada).

between Georg Cohn (with documents signed in his own handwriting), Frede Castberg and Professor Torsten Gihl, who headed legal efforts on behalf of the Swedish Foreign Ministry.[24] These documents prove beyond doubt that both Sweden and Norway were well aware of Cohn's intention to propose his amendments in Stockholm, in exactly the same manner as he later shared with his Nordic counterparts his prepared set of amendments for the 1949 Geneva Conference of Plenipotentiaries.[25]

Now consider the sequence of speakers over those two days of 24 and 25 August 1948 in Stockholm's Sub-commission III. Georges Cahen-Salvador's calling on Frede Castberg immediately after the scepticism voiced by the ICRC's Claude Pilloud was certainly not incidental. Castberg was one of the ICRC's biggest international supporters. Back in 1944, his voice had been a vital one in the decision of the Nobel Committee to award the 1944 Peace Prize to the ICRC for its actions and efforts on behalf of the Second World War's war victims[26] (Figure 18).

Castberg maintained some of the most humane positions during the 1949 Plenipotentiaries Conference, again in a coordinated manner with the Danish Cohn and with Gihl from Sweden, especially during the harsh debates concerning the final adoption of the text for Common Article 3.[27]

Interestingly enough, and directly after Castberg had poured cold water on Pilloud's remarks due to the ICRC's untenably rigid reaction to Cohn's motion, Cahen-Salvador decided to give the floor to none other than the Swedish delegate, who proposed the separate discussion of Cohn's amendment. Let us not forget the venue here. Sweden was also acting as the host of the 1948 Red Cross Conference,

24. Swedish Royal Archives ('Riksarkivet') Stockholm, General File # UD, 1920 ärs dossier system HP 1427, AvD: 508, group: 30, sub-file # XIX (1943–7), sub-file # XX (July 1947–December 1948 including the Stockholm Conference), sub-file # XXI (January 1949–March 1949 including all correspondences between Gihl, Cohn and Castberg in preparation for Geneva 1949), and sub-file # XXII (Geneva Conference of Plenipotentiaries – April to July 1949.

25. Swedish Royal Archives ('Riksarkivet') Stockholm, General File # UD, 1920 ärs dossier system HP 1427, AvD: 508, group: 30, sub-file # XXI (January 1949–March 1949), Letter from Cohn to Gihl 25 March 1949, attached to Cohn's 5-page memorandum (Doc. HP 30 B), following Stockholm, and in preparation for the upcoming Geneva Conference of Plenipotentiaries.

26. On Castberg's vital role in the nomination of the ICRC for the Nobel Peace Prize, see Ivar Libæk, 'The Red Cross: Three-time recipient of the Peace Prize', published 30 October 2003, subsection 'The 1944 Peace Prize: Humanitarian activities and services to prisoners of war'. Available from the website of the Nobel prize committee: https://www.nobelprize.or g/prizes/themes/the-red-cross-three-time-recipient-of-the-peace-prize.

27. For Castberg's and Cohn's continuous push in favour of the rights of so-called unlawful combatants during the 1949 Geneva Plenipotentiaries' Conference, see Knut Dörmann, 'The legal situation of "unlawful/unprivileged combatants"', in *International Review of the Red Cross*, vol. 85, no. 849 (March 2003), pp. 45–74 at 56–7, n. 30.

Georg Cohn

Claude Pilloud
Jean Pictet

Figure 18 Opening ceremony of the XVIIth Red Cross Conference in Stockholm, 20 August 1948. In the circles from left to right: the young Jean Pictet, Claude Pilloud and Georg Cohn. © ICRC Photo Archives – Geneva 2018.

with Bernadotte, the Geneva ICRC's arch-rival, as its chair and with Judge Sandström as the legal commission's overall president. Cahen-Salvador's own views, both as chairman of the Civilian Convention's Sub-committee III and as the French delegate to the conference, were certainly in line with those of Cohn, Castberg and Sweden. Under these political circumstances, and with the United States finally also coming on board in favour of Cohn's amendment during its second reading (25 August 1948), the ICRC could, in the end, do little but support Cohn's text during its last reading. This text, which finally became paragraph 6 of Article 49, was never discussed during the 1949 Geneva Conference of Plenipotentiaries as it was unanimously supported upfront by all the state parties present there – this time including Canada.

The international criminalization of Cohn's prohibition on settlements: 1977–98

With GC-IV's drafters' painful personal experiences of their deportation as civilians during the Second World War fresh in their minds, it should come as no surprise that GC-IV, as in the Convention for Civilians, explicitly includes deportations as an act worthy of criminal prosecution under its Grave Breaches clause (GC-IV Article 147).[28] What might come as a surprise, however, is learning that it is the only one of the four Geneva Conventions to do so. Neither GC-III (Prisoners of War) nor GC-II (shipwrecked), both of which include an Article detailing the offences amounting to Grave Breaches (Article 130 and Article 51, respectively), lists deportations among their immediately prosecutable crimes.[29] This is most probably because deportations are first and foremost associated not with combatants but with civilians, whom a conquering state wishes to do away with as it acquires its new territory.[30]

In his 1958 commentary, Pictet lamented the conflation within the same GC-IV Article between the prohibition on the transfer of one's own population *into* a conquered territory and the prohibition on deportation of native populations *outside of* a conquered territory.[31] As the global process of decolonization was gathering pace, the prospect of a colonial resurgence and a revival of *Grossraum's* signal historical mechanic of 'Annex – Deport – Repopulate' seemed to Pictet hypothetically quite remote.

Ultimately, however, history would prove Pictet's mild optimism wrong and would confirm Cohn's worst suspicions about states' fetish for territorial appropriation and the dangers to native civilian populations lurking in the practice of conquest. Less than a decade after writing his commentary, Pictet could, if he had so wished, have witnessed first-hand how a defensive war against aggressors can turn on its head – morphing into colonization by an accidental conqueror. Israel's victory in 1967 over the combined Arab armies of Egypt, Syria, Jordan and Iraq resulted in its decision to settle permanently in militarily occupied Hebron merely ten months after conquering it, in April 1968. In the course of that same conflict, over 200,000 Palestinian civilians either fled or were actively

---

28. On the drafting of the Grave Breaches clauses in the various Geneva Conventions of 1949 and how these related to the rise of the idea of international criminal justice, which eventually evolved into the Rome Statute and today's International Criminal Court in The Hague, see Lewis, *The Birth of the New Justice*, pp. 260–8. On the legal importance of the Geneva Conventions' Grave Breaches clauses and their current application to universal criminal jurisdiction, see Paola Gaeta, 'Grave Breaches of the Geneva Conventions', in Andrew Clapham, Paola Gaeta and Marco Sassoli (eds.), *The Geneva Convention of 1949: A Commentary* (Oxford: Oxford University Press, 2015), pp. 615–46.

29. Stanislav Nahlik, 'Le Problème des Sanctions en Droit International Humanitaire', in Christophe Swinarski (ed.), *Studies and Essays on International Humanitarian Law and Red Cross Principles in Honour of Jean Pictet* (The Hague: Martinus Nijhoff, 1984), pp. 469–81 at 477.

30. On the unanimity of the drafters concerning the prohibition on deportations, see *Pictet Commentary*, p. 279.

31. Ibid., p. 283: 'This clause was adopted after some hesitation, by the XVIIth International Red Cross Conference … It would therefore appear to have been more logical … to have made the clause in question [i.e. Article 49 paragraph 6] into a separate provision distinct from Article 49'.

deported away from the West Bank into neighbouring Jordan.[32] Less than two decades after Pictet's commentary, following the 1974–5 Turkish invasion of Cyprus, thousands of Turks from Anatolia actively colonized the northern part of that island following a Turkish-led premeditated expulsion of Greek Cypriots from its northern portion. The reciprocal expulsion of Turkish Cypriots from the island's south soon followed, in what Christian Tomuschat (the current president of the OSCE's Court of Conciliation and Arbitration) has recently referred to as an 'exchange of populations'.[33]

In the aforementioned instances, the transfer of the occupier's population either precipitated a long period of subjugation of the occupied territory and its people (Palestine) or led to that civilian populations' outright ethnic cleansing (Cyprus). In each case, an annexation (of sorts) soon followed – and in both cases, the occupiers have refused to recognize the continued applicability of the law of occupation to these conquered territories.[34]

In 1977, after a three-year drafting period, the Additional Protocols to the Geneva Conventions were adopted by the Conventions' state parties. These additional protocols, which entered into force in 1978, have since been signed and ratified by an overwhelming majority of the world's states.[35] Article 85 (4) (a) of

32. Tom Segev, *1967: Israel, the War, and the Year That Transformed the Middle East* (New York: Macmillan & Henry Holt Books, 2007), p. 410.

33. Tomuschat, 'Prohibition on Settlements', pp. 1551–74 at 1558. The fact that Tomuschat, author of the most authoritative of GC-IV's contemporary legal commentaries, chose to call his chapter on Article 49 paragraph 6 'Prohibition on Settlements' – and that, in that chapter, he chose to refer to this very paragraph in terms directly related to the practice of forced population exchange – speaks volumes about the historical setting that surrounded Georg Cohn's original prohibition, drafted back in 1948. The concept of 'forced population exchange' was shamefully born in 1923, during the elaboration of the Treaty of Lausanne, to allow for the reciprocal uprooting of Greek and Turkish populations during the League of Nations' early years. This practice was then repeated and applied in tandem by the Nazis and the Soviets as they carved up Europe between 1939 and 1941 under the terms of the Ribbentrop–Molotov Agreement (officially, the Treaty of Non-aggression between Germany and the Union of Soviet Socialist Republics). For a state-of-the-art overview of the history of forced population exchange, see Adamantios Theodor Skordos, *Interdependenzen regionaler und globaler Prozesse: Die Prägung des modernen Völkerrechts durch die Konfliktgeschichte Südosteuropas* (Wien & Köln: Böhlau Verlag 2020). For the specific practices of forced population exchanges and transfers between 1939 and 1945, see Joseph B. Schechtman, *European Population Transfers 1939-1945* (Oxford: Oxford University Press, 1946).

34. For a thorough discussion and literature on both cases, Turkey and Israel, see Tomuschat, *Prohibition on Settlements*, pp. 155–1559.

35. To date, out of 194 UN member states, 174 have signed and ratified Additional Protocol I, and 168 states have signed and ratified Additional Protocol II of the Geneva Conventions.

Additional Protocol I brought Georg Cohn's prohibition on colonization under the umbrella of prosecutable Grave Breaches. In 1998 – during the adoption of the Rome Statute, which established the International Criminal Court at The Hague – Cohn's prohibition became a prosecutable international war crime under Article 8 of that statute.[36]

This international criminalization of the transfer of an occupier's population into a conquered territory was directly linked to Israel's outright abrogation of this prohibition. Its criminalization in the ICC's Rome Statute was adopted in direct response to Israel's colonization of Palestine and the dire ramifications that this had entailed (and continues to entail) for the lives of the Palestinians.[37] Israel, for its part, had declined to sign and join the statute precisely because it did not see its colonization and oppression of the Palestinians as a war crime meriting international prosecution.[38]

Article 49 paragraph 6 as seen with the benefit of hindsight

Now that half a century has elapsed since Israel's first occupation of Palestinian territory, one must return to the original logic that underpinned the international support for Georg Cohn's drafting of Article 49 paragraph 6. Cohn's paragraph 6 was drafted solely with the interests of native peoples in mind. As we saw above, Frede Castberg's argument as to why Norway had supported Cohn's text in Stockholm was precisely the pressure of requirements for 'feeding etc.' that incoming colonizers would exert on the natives of an invaded territory.[39] The specific historical Danish context should not be forgotten here either. From 1944 onwards, Denmark hosted an increasing number of German refugees who had fled Eastern Europe ahead of the forward march of the Red Army. By the end of the war, Denmark was home to some 300,000 German refugees, who were

---

36. Rome Statute of the International Criminal Court, Article 8 (2) (b) (viii).

37. Michael Sfard, *The Wall and the Gate: Israel, Palestine, and the Legal Battle for Human Rights* (New York: Macmillan & Henry Holt Publishers, 2017), p. 135, n. 21.

38. The direct relationship between the elaboration of the prohibition on settlements in the Rome Statute and Israel's colonization of Palestine was already evident during the Rome Statute's drafting phases. The Israeli delegate to the drafting of the statute, Eli Nathan, rhetorically questioned the inclusion of the prohibition on settlements within Article 8's scope: 'Can it really be held that such an action as that listed in Article 8 above really ranks among the most heinous and serious war crimes, especially as compared to the other, genuinely heinous ones listed in Article 8?' In the end, it was this international criminalization of settlements that triggered Israel's walkout of the ICC. See Michael G. Kearney, 'On the Situation in Palestine and the War Crime of Transfer of Civilians into Occupied Territory', *Criminal Law Forum*, vol. 28 (2017), pp. 1–34 at 2 n. 1. Available at: https://link.springer.com/content/pdf/10.1007/s10609-016-9300-9.pdf.

39. See above, p. 158, n. 349.

dispersed across the country and who were being fed and cared for at the expense of the already-impoverished Danish local population.[40] Add the ideological tenets of *Grossraum* and one gets the full historical picture.

At the very core of Israel's refusal to admit the application of Cohn's text to its occupation of Palestinian territory lies its simple disregard for the people whom it has occupied. The logical supremacy that Israel ascribes to the status of territory itself, over and above the impacts of its occupation on its native peoples, is knowingly flawed and intellectually dishonest. Paragraph 6 of Article 49 back in 1948, which the Holocaust-surviving Rabbi Georg Cohn wrote after his experiences in Nazi-occupied Denmark, had *people* rather than territory as its focus. As Theodor Meron – the former president of the ICTY – recently put it,

> Those who argue for the non-applicability *de jure* of the Fourth Geneva Convention to the West Bank on the ground of the disputed character of the territory also, and importantly, disregard the character of the Geneva Convention as a humanitarian convention *par excellence*, i.e., a convention that is not concerned with legal or formal claims to a territory, but that has as its principal object and purpose the protection of the civilian population of occupied territories.[41]

This passage by Meron is crucial – because of the identity of the speaker and, not least, its context. Born into a Jewish family in Poland in 1930, Theodor Meron survived the Holocaust himself but lost most of his family and loved ones to it. Thanks to his undoubted legal brilliance – and following his studies at the Hebrew University, Harvard and Cambridge – Meron climbed the ranks in Israel's young foreign ministry and was nominated its legal adviser in August 1967, in the aftermath of the Israeli victory in the Six-Day War. Barely a month had passed since Meron's appointment before the Israeli prime minister Levi Eshkol requested his legal opinion concerning the possibility of building settlements in the territories recently conquered. Israeli law had already been formally applied to East Jerusalem some two months earlier, in June 1967, through a legislative act of parliament, in one of the bluntest contraventions of international law seen thus far. Meron was walking into a legal minefield when he took up the position of chief legal counsel to the Israeli Foreign Ministry – and he knew it. Israel's entire governmental legal

---

40. On the dire impact of the forced housing of well over a quarter of a million German refugees in Denmark, to the detriment of the local Danish population, see Herbert, *Best: Biographische Studien über Radikalismus*, pp. 396–9. On the specific importance of the Danish experience under the German conquest of Danish Schleswig-Holstein and South Jutland, see Korman, *The Right of Conquest*, pp. 84–5.

41. Theodor Meron, 'The West Bank and International Law on the Eve of the Fiftieth Anniversary of the Six-Day War', *American Journal of International Law*, vol. 111, no. 2 (April 2017), pp. 357–75 at 367 ('The Fourth Geneva Convention as a People-Oriented Convention').

apparatus was being mobilized in an effort to argue away GC-IV's applicability to the newly conquered territories – especially the West Bank, the geographical cradle of Jewish biblical civilization.

On 14 September 1967, Meron replied to Prime Minister Eshkol. In a four-page memorandum, he did not hesitate to emphatically counter the legal positions endorsed by Israel's governmental legal establishment. Referring directly to Georg Cohn's text as embedded into GC-IV's Article 49 paragraph 6, Meron wrote,

> [text in Hebrew] ... concerning the possibility of Jewish settlements in the West Bank and on the Golan Heights ... I am afraid there exists a great international sensitivity concerning the entire question of Jewish settlement in the newly seized territories, and that our legal argumentation ... will not alleviate the great international pressure which shall be exerted upon us ... based upon the Geneva Convention number 4 ... from the perspective of public international law, its main directive is the paragraph which is included in its Article 49 of Geneva Convention number 4. Israel of course is a state party to this convention. This paragraph states that:
>
> 'The occupying power shall not deport or transfer parts of its own civilian population into the territory it occupies'
>
> [Text in Hebrew] the prohibition is therefore categorical and does not depend on the motivations for this transfer of population nor on its objectives, as it is meant to counter the settlement in the occupied country by the natives of the occupying state.[42] (Figure 19)

Meron thus referred his own government to Cohn's original text from 1948 as drafted by Cohn in Stockholm. Contemporary readers perhaps less conversant with the political and religious messianic pressures that engulfed Israel after its June 1967 victory might overlook the remarkable intellectual courage demonstrated by Meron here. During the subsequent fifty years, as Meron ascended the highest echelons of international legal practice and judiciaries, he never mentioned his courageous stance against the Israeli government's blunt contravention of the international law of belligerent occupation concerning its obtrusive construction of settlements, and his own heroic failure to prevent it. It was only revealed in 2015, as Meron's top-secret memo to Eshkol came to light thanks to the dedicated and painstaking work of archive-based historians working for an Israeli human-rights NGO.[43]

---

42. This document was uncovered by Gershom Gorenberg at Israel's state archives and is included in his book *The Accidental Empire: Israel and the Birth of the Settlements 1967-1977* (New York: Henry Holt Publishers, 2007), p. 102, n. 9. Israeli State Archives file # 153.8/ 7921/ 3A. A scan of this document is also available on Gorenberg's blog. Available at: http://southjerusalem.com/wp-content/uploads/2008/09/theodor-meron-legal-opinion -on-civilian-settlement-in-the-occupied-territories-september-1967.pdf.

43. Gershom Gorenberg, 'Israel's Tragedy Foretold', *The New York Times*, 10 March 2006. Several of Meron's other memos concerning his legal counsel against the deportation

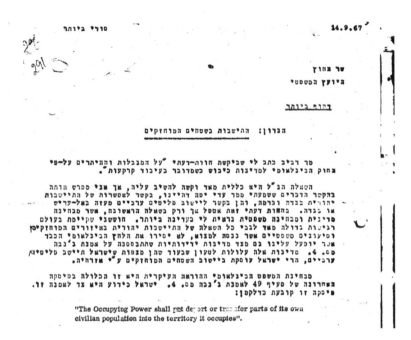

Figure 19 Theodor Meron's September 1967 memorandum.

Nowadays, half a century after Meron wrote his memorandum to the Israeli government, and despite over half million Israeli settlers now living beyond the 1967 'Green Line', the persistent qualification of the West Bank as 'occupied territory' by an overwhelming majority of the world's states (with the exception of Israel and perhaps the United States) and its international organizations, seems

of Palestinian militants from the occupied territories, due to the prohibitions enshrined in GC-IV's Article 49, and against Israel's highly problematic endorsement of Palestinian house demolitions have also been uncovered by the Israeli NGO AKEVOT ('Footprints'), which has taken upon itself a thorough examination of Israel's state archives, and has unearthed the story of how the occupation of the Palestinians was masterminded and orchestrated by the Israeli state from the earliest days of the June 1967 victory onwards. See www.akevot.org.il.

Meron's unequivocal opinion validating the non-legality of Israel's West Bank deportation policy, from December 1967 (including the full English translation of this memorandum), can be found at: https://akevot.org.il/en/article/deportation-policy-memo/#popup/bfeae6 4af62460ba7a8f9c15e326122a

On the illegality of the annexation of Jerusalem, with Meron explicitly quoting GC-IV's Article 47, and on the illegality of house demolitions according to GC-IV's Article 64, see his memorandum from 12 March 1968 (also in English translation) Available at: https://akevot. org.il/en/article/theodor-meron-opinion/#popup/0a68d7247ba49f9a0a2dd3bd67d44ce0.

rather remarkable. Seen in retrospect, the concept of 'occupation' as specifically applied to Palestine has shown a rather remarkable resilience over time. When one considers the inconsistency of expert opinions as to what Israel's control over the West Bank in fact amounted to, from the late 1960s until the mid-1980, it would be safe to say that the understanding that this is indeed 'occupation' with all that it entails in fact strengthened over the years.

At the heart of occupation's conceptual resilience vis-à-vis Palestine lies the demise of the concept of *debellatio*. As we saw, in the introduction to Part Two with Max Huber and even with Hans Kelsen's positions vis-à-vis defeated Germany, the concept of *debellatio*, and the idea that a totally subdued territory could now be subjected to the sole mercy of the conqueror, was not entirely 'off the radar' post Second World War. Without indulging in a complex debate as to whether ontologically – Israel's 1967 victory indeed amounted to *debellatio* – or not, in its *legal* sense, and in terms of its *political* affects, there is virtually no doubt that this was one reasonably possible interpretation of reality after Israel's victory in 1967.

By the end of that war, Jordan had retreated completely from the West Bank. In fact, in 1967, in the eyes of many respected international legal commentators, *debellatio* was still a legally viable option. In 1968 (i.e. one year after Meron's memorandum), Georg Schwarzenberger, the undisputed authority concerning the law of occupation at that time, explicitly endorsed the right of conquest under *debellatio*.[44] Being somewhat of an apologist for the Israeli, Yoram Dinstein's opinion from 1988 was that annexation of a territory lost by an aggressor to the conquering state was 'not without its legal logic: let the aggressor pay for his crimes'.[45] Even as late as 1982, a renowned international legal expert such as Michael Bothe, writing for the *Max Planck Encyclopaedia of Public International Law*, could contend that 'annexation would no longer be unlawful' in 'cases of *debellatio* or subjugation'.[46]

Nowadays, and thanks in particular to Eyal Benvenisti's erudition in the realms of the international law of occupation, we no longer accept *debellatio* as a ground

44. Georg Schwarzenberger, *International law as Applied by International Courts and Tribunals Vol. 2* (London: Stevens & Sons, 1968), p. 297: 'If as a result of legal, as distinct from illegal, war, the international personality of one of the belligerents is totally destroyed, victorious Powers may … annex the territory of the defeated State, or hand over portions of it to other states.' Quoted in Korman, *The Right of Conquest*, p. 222, n. 116.

45. Quoted in: Korman, *The Right of Conquest*, p. 222, n. 118. In contrast to Theodor Meron's standing against Israeli governmental pressures post 1967, Dinstein's international legal objectivity has been recently tainted (if not severely stained) as investigative journalists from *Haaretz* newspaper uncovered documents within the Israeli Foreign Ministry archives proving his covert and secret cooperation with the state, as he himself headed the Israeli branch of the well-respected international human-rights NGO Amnesty International during the 1970s, in direct contravention of that NGO's policies. See Uri Blau, 'Documents reveal how Israel made Amnesty's local branch a front for the Foreign Ministry in the 70s', in *Haaretz*, March 18 2017.

46. Quoted in: Korman, *The Right of Conquest*, p. 222, n. 117.

for ceasing to recognize a territory as occupied.[47] Almost thirty-five years after his 1982 opinion in favour of the legality of territorial annexation under the conditions of *debellatio* or complete subjugation, cited above, Michael Bothe would also come around to Benvenisti's and Tomuschat's conclusion concerning its implicit and perpetual wrongfulness – thus diametrically opposing his own previous opinions on the matter.[48]

At the heart of *debellatio*'s decisive epistemologically refutation lies GC-IV's Article 47. If, immediately after the Second World War, despite Germany's and Japan's complete and uncontested surrender, GC-IV's drafters still went the full legal length to unequivocally secure conquered civilians' rights and verify that these could not be altered as a result of regime changes, peace agreements, annexations or any other political alternation in their territory's declared status, then *debellatio* was simply meaningless.[49] If *no change* in the original rights of a given civilian population could come about, despite the fact that a given armed conflict indeed occurred on that territory, then *debellatio* – which is ipso facto a concept associated with *affirmative change* in a territory's stature (as in the cessation of a given state's existence) – was invalid.

This realization concerning *debellatio*'s refutation is indeed novel and has only fully materialized over the past two decades. As we have seen from the thoughts of Schwarzenberger Botha and the like from the late 1960s to the early 1980s, the possibility of a fundamental change in a territory's nature, and consequently – in the rights of its civilian inhabitants was still plausible. Yet for the young Theodor Meron, as early as 1968, things were crystal clear. Occupation could not morph into territorial title, and the construction of settlements in the West Bank was entirely illegal under international law, irrespective of arguments made already back then that argued that Israel's victory amounted to a *debellatio* and hence – permitted such changes in the West Bank's territorial stature, and consequently – in the rights of its subjugated inhabitants. With the benefit of historical hindsight, and faced with the immense political pressures of that period, it is rather remarkable to note just how correct the young Meron really was in his legal understanding of GC-IV's substantive legal meaning.

As he himself noted on the pages of the *American Journal of International Law* some fifty years later, GC-IV's drafters – Georges Cahen-Salvador, Frede Castberg

---

47. Benvenisti, *The International Law of Occupation*, pp. 161–4. Christian Tomuschat, in the recent and definitive Oxford Commentary on GC-IV, fully endorses Benvenisti's understanding that the concept of *debellatio,* and its alleged resulting right of territorial annexation, has become fully and totally obsolete and is not recognized nowadays. See Tomuschat, *Prohibition on Settlements*, p. 1554, n. 7.

48. Michael Bothe, 'The Administration of Occupied Territory', in Andrew Clapham, Paola Gaeta and Marco Sassoli (eds.), *The 1949 Geneva Conventions: A Commentary* (Oxford: Oxford University Press, 2016), pp. 1455–84 at 1466, para 32.

49. This is essentially Benvenisti's argument against *debellatio*'s conceptual validity. See: *The International Law of Occupation*, pp. 161–4.

and, most notably, Georg Cohn – were thinking of war's *human victims* when they came to draft that Convention for Civilians in 1949 – not its territory. They had intended to draft, in Meron's words, a 'people-oriented Convention'.[50] Cahen-Salvador, Cohn and Castberg's motivations were 'classically' humanitarian – that is, *humanly* oriented. Humanity dictated that an indigenous people's land ought not to be violently expropriated from them, for the sake of other people's colonial needs, contrary to their indigenous benefit. GC-IV's entire rationale was premised on humanity – not geography.

---

50. One of the first commentators to take up Meron's term 'people-oriented Convention' was the US State Department's legal adviser, in a symposium held in Israel in 1971 and chaired by Yoram Dinstein. See Stephen M. Boyd, 'The Applicability of International Law to the Occupied Territories', *Israel Yearbook on Human Rights,* vol. 1 (1971), pp. 258–82 at 259.

Chapter 7

GEORG COHN'S CRUSADE AGAINST THE DEATH PENALTY – ARTICLE 68

A resurgent colonialism

The inevitable confrontation between an occupying power and the occupied civilian population under its control is heightened under conditions in which active armed resistance to the occupier takes place. Of the GC-IV Articles that were drafted to regulate the legal aspects of this confrontation between occupier and occupied, Article 68, which deals with penalties to be borne by occupied civilians who have offended against the occupier, is of prime importance. Its text frames the reasonings and conditions for both incarceration of occupied civilians and, more importantly, sets out the terms under which the occupier is entitled to impose capital punishment (i.e. the death penalty) on members of the occupied population. Article 68 states in quite clear terms that occupied civilians who have taken action so as to harm the occupier without the intention of causing grave harm, serious damage or the death of the occupier's forces would be liable for imprisonment. The death penalty can only be imposed in cases of espionage, sabotage to the occupier's installations or death caused by the actions of that occupied civilian. Most importantly, a death sentence can only be imposed if the actions carried out by the accused would have resulted in the application of the death penalty for those same actions according to the law of the occupied land *prior to* that occupation's beginning. In the words of the convention, the death penalty could only be imposed if it 'was provided for similar cases under the law in force before the occupation began'.[1]

With its clear wording and narrow margins for divergent interpretations, commentators have for the most part been of one mind regarding the application of the death penalty in Article 68.[2] As Jean Pictet stressed, a crucial phase in

---

1. Pictet, *Commentary on the Geneva Convention Relative to the Protection of Civilian Persons in Time of War 12 August 1949*, pp. 342–7 at 345.

2. Yutaka Arai-Takahashi, 'Law making and Judicial Guarantees in Occupied Territories', in A. Clapham, P. Gaeta and M. Sassoli (eds.), *The Fourth Geneva Convention of 1949: A Commentary* (Oxford: Oxford University Press 2016), pp. 1446–9.

the wording of Article 68 (then still known as Article 59) took place during the 1948 Stockholm Conference, where this *conditio* sine qua non regarding the pre-existence of a death penalty in a given territory was first introduced.[3] Once this condition was 'set in stone' at Stockholm, the 'realist' powers (with the UK at their helm), who at the 1949 Conference of Plenipotentiaries wished to legally condemn this qualifying condition, found themselves diplomatically cornered by the delegations that advocated its continued inclusion in the already-endorsed Stockholm draft text.[4]

The whole diplomatic battle over the terms of application of the death penalty in the Civilian Convention text actually revolved around one single theme, which ran through GC-IV's entire drafting process – namely, *colonialism*. While this word itself does not appear anywhere in GC-IV's text, thanks to its removal by Georges Cahn Salvador during the final stages of the discussions concerning Common Article 3 in Stockholm, its sub-textual impact was clear and incontrovertible to all present.

The UK stood at the forefront of the struggle to retain the option of imposing the death penalty in occupied territories. The UK's myriad of military commitments – from official occupation in the newly constituted West Germany to semi-occupation in Greece and Cyprus, to its now-resurgent colonialism in Malaya and even to colonies of other countries that it now controlled (e.g. Indonesia, formerly colonized by the Netherlands) – meant that the last thing its generals wanted was to have their hands tied by newly devised international treaties. The UK's attorney general did not mince his words as he overtly opposed Britain's entry into 'any Convention which would prevent our treating insurgents as traitors' – asserting, 'we are a colonial power'.[5] The problem with the UK's stance was its historical timing, as occidental colonialism was now slowly beginning to unravel. After the experiences of the Second World War, along with the mass executions of civilians at the hands of the Nazis and the Japanese within their occupied territories, the UK's position in favour of the death penalty was simply inadmissible. This was especially true in the minds of people such as Georges Cahen-Salvador and Georg Cohn, who were now seated at that same drafting table as the UK.

The limitation of the death-penalty clause at Stockholm

The text of Article 68 (draft working Article 59) was first introduced by the ICRC in the proposed Civilian Convention text drawn up in preparation for the 1948 Stockholm Conference.[6] This early version of the Article, concerning penalties to

---

3. Pictet, *Commentary*, p. 345.

4. Ibid.

5. Best, *War and Law since 1945*, p. 173, n. 102.

6. XVIIth International Red Cross Conference (Stockholm, August 1948) Draft Revised or New conventions for the Protection of War victims, Geneva May 1948, p. 153

be imposed on occupied civilians by the occupier, already maintained a clear-cut division between felonies that would trigger imprisonment, and grave felonies (homicide, espionage and the like) that would allow for the application of the death penalty. Courts could only pronounce the death penalty against people convicted of homicide or acts that directly caused the deaths of others.

Discussions at Stockholm concerning GC-IV's prospective conditions for the application of the death penalty took place during the morning and afternoon sessions of 24 and 25 August 1948.[7] These were the very same sessions in which Georg Cohn brought forth his proposal for the prohibition of colonization (Article 49 paragraph 6) and the transfer of the occupier's own population into conquered territory, discussed in Chapter 6.

The drafting of the clause concerning the application of the death penalty in occupied territories was first raised by Sweden, as its delegate, Holmgren, duly raised the cardinal issue of the competencies of military courts appointed by the occupier to carry out death sentences impartially.[8] Before the events of the Second World War, and certainly after them, there arose serious international doubts as to whether military courts could really ever be just and impartial. While the Nazi occupation forces in Eastern Europe seldom bothered themselves with court proceedings prior to the summary execution of prisoners and hostages, the German occupation authorities of Western Europe did in fact resort to military judicial procedures. However, experience in France, Belgium, Denmark and other western territories merely demonstrated that, more often than not, German military courts had constituted little more than a procedural 'rubber stamp' for the summary execution of civilians under occupation. Duly accepting Holmgren's concern, the US delegate, Albert Clattenburg, assured his Swedish colleague that the United States planned to propose an amendment to Article 59 concerning the death penalty – one which would provide for a sensible compromise and reasonable safeguards on this issue.

(hereinafter '*Civilian Convention Text BEFORE Stockholm*), pp. 180–1. This Article read: 'When a protected person commits an offence with intent to harm the occupant, but which but does not constitute either an attempt on the life or limb of members of the occupying forces or administration, or a grave collective danger, or serious harm to the property of the occupant or of the installations used by him, the only penalty depriving him of liberty to which he is liable shall be internment as foreseen in Part III, Section IV. The courts of the occupying Power may not pass the death sentence on a protected person unless he is guilty of homicide or of some other wilful offence which is the direct cause of the death of one or several persons. The two preceding Sections do not apply to the case of a protected person who is guilty of espionage to the detriment of the occupying Power.'

7. *Stockholm XVII Red Cross Conference, Debates of the Sub-Commissions of the Legal Commission, afternoon session of Saturday 21ˢᵗ August 1948*, pp. 61–79. Emphasis added. Available from the website of the ICRC Library at: https://library.icrc.org/library/docs/DOC/11670.pdf.

8. Ibid., p. 66.

The next day, the United States presented its amendment to Article 59.[9] It is this Stockholm text, adopted by that Red Cross Conference (with some minor changes), that finally made it into GC-IV's text as we know it today – albeit not without a crucial diplomatic contest over it in Geneva. Clattenburg's amendment introduced two crucial limiting components into Article 59. The first stressed the fact that occupied civilians are not bound by any allegiance to the occupying power.[10] This limitation made its way into the final text as well: it was adopted at the 1949 Geneva Conference of Plenipotentiaries and is known today as Article 68 paragraph 3. Clattenburg's second limitation was the more crucial, as it stipulated that the death penalty could not be prescribed unless it already existed within the official penal code of the occupied country prior to its conquest:[11]

> The courts of the occupying Power shall not pass the death sentence on a protected person unless he is guilty of an offence which was punishable by the death penalty under the law of the occupied Power at the outbreak of hostilities.[12]

With these two limitations incorporated into its paragraph 2, GC-IV's Article 59 concerning the application of the death penalty left Stockholm and was presented as the opening text for the Geneva Conference in April 1949.

George Cohn's struggle to limit the death penalty's application in Geneva 1949

Nothing, therefore, could have prepared Georg Cohn for the upcoming diplomatic clash concerning the limitation of the death penalty at the 1949 Geneva Conference of Plenipotentiaries. At the opening of this conference, Canada, clearly acting on the UK's behalf, submitted an explicit amendment for the complete removal of Article 59's paragraph 2. This was the very clause that provided for the limitations of the death penalty, as inserted in Stockholm by the US delegate Clattenburg. In Canada's view, an error had occurred during the Stockholm deliberations in

---

9. Ibid., pp. 78–9.

10. Ibid., p. 79. The original amendment by Clattenburg read as follows: 'The death penalty may not be pronounced against a protected person unless the attention of the Court has been particularly called to the fact that the accused, not being a national of the occupying Power, is not bound to it by any duty of allegiance and is in its power by reason of circumstances independent of his will.'

11. Ibid., p. 79.

12. *Revised and new Draft Conventions for the protection of war victims: texts approved and amended by the XVIIth international Red Cross Conference*, Geneva October 1948, p. 132 (text in italics). Available at: https://library.icrc.org/library/docs/CDDH/CI_1948/CI_1948_PROJET_ENG_04.pdf

this regard, and this was the place to correct it.[13] The United States, for its part, submitted a new amendment to Article 59 that opted to strike out any reference to the law of the occupied territory prior to its occupation – the very protection that it had itself argued for in Stockholm – thus effectively gutting the protection afforded by paragraph 2. The United States went on to question the protection from the death penalty accorded to minors (persons under eighteen years of age), a qualification that it had also backed in Stockholm.[14] As per the diplomatic conference's routine procedure, Georges Cahen-Salvador, Committee III's chairman now re-elected for the proceedings in Geneva, duly referred both the Canadian and the US amendments to a special drafting committee.[15]

The discussions within this first drafting committee for Article 59 were dominated by the United Kingdom, the United States and their allies, with the Soviet Union consistently and adamantly pushing in favour of retaining Stockholm's draft exactly as it stood. Overriding the Soviet Union, the committee finally came up with a new draft Article 59. This not only removed paragraph 2's protection but went even further, enumerating the spectrum of actions that could merit the pronouncement of a death-penalty verdict by the occupier's military courts. These now included 'actions which constitute serious public dangers' and 'serious damage to the property of the occupying forces or their administration' in addition to 'sabotage', 'unlawful hostilities by civilians' and 'marauding'.[16] On 7 July 1949, Committee III's plenary was presented with the results of the UK–US dominated drafting committee's text.[17]

Diplomatic cunning was not exclusive to the United Kingdom and the United States, however. Rather than confronting the Anglo-Saxons head on (yet again – after forty days at the drafting committee), the Soviet Union opted for a more knowing diplomatic manoeuvre. The Soviet delegate, Platon Morosov, simply demanded to hear the ICRC's views concerning Article 59's newly proposed text, as produced by the UK–US dominated drafting committee.[18] The speaker on the ICRC's behalf was none other than Claude Pilloud – the irreproachable and well-respected director of the International Committee's legal division. Pilloud wasted neither time nor words, but simply went on to pour a healthy dose of 'diplomatic cold water' on the UK and US efforts, stating that he

13. *Final Record* Vol. II A, p. 673, statement by Wershof (Canada) afternoon session of Wednesday, 18 May 1949 1.00 pm of Committee III (Civilian Convention) chaired by Georges Cahen-Salvador.

14. Ibid., p. 673, statement by Ginnane (US).

15. Ibid., p. 674.

16. Ibid., p. 767 statement of Day (UK).

17. Ibid., pp. 763–70, morning and afternoon sessions of the 7 July 1949, all chaired by Cahen-Salvador.

18. Ibid., p. 766. Statement by Morosov (USSR).

greatly regretted the wording of the second paragraph of the Article. The list of offences for which the death sentence was provided had been made so comprehensive that there would apparently be no change from the practice followed in occupied countries during the last war. The decision taken by the Drafting Committee was a bitter disappointment to those who had hoped that the Draft adopted at Stockholm would be accepted. He earnestly hoped that Committee III, after considering the matter afresh, would decide to reverse the Drafting Committee's decision.[19]

Thus, according to the ICRC's view, were this UK/US-sponsored text to be adopted, it would mean that actions similar to those undertaken by the Nazis during the previous war would not be illegal. Morosov happily put the final nail in the coffin of the UK–US drafting proposal as he reiterated his view that the conference ought to return to the Stockholm text – the very wording drafted by the US delegate, Clattenburg, one year earlier.[20]

As with so many instances of diplomatic deadlock throughout GC-IV's three-year drafting process, it was Cahen-Salvador who came to the rescue. On his instruction, France tabled a motion of compromise between the Anglo-Saxon 'realists' and the humanitarian camp lead by the Soviet bloc and the Scandinavian countries. Carried forward by Lamarle on France's behalf (given Cahen-Salvador's chairmanship), the new French amendment proposed the inclusion as acts warranting the death penalty of some of those mentioned by the UK (most notably, espionage, grave acts of sabotage and death-causing acts), while still qualifying the death penalty's administration upon its pre-existence within the occupied country's penal code (Clattenburg's qualifying clause). It was this text that was finally adopted by the Plenipotentiaries' Conference, and which is today known as Article 68 paragraph 2.[21] Pilloud's swift signing off on this French motion on the ICRC's behalf certainly points to its pre-orchestrated and advanced coordination with the ICRC.[22] Much the same could be said of the Soviet bloc's response to it, carried forward by Committee III's Soviet vice chairman Nissim Mevorah, who stated that 'the effort made by the French Delegation was worthy of praise' and that the Soviets would 'be able to support it'.[23]

19. Ibid., p. 766. Statement by Pilloud (ICRC).

20. Ibid., p. 766. Statement by Morosov (USSR).

21. Ibid., p. 767. Statement by Lamarle (France), which reads, 'The penal provisions promulgated by the Occupying Power in conformity with Articles 55 and 56 may only impose the death penalty on a protected person in cases where the person is guilty of espionage, of serious acts of sabotage against the military installations of the Occupying Power and of intentional offences which have caused the death of one or more persons, provided that such cases were punishable by death under the law of the occupied territory in force before the occupation began.'

22. Ibid., p. 768. Statement by Pilloud (ICRC).

23. Ibid., p. 767. Statement by Mevorah (Bulgaria).

As per the rules of procedure, a second drafting committee – this time, comprising the UK and France – was charged with providing Committee III with the final text of Article 59 paragraph 2 for adoption. A week later, as the desired text surfaced during the afternoon session of 14 July 1949, the Soviet and Scandinavian delegates were amazed to see that once again the UK had managed somehow to persuade the second drafting committee of Article 59 to drop Clattenburg's protective clause of paragraph 2 concerning the limitation of the death penalty. Denmark and the Nordic countries under Georg Cohn's leadership would have none of it.[24] Neither would the Soviet Union under General Slavin.[25] Committee III could either vote on the French text exactly as it had been formulated one week earlier when presented by Lamarle or revert to Clattenburg's original Stockholm text. Both delegates, with all their allied member countries behind them, now pressed Chairman Cahen-Salvador to go to a vote on all the various proposed options. Paragraph 2 of Article 59, in its French compromise-draft form, received 21 votes to 11. The United Kingdom and the United States appeared to have been defeated.

The closing chapter in this Article 59's history of development was the United Kingdom's and United States's last-ditch attempt to reintroduce (yet again!) their amendment of the Article's paragraph 2. A week before GC-IV's final signing ceremony, the UK audaciously argued that deterrence necessitated the death penalty's non-limitation so as to keep occupied civilian populations at bay. Without the threat of the death penalty – so claimed Sir Robert Craigie, the UK's head of delegation – civilian populations might rise up against their occupier more forcefully, thus triggering an even harsher reaction from the latter.[26] The US delegate, Leland Harrison, fully concurred with his UK counterpart.

Taking the floor after Craigie and Harrison, Georg Cohn decided that it was high time to bring some of his recent personal experiences to the drafting table. Arguing against Craigie's line of argument, which stressed the 'necessities' of the occupying power, Cohn replied,

> The Delegate of the United Kingdom, with the support of the Delegate of the United States of America, has here recalled the past experiences of belligerent Powers. He has stressed 'necessities' which, in this special case, I cannot myself recognize. Allow me to draw your attention to the bitter experience of the populations of occupied countries during the war, and to recall the long series of crimes perpetrated and death sentences pronounced by the belligerent Powers against the civilian population, in defiance of every law and moral principle. ... We must, therefore, in the name of the countries which have suffered from such acts committed by belligerents, call for the maintenance of a text ensuring

24. Ibid., pp. 788–9. Statement by Bagge (Denmark) upon instruction from Georg Cohn – the head of the Danish delegation.
25. Ibid., p. 789. Statement by General Slavin (USSR).
26. *Final Record*, Vol. II -B, pp. 424–5, Statement of Craigie (UK).

generous and effective protection for civilians … the Danish delegation recommends the Assembly not to give its vote to another new text, the adoption of which might, in the event of another war, serve as a pretext for a belligerent, once more to commit atrocities of the kind which aroused the indignation of the whole world during the last world conflict.[27]

Craigie was defeated – and he knew it. Writing back to the UK Cabinet, he could do no more than contemptuously scorn Cohn's diplomatic victory:

The Scandinavian delegations which appeared to be very much under the narrow and obstinate leadership of Dr. Georg Cohn, the leader of the Danish delegation, were a great disappointment. … This appeared to be due to the somewhat exaggerated conception by the Danes of their suffering under German occupation. Monsieur Cohn, who exercised the main influence over the Scandinavian delegations was impervious either to reason or argument.[28]

At the final count, Article 59, including its protective paragraph 2, was adopted by 33 votes to 5, with 5 abstentions.[29] As things later transpired, during the horrors of Britain's colonial unravelling, this defeat for the UK actually meant nothing for its policy vis-à-vis guerrilla fighters. The death penalty that it had not been able to legalize in Geneva in 1949, it simply executed in Kenya less than a decade later.[30]

The illegitimacy of the occupier's justice when applied by his military courts

At the heart of all the debates concerning the death penalty during GC-IV's drafting lay the fundamental issue of the illegitimacy of the occupier's justice system. This illegitimacy would come to the fore sooner than later for France, in this case – concerning its decolonization war in Algeria. In 1957, Albert Camus published his *Reflections on the Guillotine*, his famous call for a permanent abolition of the death penalty.[31] The Algeria-born French author had just won the Nobel Prize in literature, so there could be no better timing for him to mobilize his writing skills against the death penalty, and in favour of the moral objective

27. Ibid., p. 426 Statement of Cohn (Denmark).

28. Royal National Archives (London Kew Gardens), File # F.O. 369/4164, Final Report by Sir Robert Craigie to Foreign Office S. W. 1., November 1949, paragraph 85, p. 18.

29. Ibid., p. 431 at the bottom.

30. See Chapter 9.

31. Albert Camus, 'Réflexions sur la guillotine', dans Albert Camus and Arthur Kœstler (eds.), *Reflexions sur la peine Capitale* (Paris: Calmann-Lévy, 1957). English edition and translation by Justin O'Brian (ed.), *Albert Camus: Resistance, Rebellion, and Death* (New York: The Modern Library, 1963), pp. 131–79.

in which he fundamentally believed. One year earlier, in 1956, the then French minister of justice, François Mitterrand, had decided to reintroduce the death penalty in Algeria, where France was bearing down on the nationalists in its fight against the FLN, the country's National Liberation Front. Of all the execution methods available, Mitterrand deliberately decided to adopt the most notorious and historically laden practice of them all – decapitation by guillotine. By the time Camus wrote his polemic in 1957, some forty-five Algerian Muslims had already been executed in this fashion.[32] However, Algeria was not referred to in the *Reflections*;[33] Camus's objective was to set forth a general argument against the death penalty, not a specific statement about politically contested Algeria.

That said, contemporary readers needed very little introductive contextualization in order to grasp what Camus was referring to. It was on Algeria, not on metropolitan France, that Camus set his sights when he wrote his *Reflections*. By 1957, the worst and most violent phase of the Algerian war of independence (1954–62) had begun. The notorious battle for the Kasbah of Algiers waged by French armed forces against the FLN took place that very same year, and Jean-Jacques Servan-Schreiber, Camus's editor at the magazine *L'Express*, had just published an account of his own experiences serving with the French army in Algeria. The French had by now openly resorted to summary executions, torture and the oppression of civilians in their fight against the FLN.[34]

Camus's approach to the war in Algeria was complicated. Yet on guillotined death penalties, his voice was loud and clear – and it was exactly the silence and invisibility of the guillotined executions that bore the brunt of his ire. During the French Revolution (the guillotine's heyday), executions had been conducted in broad daylight, on the Place de la Concorde in central Paris, for all Parisian passers-by to observe *in coram publico*.[35] By contrast, in Algeria, guillotined executions were now being conducted behind the walls of secluded prisons, far away from the public eye. If these executions were indeed so legally and morally justified, why did the state not conduct them in broad daylight as it did in the past? The guillotine was thus a measure of colonial repression, its key colonial feature being its exclusive application in the colony and not in the colonizer's motherland.

If an occupation is intended to be temporary from an international legal perspective, then the occupier's justice system and the consequences of its verdicts ought also to be equally temporary to the maximum extent possible. As such, the

---

32. On Mitterrand's reintroduction of guillotine deaths to Algeria as the French justice minister, see François Malye et Benjamin Stora, *François Mitterrand et la guerre d'Algérie* (Paris: Calmann-Lévy, 2010), Ch. 5 'Les Guillotinés, pp. 130–74.

33. Save for one personal recollection of his father in Algeria back in 1914 (p. 131), Camus deliberately did not refer to the French–Algerian war anywhere in the text, consistent with his objective of making a general claim against the usage of the death penalty; he wished to avoid a specific debate about the Algerian situation.

34. Jean-Jacques Servan-Schreiber, *Lieutenant en Algérie* (Paris: Julliard, 1957).

35. Camus, *Reflections on the Guillotine*, p. 137.

occupier ought not, in all conscience, apply the most permanent and irreversible measure of punishment – namely, the death penalty. That the death penalty was illegitimate on its own account was confirmed by the authors of the European Convention on Human Rights in November 1950. France in fact delayed its ratification of this treaty – which was partially drafted by its own jurist, René Cassin – on account of it being in breach of it, over its conduct in Algeria.[36] Thus, its illegitimacy was twofold. First, it was carrying out a punishment that was no longer valid in Europe. Second, in order to do so, it was issuing death penalties solely through the military courts in Algeria – a territory over which French colonial rule was now being internationally challenged.[37] To be sure, similar death penalties via guillotine were obviously not being executed in metropolitan France, but were reserved solely for colonial territories such as Algeria. Thanks to his literary sensibilities, Camus grasped all too well this twofold measure of illegitimacy – of the death penalty itself, and on top that, its issuance by the occupier's hostile judicial mechanism. His example of this two folded illegitimacy at the beginning of the *Reflections* is rather telling:

> When the Nazis in Poland indulged in public executions of hostages, to keep those hostages from shouting words of revolt and liberty they muzzled them with a plaster-coated gag. … We smother under padded words with a penalty whose legitimacy we could assert only after we had examined it in reality.[38]

Camus here questions the illegitimacy of the penalty under the most illegitimate of regimes – the Nazi *Grossraum* occupation of Poland. He then charges his example with the second measure of illegitimacy – that of the German military-courts system that stipulated these executions. The legitimacy of an occupier's military courts is always in question. As we saw above, the entire effort to limit the death penalty within GC-IV was the result of exactly this problematic, raised during the Stockholm Conference by the Swedish delegate Holmgren, to which the US delegate Clattenburg responded with his important qualification of Article 59. The whole point behind the idea of premising the applicability of the death penalty in occupied territory on its pre-existence in the occupied country's penal code is one of legitimacy. If there is any situation in which the death penalty can still apply, it surely must be derived from the state's normative order prior to its entry into occupation's legal abnormality and moral illegitimacy.

36. Marco Duranti, *The Conservative Human Rights Revolution: European Identity, Transnational Politics, and the Origins of the European Convention* (Oxford: Oxford University Press, 2017), pp. 316–17.

37. On the world's option of the illegitimacy of French colonial rule in Algeria from 1958 onwards, and the repeated motions at the UN General Assembly against it concerning this issue, see Horne, *A Savage War of Peace*, pp. 467–9.

38. Camus, *Reflections on the Guillotine*, pp. 133–4.

The mandating of Israeli military courts to issue the death penalty against Palestinians in the occupied territories – 2018

In January 2018, the Israeli Knesset initially approved legislation that would allow for Israel's military tribunals in the occupied territories to pronounce the death penalty on Palestinians found guilty of grave attacks that resulted in the deaths of Israelis.[39] Unheeded by the Israeli attorney general's alarm at this measure, the Netanyahu government succeeded in garnering the necessary majority in parliament to pass this legislative vote in its first roll call.[40] The drafting history of GC-IV's Article 59 provides some rather macabre parallels with this Israeli legislative motion. As with France and Algeria, here too, the authority to issue the death penalty would be administered solely by the military courts situated outside Israel's metropole – exclusively in the Occupied Palestinian Territories (OPT). Since the establishment of the State of Israel, the one and only person to have been executed on a court's verdict had been former SS-*Obersturmbannführer* Adolph Eichmann, who was found responsible for the extermination of over six million Jews; Israel's death penalty had not been resorted to since. As if in a deliberate attempt to emulate the Algerian situation, therefore, Israel had decided to adopt *both* aspects of illegitimacy evident in Camus's *Reflections on the Guillotine*: the general illegitimacy of the death penalty and the specific illegitimacy of the occupier's justice system – in this case, Israel's military courts in the OPT.

At the heart of military courts' legitimacy lies the problem of impartiality – or, rather, the absence thereof. The historical context is important here. The earliest stages of GC-IV's drafting directly coincided with the unfolding of the Nuremberg trials, officially known as the 'International Military Tribunal'. Not without cause, one of the hardest hurdles facing the Nuremberg prosecution was the claim forwarded by none other than former *Reichsmarschall* Hermann Göring that the entire trial constituted nothing more than 'victor's justice'. One of Nuremberg's key features was precisely the lengths to which its prosecutor, Justice Robert Jackson, went in order to counter this impression. In contrast, and despite the circumstances of his kidnapping in Argentina, Eichmann's trial in Jerusalem's District Court over a decade later, pleaded before Justice Landau's three-judge bench, which resulted in an executed death penalty, was perceived without any measure of doubt to be legally impartial – even by its most famous ideological critics, such as Hannah Arendt.[41]

39. Moran Azoulay, 'With a Narrow Majority, the Knesset Approved the Law for the Death Penalty for Terrorists', *YNET*, 3 January 2018 [in Hebrew]. Available at: https://www.ynet.co.il/articles/0,7340,L-5065912,00.html.

40. Tova Zimuki, 'Attorney General Mandelblit Is Opposed to the Proposed Legislation Allowing for the Imposition of the Death Penalty for Terrorists', *YNET*, 19 December 2017 [in Hebrew]. Available at: https://www.ynet.co.il/articles/0,7340,L-5058908,00.html.

41. Ben-Nun, 'The Victor's Justice Dilemma', pp. 7–19.

As with the story of the drafters of GC-IV themselves, in the case of this 'Trial of the Century', personalities also mattered. One of the greatest judicial giants ever to sit on Israel's Supreme Court bench was its interim president, Justice Chaim Cohn. Born in 1911 in the German Baltic city of Lübeck to an ultra-religious Jewish-German family, Cohn received the usual dual education of rabbinical and secular studies and submitted his PhD thesis in Law to the University of Frankfurt several months prior to the Nazis' rise to power. Emigrating to Israel in 1933, Cohn rose through the legal ranks to become the quintessential voice of humanity on Jerusalem's High Court bench.[42] In 1960, as Eichmann was captured in Buenos Aires, Cohn was still serving as Israel's attorney general. With much of his own family having been exterminated in the Holocaust, Cohn personally knew that as attorney general he would be expected to request the death penalty for Eichmann once the trial was set in motion. Preferring to follow his conscience rather than demand the death penalty for the accused, Cohn resigned as attorney general and relinquished his role as chief prosecutor in what was evident to become one of the most famous trials of the twentieth century. His successor, Gideon Hausner, stepped into that historic limelight.[43]

Roughly around the time that Cohn resigned his post, another of Israel's German-born judicial titans, the Danzig-born Meir Shamgar (Sternberg), began charting his path in the country's legal history. As the advocate general of the Israeli army, in 1963, Shamgar set out the strategic planning for the eventuality in which, in an upcoming military confrontation with the Arab world, Israel would find itself a military occupier of further Arab lands.

As the army's chief legal officer, Shamgar was well acquainted with the highly problematic role that had already been played by military courts within Israel – specifically, under the rule of the UK's armed forces, who had executed Jewish vigilantes on account of their anti-British actions. Shamgar was personally subjected to deportation to East Africa in 1946 by those same British military courts, due to his membership of the Anti-British Irgun underground group. As a stern believer in the rule of law, Shamgar rejected the idea that post 1949, Palestinian residents of Israel would be subjected to military courts while Jewish Israelis came under the jurisdiction of the state's civilian court system. To this end, from 1955 onwards, the Israeli legislator began to significantly limit the role of military courts, gradually transferring all of their functions to the regular

42. On Chaim Cohn's refusal to demand the death penalty for Eichmann, and his turnover of the prosecutor's roles in this trial to Gideon Hausner, see Professor Daniel Friedman's obituary for Cohn: Daniel Friedman, 'In Memoria- Chaim Cohn', in *Hamishpat* ['The Trial' – Hebrew], vol. 14 (July 2002), pp. 4–8, at 4. Available at: http://hamishpat-arc h.colman.ac.il/heb/Issues/Issue14/article,675.

Cohn never had the chance to defend his doctoral thesis at the law faculty of the University of Frankfurt am Main back in 1933. In the 1950s, he was offered the chance to come and defend his thesis and duly receive his doctoral title, which he cordially declined.

43. Ibid., p. 6, n. 9.

court system. By 1966, as the country's Arab residents had come to receive Israeli citizenship, the military court system had become virtually redundant.[44]

By the end of the 1967 war, Israel had almost quadrupled its territory, which now also included the Sinai Peninsula, the Gaza Strip, the West Bank and the Golan Heights. The reinstatement of the military court system was the only way in which the state could effectively exert immediate legal control over these vast newly conquered territories and their peoples. Pursuant to GC-IV's stipulations, Shamgar's preparations stipulated that the *jus ante* (the law preceding Israel's occupation) would remain valid and in place and would only be superseded by the military commander's decrees, or by the judicial injunctions of the newly established military courts.

By 2017, five decades after Israel's enactment of its military court system in the West Bank, the extent to which this military judicial system had morphed into an arm of the state geared exclusively towards the continued subjugation and oppression of occupied civilian Palestinians came to light. While Israeli human-rights NGOs had long bemoaned the evil implicit in this system, it was down to *Haaretz* newspaper's investigative journalism that the true Kafka-like nature of this system was made public.[45] The level of guilty verdicts pronounced by the military court in the OPT was 99.76 per cent. In the case of requests for administrative detention – that is, an indefinite incarceration in jail prior to any indictment – the military courts' approval rate was 98.77 per cent.[46] What Sharon Weill has termed a military 'judicial domination' had materialized. Israel's system of military courts in the OPT had evolved into yet another state arm whose sole purpose was the unending occupation of the Palestinian people.[47]

In 1946, as Georg Cohn returned from his exile in Sweden, Werner Best, then in Allied custody, was tried in Denmark in absentia. He was convicted of multiple murders, and numerous other crimes committed by the Nazis during his tenure as the German plenipotentiary in Copenhagen and sentenced to death by the Danish court. Languishing in an Allied jail and awaiting the results of his interrogation by the Allied prosecutors in Nuremberg, Best's survival chances seemed bleak. Yet in 1948, and following his release without prosecution from the hands of the Allied

44. Menachem Hofnung, *Israel- Security Needs vs. The Rule of Law* (Jerusalem: Nevo Legal Publishers, 1991), pp. 154–5 [in Hebrew], 1991 ירושלים: נבו הוצאה לאור מנחם הופנונג, ישראל- בטחון המדינה מול שלטון החוק: 1948-1991

45. Chaim Levinson, 'The Israeli Military Courts in the West Bank: Only a Third of Appeals Are Admitted', *Haaretz*, 29 November 2011 [in Hebrew] Available at: https://www.haaretz.co.il/news/law/1.1578247.

See also report by *Btselem: The Military Courts*, briefing 11 November 2017. Available at: https://www.btselem.org/military_courts.

46. Ibid.

47. Sharon Weill, 'The Judicial Arm of the Occupation: The Israeli Military Courts in the Occupied Territories', *International Review of the Red Cross*, vol. 89, no. 866 (2007), pp. 395–419 at 419.

authorities in Germany, the Danish court decided to clear the executor of Schmitt's *Grossraum* ideology and revoke his death penalty.[48] With Best now a tried foreign national, his entire file, along with the Danish requests for his extradition, were all being handled by Georg Cohn, who by that time was back at his desk at the Danish Foreign Office overseeing its international law department. In all probability, Cohn was relieved at Best's having been cleared. In 1948, it would have seemed much more important for him to dedicate his efforts towards the future international legal prohibition of the kind of acts for which Best had become notorious – rather than trying to persecute this Nazi, who would go on to live out the rest of his days in infamy until his death some four decades later.

That same year, in 1948, the young Chaim Cohn flew from Israel to Copenhagen, to meet with Georg Cohn. Following the creation of the State of Israel, David Ben-Gurion, its first prime minister, ordered Chaim Cohn to consult with prominent Jewish jurists around the world concerning a prospective constitution for the newly born Jewish state.[49] Both Cohns were renowned jurists in their respective countries. Both had been born into German religious Jewish families. Both experienced a similar upbringing and education, which included a PhD in law coupled with rabbinical learning and ordination. As the Nazis took over their birth-countries, both had fled for their lives. And, at the end of the day, both were repelled by the idea of pronouncing the death penalty on their persecutors – be it Georg Cohn over Werner Best in 1948, or Chaim Cohn over Best's SS subordinate Adolf Eichmann in 1960.

During their meeting in Copenhagen in the winter of 1948, did they share views concerning the application of capital punishment?

Was it just a coincidence that both men saw eye to eye on the need to never impose it – not even on Nazis such as Best and Eichmann?

Might Chaim Cohn, the younger of the two have been influenced by Georg Cohn's abhorrence of the death penalty – in the very same manner in which the elder Cohn pleaded against it in Stockholm two months prior to their meeting?

The material in the archives is silent on this point.

In 2018, the Israeli Knesset affirmatively approved the first reading of legislation that would allow its military courts in the occupied territories to sentence Palestinians to death, in cases in which the military judges' bench unanimously agreed with the imposition of capital punishment.

Georg Cohn's and Chaim Cohn's legal legacies had been resigned to their fate, and were now comfortably and cordially forgotten.

---

48. Herbert, *Best: Biographische Studien über Radikalismus,* pp. 444–8.

49. Georg Cohn advised Chaim Cohn to separate religion from the state – as was the case in Denmark.

Part Three

THE STRUGGLE AGAINST NON-APPLICABILITY

Ever since its adoption and entry into force, states have had a difficult time keeping up with GC-IV's stipulations. Consequently, and rather than trying to live up to their responsibilities under this Convention, they have for the most part attempted to exempt themselves altogether from its stipulations – repeatedly arguing that it does not apply in their specific case.

The question of applicability and, perhaps more importantly, who decides whether the Convention applies or not in a given conflict was, in fact, well within the sights of the GC-IV's drafters. Chapter 7 looks at the evolution, throughout its various drafting stages, of ideas concerning judicial oversight over the Convention's implementation – along with the eventual (and very last-minute) rejection of the ICJ's authority over the Convention back in 1949, and the historical turnaround of events that, some three decades later, brought GC-IV firmly under the ICJ's purview. As we shall see, the rejection of the ICJ oversight clause at GC-IV's very last reading during the final days of the 1949 Geneva Conference of Plenipotentiaries had less to do with any resentment of the idea of such control and much more to do with political Cold War considerations and the deadlock between the Soviet Union and the United States, at the UN Security Council concerning UN' membership.

In marked contrast to the conduct of states, the reaction – indeed, the enthusiasm – with which the ICRC endorsed GC-IV was nothing less than remarkable. From having read the Geneva Conventions of 1929 in the most reticent and narrow legalistic manner which brought it not to address the mass extermination of Jews, Eastern European civilians and Soviet POWs during the Second World War, the ICRC– once GC-IV came through – embraced its humanitarian mission with an almost religious fervour. If in 1945, Carl Burckhardt could – as seen in Chapter 1 – still bend over backwards in his disingenuous reading of the POW Convention so as not to apply it to Allied Jewish POWs whose rights had been violated by Nazi Germany, by 1955 the ICRC was going out of its way – as we shall see in Chapter 8 – to convince the French authorities in Algeria and their colonial British counterparts in Kenya and Cyprus to apply the Convention to both civilians and guerrilla fighters.

This radical change of heart by the ICRC was accompanied by a revision of the federation of Red Cross and Red Crescent societies' statutes, undertaken by Jean Pictet, in view of the conscription of the German and Japanese National Societies in favour of those countries' war efforts during the Second World War.

These developments catapulted the ICRC to the very forefront of humanitarian action – especially in favour of civilians – far ahead of other contemporary international organizations such as the nascent UN agencies. Chapter 9 looks deeper into this mobilization by the ICRC in favour of its humanitarian causes, the initiation of its infallible character in favour of victims, and in its firm – albeit always confidential – stances *against* states, as these continued their attempts to circumvent their obligations under the Geneva Conventions that they had signed and ratified.

Chapter 8

ARBITRATION, JUDICIAL SETTLEMENT AND THE ICJ'S ROLES VIS-À-VIS GC-IV

The International Court of Justice's advisory opinion on 'The Wall' in the West Bank

On 9 July 2004, the Israeli–Palestinian conflict experienced a mild 'legal earthquake'. In its advisory opinion delivered that day, the ICJ in The Hague proclaimed that the separation barrier that Israel had erected in the heart of Palestine's West Bank territory was illegal, and that it breached international law. This barrier ('The Wall') had materialized after a wave of suicide attacks by Palestinian militants in Israeli cities and areas of high population density, following the collapse of the Oslo peace process and the eruption of the second Palestinian uprising (*Intifada*). Gradually, from 2002 onwards, as it became clear that Israel could not hermetically seal itself off from Palestinian suicide bombers crossing into its territory, a firm majority of Israelis – and, with them, the upper echelons of the country's political establishment – opted for the construction of 'The Wall'. As it additionally became clear that Israel was not going to build this barrier on its own sovereign territory but would, in fact, use its construction as a pretext to carve up the West Bank and incorporate large swaths of its territory into the Israeli side, Palestinians opted to challenge its international legality. It was, after all, being erected directly on land that was destined to eventually become part of an envisaged Palestinian state.

In particular, the court found that Israel had breached its obligations as a signatory to the GC-IV, and was thus liable for the consequences of its actions as the Occupying Power under the terms of this treaty. Several months earlier, the ICJ had been requested by the UNGA to render its opinion with regard to the following question:

> What are the legal consequences arising from the construction of the wall being built by Israel, *the occupying power*, in the Occupied Palestinian Territory, including in and around East Jerusalem, as described in the report of the Secretary-General, considering the rules and principles of international law,

including the Fourth Geneva Convention of 1949, and relevant Security Council
and General Assembly resolutions?[1]

In the drafting (and crafting, for it is a true craft) of UN resolutions, every word
counts – and the General Assembly's framing of this specific, legal question for
the ICJ's consideration was no exception. The explicit reference to GC-IV in the
body of the question and the specific qualification, between separating commas,
of Israel – designating it as 'the occupying power' – were no coincidence. One of
the key objectives of the UNGA was deliberately to refute, once and for all, Israel's
claim for non-recognition of the applicability of GC-IV to occupied Palestine. This
legal view by Israel was summed up by the UN secretary general, in his preparatory
report to the General Assembly mandated to discuss the requested ICJ opinion, in
the following terms:

> Despite having ratified the Fourth Geneva Convention, Israel has not
> incorporated it into its domestic legislation. Nor does it agree that the Convention
> is applicable to the occupied Palestinian territory, citing the lack of recognition
> of the territory as sovereign prior to its annexation by Jordan and Egypt and
> [claiming that it is], therefore, not a territory of a High Contracting Party as
> required by the Convention.[2]

In simple terms, the Israeli position ran as follows: since Israel seized the West Bank
from Jordan in 1967, and since the incorporation of this territory into Jordan after
the 1949 Rhodes armistice agreement was never recognized by the international
community, the legal status of the West Bank was that of a 'disputed territory'.
Accordingly, Israel's occupation of Palestine was not subject to the provisions of
GC-IV, thus triggering Israel's repeated (and solitary – for no other state on earth
has accepted its position here) refusal to recognize GC-IV's legal applicability to
its occupation of Palestine.

Despite this, it was far from self-evident that the ICJ would indeed rule against
Israel. In the wake of the wave of Palestinian suicide bombings that had engulfed
the country since 2000, and against the international backdrop of the 11 September
2001 attacks on New York's World Trade Centre, self-defence and military necessity
were certain to be high on the court's list of judicial considerations. In an interview
with Associated Press that morning, the Palestinian delegate to the UN, Nasser

---

1. UNGA Emergency Session, 23rd Plenary Meeting, 8 December 2003, UN Doc. A/
RES/ES-10/14 (italics added). Available at unispal.un.org/DPA/DPR/unispal.nsf/0/F95
3B744269B9B7485256E1500776DCA (accessed 14 December 2016).

2. 'Report of the Secretary-General prepared pursuant to General Assembly resolution
ES-10/13', UN Doc. A/ES-10/248, 24 November 2003, Annex I, point 3. For Israel's
statement to the UN Security Council (the full discussed annex), see Annex 1 of unisp
al.un.org/DPA/DPR/unispal.nsf/0/BDD222DF1DF3712185256E4C006C1D75   (accessed
14 December 2016).

Al-Kidwa, displayed a reserved and cautious comportment, not knowing which way the ruling would go or how unequivocal it would be.[3] In retrospect, Al-Kidwa could not have wished for a more decisive legal opinion from the ICJ's fifteen-judge bench.

In the event, the court ruled 14 to 1 in favour of the non-legality of 'The Wall' under international law. While Israel had boycotted the ICJ proceedings, it had, however, launched a combative media campaign against the ICJ's decision to deliver its judicial opinion on the matter. In the midst of this media blitz, Israel delivered to The Hague the burnt carcass of a bus that had been blown up by a Palestinian suicide bomber a mere four months prior to the publication date of the court's opinion.[4] In his dissenting opinion, Judge Thomas Buergenthal criticized his peers for not rejecting the initial request from the UNGA for the ICJ's advisory opinion, given that the court 'lacked sufficient information and evidence to render the opinion.'[5] Yet, at least in one respect, all the judges (including Judge Buergenthal) were unanimous: the GC-IV of 1949 applied in full to the OPT, and Israel was bound by it whether the country liked it or not.

Of all the negative aspects of the ICJ ruling on 'The Wall', this unanimous application of GC-IV to the West Bank must have tasted bitter as wormwood to Alan Baker's palate. As the British-born deputy director and chief legal counsel of the Israeli Foreign Ministry, Baker had spent much of his career defending the legal legitimacy of Israel's occupation of Palestine. A settler himself, from the nearby Jerusalem settlement of Kfar Adar, Baker had been assigned the task of preparing Israel's legal position vis-à-vis the ICJ proceedings. A veteran of negotiations with the Palestinians all through the Oslo years, he had, before emigrating from the UK to Israel, studied law at the University College London and later completed his studies at the Hebrew University Law Faculty in Jerusalem.[6] A former military prosecutor and senior legal advisor to the Israel Defence Forces (IDF) with a sharp legal mind, Baker was well acquainted with the intricacies of Israel's long-

3. Interview with Al-Kidwa, *Associated Press*, 9 July 2004. Available at www.aparch ive.com/metadata/youtube/e9d5792e6141cbcb2c908ccd5088dfe5 (accessed 14 December 2016).

4. Footage of this demonstration, by Israeli medical-aid workers and other supporters, in front of the ICJ's Palace of Justice in The Hague (*Associated Press*, 24 February 2004) is available at www.aparchive.com/metadata/youtube/664fb399674e2dba6b7490ada267598a (accessed 14 December 2016).

5. 'Declaration of Judge Buergenthal', International Court of Justice Advisory Opinion: Legal Consequences of the Construction of a Wall in the Occupied Palestinian Territory, 9 July 2004. Available at www.icj-cij.org/docket/files/131/1687.pdf (accessed 14 December 2016).

6. Moshe Gorali, 'Legality Is in the Eye of the Beholder: The international community believes the settlements violate the Fourth Geneva Convention and may even be a war crime under the terms of the International Criminal Court. Israel disagrees', *Haaretz*, 25 September 2003.

standing, and futile line of argument, which maintained that the country was not an occupier of Palestine. On 29 January 2004, Baker had sent the ICJ Israel's official position in a lengthy, 240-page document packed with legal argument and source materials. Among his myriad of legal claims, Baker contended that the ICJ was not competent to answer the question put before it by the UNGA, since that question itself was of a *political* rather than a *legal* nature. Palestine was not a recognized state, and therefore had no standing in the World Court (i.e. the ICJ), which, as per its statute, is restricted exclusively for state parties. Other legal arguments revolved around the non-applicability of the court's previous opinions and rulings on other occupied territories – most notably, the 1971 decision on Namibia and its 1975 ruling on Western Sahara.

Yet despite all the arguments that Baker presented, there was one argument that he deliberately *did not* make – and which was glaring in its absence: according to GC-IV's *travaux préparatoires* and its annexed resolutions, the ICJ's jurisdiction over this specific convention had been forcefully and deliberately *removed and rendered void* by its drafters back in August 1949. If the UNGA's question was indeed predicated on the applicability of GC-IV to occupied Palestine, and the ICJ's judicial authority had been explicitly removed from adjudicating over matters concerning this convention, then the ICJ would be compelled *not* to adjudicate over the question just placed before it by the UNGA. This was exactly the legal result that Baker wished for. So why didn't he argue for it? The answer lies in GC-IV's intricate, historical evolution and how much of it eventually came to be considered an integral part of customary international law.

The meandering nature of treaty-making and the 'compromise paradigm'

Historical scholarship has broadly viewed GC-IV as a paradigm of sensible compromises between universal, humanitarian norms on the one hand and the safeguarding of national sovereignties on the other.[7] Recent scholarly contributions have repeated this modality of compromise vis-à-vis the insertion of references to ICJ into the convention's final text.[8]

At the heart of this 'compromise paradigm' lies the age-old conflict between nation-state sovereignty and international legal universalism. One of the most striking areas in which this compromise is evident is in the glaring lack of any substantial legal enforcement mechanisms within the GC-IV text. The only textual reference (of sorts) to an international oversight body outside the purview of the belligerents themselves is a now-forgotten, legally weak reference to the ICJ,

---

7. Best, *War and Law since 1945*, pp. 80–179; George Aldrich, 'Some Reflections on the Origins of the 1977 Geneva Protocols', in Christophe Swinarski (ed.), *Studies and Essays on International Humanitarian Law and Red Cross Principles in Honour of Jean Pictet* (The Hague: Martinus Nijhoff, 1984), pp. 129–37 (hereinafter 'Aldrich 1984').

8. Lewis, *The Birth of the New Justice*, pp. 229–73.

inserted at the end of the convention text as a non-binding resolution upon its High Contracting Parties. It reads:

> The Conference recommends that in the case of a dispute relating to the interpretation or application of the present Convention which cannot be settled by other means, the High Contracting Parties concerned endeavour to agree between themselves to refer such dispute to the International Court of Justice.[9]

A textual reading of this resolution gives the impression that the relinquishing of state sovereignty before this international jurisdiction was, at best, a weak recommendation – an amicable suggestion to be considered by state parties, just in case they might have forgotten or overlooked this possibility. In fact, this resolution has been rendered so meaningless that it is no longer attached to the official text of GC-IV, nowadays fully available online from the ICRC website, leaving the reader to search for it through the volumes of the original diplomatic proceedings or in designated web pages.[10]

Yet was this the real intention of the drafters who inserted this resolution? Did the drafters of the most important international treaty for civilian protection during armed conflict really intend to release state parties from the ICJ's judicial oversight, and relinquish all disputes to bilateral bargaining between warring parties?

In fact, the original intention of a solid majority of the drafters was to incorporate within the treaty itself a concrete reference to a judicial mechanism for the interpretation, and ultimate settling, of disputes between belligerents. This judicial-oversight capacity was originally envisaged as being entrusted to the highest international legal authority at the time – namely, the International Court of Justice at The Hague. This intention – to have a substantial judicial mechanism for the settlement of disputes (rather than the classic diplomatic means of negotiation and conciliation and, if necessary, the weak, legal mechanism of arbitration) – had existed from GC-IV's earliest drafting stages, and it gathered momentum through the convention's three years of *travaux préparatoires*. The 'gutting' of the ICJ mechanism from the Convention text was not the result of any *legal* re-evaluation, however. It was, rather, due to very specific *political* circumstances in which a small minority of state parties from the Soviet bloc threatened to sabotage the entire convention project should any such sovereignty-limiting mechanism be inserted

9. *Final Record of the Diplomatic Conference of Geneva of 1949* (hereinafter 'Final Record'), vol. 2 Section B (Berne: Federal Political Department of Switzerland, n.d.), p. 432. Available on the US Library of Congress website at www.loc.gov/rr/frd/Military_Law/pdf/ Dipl-Conf-1949-Final_Vol-2-B.pdf (accessed 14 December 2016).

10. See the official text of the 'Geneva Convention (IV), relative to the Protection of Civilian Persons in Time of War' (signed Geneva, 12 August 1949) at www.icrc.org/ihl/385 ec082b509e76c41256739003e636d/6756482d86146898c125641e004aa3c5 (accessed 14 December 2016).

into the text. Furthermore, the Soviet insistence on removing the ICJ's oversight capacity had much more to do with external considerations concerning the contemporary 'diplomatic war' over UN membership at the UN Security Council than existing historical accounts allow, and much less to do with the humanitarian issues at hand – in this case, concerning the making of GC-IV.[11] Ironically, it was the very same person (Soviet jurist Platon Morosov) who 'shot down' the proposed ICJ clause in 1949 and then came to reinstate the ICJ's international authority over GC-IV vis-à-vis state parties some four decades later, when he sat as a judge on the ICJ's bench as this court rendered its landmark verdict in *Nicaragua vs. United States* (1986).[12]

11. Best, *War and Law*, pp. 156–8. Geoffrey Best based his reading of the Final Record proceedings on Paul de la Pradelle's account of this episode: *La Conference Diplomatique et les Nouvelles Conventions de Genéve du 12 Août 1949* (Paris: Les Éditions Internationales, 1951) (hereinafter 'La Pradelle 1951'), pp. 265–84. Best's unqualified acceptance of La Pradelle's version of events has, ever since, acted to the detriment of both historical scholarship and a full understanding of the extent to which the drafters in fact intended universalist values to prevail over narrow state interests in the Geneva Conventions. At the heart of both Best's and La Pradelle's accounts lay the overt claim that the Soviet bloc was motivated by narrow, Machiavellian, *étatist* interests rather than true humanitarianism. Consequently – so went the assumption – the Soviets would have been against any sovereignty-limiting mechanism in the convention texts concerning disputes on the application and breaches of the conventions. The problem with this line of argument is the fact that of all the UN Security Council Permanent Five (UNSC P-5) members present at the drafting table, the Soviets were, alongside France, by far the most favourably disposed towards the Civilian Convention, with the UK certainly being the most hostile to this humanitarian, legal endeavour. In fact, as Mark Lewis has exposed in documents from the ICRC archives (Pilloud's final report after the Conference of Plenipotentiaries – September 1949), it was mostly thanks to the Soviets that the Civilian Convention was concluded. See Lewis, *Birth of the New Justice*, p. 268, n. 162. Best could be excused his reading, having had no access to the ICRC archives. Yet even so, he should not have overlooked the fact that it was Morosov himself who proposed widening the scope of protections for victims in cases of disputes between state parties, as it was the Soviet delegation that proposed extending the mechanism of arbitration (originally envisaged only in the case of the Maritime Convention) to all the Conventions – and especially to the newly created Civilian Convention. See statement of Morosov at the 8th meeting of the Special Committee, 23 May 1949, *Final Record*, vol. 2 B, p. 52. As for La Pradelle (who was personally present during all the deliberations on the intended ICJ oversight mechanism) and his false representation of the motivations behind the Soviet position against ICJ oversight – this probably had more to do with the fact that he (together with Georg Cohn, from Denmark) viewed the mechanism as his own personal mission in this convention, and that once it had been struck out due to the Soviet intervention the latter were, in his opinion, the ones to blame.

12. *Military and Paramilitary Activities in and against Nicaragua* (*Nicaragua vs. United States of America*) (Merits: Judgment), delivered 27 June 1986, International Court of

*Arbitration – the initial French ideas for an ICJ oversight mechanism
for GC-IV's ultimate resolution of disputes*

Before delving into the intricate details of the evolution of this judicial-oversight clause, a brief reminder of the GC-IV drafting timeline might prove useful. The project of revising the conventions and adding a special one for the protection of civilians had been envisaged at the ICRC Tokyo Conference of 1934; yet, as the world entered the Second World War, the planned follow-up conference of 1940 was postponed. In February 1945 (three months prior to the end of the war in Europe), ICRC president Max Huber sent out invitations for an informal consultation session in Geneva. As we saw in Chapter 1 a French interministerial committee (see below) first met in July 1946. It immediately created three sub-commissions: one to study the revision of the Prisoners of War Convention, a second to study the revisions of the Sick and Wounded Convention and a third charged with the new Convention for Civilians.[13] The ICRC replicated this process during the 1949 Geneva Conference of Plenipotentiaries, adding a fourth committee charged with the coordination of Articles common to all three conventions. As the International Committee pushed forward and pre-scheduled the governmental experts' meeting for April 1947, the interministerial committee came under ever-growing time pressures to conclude its first French draft of the proposed Civilian Convention. During the Stockholm Conference of August 1948, the first full draft of this new convention was presented. The Geneva Conference of Plenipotentiaries (April to August 1949) worked on all the texts until the endorsement of the Final Act on 12 August 1949. The ICRC individually also consulted with several international legal experts (Hersch Lauterpacht among them) so as to improve the Stockholm text prior to the 1949 Geneva Plenipotentiaries' Conference.[14]

From the outset, France held a special intermediary status between the 'realist' and 'universalist' camps – and also lay somewhat between the US and Soviet camps of the now-open Cold War. Aside from Switzerland, it was the state most supportive and most intimately connected to the ICRC in the efforts to promote the Geneva Conventions' revisions, with special emphasis on the new Convention for Civilians. Since the UN's creation in 1945, France had been a permanent veto-

Justice Reports 14, pp. 113–14 § 216–21, pp. 129–30 § 254–6 (hereinafter 'ICJ – Nicaragua'). Available at www.icj-cij.org/docket/?sum=367&p1=3&p2=3&case=70&p3=5 (accessed 14 December 2016).

13. French Foreign Ministry Archive (FFMA), new archiving filing numbers, File # 768 SUP/ 160-bis. *Révision des conventions de Genève- procès-verbaux des réunions de la commission interministérielle au sujet de la révision des conventions de Genève, documents; conférence officieuse en vue de la révision et de l'extension des conventions de Genève de juillet 1929 (avril 1947)*, session of 23 July 1946, presided over by Monsieur Bousquet – director of administrative conventions at the French Foreign Ministry (also known in its nickname 'the Quai d'Orsay').

14. Best, *War and Law*, pp. 160–1.

carrying member of its Security Council. Following the Yalta Conference, it also became a military Occupying Power – both in Berlin and in southwest Germany. In early 1946, French foreign minister Georges Bidault issued a governmental decree that created the interministerial committee comprising selected experts from the various branches of the French executive and tasked it with studying the GC-IV revision and drafting a full convention text consistent with French views.

The interministerial committee worked sequentially; it first dealt with the revision of the Prisoners of War and Sick and Wounded Convention texts, and only then proceeded to work on the new Civilian Convention text.[15] The representative of the General Staff of the Armed Forces within the interministerial committee was Colonel Roussenne, who was closely associated with Lamarle and Georges Cahen-Salvador.[16] Roussenne was the first person to make an explicit reference to an ICJ judicial-oversight role, within the proposed Prisoners' Convention text. In his textual corrections for Section II (dubbed the 'control organ'), Roussenne redrafted the proposed Article 87 in his own handwriting, and added in the ICJ mechanism:

> *Article 87*: In the case of a disagreement between the belligerents regarding the application of the dispositions of this present Convention, The Protecting Powers ought, to the measure possible, bring forth their good offices with the objective of regulating the differences.
>
> The Permanent Court of International Justice shall designate, in the case of a conflict, at least three PERSONALITIES FROM NEUTRAL POWERS [handwritten strike out over the word 'judges'] charged with instructing the belligerent powers, ON THE CASE AT HAND [added in handwriting], relative to the application of the present convention. The belligerents will be obliged to follow through upon these instructions ('*Les beliligérants seront tenus de donner suite à*).[17] (Figure 20)

15. FFMA, new archiving filing numbers, File # 768 SUP/ 160-bis. *Révision des conventions de Genève*. During this session, the future dates of the committee for the Prisoners of War, and Sick and Wounded Conventions were set out. The discussions on the Civilian Convention were to be postponed to a later date once the first two conventions' texts were sufficiently developed. See p. 7.

16. FFMA, new archiving filing numbers, File # 768 SUP/ 160-bis. *Révision des conventions de Genève*. At the end of this file are deposited the private papers of Colonel Rousenne, bound by a paper written in red (hereinafter 'FFMA – Roussenne Papers'). The file contains an exchange of several handwritten notes between Lamarle and Rousenne, written in personal, non-formal and friendly language, indicating their long-time acquaintance.

17. FFMA – Roussenne Papers, 'Interministerial commission for the revision of the Geneva Convention of 1929, Drafting Committee of the Text to be Approved by the Commission, drafted by: JACOB, CHAYET, PERRIN'. This draft convention text has eighteen pages (not numbered), and is full of handwritten corrections in turquoise fountain-pen ink over the printed black-and-white text. The corrections to Article 87 are on the last

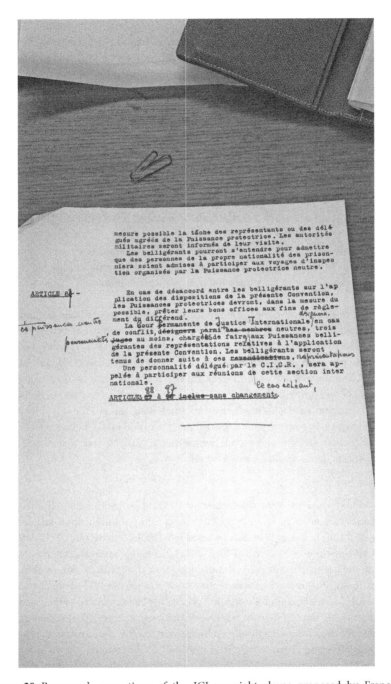

Figure 20 Rousenne's corrections of the ICJ oversight clause proposed by France – February 1947. The very first French draft text for the revision of the 1929 Prisoners of War Convention at the French interministerial committee of the Quai d'Orsay. © French Foreign Ministry Archive La Courneuve. Photo by Gilad Ben-Nun.

One must point out that Rousenne's thinking here is one of *arbitration* and not *judicial settlement*, since it is the belligerents themselves who are choosing the judges and the legal procedure (and probably the legal code too, had this measure come into force) that was to be applied. To this extent, while Rousenne was undoubtedly sincere about his intention to rein in states and oblige them to submit to universal humanitarian norms, his proposed means – arbitration – was insufficient to the task. It was a 'classical' relic of the days of the League of Nations, when state sovereignty reigned supreme above all else and was considered the 'sacred cow' of international law. Yet for Cahen-Salvador and others, after the atrocities of the Second World War, arbitration was simply not seen as a sufficiently strong legal mechanism.[18]

From arbitration to judicial settlement in France's first 'blueprint' for GC-IV

As Roussenne came to advise Sub-commission III, charged with the Convention for Civilians (which included a certain number of participants not present in the other sub-commissions), he somewhat optimistically explained,

> It will be positive to envisage the existence of an international tribunal composed of the representatives of all the signatory powers [it is clear from the context that the UN Security Council Permanent Five members (UNSC P-5) are meant here] of the Convention, who would rule over all issues before them. This tribunal would continue to work all through hostilities and would rule over all accounts brought before it by the belligerents. In the case where the combatant countries also participate in its judiciary, this tribunal shall [be composed] solely of neutral judges, in front of whom the belligerents would plead their cases, and to whose decisions they would submit themselves. … Such a public instance, at the international level, would be very efficient.[19]

page – 18. One should note here that Roussenne is still thinking within the political terms of the League of Nations, as he refers to the Permanent Court of International Justice (PCIJ), which by that time had already metamorphosed into the ICJ – under the UN Charter.

18. One must also stress here that Roussenne's inclination towards arbitration has also to do with the fact that he was charged with considering the Civilian Convention from the 'vanguard' of the Prisoners of War Convention of 1929, when the mechanism of arbitration already existed in the Maritime Convention yet had *not* been extended to the Prisoners of War Conventions. Thus, Roussenne was still thinking in terms very much associated with the League of Nations. Cahen-Salvador's push forward towards a mechanism that would be significantly stronger in legal terms within the Civilian Convention – not yet in existence – was already very reminiscent of universalist modalities of thinking, which were much more characteristic of the intellectual tendencies within the international system after the traumas of the Second World War and the creation of the UN.

19. FFMA – Roussenne Papers. Within this sub-file is a copy of the first 'concept paper', which the French interministerial committee elaborated *prior* to the commencement of the

Within the same interministerial committee, and very early on (November 1946), Chairman Cahen-Salvador also stressed the need for legal universality. When Lamarle requested the former's seasoned advice as to the most important issues to which attention should be paid in the upcoming Geneva Conventions – issues that he ought to raise with other permanent UN Security Council members in his upcoming trip to the UN's first General Assembly in New York – the old *éminence grise* replied that

> the cardinal question concern[ed] this Convention's effectiveness. He [i.e. Cahen-Salvador] estimated the problem of breach and the corresponding sanction in the case of a violation of the Convention's dispositions to be of the most fundamental importance and merits a deep and detailed study … this control, to be really effective, must be exercised by an international protecting body, and within [the] immediate disposition of all belligerents, accepted and recognized in one single text … this role could in the best of cases be confided to the International Committee of the Red Cross. In this case, though, the status of its delegates must not be based on bilateral agreements between the ICRC and each and every belligerent singularly, but must be based upon an obligatory Convention for all signatories – current and future. In order to give it even more authority this future organ would best be attached to the UN.[20]

As Sub-commission III continued its work, these universalist ideas filtered into the 'blueprint' for the Civilian Convention, the initial version of which appears to have been written probably around January 1947.[21] Lamarle brought with him to Geneva a revised version of this first draft, and handed it over to the ICRC in the governmental experts' meeting of April 1947. Article 30 of this revised draft convention text, which was submitted to the government experts' meeting between 14 and 26 April 1947, read,

drafting of a full-blown proposal for the Civilian Convention. See printed report entitled 'report regarding the necessity of elaborating a project of a Convention for the protection of the civilian population during times of war- principle which ought to govern its drafting', pp. 7–8. The report is not dated, but was definitely prepared before the tabling of the official French draft for the meeting of governmental experts in April 1947 – thus placing it somewhere between July 1946 and March 1947.

20. FFMA, new archiving filing numbers, File # 768 SUP/ 160-bis. *Révision des conventions de Genève*, Procès verbale, 14 November 1947, pp. 7–8.

21. FFMA, new archiving filing numbers, File # 768 SUP/ 160, *Commission interministérielle chargee de l'etude des additions et modifications a apporter aux Conventions de Geneve de 29 Juillet 1929: Sous-Commission pour l'elaboration du projet de la convention relatif a la protection des civils en temps de guerre.* In this draft document, the clause concerning the international tribunal is Article 29 on p. 7.

In the case of a disagreement between belligerents over the application of the dispositions of the present Convention, the international organ [the ICRC] shall have the right to attempt to undertake measures to overcome the differences. The high contracting parties shall execute the decisions of the International Tribunal competent to rule regarding the legality of any measure taken by the occupying power. This Tribunal could be summoned either by that power, or by an interested plaintiff, or by the securing agencies [i.e. the ICRC or other humanitarian organizations].[22] (See Appendix 1)

Yet not all was 'plain sailing' for the supporters of universalism – not even those at the Quai d'Orsay itself. In its efforts to compile the best draft that it could muster, the interministerial committee also invited recognized external experts to advise it on the proposed convention texts. One such expert was the Sorbonne law professor Marcel Sibert of the French Institute for High International Studies, a recognized authority in the field of public international law and the author of what became the key contemporary textbook regarding issues of war and peace.[23] Sibert unequivocally rejected the notion that the ICJ could perform the task envisaged for it by Roussenne without fundamentally overstepping its mandate:

Monsieur Professor Sibert observed that the International Court of Justice could not, without overstepping its own Terms of Reference, play the role Chief of Compliance ('*censeur*') for the Convention's application. He thought this role could be confided with the envisaged special international organ – the International Committee of the Red Cross. The ICRC possesses a moral authority which is not at all negligible which has, amongst other things, the advantage of existence and readiness to function in such circumstances. After a short debate the commission decided to modify the Second paragraph of the proposed Article 87 into the following: 'The International Committee of the Red Cross or another International organ shall designate, in the case of a conflict, at least three personalities from neutral powers, who shall be charged with examining the disagreement, and who could submit their observations and conclusions to the interested belligerent powers.'[24]

22. FFMA, new archiving filing numbers, File # 768 SUP/ 160, *Project of an International Convention concerning the condition and protection of civilian enemy nationals located on the territory of a belligerent or on a territory occupied by him*. The draft is not dated – but was most certainly tabled officially by France at the governmental experts' meeting in April 1947 and was amended during the Stockholm Conference one year later in August 1948. Title III 'The Convention's execution', p. 6.

23. Marcel Sibert, *Traité de Droit International Public: La Droit de la Paix* (Paris: Éditions Dalloz, 1951).

24. FFMA, **new** archiving filing numbers, File # 768 SUP/ 160-bis. *Révision des conventions de Genève*, Procès verbale, 8 January 1947, pp. 7–8.

A comparative reading of Roussenne's text with that finally endorsed at Sibert's instigation is revealing. Roussenne and Cahen-Salvador both opted for the possibility of overriding national sovereignty, as a measure of last resort, as they evoked the ICJ's judicial supreme authority over belligerent state parties. Sibert, on the other hand, not only did away with the ICJ's oversight but also replaced it with a weak and voluntary ICRC 'good offices' function – one that had no binding force whatsoever over state parties. This corresponded with Sibert's very restrictive legal views regarding the inviolability of national sovereignty – the 'sacred cow' of international legal principles during the interwar period. The clash between Roussenne and Cahen-Salvador on the one hand and Sibert on the other surfaced yet again during the contentious debate about the extension of the Geneva Convention's protections to conflicts far and wide, beyond the strict international definitions of the 1929 Conventions. On that occasion, Roussenne declared that

> it is indispensable to guarantee the essential rights of any person, including the respect for human dignity for persons who, whatever the title they have, will be in the hands of the enemy. It seems, in effect, that in a future conflict, the first war operation shall consist of massive arrests of enemy nationals. These people shall be for the most part civilians. It is important to protect them. That is why he thought the formula of one convention for both civilians and for prisoners of war was better.[25]

To this, Sibert replied that

> he estimated that the qualities of war prisoner will be legally recognized exclusively towards the armed forces.[26]

Therein lay the fundamental difference in world views between those who regarded the upcoming conventions from a universalist perspective and those who upheld a legally strict and thematically fragmented application of the issues. The fact of the matter was that those who had suffered the most from war tended – like Colonel Roussenne and Cahen-Salvador – to advocate universalism. The 'old guard jurists' from the days of the League of Nations came down on the side of restricting any form of forced intervention and upholding the supremacy of national sovereignty. As we saw in Chapter 2 a similar clash of legal visions was simultaneously taking place within the higher echelons of the ICRC between Max Huber's narrow, legalist approach and the expanded legal vision of the younger guard of jurists represented by Jean Pictet. In the end, it was the universalism of Pictet, Roussenne and Cahen-Salvador that prevailed, as its supporters managed to secure the endorsement of Common Article 3 and to refute Sibert's prediction regarding 'the qualities of war prisoner'.

25. Ibid., p. 3.
26. Ibid.

Nevertheless, Sibert stressed one fundamental point that, in the strict international legal sense, could not be avoided: it was not entirely clear whether the International Court of Justice could have jurisdiction over the prospected Geneva Conventions. Article 35 of the ICJ's Statute restricted that body's purview exclusively to UN member states. Therein lay the legal grounds for Sibert's objection to the possibility of an ICJ oversight with respect to the conventions. While other legal interpretations would stress the ICJ's merited jurisdiction due to the statute's Article 36 (also known as the 'optional clause'), this legal conundrum would return to haunt Cahen-Salvador with a vengeance two years later.

The removal of the ICJ oversight clause – from Geneva (April 1947) to Stockholm (1948)

The initiation and drafting of the ICJ oversight clause as described above had thus far been restricted to the higher echelons of the French government, as part of the internal deliberations and draft elaboration undertaken by Cahen-Salvador's interministerial committee. Based on accumulated institutional experience from the eighty-odd years that had elapsed since the first Geneva Conventions had been endorsed, Cahen-Salvador was well prepared for the upcoming stages in the drafting process. Once the French draft had been brought to the Governments Experts' Conference, between 14 and 26 April 1947, and under the most favourable assumptions that the ICRC and member states would indeed endorse the French draft (something that was anything but obvious at the time, given the existing Tokyo 1934 draft for a Convention for the Protection of Civilians), the entire drafting process would be assumed by the ICRC. This would then reduce France's position to that of a mere member state among many – no more important than other members of the UN Security Council. The issue of who was in charge of signing off on the final draft, and who would have 'the last word' in the texts that made it through to the next stage within this three-year drafting process, was no mere detail but could crucially impact on the substance of the draft. This was all the more important, as we shall discover below, given that the ICRC was tacitly, but firmly, opposed to Cahen-Salvador's ICJ oversight clause.

As mentioned in Chapter 2 the period immediately following the Second World War was marked by a significant rift between the ICRC and the League of Red Cross and Red Crescent Societies. The decision to convene the international conference of Red Cross National Societies, together with the ICRC in Stockholm, was already foreseen in 1946 – and for Cahen-Salvador and his French peers, this issue was certainly at the back of their minds. Swedish diplomat Folke Bernadotte, who was destined to preside over this Red Cross Conference, sought to break the ICRC's monopoly on action during wartime – a feat that he had effectively already accomplished during the closing months of the war in Europe with his rescue of Danish and other Scandinavian prisoners of war from Himmler's clutches. The distinction between wartime and peacetime activities would also later come to play a role in the proceedings of the Conference of Plenipotentiaries, with regard to the desired functions of the ICJ's oversight mechanism.

The rift between the ICRC and the League of Red Cross and Red Crescent Societies was most apparent over the question of who would have the last word concerning the drafting of the upcoming new Geneva Conventions, as is evident from the ICRC's report on the preliminary meetings held in Geneva between July and August 1946.[27] Agenda item number 10, which was concerned with the creation of a 'special commission for the study of the new draft Geneva Conventions', stipulated that

> the Conference decides to appoint a Commission which shall remain in close touch with the ICRC, and to which the latter [the ICRC] shall submit the texts it has drafted, before sending them to other National Societies. This Commission shall be appointed by the Executive Committee of the League.[28]

This was certainly a break with the past. Previously, it had been strictly up to the ICRC to prepare drafts for subsequent endorsement by the League, which encompassed all National Societies. Now, however, it was the National Societies (represented in the League) who were going to have the last word as to what the drafts of the proposed new Geneva Conventions would include. The novelty, if not outright revolutionary character, of this new arrangement did not escape the attention of the deeply controversial ICRC president, Carl Burckhardt:

> The President of the International Committee explained that hitherto it was the International Committee who prepared the draft conventions, always in cooperation with experts delegated by National Societies and by Governments, sitting in Commissions summoned by the Committee. The latter [i.e. the ICRC] of course claimed no monopoly on the work of revising the Conventions; it had no objection that the experts should, if the National Societies so desire it, be nominated by the Executive Committee of the League. The International Committee would continue to undertake the preparatory work and to draw up the preliminary drafts as it has done successfully for the past eighty-four years. This thankless task requires a sustained effort of several years and the whole-time assistance of specialists. The International Committee would submit its drafts to the proposed special Commission contemplated [i.e. to the *joint* Commission composed of both ICRC and League representatives], before presenting them to the International Red Cross Conference. The International

27. *Report on the Work of the Preliminary Conference of National Red Cross Societies for the study of the Conventions and of various Problems relative to the Red Cross* (ICRC: Geneva, 26 July–3 August 1947). Available on the US Library of Congress website at www. loc.gov/rr/frd/Military_Law/RC_Report-prelim-conference.html (accessed 16 December 2016).

28. Ibid., pp. 140–1.

Committee, however, obviously reserved its entire liberty to express its views at the International Conference, should they differ from those of the Special Commission, and to submit its own drafts to the Conference. After a debate, the decision quoted above was passed by a majority vote.[29]

The 1947 Government Experts' Conference was the first international forum at which the French, represented by Albert Lamarle, presented their draft for the revised Conventions – including the draft for the new Civilians' Convention, in which the ICJ oversight clause appeared under Article 30. Despite the partial endorsement that this French draft received from the conference, the ICJ oversight clause did not make it into the next drafting stage at Stockholm a year later, in August 1948. There, the only two remaining mechanisms for resolving differences arising between one or more belligerent parties were those of conciliation and of inquiry in the case of an alleged violation of the convention.[30] The only reference to the high international court in the entire convention text was to be found in the provisions concerning the election of the members of the enquiry committee within the inquiry mechanism.[31]

Where and when the ICJ oversight clause drafted by Cahen-Salvador, Lamarle and Roussenne was knocked out of the conventions' working drafts is not exactly clear. Given that it was not included in preparatory drafts for the Stockholm Conference, which the ICRC distributed to all National Societies and member-state delegates in May 1948, one can safely assume that this removal occurred between April 1947 and May 1948. The answer as to who was responsible for this removal is, however, fairly clear. Given that the ICRC was in charge of consolidating the draft – which was only to be *approved* by the special commission (mentioned above) that was created in August 1946 – there can be little doubt that it was upon the ICRC's instigation that the French ICJ oversight clause was removed from the text. Before examining the archive material, which unequivocally points to the ICRC's responsibility for this removal, one needs to ask why the International Committee would have been at odds with the French ICJ oversight clause in the first place.

29. Ibid., p. 141.

30. In this regard, conciliation essentially means the facilitation of talks and contacts between belligerent parties through the good offices of a neutral envoy, overwhelmingly implied as being an ICRC delegate. See Best, *War and Law*, p. 156; for the text of the respective Conventions, see Chapter 1 Article 11 of the Sick and Wounded GC-IV. The inquiry mechanism was intended to be launched independently and in a coordinated manner by any party contending that a violation of the laws of war had been committed by the belligerents of another party. See Best, *War and Law*, pp. 156–8; for the text of the respective Conventions, see Chapter 9 Article 41 of the Sick and Wounded GC-IV.

31. *Final Record*, vol. 1, p. 55: 'The plaintiff and defendant States shall each appoint one member of the Commission. The third member shall be designated by the other two, and in case they cannot agree, by the President of the Court of International Justice.'

As we have seen in other chapters, biographical details provide for a good starting point from which to explore these issues. Very few institutions provide personnel who could claim as close and intimate a connection with, and internal knowledge of, the intricacies and workings of the ICJ (or, rather, its predecessor: the PCIJ) as could the ICRC. First, there was Max Huber, the chairman of the convention's drafting committee and the undisputed 'father figure' of the entire Red Cross movement.[32] Huber was the former two-time president of the PCIJ and its judge for nine years. He declined a third PCIJ presidential term so as to take up the ICRC presidency in 1928.[33] Second, Paul Ruegger – the incumbent ICRC president from May 1948 onwards, following Carl Burckhardt's highly controversial stint in that role – was a former judge ad hoc at the PCIJ and its registrar under its Swedish judge, Aka Hammarskjöld (himself the brother of the later renowned UN secretary general Dag Hammarskjöld).[34] Thus, at least in terms of sheer knowledge, few institutions had staff who could better understand the implications of providing a good set of 'legal teeth' to the upcoming Geneva Conventions under the ICJ´s purview than the ICRC itself. Intuitively, one would assume that Huber and Ruegger, who were undoubtedly committed humanitarians at heart, would have rejoiced at the idea of member states voluntarily binding themselves to oversight by the world's highest international court. Yet definitely, Huber – and probably Ruegger too – had his good legal and political reasons for opposing the ICJ oversight clause.

At its core, the legal framework on which the ICRC's work was premised was fundamentally non-coercive. The unquestionable respect that the International Committee received from state parties and the moral aura with which it was inherently vested prescribed a very specific, non-public type of diplomacy. In hindsight, the ICRC's diplomatic approach, at least until after the enactment of the 1977 Additional Protocols to GC-IV, certainly had much in common with elements in Joseph Nye's concept of 'soft power' (albeit without the financial-incentive component of that theory).[35] At their very best, both Nye's concept and the ICRC's approach were all about co-option and persuasion. Coercion, especially of a 'top-down' nature, had no place in the ICRC's work; it could not be further from the fundamental diplomatic logic inherent in persuasion. Accession to the Geneva Conventions was, in any case, voluntary. Neither the International

---

32. This was the literal term used by many outside the ICRC with respect to the Red Cross League. Henrik Beer, the secretary of the Stockholm Conference, refers to Huber as 'our revered father figure' – see Beer, 'Jean Pictet and the National Societies', pp. 855–60.

33. Dietrich Schindler, 'Max Huber', *European Journal of International Law*, vol. 18, no. 1 (2007), pp. 81–95, at 93.

34. A state party to a case before the ICJ that does not have a judge of its own nationality on the bench may choose a person to sit as judge ad hoc in that specific case.

35. Joseph S. Nye Jr., 'Soft Power', *Foreign Policy*, no. 80 (1990), pp. 153–71. For a more detailed version, see his book *Soft Power: The Means to Success in World Politics* (New York: Public Affairs Press, 2005).

Committee nor other member states could coerce any specific country to accede to the conventions, nor could they prevent that country from withdrawing from them if it chose to do so. By its very nature, therefore, the ICJ oversight clause was diametrically opposed to the voluntary, legal quality of the ICRC's work since it intrinsically entailed the possibility of compelling a state to do something or to shoulder responsibility for its actions, via imposition by a mechanism outside itself. In Max Huber's legal world, in which all principles were secondary to and circumscribed by the 'sacred cow' of state sovereignty, a coercive mechanism within a convention that was essentially voluntary would be a legal contradiction in terms.

Yet this was now the official position – through its representative, Georges Cahen-Salvador – of France, by far the ICRC's strongest political supporter in the international arena. Thus, before the ICRC could delve into the *legal* difficulties that the adoption of an ICJ mechanism would entail, it had first to deal with the immediate *political* problem of how to convince France to abandon its universalist legal view without alienating the country altogether. As the International Committee prepared its proposed GC-IV texts for the upcoming Stockholm Conference, its rank and file knew full well that this conundrum would have to be dealt with – at the very latest, once it dawned on the French delegation that the ICRC had single-handedly 'gutted' its proposed ICJ oversight mechanism from the draft conventions without its consent.

As mentioned in Chapter 2, seldom did the ICRC experience such a threat to its very existence as it did between the end of the Second World War and the Toronto Conference of 1952. During this time, which Dominique Junod has rightfully termed 'a period of peril', no single event would be as dangerous to it as the Stockholm Conference of August 1948, prior to Count Bernadotte's assassination.[36] The latter's primary objective during this conference was to weaken the International Committee so that, as we saw above, its monopoly role during times of war could be infringed upon – if not assumed outright – by the League of Red Cross and Red Crescent Societies.[37] In his final report to the French foreign minister, Robert Schuman, Albert Lamarle explained the political logic underpinning the rejection of any ideas that would add additional international oversight bodies alongside the ICRC:

> In relation to the question of a Protecting Power, the French delegates at the legal committee [i.e. Lamarle] underscored the vested interest in envisaging the creation of an international organ capable of substituting for a protective power under the hypothetical situation whereby there shall be even [fewer] neutral parties to a future conflict as was the case in the last one [i.e. during the

36. Dominique D. Junod, *The Imperilled Red Cross and the Palestine-Eretz-Yisrael Conflict 1945-1952* (London: Paul Kegan and The Graduate Institute for International Studies Geneva, 1998).

37. Best, *War and Law*, p. 86.

Second World War]. Despite the instance of our delegation, the majority of the delegations did not see the urgency of this project. *Many, so it seemed, estimated that the proposed international organ would compete with the ICRC.*[38]

In essence, then, this argument against any oversight body was of a *political* nature – not a legal one. The message that supporters of the Geneva ICRC were sending to the French ran as follows: given the already prevalent anti-ICRC sentiment, both from the League of Red Cross and Red Crescent Societies and from the Soviet bloc, any proposal that could serve to weaken or undermine the exclusivity of its roles or to substitute for any of its functions – especially during periods of heightened conflict – would be dangerous, and is not to be contemplated at this stage. This was not the time to raise ideas that would curtail any of the ICRC's powers or exclusivity – and the oversight mechanism would have directly encroached upon the ICRC's 'turf' of conciliation and mediation during times of heightened armed conflict. The seasoned Lamarle was well aware of these issues, and hence chose not to pursue his agenda for a universal oversight function within GC-IV during the Stockholm Conference. In any case, Stockholm, being a conference of the Red Cross movement *and not* of member states, was certainly not the appropriate venue at which to discuss this issue. That occasion would arise in any case during the prospective Conference of Plenipotentiaries, which most delegations (most notably that of the United States) wished to speed up.[39] There, France would be among a small, exclusive 'club' of UN Security Council permanent members who wielded much more influence than they could at a non-governmental gathering such as Stockholm. As Lamarle assured Schuman, France had not uttered its last word on this issue:

> In this regard, there will be still a great effort to be made so as to clarify and persuade the other delegations.[40]

While the current author has not managed to find any trace in the archives of an official ICRC request to the French to drop their oversight-mechanism idea during Stockholm (in all probability, such a request would have only been made verbally and not in writing – if at all), the International Committee's *legal* position

---

38. FFMA, new archiving filing numbers, File # 768 SUP/ 159 ter, Lamarle to Schuman, 3 September 1948, pp. 2–3 (italics added).

39. Albert E. Clattenburg Jr., *Department of State Bulletin* (as in n. 30 above): 'In common with the majority of their fellow delegates, the United States Delegation felt that this schedule is too leisurely and will recommend that steps be taken to advance the dates of the meetings as much as possible. ... Modern conditions have created such wide gaps in international law on these subjects that all the delegates to the Geneva meeting were convinced of the urgency of immediate remedial action.'

40. FFMA, new archiving filing numbers, File # 768 SUP/ 159 ter, Lamarle to Schuman, 3 September 1948, p. 2.

against the oversight mechanism was unequivocal. Max Huber fundamentally did not believe in anything that could supersede state sovereignty – the very process that the oversight mechanism involved.

The central organ in the ICRC within which judicial issues were debated was (and still is) the legal commission (*Commission juridique*), which reports directly to the International Committee's directorate. The minutes of the legal commission's sessions are an invaluable source of information for historians and legal scholars alike, since within these deliberations one can observe the authentic positions under which the ICRC as an organization was operating and which served as its legal guidelines. To be sure, the International Committee was well aware, and from very early on, of the full extent of French ideas in favour of the insertion of mechanisms for judicial settlement of disputes within all the conventions being discussed: both the existing conventions (Prisoners, Maritime, and Sick and Wounded) as well as the new Civilian Convention, which was still in the making.[41]

The final session of the ICRC's legal commission before the Conference of Plenipotentiaries, which began in April 1949, was held on Wednesday, 16 March – five weeks prior to the conference's opening ceremony.[42] During this session, several crucial issues were discussed – among them, the ICRC's participation in the Conference of Plenipotentiaries, and the composition of its team; the International Committee's right to take initiative on its own accord; and the ICRC's relations with the Swiss federal authorities. Three pages of that day's minutes were dedicated to the question of oversight of the upcoming GC-IV. The two interlocutors who politely exchanged views on these issues were Max Huber and Jean Pictet:

> Pictet: Concerning the question of the competent international organ, which attitude should we adopt? The best would be without a doubt to declare that at this stage no concrete proposal has been tabled, and [that] when that shall be the case the ICRC would be ready to study that proposal.
> Mr. Cahen-Salvador, it seems, will propose The Hague [i.e. the ICJ] as the 'Competent International Organ'.
> Huber: Thinks that neither the Court [i.e. the ICJ], nor the ICRC could play this role. In any case it seems doubtful to him that States would in any way go beyond the generalities on this subject.
> Pictet: Evoked the possibility of other general measures. The proposed project for the protection of civilians [i.e. the new GC-IV for civilians, yet to be

---

41. A copy of Roussenne's original clause for judicial settlement, which he initially envisaged for the Prisoners of War Convention, is located at the ICRC archive at AICRC – CR- 240/ 3. This is a one-page document marked in the upper-left corner as 'France- Min. Prisonniers, Déportés, Refugiés, – Compte-rendu Mournées détudes des HC – 1945'. The title is then 'P.G. Art. 87' (which would stand for *Prisonniers de guerre*) and the main subtitle is 'Tribunal International'. The use of '1945' seems to be a reference rather than the actual date, as Roussenne only wrote this sometime around July 1946.

42. AICRC File # CR -211, Procès verbeaux, Vol 1, 0 à 35, 16 March 1949.

adopted] is largely based upon The Hague Conventions. Why in this case not replace The Hague Conventions with the Geneva Conventions? That might be the correct question to pose.

Huber: Indicated that The Hague movement had begun *as one of arbitration*. That is a separate and other branch of international law. We are dealing here with the laws of war, of neutrality, and of victims at sea etc. It did not seem to him that the ICRC would be at an advantage to become the guardian of the laws of war. With regard to the Atomic bomb, that subject is already posed to the UN.[43]

The above passage is fascinating in several regards, since it exposes multiple rifts in the interpretation and understanding of the essential character of international humanitarian law. In the first place, it exposes the ICRC's fundamental legal position vis-à-vis the very idea of some form of oversight that could or would ensure nation states' compliance with the Geneva Conventions. Pictet and Huber exhibit here a fundamental divergence in their understanding of how the laws of war ought to function, and in their views concerning the role of the international community and the ICRC in enforcing those laws. Huber cleaved to the view that the application of the laws of war to the behaviour of actual member states was, at its core, voluntary. In the Huberian world view, a state could – at best – be enticed, allured, tempted or, perhaps, persuaded to uphold the laws of war. It could not be forced or compelled into compliance. The latter was precisely what Cahen-Salvador was advocating with his proposed oversight mechanism, which would (hopefully) exert enforcement over a delinquent member state.

We saw earlier in – Chapter 3 – how Pictet and Huber diverged over the application of GC-IV to internal conflict and civil wars, during Pictet's relentless push for the adoption of Common Article 3. The same principal dichotomy was at play here. In Huber's relativist world prior to the Second World War, one could safely advocate for the supremacy of state sovereignty. In the world post Auschwitz and Nuremberg, that was no longer possible. A sensitive reader of the passage above might also sense the generational rift between the two men alongside the obvious (and well-merited) respect that the younger Pictet had for his wartime mentor. Huber was still thinking in terms belonging to the world of the League of Nations; Pictet was already reasoning within a world governed by the UN, which included the possibility (and even desirability) of military enforcement through the powers vested in the Security Council under Chapter VII of the UN Charter – something that would have been unthinkable during Huber's tenure at the PCIJ.

Therein lay another fundamental rift between the two – concerning the ICRC's role in the interpretation, application, maintenance and development of the laws of war. Nowadays, Huber's exhortation that the International Committee could not become the guardian of the laws of war is diametrically opposed to the very

---

43. Ibid., pp. 3–4 (italics added).

essence of what the ICRC is all about. It is, a fortiori, the most prominent guardian, not to say the prime representative, of the laws of war.

One simple example can be drawn from the theme with which this chapter began: the question as to whether Israel's rule over the West Bank constitutes an occupation – and therefore does, in fact, trigger the application of the Fourth Geneva Convention. In its 2004 advisory opinion on the illegality of the separation barrier, the ICJ explicitly drew on the International Committee's own legal determination as to GC-IV's applicability to the West Bank in an exclusive paragraph, which it dedicated to the ICRC's position:

> 97. Moreover, the Court would observe that the ICRC, whose special position with respect to execution of the Fourth Geneva Convention must be 'recognized and respected at all times' by the parties pursuant to Article 142 of the Convention, has also expressed its opinion on the interpretation to be given to the Convention. In a declaration of 5 December 2001, [the] ICRC recalled that it 'has always affirmed the *de jure* applicability of the Fourth Geneva Convention to the territories occupied since 1967 by the State of Israel, including East Jerusalem'.[44]

That the ICJ would explicitly establish its own legal opinion pursuant to what the ICRC would determine as the correct de jure application of the international treaty known as the GC-IV would have been unthinkable to Huber – the PCIJ's former two-term president. Precisely what Huber *did not* think would happen, happened. Half a century after Pictet's and Huber's debate, the ICRC became the central guardian, global custodian and senior legal interpreter of the laws of war.

The ICJ enforcement mechanism at the Geneva Conference of Plenipotentiaries – from April to August 1949

As we saw in 'Omission 4' in the Introduction when the Geneva Conference of Plenipotentiaries opened on 21 April 1949 the blockade of Berlin by Soviet forces – which had begun some ten months earlier, just before the Stockholm Conference – was still in effect. By all accounts, the arrival of the Soviet delegation in Geneva, headed by General Slavin and Platon Morosov, gratified all the delegations present – the Americans and British included.

The account of what transpired at the Conference of Plenipotentiaries with regard to the story of the oversight mechanism carries all the qualities of a gripping legal drama. In its essence, it portrays the rise, refining, approval and then, at the eleventh hour, the sacrifice of the oversight mechanism on the altar of diplomatic unity as the Soviet delegation ultimately positioned it as a 'deal breaker' for its

---

44. ICJ Advisory Opinion of 9 July 2004: Legal Consequences of the Construction of a Wall in the Occupied Palestinian Territory, ICJ Reports 2004, pp. 175–6, § 97.

entire participation in the convention. It is a tale of how the process of negotiation of a given treaty can subvert the overt and explicit intentions of a solid majority of its drafters, and end up with the minority coercing that majority to cave in to its demands for fear of a walkout and the breakdown of talks.[45] A corroborating effect of this drama also concerned the biographical backgrounds of the drafters who headed the key delegations at the helm of the various political camps within the Conference of Plenipotentiaries. In hindsight, it is quite remarkable to see just how many of the world's leading international jurists came to find themselves sitting around – and, in many cases, on opposing sides of – the same drafting tables.

As mentioned above, while the ICRC did most of the groundwork in preparing the drafts for the Plenipotentiaries' Conference, these drafts were by and large shaped and formulated according to the committee's own meta-logical understanding of international law's voluntary nature and the inability to resort to coercive measures within it. This understanding was most certainly shared by the Soviet bloc as a whole. It might even have partially appeased certain realist elements within the US administration who wished to avoid having their actions as occupiers curtailed and scrutinized by external international organs. Yet to the large majority of the drafters, who held firm ideas about the need to universalize the laws of war through providing them with a set of legal teeth, the ICRC drafts that emerged from the Stockholm Conference – and even those that went through the scrutiny of a special group of experts (which included Hersch Lauterpacht) in December 1948 – fell significantly short of the expectation for a real and effective legal mechanism that would ensure compliance.

The two most vocal critics of the International Committee drafts were Denmark´s Georg Cohn, and Paul de La Pradelle, the delegate from Monaco. De La Pradelle was a senior international law professor at Aix-en-Provence, who would later establish the well-known school for political science there ('Sciences Po Aix', as it is known today). He was also – and perhaps more importantly – the son of Albert de La Pradelle, who had been a judge at the PCIJ and a key drafter of its statute back in 1919–20. Concerning the measures for assuring compliance with the proposed new Geneva Conventions in opening drafts, elaborated by the ICRC and provided to the delegates, he wrote,

> The necessity exists to preconceive in one or several Common Articles in the Conventions' text of modes for the peaceful settlement, susceptible both in times of peace as in times of war, of differences and contentions concerning the Convention's interpretation [of] the applications of their dispositions.
>
> This reasonable perspective justified putting in place a complete mechanism for settlements, so as to put definitive sources of technical resources for

---

45. The rise, debates around and eventual rejection of the ICJ enforcement clause – originally tabled as a Danish amendment, proposed as an additional common clause to all three Conventions – have been partially explained by La Pradelle and briefly summarized by Best. See *La Pradelle 1951*, pp. 223–84; and Best, *War and Law*, pp. 142–60.

international disputes in service for the protection of war victims [...] with regard to this ideal scheme, the texts adopted in Stockholm were insufficient. Far from achieving progress over the text of the 1929 Conventions, they marked a regression.[46]

Ultimately, asserted de La Pradelle, 'in the definitive, the contentious dispositions arrived at in Stockholm presented a defective result'.[47]

The defect to which La Pradelle was referring was, of course, the lack of any agreed, structured procedure whereby breaches of the convention could be brought before an objective, international body capable of enforcing its verdict. In an unusually candid exposition to the plenary of the Plenipotentiaries' Conference, the drafting group mandated to work on the text of a proposed oversight clause explained the defect that they were trying to remedy. In their account, the group's members elaborated on the perennial problems of enforcement in international law:

> To deplore the inadequacy of the procedure for settling disputes under international law is almost a commonplace. Whereas national legislations generally provide for the repression of any infringement of their rules, and whereas all legal disputes are settled by the national courts of justice, the dogma of State sovereignty in international law has proved an insurmountable obstacle to any generalization of a system of compulsory international jurisdiction.[48]

Their language is very reminiscent of Cahen-Salvador's words to the French interministerial committee three years before: 'The problem of breach and the corresponding sanction in the case of a violation of the Convention's dispositions are of the most fundamental importance.' In all probability, however, the 1949 wording was a joint effort led by Georg Cohn, the drafter of the Danish amendment who articulated the idea of having an oversight body, together with La Pradelle – with Cahen-Salvador supporting this effort 'from the rear'.

On 4 May, the Danish delegation submitted to the plenary its proposal for an oversight mechanism for the resolution of disputes in all four Geneva Conventions.[49] While the amendment itself was presented by Denmark, it was officially submitted

---

46. Ibid., p. 266.
47. Ibid., p. 271.
48. *Final Record*, vol. 2 B, p. 131.
49. Prior to his submission of the Danish amendment, Georg Cohn informed the Joint Committee (i.e. the committee of the conference designated to deal with Articles common to all four Geneva Conventions) of his intention to submit 'an amendment providing for a procedure for a final solution of disputes which might arise in connection with implementation of these Conventions' without going into the exact details of his proposal for an ICJ oversight clause. Given that this topic was at that early stage beyond the terms of reference of the Joint Committee, the Belgian chairman opted to send this issue to the

on behalf of Austria, Finland, France, Monaco and the Netherlands. This cohort of states was in fact the crux of the 'universalist' political camp present at the making of GC-IV. Cohn, de La Pradelle and Cahen-Salvador would carry this effort to provide some legal teeth to the upcoming conventions through several stages of negotiations over the following three months. The Danish amendment originally read,

> In the event of two or several contracting States differing as to the interpretation or application of the stipulations of the present Convention, or as to the indemnity due to one of their nationals or to one of the persons placed under their protection, or as to other legal consequences arising from infringement of the said stipulations, each of the parties may, in the form of a request, submit the difference to the International Court of Justice set up by the United Nations Charter. The Parties undertake to abide by the decisions of the Court.[50]

That this was an issue of legal universalism was made emphatically clear by Cohn's explanatory words to the plenary:

> The Conventions for the Protection of War Victims which we are engaged in drawing up, constitute a very important piece of international legislation … the practical effect and importance of this essential work of legislation would certainly be consolidated if it were possible to begin creating a competent international body to which the parties concerned could refer in order to obtain an impartial and final solution of difficult and doubtful cases … the difference between vague principles with no binding force … and a prescription of law consists precisely in this; is there, or is there not, in existence an impartial competent body to give a final decision. … The best way of making certain of an objective solution would undoubtedly be to submit cases of this kind to the Permanent Court of International Justice at the Hague, which fulfils all the requisite conditions for taking the necessary decisions.[51]

The erudite, explanatory words of Paul de La Pradelle took over where Cohn left off. La Pradelle explained the Convention's various resolution mechanisms (inquiry, conciliation and judicial enforcement); how these differed from the

---

Special Committee for procedural approval of the entire issue. See *Final Record*, vol. 2 B, p. 23, recording the morning session of 4 May 1949.

50. *Final Record*, vol. 2 A, p. 34 – CDG/MIX.4, 4 May 1949. The original text was in French; this translation was the official one made by the ICRC during the conference's proceedings. The original reference of the Danish amendment was CDG/ Plen.10.

51. *Final Record*, vol. 2-A, p. 33, 6th Plenary meeting, Tuesday 10 May 1949, session of 15:00 hours.

previous Geneva Conventions and why the Danish amendment merited support.[52] After some procedural discussions, and with the agreement of all the delegates, the issue was turned over to a working group within the special committee. This group was tasked with discussing the proposed Danish amendment and, in the event of agreement, with drafting the text that would be presented to the plenary for voting and final adoption. The first full discussion concerning the Danish amendment took place on 23 May. Much of what transpired in that session pointed to cardinal issues that would arise later in the course of discussions during the summer months, up until the endorsement of the Final Act in August 1949.

An established – though unofficial – procedure was for the director of the ICRC's Legal Department, Claude Pilloud, to speak first and present the International Committee's view of the issue under discussion. In line with the policy decisions that the ICRC had adopted during the previous session of its *Commission juridique,* Pilloud put forward his moderately critical evaluation of the Danish amendment:

> It would be the task of the Protecting Powers to seek a solution to the disputes which might arise in connection with the interpretation and application of the Conventions. Referring to the two categories of possible disputes, those which arose in peacetime and those which occurred in wartime, the Representative of the International Committee of the Red Cross noted that the former were a rare occurrence. In connection with the latter, experience had proved that to be effective, the investigation had to follow immediately the violation. Furthermore, Mr. Pilloud pointed out that it was difficult to foresee the international body which in wartime would be capable of functioning with a view to settling disputes.[53]

Pilloud repeated almost verbatim Max Huber's objections to Cahen-Salvador's idea of an ICJ oversight clause. One should read the reference to 'Protecting Powers' for what it is – a plea to assign the ICRC the task of regulating disputes. This, of course, implied remaining within the voluntary, 'soft' boundaries of conciliatory diplomacy, which was the ICRC's trademark. Coercion was not possible within the available tools of international law, certainly not in times of war – so argued Pilloud. La Pradelle was not oblivious to the ICRC's voluntary reading of the character of international law, acknowledging that

> the Protecting Power might be involved in the dispute and that it could not be simultaneously judge and party. [La Pradelle] gave several examples of disputes occurring in peacetime between the High Contracting Parties in respect of interpretation and application of Conventions, and considered that such disputes should be referred to the International Court of Justice.[54]

52. See Statement of de La Pradelle, Ibid., p. 34.
53. Ibid., vol. 2 B, p. 51.
54. Ibid.

And Denmark's position in favour of the ICJ's oversight was stated all the more bluntly by its delegate, Peter Bagge, who spoke directly after de La Pradelle:

> Denmark was of the opinion that arbitration could have value only if it were carried out by a body exercising effective authority, such as the International Court of Justice.[55]

The debate thus far had mostly been dominated by members of the 'universalist' camp, headed by Denmark and Monaco. Now came the turn of the 'realist' members to have their say – and first among these was the US delegate. In a world in which the United States was an Occupying Power, and given the ever-present eventuality of war with the Soviet bloc – war that had so narrowly been avoided in the recent case of the Berlin Blockade, and which was bound to erupt elsewhere[56] – the United States was not in favour of submitting its disputes regarding the application and interpretation of the laws of war to any compulsory jurisdiction. Its representative bluntly advised that

> the United States Delegation would be opposed to the inclusion in the Conventions of any clause of compulsory arbitration. They were in agreement with the proposal to extend the investigation procedure to all the Conventions. However, they were not convinced of the practicability of such procedure in wartime.[57]

In a reply to the Italian delegate, who took the floor after this opening intervention and raised the well-known problem of the ICJ's jurisdiction for non-UN member states who had not recognized its legal authority to adjudicate, the American delegate revealed his final position. The United States drew a stark distinction between periods of war and those of peace, in much the same sense as had initially been outlined by the ICRC's Pilloud. Wartime was no time for ICJ deliberations; peacetime was more conducive to it, provided that one could get all the convention's participants to voluntarily recognize the ICJ's capacity to adjudicate. The UK followed suit in this regard:

> The United Kingdom was in principle in favour of the Danish amendment for the submission of disputes to the International Court in peacetime. She supported the United States Delegate's remarks and suggestions. The United Kingdom Delegation were in favour of the extension to all Conventions of some provision for enquiry. Once the latter had been held, the parties should be bound to bring to an end any violation which had taken place.[58]

---

55. Ibid.
56. As we saw in the Introduction, conflict did, indeed, erupt in Korea the very next year.
57. Ibid.
58. *Final Record*, vol. 2-B, p. 52 (statement of the UK by Guttridge).

Lastly came the position of the Soviet Union, as represented by its seasoned diplomat Platon Morosov. Instead of saying what the Soviet Union would oppose, Morosov stressed the need to unify all the arbitration and oversight clauses so that all four Geneva Conventions carried the same legal mechanism for the resolution of disputes. Rather than speaking against the ICJ, the Soviet delegate proposed inserting a clause requiring the disputed parties to agree on an arbitrator. In tabling this measure, Morosov was opting for some middle ground between the voluntary and coercive aspects of international law. As the chairman designated a working committee to deal with this issue – comprising, under de La Pradelle's chairmanship, Denmark, Italy, Monaco, the UK and the Soviet Union – Morosov performed a diplomatic gesture that would have been unthinkable just a few months earlier at the height of the Berlin Blockade. He graciously requested the chairman to call on the United States and France to take part in this group. The UK seconded his proposal. Thus came into being the working committee in which the ICJ oversight clause would be debated during the conference.[59]

On 10 June, Georg Cohn tabled his corrected amendment, designed to accommodate the request for a distinction between periods of war and peace in the application of the convention's mechanism of referring judicial disputes to an ultimate international body: the ICJ. This new proposal – as with the first Danish amendment, tabled on 4 May – was supposed to be inserted in parallel into all four Geneva Conventions so as to form a coherent and common article for them all.[60] It read:

> In the event of two or several contracting States differing as to the interpretation or application of the stipulations of the present Convention, or as to the indemnity due to one of their nationals, or to one of the persons placed under their protection, or as to other legal consequences arising from infringement of the said stipulations, each of the parties may, in the form of a request, submit the difference to the International Court of Justice set up by the United Nations Charter. The parties take to abide by the decisions of the Court.
>
> During hostilities between the parties in litigation the dispute may not be submitted to the Court before a serious effort has been made to settle it by means of conciliation, good offices or the procedure of enquiry provided in the present convention. In the event of a disagreement as to whether the conditions under which the dispute may be submitted to the Court are, or are not, fulfilled, the Court shall decide.[61]

This text, while certainly satisfying the wishes of the universalist countries (including France, the Netherlands and Belgium), with Denmark at their helm,

59. Ibid.

60. It was meant to be Article 40 in the Sick and Wounded Convention, Article 44 in the Maritime Convention, Article 119 in the War Prisoners' Convention and Article 130 in the Civilian Convention.

61. *Final Record*, vol. 3, pp. 44–5. The original reference of this new amendment was CDG/MIX.22.

also managed to allay the concerns of the United States thanks to the limitation of compulsion to address disputes to the ICJ in times of war. The United Kingdom, in tandem with the United States, supported this view.

Yet the most important objections and starkest opposition to this ICJ oversight clause came from the other 'realist' countries, with the Soviet bloc at their head and Australia following not far behind. These nations rightly stressed a simple yet crucial fact: according to the Statute of the ICJ, only UN member states were automatically bound by the World Court's authority over them (based on Article 35). As the Soviet delegate eloquently explained it, he emphatically

> objected to the addition proposed by the Working Party of a provision per which Parties signatory to the Convention would be bound by the Statute of the International Court of Justice. All countries were not members of the United Nations, and there was a difference between the status of Member countries and Non-Member countries concerning the International Court, as set out in Article 35 of the Statute of the Court. He, therefore, considered that the Working Party's draft went against the stipulations of the United Nations Charter and [was] not within the province of the present Conference.[62]

And the Australian delegate was similarly opposed to the inclusion of any ICJ oversight reference in the Convention text:

> According to Articles 34, 35 and 36 of the Statute of the International Court of Justice, some of the High Contracting Parties to the present Conventions would not be competent to apply to the Court, and the Court would not be competent to receive their applications.[63]

Both Sokirkin (Soviet Union) and Colonel Hodgson (Australia) were essentially repeating an argument very well known to the French delegation – put forward earlier by their own Professor Sibert. Sibert had, back in January 1947, raised objections to an ICJ oversight clause along the very same lines of incompatibility of the ICJ's statute with GC-IV as it stood, since a large portion of the prospected signatories were not UN member states. In a last-ditch attempt to overcome this obstacle, Cahen-Salvador suggested that, as part of the convention text, all states would specially and specifically recognize the ICJ's authority over the upcoming conventions in a voluntary manner:

> The States, Parties to the present Convention, who have not recognized as compulsory *ipso facto* and without special agreement, in relation to any other State accepting the same obligation, the jurisdiction of the International Court of Justice in the circumstances mentioned in Article 36 of the Statute of the Court,

---

62. *Final Record,* vol. 2 B, p. 103, Statement of Sokirkin (USSR), Special Committee 39th session, 11 July 1949.

63. Ibid., p. 104 Statement of Hodgson (Australia).

undertake to recognize the competency of the Court in all matters concerning the interpretation or application of the present Convention.[64]

By relying on Article 36 of the court's statute – which allowed for the extension of its jurisdiction upon all matters, in or outside the UN, so long as this was enshrined in the treaty that the court was supposed to examine – Cahen-Salvador tried to legally outmanoeuvre his Soviet and Australian realist opponents. On 11 July 1949, the text of the second Danish amendment was endorsed by the Joint Committee 10 against 1 with a single abstention, followed by another vote of confidence of 17 against 10 with 10 abstentions.[65] On 22 July, the entire Conference of Plenipotentiaries also endorsed the French text for the compulsory recognition of the ICJ's authority 'without the slightest of difficulties', according to La Pradelle's own testimony, as the delegate of Monaco who also took the vote in that same plenary session.[66]

Morosov's ultimatum and the Soviet veto over UN memberships at the UN Security Council

On Monday, 1 August 1949, during the very last reading of the entire GC-IV text – at the 'eleventh hour' in this process – the Soviet delegate, Morosov, made his move. He raised an outright objection – but *not* to the ICJ oversight clause itself (Article 41). His target was Cahen-Salvador's lopsided attempt to confer an obligatory recognition of the ICJ on all states represented at the Conference of Plenipotentiaries, whether they were UN member states or not. This was Article 41A, which called for the application of Article 36 of the ICJ Statute – as mentioned above.[67] Faithful to the Soviet view all through the Plenipotentiaries' Conference's three months of deliberations, Morosov raised yet again his legal claim that Article 35 of the ICJ Statute precluded the possibility of any reference to it in the Geneva Conventions since it applied to UN member states only. He instead tabled an amendment that demanded the removal of the already-endorsed Article 41A, which would have granted the ICJ an ability to adjudicate over the convention even though (as per Article 35) it could only adjudicate over disputes between two of more UN member states. According to Morosov, the proposed Article 41A was simply and directly in breach of the UN Charter:

> It may be emphasized that the Article under examination does not concord both with the Statute of the International Court of Justice and with the

64. *Final Record*, vol. 2 B, p. 103. See also *La Pradelle 1951*, p. 278.

65. *La Pradelle 1951*, p. 279, summarizing Plenary Session 37 of 11 July 1949, ICRC *in extenso* reference CDG/Mix/SC I CR 39, p. 5.

66. Ibid., p. 279.

67. By now, the accepted French version of the original Danish amendment was known as Articles 41A, 45A and 130D within the Prisoners of War, Sick and Wounded and Civilian Conventions respectively. See *La Pradelle 1951*, p. 32, n. 60.

United Nations Charter. As is well known, according to Article 35 of the Statute of the Court, the latter is open without further proviso to States who recognize this Statute. Moreover, the conditions of access to the Court for other countries are determined, according to the same Article 35, by the Security Council.[68]

Platon Dmitriejevitsj Morosov was one of the most able and respected jurists at the conference. Born in 1906 in St Petersburg, he was a graduate of the prestigious legal institute there (previously headed by the distinguished diplomat and jurist Fyodor Martens). Rising through the ranks of the Soviet central prosecutor's office, Morosov was chosen to lead the Russian prosecution team at the Tokyo War Crimes Tribunal in 1946. Over the same period, he served as the key Soviet jurist during the Genocide Convention's *travaux préparatoires* until their final signature in 1948. He later served as the Soviet delegate on the UN's Human Rights Commission, with a long tenure as deputy director of the Legal and Treaties Department at the Soviet Foreign Ministry. From 1960 to 1968, Morosov served as the Soviet Union's deputy representative to the UN. These were some of the toughest years in international diplomacy, encompassing the Cuba Missile Crisis; the Middle East's Six-Day War; the Congo Crisis and the assassination of that country's first post-independence prime minister, Patrice Lumumba; followed by the death of UN secretary general Hammarskjöld; and, finally, the Vietnam War. In 1970, Morosov was unanimously awarded a seat on the bench of the ICJ as a presiding judge – a token of the unbridled respect that he had garnered, especially within the diplomatic circles of his adversaries in the West.

In Geneva, the UK delegate, Sir Robert Craigie – who, as the former British ambassador to Japan and head of the UN War Crimes Commission, knew Morosov well from their joint work as prosecuting allies at the Tokyo War Crimes Tribunal – pointed to the dangers implicit in the Soviet position to international law writ large:

> The United Kingdom Delegation have always been in favour of some reference to the jurisdiction of The Hague Court in our Convention … Article 35 says, in the first paragraph, 'The Court shall be open to States Parties to the present Statute', and in the second paragraph 'The conditions under which the Court shall be open to other States shall, subject to the special provisions contained in treaties in force that is, treaties in force at the time of the dispute. … Under the words 'subject to the special provisions contained in treaties in force', any such reference in an international treaty seems to us to be perfectly in order.[69]

---

68. *Final Record,* vol. 2-B, p. 365, Statement by Morosov (USSR).

69. *Final Record,* vol. 2 B, p. 368: 22nd plenary meeting – reading of the joint Articles to all conventions, Monday 1 August 1949.

Yet this debate had more to do with power politics than legalities. A revealing insight as to why Morosov was pursuing his line of legal argumentation can be found in the subsequent paragraphs of the *Final Record*:

> The provisions of Article 41A obviously infringe [upon] both the competence of the Security Council and of the General Assembly of the United Nations; it [the Article] overthrows the procedure set up for recognition of the jurisdiction of the Court, by which States which are parties to the Statute, equally with those which are not, must recognize this jurisdiction in accordance with the conditions laid down in Article 36 of the Statute. The Conference is not competent to deal with this point, and has no right to interfere in a matter which in reality comes within the province of the General Assembly and of the Security Council of the United Nations

And finally,

> The Article completely ignores the fact that the States represented at this Conference have not all adhered to the Statute of the International Court. Similarly, the Article ignores the fact that members of the United Nations are, under Article 93 of the Charter, *ipso facto* parties to the Statute, whilst States which are not members of the United Nations may become parties to the Statute, only on certain conditions, to be determined in each case by the General Assembly of the United Nations, upon the recommendation of the Security Council. ... In practice, this provision would have no legal validity, for the simple reason that it violates the United Nations Charter and the Statute of the International Court of Justice.[70]

So there we have it – loud and clear. As per Morosov's reading, the ICJ's competence could only be invoked by UN member states. This was, of course, a completely false reading of the ICJ Statutes, and Morosov immediately stood to be corrected by Georg Cohn – a correction that Morosov himself knew was rightfully and justly called for.[71] There was indeed nothing in the ICJ Statute to prevent an international treaty being subjected to its judicial oversight. That, in fact, had been the whole point of having Article 36 (also known, since the 1920s, as the 'optional clause') inserted in the first place some thirty years previously, during the drafting of the

---

70. Ibid.

71. Ibid., Statement of Georg Cohn (Denmark): 'There is no rule, no principle of international law, which conflicts with the insertion of a clause of this kind in our Conventions; and no one will deny that all the States represented here are entitled to recognize the jurisdiction of the Court. The objections which have been made are therefore devoid of any importance and should not prevent this Conference from including such a clause among the provisions of the Conventions.'

PCIJ Statute (which is identical to the ICJ Statute) in 1920.[72] All the delegates in the room, being long-standing veterans of the League of Nations, knew this full well – including Morosov. Yet the Russian jurist was in fact cloaking a *political* claim with the mask of a legalistic (albeit false) principle.

In August 1949, there was probably no subject more divisive in diplomatic circles than UN membership. One cannot fully understand Morosov's objection to the ICJ's oversight capacity over GC-IV without putting the entire debate into its political and diplomatic context. During the first ten years of the UN's existence, between the San Francisco Conference in 1945 and the Suez Canal Crisis of 1956, the Soviet Union was the sole UN Security Council permanent member to exercise its veto power over Security Council draft resolutions with which it disagreed. All in all, during this period, the Soviet Union used its veto power some fifty-six times. Thirty of these fifty-six instances occurred between 1945 and September 1949 – that is, during the years of GC-IV's *travaux préparatoires*. And out of these 30 vetoes, 14 were made so as to specifically block Western (and Western-backed) countries that had not attended the San Francisco Conference from joining the UN. Of the nine countries whose UN membership the Soviet Union blocked during this period, six (Austria, Finland, Italy, Ireland, Portugal and Sri Lanka) were represented at the GC-IV's Plenipotentiaries' Conference. In short, the Soviet Union was inordinately 'protective' of the balance of member states as admitted to the UN during these years – especially because the Soviet bloc was greatly outnumbered by Western-aligned countries. (This was, we should remember, long before the wave of decolonization that significantly enlarged UN membership, and established the Bandung non-aligned movement.)

In endorsing Cahen-Salvador's Article 41A by forceful majority amendment, the Conference of Plenipotentiaries was in fact attempting to outmanoeuvre the Soviet-instigated partial paralysis of the entire international system – the target of which was precisely UN membership and all its corollaries. The ICJ's ability to adjudicate in world affairs and treaties was one of the most important of those corollaries. Through the introduction of Article 41A, Western states were doing much more than simply providing for an adjudication mechanism for the resolution of disputes in a given treaty (in this case, GC-IV). They were also attempting to impose a course of action that would have negated the force of the Soviet veto power on the UN Security Council, and which could be repeated and replicated in the drawing up of future treaties. This could potentially be a very dangerous development in Morosov's eyes.

The whole point of the veto power established in 1945, as understood by Moscow, was to 'corner' the entire international community in a deadlock that would demand compromises. An endorsement of Article 41A would have let the entire international community 'off the hook', so to speak, and would have reduced its willingness and incentive to seek diplomatic compromise with the Soviet bloc.

---

72. Amos Hershey, 'Judicial Settlement and the Permanent Court of International Justice', *Indiana Law Journal*, vol. 1, no. 2, Article 2 (1926), p. 75, and especially footnote 4.

This compromise was indeed achieved some six years later (and after yet another war – this time, in Korea) when Western and Soviet countries agreed to the so-called UN package deal, which enabled bipartisan membership for countries from both sides of the East–West international political divide. Georg Cohn's attempt to narrow the debate to the specificities of GC-IV was of no use in this situation, as there were much bigger issues at stake.

Morosov had previously demonstrated that he was not intrinsically against some form of international oversight for the regulation of disputes. He had, in fact, suggested widening the application of the enquiry mechanism, initially applying only to the Maritime Convention, to all four conventions and had also consented to a clause that would have nominated an agreed arbitrator between disputing parties. Morosov's view was limited to the humanitarian treaty at hand, of which he was clearly supportive. Yet, in the process of drafting this specific treaty, he was certainly not going to open doors for far-reaching precedents that would weaken the pressure that the Soviet Union could exert through its all-encompassing veto power at the UN Security Council.

The ICJ's weakness during its early years, and Cahen-Salvador's coerced compromise

There was also another perspective, of which many of the delegates were well aware but decided to ignore: the inherent political weakness, and loss of international stature, of the ICJ at this time. The period from 1946 to 1960 could, in fact, be considered as one of the worst in the court's history. In his 1958 course at the Academy of International Law at The Hague ('*Receuil des cours*'), the leading international lawyer Jacob Robinson explained the existential difficulties that the ICJ faced

> the attitude of governments to the use of the International Court of Justice is a disquieting one. The number of accessions to the compulsory jurisdiction clause is thirty-two out of eighty-five members of the judicial community. ... Governments do not seem to be ready to entrust the International Court of Justice with the solution of their justiciable quarrels, while on the other hand, they are not loath to use the Court for their own national policies. That there are large areas of the world where not a single State has accepted the compulsory clause is a disturbing omen for the rule of law in international relations, while, on the other hand, it highlights the readiness to use the law and legal organs for the promotion of selfish political aims on the theory that *jus est ancilla politicae.*[73]

73. J. Robinson, 'The Metamorphosis of the United Nations', in *Collected Courses of The Hague Academy of International Law* ('*Extract of the Recueil des Cours*'), vol. 94 (Leiden: A.W. Sijthoff, 1958), pp. 493–592, at p. 575 (hereinafter 'Robinson – Receuil 1958') (italics in the original). The linguistic formulation employed here dates back to medieval metaphysics,

Summing up, Robinson noted, 'All the friends of the rule of law have observed with great anxiety a tendency to boycott the Court and virtually put it out of business.'[74]

By blocking Article 41A of the proposed GC-IV, Morosov was certainly making a *legal* claim, but one which had *political* implications. The drafters of the UN Charter had, in fact, intended the UN's veto power to perform exactly as the Soviets were utilizing it – namely, in favour of forcing diplomatic compromises over and above the strict tenets of international legality.

Georges Cahen-Salvador was thus faced with two equally unpalatable options. A push forward for the French amendment with the overwhelming majority of votes that he had at his disposal would have, in all probability, triggered a wholesale walkout of the Soviet bloc delegations. This would have resulted either in the collapse of the entire convention-revision project or in the convention remaining a 'dead letter', never to be implemented. On the other hand, acceptance of Morosov's demand to strike out the amendment entirely would have dealt a harsh blow to the universalism that Cahen-Salvador so cherished and would have further contributed to the ICJ's demise. Cahen-Salvador opted for compromise:

> To avoid a lengthy debate which might lead to confusion, and at the same time in the conciliatory spirit which the French Delegation has always shown whenever it was possible, without detriment to the rights of the French State, we now ask you all, both the majority and the minority, to make a conciliatory gesture. … The suggestion which the French Delegation wishes to place before you is the following: to make the present clause mandatory under the Convention would be to hamper an accession which cannot be compulsory, but only voluntary. What would be feasible, would be to recommend delegations, who have not yet signed the Statute of the International Court of Justice, that they should join the international community which recognizes the competence of this High Court; *this should be recommended, but not made an obligation.*[75]

Thus came into being the non-binding resolution mentioned in the opening sections of this chapter, which itself required considerable drafting efforts.[76] As the respected president of the Civilian Convention, Cahen-Salvador was not about to shame Morosov. On the contrary, he made an explicit yet neutral reference to Morosov's legal claim, with which he did not agree, to the superiority of Article 35 of the ICJ's Statute – thus saving the Russian's diplomatic face. In return, Morosov abstained in the final vote over this resolution, rather than object outright to any proposed ICJ reference.

---

whereby philosophy's sole purpose was to service the study of theology – hence, it being 'enslaved' (*ancilla*) for the sake of a supreme ulterior objective – but had no justification in and of itself

74. Ibid., p. 571.

75. *Final Record*, vol. 2 B, p. 367: 22nd plenary meeting – reading of the joint Articles to all conventions, Monday 1 August 1949. Italics added.

76. On the different stages of this resolution, see *La Pradelle 1951*, pp. 282–4.

The afterlife of GC-IV's judicial oversight – Nicaragua, the Rome Statutes and beyond

In 1979, at the height of East–West tensions due to the recent Soviet invasion of Afghanistan, Platon Morosov was unanimously voted, for the second time, to serve another tenure on the ICJ´s bench. In late 1984, the ICJ approved adjudication of the charges brought forward by Nicaragua against the actions of the United States – specifically, the latter's support for the 'Contra' armed rebels against the Communist Sandinista regime. In 1986, the ICJ issued its momentous verdict, *Nicaragua vs. United States*, which is considered a benchmark ruling concerning armed conflict and the application of international humanitarian law within it.[77] Some eight months prior to its final delivery, in September 1985, Platon Morosov resigned from the ICJ bench due to his rapidly deteriorating health, but not before he managed to make his vital contribution to that verdict. The Soviet jurist did not live to observe in full the future legal implications of *Nicaragua vs. United States* as he passed away in May 1986, just one month before the judgement was made public.

It should be stressed that neither the plaintiff (Nicaragua) nor the defendant (the United States) had made any reference whatsoever to GC-IV in their respective motions. Rather, it was the ICJ´s bench, on its own account, that decided to introduce GC-IV and infer its relevance to the case:

> Although Nicaragua has refrained from referring to the four Geneva Conventions of 12 August 1949, to which Nicaragua and the United States are parties, the Court considers that the rules stated in Article 3, which is common to the four Conventions, applying to armed conflicts of a non-international character, should be applied.[78] (Figure 21)

It is worth remembering that the resolution which proposed that states voluntarily submit their disputes over GC-IV to the ICJ implied ipso facto that at the time of its drafting the ICJ in fact had no jurisdiction to adjudicate over this treaty. Morosov – the very person responsible for the restriction of that jurisdiction – was now, some three and a half decades later, sitting on the ICJ's bench. With this in mind, the following passage in the verdict is absolutely astounding:

> There is an obligation on the United States Government, in the terms of Article 1 of the Geneva Conventions, to 'respect' the Conventions and even 'to ensure respect' for them 'in all circumstances', since such an obligation does not derive only from the Conventions themselves, but from the general principles of humanitarian law to which the Conventions merely give specific expression.[79]

77. *Military and Paramilitary Activities in and against Nicaragua (Nicaragua vs. United States of America)* (Merits: Judgment) delivered 27 June 1986, International Court of Justice Reports 14, pp. 113–14 § 216–21, pp. 129–30 §254–6.

78. Ibid., pp. 113–14 § 216–21.

79. Ibid., p. 114 § 219.

Figure 21 Opening day of the ICJ proceedings in the case *Nicaragua vs. United States*, 26 November 1984. Platon Morosov seated on the ICJ bench on the far left. © International Court of Justice – The Hague.

The seventy-nine-year-old Morosov must have been amused by the historical irony vested in this turn of events. During the thirty-six years that had passed since his objections to Article 41A, the world had changed. UN membership had become universalized – which, in turn, had increased the ICJ's influence and stature. More importantly, the GC-IV's Additional Protocols (adopted in 1977) had become an integral part of *international legal custom* – their signing, a rite of passage for any new state wishing to join the community of recognized nations represented in the UNGA.

During the 1990s, the atrocities in the former Yugoslavia and Rwanda were prosecuted in designated international criminal tribunals (the ICTY and the ICTR – the International Criminal Tribunals for those respective nations). In this, they followed the path laid down by the ICJ through its judicial application of GC-IV in the Nicaragua ruling.[80] The 1998 Rome Statutes, which established the ICC at The Hague, provided further grounding for GC-IV's indispensability to the workings of international judiciaries.[81]

80. Theodor Meron, 'Customary International Law Today: From the Academy to the Courtroom', in Andrew Clapham and Paula Gaeta (eds.), *The Oxford Handbook of International Law in Armed Conflict* (Oxford: Oxford University Press, 2014), pp. 37–49, at 40.

81. Ibid., pp. 41–8.

Chapter 9

NON-APPLICATION FROM COLONIALISM
TO TERRORISM: 1950S–2000S

GC-IV as the ICRC's global 'credo'

The discrepancy between GC-IV's universality (all UN member states without exception being party to it) has been and continues to be a point of contestation regarding this treaty's relevance to armed conflicts. GC-IV's ability to ameliorate the conditions of civilians trapped between confronting armed forces has been, and is currently being, continuously put into question.[1] Sceptics, viewing the continued battering of civilians *after* GC-IV's entry into force, have repeatedly questioned its relevance. After all, this treaty, the only such document that all the world's states have signed and ratified, has not always yielded, in the seventy years since its adoption, a cessation of violence against civilians. This conundrum, of a treaty which has been universally ratified yet at times is harrowingly not upheld, has provided some very fertile grounds for ardent realists to question GC-IV's very existence. If states only signed and ratified GC-IV to later absolve themselves from its provisions, they argue, what was the point in having it in the first place? This debate is certainly not limited to GC-IV, and probably applies to a more general discussion on the relevance of international human-rights treaties writ large – and states' compliance with them.[2] While this general debate is far beyond the scope of this study, research into the impacts of human-rights treaties in fact points to the fundamental weakness of the realist-sceptics' criticisms. At the end of the day, such treaties have far more impact than we tend to acknowledge – if only because much of this impact simply goes unnoticed.[3]

---

1. That is, after all the intellectual thrust behind such edited volumes as Evangelista and Tannenwald (eds.), *Do the Geneva Conventions Matter?*

2. One of the most eloquent and interesting advocates of the declining relevance of human-rights treaties in general has been Eric Posner, *The Twilight of Human Rights Law* (Oxford: Oxford University Press, 2014). For a concise articulation of the book's argument, see Eric Posner, 'The Case against Human Rights', *The Guardian*, 4 December 2014. Available at: https://www.theguardian.com/news/2014/dec/04/-sp-case-against-human-rights.

3. Oona A. Hathaway, 'Do Human Rights Treaties Make a Difference?' *Yale Law Journal*, vol. 111 (January 2002), pp. 1935–2042.

However, when one comes to specifically judge GC-IV's importance, this exclusive optic centring on the conduct of states and whether or not they legally abide by GC-IV's treaty provisions is fundamentally skewed and harshly misleading. It completely overlooks the paramount impact that the ICRC's actions have had on civilians the world over during the past seven decades. The International Committee's – and, for that matter, the entire Red Cross movement's – umbilical attachment to this treaty and thus its actual impacts 'on the ground' in the amelioration of human suffering are simply undeniable. A retrospective historical examination of GC-IV's influences, undertaken specifically through a global-historical lens, yields some interesting insights in this regard.

GC-IV, the ICRC and decolonization: Kenya's Mau Mau and Algeria's independence struggle during the 1950s

During GC-IV's earlier drafting stages, the emergence of a global decolonization struggle was already evident to most observers. The preliminary concerning Common Article 3's anticipated applicability to 'civil wars and colonial conflicts' confirmed that GC-IV's drafters were well aware that they were enacting a convention that would render illegal many of the harsh actions to quell colonial rebellions. The idea that Common Article 3's provisions (no torture, no hostages, no summary executions, etc.) were going to become cardinal in upcoming colonial conflicts was voiced by the US delegation at the 1948 Stockholm Conference in rather blunt terms – all the more so given that rebels would probably not reciprocally abide by them with state parties remaining bound irrespective:

> Before we proceed to vote on this Article, I would like to underscore that should the principle of reciprocity not be adopted, all of you who possess colonial territories, you are merely binding yourselves [to this Article's provisions], but you shall not be binding the rebels.[4]

Unsurprisingly, it was none other than Jean Pictet who, speaking directly after the US delegate, poured cold water on his calling in favour of reciprocity, as he stressed that

> introducing the notion of reciprocity would be tantamount to striking out this article all together, since it would give a belligerent the opportunity to absolve

---

4. *Stockholm XVII Red Cross Conference, Debates of the Legal Commission, morning session of Friday 27ᵗʰ August 1948, discussions of Article 2,* Statement by Colonel Mott (US) p. 43. Available from the website of the ICRC Library at: https://library.icrc.org/library/do cs/DOC/18382.pdf.

himself of its dispositions, claiming that his adversary did not abide by them, and therefore these bound him no longer.[5]

With reciprocity now firmly out the picture (it remained so all through the 1949 Geneva Conference of Plenipotentiaries), France and the UK found themselves challenged ever more forcefully as their colonial dependencies began their respective long marches to freedom. In turn, both countries resorted to legal grounds in their attempt to absolve themselves of commitments under GC-IV's Common Article 3. From 1953 onwards, and with ever-growing ferocity, the colonial uprisings in Malaya, Kenya, Algeria and Cyprus placed the UK and France in an unavoidable bind. They were trying to 'keep up appearances' as the de jure harbingers of international human-rights norms post Second World War while de facto resorting to many of the same techniques that the Nazis had applied towards their victims.

As Fabian Klose has convincingly demonstrated, the breadth and depth with which the ICRC engaged, haggled, arm-twisted and many times confronted outright the UK and France over their appalling conduct in Kenya and Algeria was remarkable.[6] Caroline Elkins's Pulitzer Prize-winning account of the UK's system of detention camps in Kenya adds to this story.[7] Additionally, through Raphaëlle Branche's work on the clash between the French state and international bodies during the Algerian war of independence, one begins to get a picture of the considerable pressure that the International Committee exerted on the French government to better its conduct regarding Algerians (both combatants and civilians).[8] Once 'armed', as it were, with the Geneva Conventions firmly on its side, the ICRC considerably stepped up its advocacy powers vis-à-vis the French and British authorities, as it repeatedly attempted to secure concessions in favour of both civilians and combatants.

During both the Kenyan and Algerian liberation struggles, the colonizers refused to acknowledge the Geneva Conventions' applicability – most notably its Common Article 3. In his 1958 analysis of the Geneva Conventions, Gerald Draper, an undisputed international legal authority on the laws of war during the second half of the twentieth century, lambasted France and the UK for their

5. Ibid., statement by Pictet (ICRC), p. 44.

6. On the ICRC's confrontations with the UK government and the British Red Cross over torture, summary execution and the Kenyan system of concentration camps, see Fabian Klose, *Human Rights in the Shadow of Colonial Violence: The Wars of Independence in Kenya and Algeria* (Philadelphia: Philadelphia University of Pennsylvania Press, 2013), pp. 122–60. See also Fabian Klose, 'The Colonial Testing Ground: The ICRC and the Violent End of Empire', *Humanity*, vol. 2, no. 1 (Spring 2011), pp. 107–26.

7. Caroline Elkins, *Imperial Reckoning: The Untold Story of Britain's Gulag in Kenya* (New York: Henry Holt Publishers, 2005).

8. Branche, 'The French Army and the Geneva Conventions during the Algerian War of Independence and After', pp. 161–74.

bending over backwards in search of excuses to avoid applying even GC-IV's most minimal threshold stipulations as stated in its Common Article 3:[9]

> No doubt the first question that will occur is the meaning to be given to the phrase 'armed conflict not of an international character'. Does it cover such conflicts as have occurred in Algeria, Malaya, Kenya and Cyprus? ... Neither France nor the UK has admitted that Art. 3 of the Convention applies ... whatever might be said about the organization of the rebels in these territories, it is significant that several thousand troops were employed to quell the Mau Mau in Kenya, the terrorists in Malaya, EOKA[10] in Cyprus, and no less than 400,000 are employed in Algeria where the rebels are still active. The refusal of France and the United Kingdom to recognize that these conflicts fall within Art. 3 has, it is thought, been determined by political considerations and not by any objective assessment of the facts.[11]

From 1951 onwards, the UK deliberately refrained from ratifying GC-IV so as to avoid being bound by its provisions. In fact, it only did so in late September 1957, in tandem with the relative waning in ferocity of Kenya's Mau Mau insurgency and Britain's partial withdrawal from Cyprus, where it also came up against the ICRC over its conduct in the armed conflict on that island. Notwithstanding its signing up to GC-IV's treaty provisions, alongside its ratification of this treaty in 1957, the

---

9. Sir Gerald Draper (1914–89) served in the British armed forces during the Second World War; was a member of the UK delegation to the Geneva Conference of Plenipotentiaries and, later, as a law professor at the University of London, became one of the most respected experts on the Geneva Conventions. He continued a long-standing relationship with the ICRC, which on several occasions conscripted him for internal and confidential legal studies that it required. One such study, which would certainly interest future researchers, concerns the question as to whether the UN's own peacekeeping forces were also bound by the Geneva Conventions and could be held accountable in the event of their grave breach of the same. This study, which Draper undertook at the ICRC's request, concerned the UN's own first fully armed peacekeeping mission – that in Congo in 1960 – and, although unfortunately beyond the scope of this volume, it is nevertheless worthy of further research. For Draper's study on behalf of the ICRC, see ACICR File # B AG 202 000-003.09, *Etude de G.I.A.D. Draper sur l'application des conventions de Genève par les forces des Nations Unies, 12/06/ 1961 – 29/ 01/1966*. For Draper's full bibliography and works, see Michael Meyer and Hilaire McCoubrey, *Reflections on Law and Armed Conflict: The Selected Works on the Laws of War by the Late Professor Colonel G.i.A.D. Draper, OBE* (The Hague: Kluwer Publishers, 1998).

10. Ethniki Organosis Kyprion Agoniston – the Greek-Cypriot nationalist guerrilla organization that fought for the end of British rule in Cyprus.

11. Draper, *The Red Cross Conventions*, p. 15, n. 47.

Figure 22 Kenya's Dagoreiti Centre for Kikuyu Orphans. UK National Archives, Kew, London, file # INF 10/156 part 9, British Official Photograph Kenya, 967–64/362–73.

UK did not forget to include its reservation against Article 68's prohibition of the death penalty, stating that

> the United Kingdom of Great Britain and Northern Ireland reserve the right to impose the death penalty in accordance with the provisions of Article 68, paragraph 2, without regard to whether the offences referred to therein are punishable by death under the law of the occupied territory at the time the occupation begins.[12] (Figure 22)

The UK, which by November 1956 had already executed 1,015 Kenyans on various charges related to the Mau Mau uprising, was determined to carry on its carnage notwithstanding its own citizenry's appeals in both Kenya and London.[13]

12. Reservation made on behalf of the UK by Sir Robert Craigie, UK delegate to the 1949 Geneva Conference of Plenipotentiaries. See United Nations Treaty Series – UNTC vol. 75 (I), 1950, 970–73, p. 450. Available at: https://treaties.un.org/doc/Publication/UNTS/Volume%2075/v75.pdf.

For the UK's ratification itself, see UNTC vol. 278, 1957, I. No. 4017–4030, II. No. 574, p. 267, n. 1. Available at: https://treaties.un.org/doc/Publication/UNTS/Volume%20278/v278.pdf.

13. See, for example, the plea by D. W. Chatteley to the ICRC in Geneva on behalf of a Kenyan named Deden Kimathi, who was destined for execution by the British colonial government in Kenya, at ACICR file # B AG 225 108 -002, letter from D. W. Chattley to the ICRC dated 28 November 1956, with the reply by P. Gaillard of the ICRC dated 4 December 1956. Gaillard informs Chatteley that indeed the ICRC had approached both Her Majesty's government and the British Red Cross with a request to visit the Kenyan detention camps and had been rejected. Tellingly, however, the ICRC did take the time to forward a copy of Chattley's appeal to Lady Limerick, vice chairman of the British Red Cross.

In contrast, France had been one of the very first countries to ratify GC-IV, on 28 June 1951. After all, it was one thing for the UK – in many ways the Civilian Convention's nemesis – to withhold its accession to this treaty, yet for France, which more than any other country had helped to 'father' GC-IV and advocated for it in front of other nations, withholding ratification on grounds of colonial-political expediency was out of the question.

Furthermore, from a strictly legal point of view France probably had a marginally better argument than the UK as to why it would not apply the convention to Algeria. Tunisia and Morocco were French *protectorates*, which by 1954–5 received their independence thanks in no small part to Pierre Mendes France, by then the French prime minister. In contrast, Algeria was not a French protectorate, but rather an integral territorial part of the state, comprising three local French *départements*. Being an integral part of metropolitan France, then, the stipulations of international law simply did not apply to Algeria – at least, not in the eyes of most French people. The UN Charter was absolutely clear on this matter as well: international treaties simply had no bearing on domestic affairs, and the 'events' in Algeria were no more than criminal incidents to be dealt with by the French police – so they argued.[14]

Yet for all their legal differences, there was one factor that applied equally to Algeria and Kenya. This was the ICRC's unbridled insistence that it had the right and the duty to intervene in these conflicts, and that GC-IV's provisions applied to them both. As both Klose and Branche have convincingly demonstrated, the International Committee did everything in its power in its attempts to persuade both the British and French governments to apply GC-IV's provisions, or at the very least its Common Article 3, to Kenya and Algeria. In stark contrast to its conduct vis-à-vis Jewish civilian victims of the Holocaust during the Second World War, or concerning Jewish POWs of the Allied armed forces, the ICRC haggled, negotiated, petitioned and re-submitted its petitions in favour of both the Mau Mau and Algeria's FLN (National Liberation Front) fighters. When the

---

14. Algeria technically comprised three *départements* of the French metropole and was part of the French Republic for a longer and more continuous period of time than Strasbourg, Alsace and Lorraine, which were under German rule from 1870 until the end of the First World War. While Klose is certainly right to point to multiple points of intellectual dishonesty inherent in France's '*Ici C'est La France*' position vis-à-vis Algeria, one must not make the methodological error of anachronism here. The fact that France's geographical image in the minds of most of today's readers is that of the mainland form of *l'Hexagone*, for the average French person in the early 1950s Algeria was probably more a part of metropolitan France than Strasbourg, which was under French rule for no more than two decades during the interwar period before reverting to German hands in 1940. Klose has a somewhat problematic reading of what, in all truth, the three Algerian 'departments' of France actually consisted of – in the psyche of the average French person – granted the obviously unacceptable colonial overtones here. See Klose, *Human Rights in the Shadow of Colonial Violence*, 'The Myth of the Three North African Departments', pp. 78–84.

UK government refused access to its delegates, the ICRC pressured the British Red Cross and tacitly cooperated with British MPs who attempted to hold their own government accountable for what was happening in Kenya. When the French government argued that Algeria was a domestic affair, the International Committee moved forward with its idea of materially applying Common Article 3's provisions while acknowledging the French position regarding non-application. After much pressure, and as the Algerian issue toped the agenda of the 1958 UNGA, the ICRC managed to secure French army general Salan's agreement to accord FLN combatants the status of POWs – albeit without referring to the matter under these legal terms. From there on, the ICRC began to exercise growing visitation rights into French detention camps in Algeria.[15]

In short, the International Committee was now reinvigorated in its purpose and strengthened in the affirmation of its humanitarian mission, as evident in its aforementioned 'head-on' engagements with the UK and French governments concerning their conflicts in Kenya and Algeria. This stood in stark contrast to the conciliatory manner with which it had approached Nazi Germany's treatment of European Jews a mere decade earlier.

The internationalization of human rights post Second World War and GC-IV's intertwining with other contemporary international legal instruments

That the ICRC – and, more generally, the entire Red Cross movement – would rapidly embrace the revised Geneva Conventions and highlight the importance of the newly achieved Civilian Convention was to be expected. Yet the political and public-opinion leverage that the International Committee could now exert on abusive governments, from the 1950s onwards, had as much to do with the interaction between the new Red Cross Conventions and the parallel adoption of other international legal instruments. The latter included the Universal Declaration of Human Rights (1948), the Genocide Convention (1948), the Refugee Convention (1951), the Convention on Statelessness (1954) and, on the regional level, the European Convention on Human Rights (1950). The cumulative effect of the coming into force of these multilateral humanitarian and human-rights instruments served as an amplifier for the ICRC's efforts to reign in abuses by delinquent governments.

Bearing this rise of multilateralism in mind, one can better grasp the actual *difference* between the cases of Algeria and Kenya. In the former, the FLN

---

15. On the ICRC's 'Salan Accord', see Francoise Perret and Francois Bugnion, 'Between Insurgents and Government: The International Committee of the Red Cross's Action in the Algerian War (1954–1962)', *International Review of the Red Cross*, vol. 93, no. 883 (September 2011), pp. 707–42. The accord itself, and the French government's documents attesting to it, are annexed to this article on pp. 737–42 (Appendixes 1–4).

managed to harness this new international reality in its favour, topping the agenda of the UNGA repeatedly from 1957 onwards and thus humiliating the French political and diplomatic establishment. By contrast, the Kenyan Mau Mau uprising failed to muster a comparable level of international influence.[16] Building on the strong support of one John Fitzgerald Kennedy (at the start of this process, still a US senator), both on Washington's Capitol Hill and at the UN in New York, by the early 1960s, as the new Kennedy administration began to assume its executive duties, the pressure on France shifted from weak diplomacy to painful economy. Because of Algeria, Kennedy (now the US president) decided to cut his country's military aid to France and refused to renew US international loan guarantees that underpinned the French economy.[17]

Another front on which diplomatic pressure was exerted, both on France and the UK, was in the Council of Europe through the provisions of the European Convention on Human Rights (ECHR), concluded in November 1950. With the French jurist René Cassin being one of the European Convention's founding fathers (in parallel to his membership of the UN Commission on Human Rights), France found itself in the awkward position of being unable to ratify the ECHR – and this, ironically, with the Council of Europe itself being seated in the French city of Strasbourg. The UK, which had ratified the European Convention in 1951, continued to argue that it did not apply to Kenya thanks to its Article 15, which allowed for its suspension in cases of national emergency.[18] In another ironic twist, the original author of the ECHR's Article 15 was none other than the UK's own delegate to that treaty's *travaux préparatoires*, Maxwell Fyfe, who, four years earlier, had served as the UK's chief prosecutor at the Nuremberg trials of Nazi war criminals.[19]

It is within this myriad of international human-rights treaties, and the various attempts by European colonial powers to invoke exceptions and derogations on account of emergency clauses, that one must understand the additional pressure that the ICRC brought to bear as it invoked the applicability of GC-IV's Common Article 3 to Kenya and Algeria.[20] From 1956 onwards, the FLN, which had insisted all along that the Geneva Conventions applied to its Algerian struggle, decided to abide by their provisions concerning its captured members of the French armed forces. The latter were independently accorded POW status by the National Liberation Front, notwithstanding the fact that France continued to summarily execute FLN fighters that it had captured. This seizing of the moral

16. Klose, *Human Rights in the Shadow of Colonial Violence*, pp. 193–242.

17. Horne, *A Savage War of Peace*, p. 463.

18. Elkins, *Imperial Reckoning: The Untold Story of Britain's Gulag in Kenya*, p. 96.

19. J. F. Hartman, 'Derogations from Human Rights Treaties in Public Emergencies', *Harvard International Law Journal*, vol. 22, no 1 (1981), pp. 4–5.

20. On the specific usage of emergency clauses in both Algeria and Kenya, see Klose, *Human Rights in the Shadow of Colonial Violence*, pp. 92–137.

high ground by the FLN through its unilateral application of the Geneva POWs Convention put France in an untenable international position, and placed it further on the diplomatic defensive. When, in 1959, the FLN independently declared the establishment of the Algerian Red Crescent, despite vocal French objections, and when the international Red Cross movement embraced and recognized its new Algerian National Society, France's diplomatic weakness merely gathered pace.[21] By 1960, as the ICRC's own explosive report on the rampant use of torture by the French state in Algeria made the headlines of the respected Paris-based daily newspaper *Le Monde*, there was little diplomatic face left for France to save.[22]

The impacts of GC-IV's internationalization also went beyond the aforementioned colonial uprisings. While the 'West' was being confronted with its human-rights béte noire in its continued colonial rules over Algeria, Kenya, Congo, Indonesia and the like, the Eastern bloc was engaging in its fair share of top-down oppressive actions over civilians. In 1953 as the Soviet Union invaded East Germany, and in 1956, as it invaded Hungary, and while Russian forces murdered, tortured and summarily executed thousands of Hungarian civilians, the ICRC's appeal to apply GC-IV's provisions vis-à-vis civilians was overtly refused by the Soviets. These events notwithstanding, the ICRC's advocacy efforts abroad yielded some rather remarkable results.[23] As roughly 10 per cent of the Hungarian population fled to Western Europe as refugees, it was in no small part thanks to the ICRC's efforts that a large number of them received Swiss and Austrian rights of asylum.[24] Given the Swiss government's very close relationship with the ICRC, one would be hard pressed to separate that government's favourable conduct towards Hungarian refugees from the clear and open advocacy appeals undertaken by the International Committee during this period.

21. Raphaëlle Branche, *Prisonniers du FLN*, Paris: Payot 2014, pp. 137–65. For an explanation by Branche of the creation of the Algerian Red Crescent and its relationship with the delegitimation of French rule there, see https://www.youtube.com/embed/GTaPm UsYx04 , Minutes 10:30–11:15.

22. For the story of how the ICRC's confidential report on French use of torture in Algeria came to light in *Le Monde*, see Luis Lema, 'Torture en Algérie: le rapport qui allait tout changer' in *Le Temps* 19 Août 2005. An English translation of this French article is available from the ICRC website at: https://www.icrc.org/eng/resources/documents/article/ other/algeria-history-190805.htm.

23. Mark Kramer, 'Russia, Chechnya, and the Geneva Conventions, 1994-2006: Norms and the Problem of Internalization', in Matthew Evangelista and Nina Tannenwald (eds.), *Do the Geneva Conventions Matter?* (Oxford: Oxford University Press, 2017), pp. 161–74.

24. On the role of Red Cross societies in the absorption of Hungarian refugees post-1956, see Michael Marrus, *The Unwanted: European Refugees from the First World War through the Cold War* (Philadelphia: Temple University Press, 2007), pp. 360–1.

Territorial arguments for non-application: Israel 'crosses a legal Rubicon' in Palestine

For half a century now, Israel's official position vis-à-vis the legal status of the OPT has rested on a structural ambiguity that its legal scholars laboured tirelessly to construct. The condition of the 'occupied territories' (this term itself being contested by Israel) was to remain perpetually undefined and in a legal limbo – a sui generis case, to which none of the world's universal international laws would fully apply – so hoped Israel. Its presence in the OPT was thus stoically Ciceronian: *tamquam ex hospitio, non tamquam ex domo* ('as if from a temporary hostel, not from a permanent home').[25] As scholars such as Eyal Gross and gifted practitioners such as Michael Sfard have both recently (and convincingly) demonstrated, the deep legal ambiguities associated with military occupation's conceptual bearings have most certainly aided Israel in her continued forceful appropriation of the West Bank, East Jerusalem and the Golan.[26]

As Israel came to consolidate its grip over the OPT, towards the end of the 1960s, the idea that forceful conquest cannot give birth to legitimate territorial title over the conquered area was still not entirely accepted by all legal scholars. In 1971, ten years prior to the commencement of his twenty-year period on the ICJ's bench (the last three as its president, 1997–2000), US jurist Stephen Schwebel indeed joined Georg Schwarzenberger and Michael Bothe in their partial acceptance of the acquisition of territory by force. Only one year after the UNGA's unanimous endorsement of Georg Cohn's principle that 'the territory of a State shall not be the object of acquisition by another State resulting from the threat or use of force', Schwebel emphatically stated that since[27]

> the West Bank, East Jerusalem, and Gaza were not part of the territory of a State in the contemplation of the law, then that principle would not be violated by Israeli occupation of portions of the West Bank, East Jerusalem and the Gaza Strip.[28]

In the face of these differing, contested and non-uniform views of what Israel's 1967 conquest really amounted to, there was, however, at least one international

---

25. Cicero, *De Senectute* [On Old Age], p. 84.

26. Eyal Gross, *The Writing on the Wall: Rethinking the International Law of Occupation* (Cambridge: Cambridge University Press, 2017), pp. 17–52. Michael Sfard, *The Wall and the Gate: Israel, Palestine, and the Legal Battle for Human Rights*, New York: Metropolitan Books, 2018, pp. 37–52.

27. UN General Assembly, Res. 2625, 24 October 1970, *Declaration on Principles of International Law concerning Friendly Relations and Co-operation among States in accordance with the Charter of the United Nations*. Available at: http://www.un-documents. net/a25r2625.htm

28. Symposium on Human Rights in Time of War, Statement by Stephen Schwebel in response to Boyd and Greenspan, *Israel Yearbook on Human Rights*, vol. 1 (1971), p. 375.

body that was emphatic, unrelenting and clear in its legal position vis-à-vis the nature of Israel's conquest of the West Bank and Gaza – the ICRC. From its very first engagements with Israeli military forces in the aftermath of the Six-Day War, and consistently over the past half-century, the International Committee has always maintained that the Palestinian territories are occupied, that GC-IV's terms apply to them in full and that Israel's settlement policy explicitly violated GC-IV's Article 49 paragraph 6. Documents from Israel's state archives overwhelmingly confirm the consistency of the ICRC's demands of the country to recognize GC-IV's applicability, along with the latter's continuous refusal to do so.

The ICRC first approached the Israeli government in May 1968 with an official brief requesting it to explicitly recognize GC-IV's applicability to the OPT. The government officially responded to the International Committee in June that year, saying that it would *practically* apply GC-IV's provisions where possible, yet would not *officially* recognize its applicability so as not to prejudicially weaken its bargaining position vis-à-vis Arab countries in any upcoming final-status negotiations over the future of these territories.[29]

In the winter of 1971, the ICRC's leadership undertook a coordinated visit to the Middle East, with its highest dignitaries simultaneously visiting Israel, Egypt, Jordan and Syria in an effort both to broker a four-way POW exchange and to try and get Israel to recognize GC-IV's applicability to the OPT. Max Petitpierre – the former president of the Swiss Federal Council, and the person who back in 1949 had presided over GC-IV's Plenipotentiaries Conference – was sent to Cairo. Frederic Siordet, who had headed the International Committee's delegation to the 1949 Plenipotentiaries Conference, took on the visits to Damascus and Amman.[30] Victor Umbricht – accompanied by Michel Marten, who had headed the ICRC's delegation in Israel–Palestine during and after the Six-Day War – visited Jerusalem.[31] In its top-secret briefing paper in the run-up to Umbricht's

29. See the Israeli Foreign Ministry's memorandum entitled 'Background paper for the forthcoming visit of Victor H. Umbricht, Member of the Presidency of the ICRC, 4-8 December 1971', p. 3 point 1. Uncovered at the Israeli State Archives thanks to the efforts of Akevot – the Israeli centre for the research on the occupation (hereinafter '*Umbricht Document*'). Available from the Akevot website at: https://www.akevot.org.il/en/article/umbricht-brief

30. Ibid., p. 1.

31. Ibid., p. 5. The Israeli Foreign Ministry paid Mr Marten a unique complement in this top-secret report, seldom attributable to functionaries of international organizations who are habitually seen as *a priori* hostile to Israel, stating that 'Mr. Umbricht will be accompanied by the director of the ICRC's Middle East department Mr. Michel Marten. Mr. Marten served in Israel as head of the ICRC's delegation here in 1967-68 and is very well versed in the affairs of the region. Despite his stringently harsh neutrality, as befitting a Swiss citizen who is a senior official in the ICRC's administration, his approach to Israel is warm and positive.'

arrival, the Israeli Foreign Ministry spelt out quite clearly the reasons for Israel's refusal of GC-IV's application:

> Since the Six-Day War, the ICRC has been consistently pressuring us to declare our willingness to apply the Geneva Convention for Civilians. Due to the following principal grounds, we refuse to apply this convention to the territories:
>
>   a. Our actions in Jerusalem since June 1967 stand in stark contrast to this Convention's written letter
>   b. This Convention enables for the nomination of an international protective power *in lieu* of the ICRC
>   c. This protective power would delve and interfere into issues we have no desire of interference thereof.
>
> The Arabs also refuse to nominate a protecting power, since this would officially imply their recognition of the State of Israel.[32]

The most telling part of the above-quoted paragraph lies in its point 'a'. Israel had officially applied its laws to East Jerusalem thus forcefully incorporating this part of Palestine into its own territory, in direct opposition to GC-IV's very spirit, as was evident from its Article 47. By taking this step, Israel had crossed a legal 'Rubicon', which considerably diminished the possibility of it applying GC-IV to the other territories that it occupied. With the benefit of historical hindsight, Israel's non-application of GC-IV to East Jerusalem, and most probably from there on to the entire West Bank (the land most biblically associated with its psyche), seems to have been less of an 'historical accident'. Nor was it solely due to its desire to wait for Arab countries to come and sit around the peace-negotiating table with it. Rather, it was probably based on the premeditated assumption that Israel would never be able to apply GC-IV to the West Bank in the first place, since it was already legally 'too far gone' once it had forcefully territorially appropriated East Jerusalem merely two weeks after that area's conquest. In short, from day one of the now fifty-year-old occupation of Palestine, Israel's senior policy makers knew full well that they were legally 'in the red' vis-à-vis GC-IV's provisions.

In theory, Israel could have excluded East Jerusalem from GC-IV's purview and applied this treaty to all the other territories that it had conquered (the West Bank, Gaza, the Sinai Peninsula and the Golan Heights). Its choice not to do so has given rise to the suspicion that this non-application of GC-IV to any of these territories was due to some sort of predetermined *a priori* plan to help it retain these territories in perpetuity.

Nevertheless, these views of an alleged premeditation on Israel's part were proved decisively wrong once it retreated from the Sinai and evacuated all its settlements there, following the Egyptian–Israeli Camp David Peace Accords of

---

32. *Umbricht Document*, p. 3 point 1, sub-points א-ג.

1978.[33] These ideas of premeditation were further refuted when Israel once again retreated unilaterally and evacuated its settlements – this time, in Gaza in 2004. By contrast, with the appropriation of East Jerusalem (1967) and the Golan Heights (1980), Israel did decide to actively disregard both international law and world opinion. In short, the reality seems to have been much more complex than some simple notion of Israeli premeditation for the retention of all its 1967-conquered territories.

Some of the fiercest challenges to GC-IV's applicability have been mounted by governments on account of the fact that they were fighting what they collectively termed as 'terrorists', to whom – so they claimed – GC-IV's protective provisions, including those of its universally recognized Common Article 3, did not apply. While this argument is certainly not new and goes back to the colonial conflicts in Algeria and Kenya, subsequent uses of the terrorism argument fundamentally differed from colonial-era arguments due to their contexts. In contrast to the long-standing presence of the colonizers in their held territories, these new non-applicability arguments were being drawn up by Western countries that invaded territories from where fighters accused of 'terrorism' originated. The most famous (or rather, infamous) of these cases concerns the United States torturing its ex-territorially held inmates in Guantanamo Bay, south-eastern Cuba – detained individuals captured in Afghanistan and Iraq. Another famous case is the torture of Iraqis in Abu Ghraib prison in Baghdad. A third, less known yet equally important, example concerns Israel's occupation of Lebanon (1982) and its treatment of captured combatants there.

The case of the US administration's torture programme for terrorism-suspected detainees post 9/11 has been well documented by Philippe Sands.[34] Following the attacks on the World Trade Center's Twin Towers in New York, the administration's legal counsellors, John Yoo and Jay Bybee, issued their legal opinions in favour of the torture of detainees suspected of terrorism. Yoo and Bybee explicitly claimed

---

33. The literature on the Israeli–Palestinian conflict, and the history of Israel's occupation, is voluminous. For the arguments of supporters of the view that Israel was inherently predetermined in its colonial desire to keep all of the territories it occupied, irrespective of the fact that the history of the past five decades has proven its arguments quite wrong, see Maxime Rodinson, *Israel: A Colonial-Settler State?* (New York: Pathfinder Press, 1973). Rodinson's followers, who have been far less eloquent or original as he initially was back in the late 1960s, include Lorenzo Verancini, *Israel and Settler Society*, London: Pluto Press, 2006. Supporters of the incremental approach to this history, which seems far more plausible to the current author, include the account of the first Israeli administrator of the occupied territories, General Shlomo Gazit: *Trapped*, Tel-Aviv: Zmora Bitan Publishers 1999 (in Hebrew), and the majestic (and probably historically most accurate) account by Gorenberg, *The Accidental Empire*.

34. Sands, *Torture Team*. See also Philippe Sands, *Lawless World: The Whistle-Blowing Account of How Bush and Blair Are Taking the Law into Their Own Hands* (New York: Penguin Books, 2006), pp. 155–70, 205–29.

that these suspects were not covered by the stipulations of the GC-III, and were not even eligible for protection under its non-derogable Common Article 3.

In response to a plea by a tortured detainee in Guantanamo Bay, the US Supreme Court was eventually compelled to adjudicate as to whether the Geneva Conventions indeed applied also to captured terrorists (or suspects of terrorism) and, more importantly, whether the US government could absolve itself from its international obligations under Common Article 3. In *Hamdan vs. Rumsfeld* (2006), the court did just that. Not only did the court stipulate that the United States was bound by GC-IV's stipulations against torture but it also found, subsequently, that the US government lawyers who advised in favour of torture were potentially liable for criminal indictment.[35]

Equally interesting are the Israeli Supreme Court's decisions concerning both the rights of incarcerated Palestinian fighters and Israel's overall responsibility for what took place within the areas it occupied in Lebanon, and with regard to GC-IV's applicability there. Following Israel's 1982 invasion, which saw a third of Lebanon under Israel's military rule (including the capital city, Beirut), two instances triggered the Israeli High Court's opinion as to whether or not Lebanon was indeed occupied territory according to GC-IV. The first came in the shape of an investigation commission (the 'Kahan Commission') concerning the massacres of Palestinian civilians in the Sabra and Shatila refugee camps in West Beirut in September 1982.[36] The second, and somewhat less known, instance concerned an appeal (*HCJ 102/82*) by Israeli human-rights lawyers Lea Tzemel and Avigdor Feldman in favour of some 4,500 incarcerated Palestinian detainees who had been placed in administrative detention without trial at a makeshift detention facility named Ansar Prison near Jezzine in central Lebanon.[37]

35. Stephen Gillers, 'The Torture Memo: How Could Two Really Smart Government Lawyers Authorize Torture in Arguments That Have No Foundation in Law?' *The Nation*, 9 April 2008. Available at: https://www.thenation.com/article/torture-memo.

36. Between 16 and 19 September 1982, Lebanese Christian Phalangist forces entered the Palestinian refugee camps of West Beirut, which were surrounded by the IDF, and massacred between 1,000 and 2,500 civilians there, significant portions of whom were women and children. For a balanced and authoritative account of the massacres, see Robert Fisk, *Pity the Nation: Lebanon at War* (Oxford: Oxford University Press, 2001) (updated edition), pp. 459–301.

37. HCJ 102/ 82 *Lea Tzemel* vs. *Minister of Defence and the Commander of Ansar Camp*, judgement delivered 13 July 1983. For a good English translation of this High Court ruling, see *Palestinian Yearbook of International Law*, vol. 1 (Nicosia: Al Shaybani Society of International Law Ltd., 1984), pp. 164–75. Available also from Google Books at: https://books.google.it/books?id=p73lu61ZnCYC&pg=PA165&lpg=PA165&dq=HCJ+102/82&source=bl&ots=FxKJnE9Ze5&sig=pu4MTVbBYZKrgkQa-Aa9fsjtx_s&hl=de&sa=X&ved=2ahUKEwjuwZLfxpTdAhWOl4sKHcRTDh0Q6AEwAHoECAAQAQ#v=onepage&q=HCJ%20102%2F82&f=false.

The same legal question lay at the heart of both the Kahan Commission and *HCJ 102/82*: What was the responsibility of a military occupying power once it had established its firm grip on a certain area within an armed conflict? While *HCJ 102/82* was specifically targeted to ask the court whether and to what extent GC-IV indeed applied to the Palestinian detainees in Lebanon, the Kahan Commission made no explicit mention of the Geneva Conventions in its report. It did, however, choose to go down the route of referring to their basic principle of the occupier's overall responsibilities, interestingly enough – drawing heavily also from the principles of religious Jewish and Talmudic law.[38]

38. The Kahan Commission did not find Israeli officials directly responsible for the Sabra and Shatila massacres. It did, however, find Defence Minister Ariel Sharon, IDF chief of staff Raphael Eitan and General Amos Yaron responsible indirectly for them. In a fascinating reference to the general responsibility of magistrates according to ancient biblical Jewish Law, the Kahan Commission made what is probably the first full reference to the principle enshrined in the Geneva Conventions that renders an occupier fully responsible for all that takes place within their occupied territory, and especially towards the deaths of innocent civilians in that territory. According to written Jewish Law as prescribed by the Torah, under no circumstances can a state's magistrates avail themselves of their responsibilities when the corpse of a dead person is uncovered, and the circumstances of that death are unknown. This stipulation appears in the Bible in Deut. 21:6-7. Upon discovery of a dead person whose circumstances of death could not be determined, the Israelite authorities were compelled to measure the distance to the closest city. The magistrates of that city, being its elders, were then compelled to take a young heifer, bring it down to the stream, slaughter it and wash their hands, swearing that their hands did not spill the dead person's 'clean blood'. The ritual is not haphazardly placed in the Torah, but rather *directly relates to the circumstances of war*. Deuteronomy 21 follows directly upon Ch. 20 of that book, which stipulates the laws of war of both *jus ad bellum* and *jus in bello* in the Torah. The reason the stipulation of the beheaded heifer follows directly upon the laws of war concerns the fact that in the ancient world many battles would end with the combatants lying dead in the field – unrecognized. The ritual came to clearly demarcate the distinction between civilians of the closest city to that battlefield, and the combatants in it.

Consistent with the constitutional construction of the Israeli judicial system – a hybrid of British Common Law, which existed during the British Mandate for Palestine prior to Israel's independence, and Jewish Religious and Talmudic law – as the legal basis of the Jewish State, the Kahan Commission saw fit to base its conclusion as to the indirect responsibility of Israeli state officials on the tenets of this ancient law. Sharon's, Eitan's and Yaron's indirect responsibility was based, so concluded the commission, on the fact that the massacres could have well been anticipated by these dignitaries, as they could probably guess quite accurately what would take place should Christian Phalangists enter Sabra and Shatila refugee camps. The biblical reference to this overall responsibility for the spilt blood of innocent Palestinian civilians was formulated by Kahan in the following terms:

A similar indirect responsibility also falls on those who knew of the decision [i.e. to let the Phalangists enter the camps]; it was their duty, by virtue of their position and their office,

By 1982, Israel's non-recognition of GC-IV's applicability over Palestine had evolved into a semi-official state policy. No matter where it fought, or where and how it would fight in the future, Israel would always claim that GC-IV did not apply. Accordingly, now in Lebanon, Israel refused to recognize GC-IV's applicability to its invasion there in the course of what amounted to a textbook case of IAC between two sovereign state parties to the Geneva Conventions. Israel, so ran the state's argument, did not officially install a military regime with military courts in Lebanon; furthermore, significant portions of that country's territory were not subject to Israeli military presence. These two criteria alone seemed sufficient, in the eyes of Israel's state attorneys, to rule out the idea that the IDF were Lebanon's de jure military occupier.

By the time that *HCJ 102/82* came to be adjudicated on by the Israeli Supreme Court (July 1983), the ground had completely shifted under the state attorney's feet. Some 10 months earlier, well over 1,000 civilians had been slaughtered in the Sabra and Shatila refugee camps by Lebanese vigilantes under the IDF´s watchful eyes, which had also provided these Phalangists with logistical support for their massacres. Four months prior to *HCJ 102/82*'s ruling, in February 1983, the Kahan Commission found that Israel's defence minister Ariel Sharon, the IDF chief of staff Raphael Eitan and Brigadier General Amos Yaron (the local area commander for West Beirut) were all indirectly responsible for allowing the massacres to happen on their watch, and were hence guilty of negligent behaviour in failing to stop them.[39]

to warn of the danger, and they did not fulfil this duty. It is also not possible to absolve of such indirect responsibility those persons who, when they received the first reports of what was happening in the camps, did not rush to prevent the continuation of the Phalangists' actions and did not do everything within their power to stop them. ... A basis for such responsibility may be found in the outlook of our ancestors, which was expressed in things that were said about the moral significance of the biblical portion concerning the 'beheaded heifer' (in the Book of Deuteronomy, Chapter 21). It is said in Deuteronomy (21:6–7) that the elders of the city who were near the slain victim who has been found (and it is not known who struck him down) 'will wash their hands over the beheaded heifer in the valley and reply: our hands did not shed this blood and our eyes did not see'. Rabbi Yehoshua ben Levi says of this verse (Talmud, Tractate Sota 38b): 'The necessity for the heifer whose neck is to be broken only arises on account of the niggardliness of spirit, as it is said, "Our hands have not shed this blood." But can it enter our minds that the elders of a Court of Justice are shedders of blood! The meaning is, [the man found dead] did not come to us for help and we dismissed him, we did not see him and let him go.' Kahan Commission Report, p. 12. Available from the website of the Israeli Foreign Ministry at: http://www.mfa.gov.il/mfa/foreignpolicy/mfadocuments/yearbook6/pages/1 04%20report%20of%20the%20commission%20of%20inquiry%20into%20the%20e.aspx.

39. Linda A. Malone, 'The Kahan Report, Ariel Sharon and the Sabra-Shatilla Massacres in Lebanon: Responsibility Under International Law for Massacres of Civilian Populations', *Utah Law Review*, vol. 373, no. 2 (1985), pp. 373–433.

The *HCJ 102/82* verdict was delivered some hundred days after the publication of the Kahan Commission's report, which was chaired by the president of that very same High Court. In addition, Justice Aharon Barak (later also the court's president) sat on the Kahan Commission bench and was a presiding judge on *HCJ 102/82*'s bench. Lastly, in both Kahan and in *HCJ 102/82*, the court's then president was part of the judicial quorum – Yizhak Kahan in the commission bearing his name, and Meir Shamgar (as the court's acting president) in *HCJ 102/82*.

When read sequentially, the Kahan report and *HCJ 102/82* expose the Israeli High Court's fundamental views as to the Israeli attorney general's argument of GC-IV's alleged non-applicability to Israel's military presence in Lebanon. If in Kahan, the judges chose not to adjudicate as to whether GC-IV indeed applied or not, but rather based their conclusions of Israel's indirect responsibility for the Sabra and Shatila massacres on customary principles, in *HCJ 102/82* the judges tackled the issue of GC-IV's applicability 'head on'. Their conclusion was unequivocal: the Geneva Conventions applied to Israel's military occupation of Lebanon in full. Thus, when read in hindsight, if, in 1982, GC-IV applied to the detainees in Lebanon's Ansar Prison, then it applied every bit as much to the IDF's actions surrounding Sabra and Shatila that same year and within the exact same geopolitical context. Occupation was occupation – especially if it took place in the same conquered country which was overrun by that same army during the same war. At the level of their supreme courts then, both the United States and Israel had to accept that the notion of automatic non-application to which these states had resorted vis-à-vis GC-IV's protective purview was simply not tenable – especially when dealing with the 'classical' case of its application: in IAC. Even the crudest form of state-sponsored intellectual dishonesty had its limits, especially when it came up against unbiased high courts' judicial review.

CONCLUSION: EXCLUDING THE EXCLUSIONS

No single individual or organization embraced the new Geneva Convention for Civilians more enthusiastically than the ICRC. In 1994, forty-seven years after Georges Cahen-Salvador and Gerhart Riegner inserted into GC-IV's Stockholm draft the idea that the ICRC would be entitled to intervene in a conflict in which a government was targeting its own nationals, the organization found itself yet again in the midst of a genocide – this time in the tiny East African republic of Rwanda. As the UN inexcusably abandoned the country and its UN peacekeeping commander, General Roméo Dallaire, to their fates, the ICRC, under the leadership of its country delegate Philippe Gaillard, significantly scaled up its Rwandan rescue operations. Thanks to unwavering support from its Geneva headquarters, and Gaillard's outright heroism, the International Committee managed to save well over 65,000 lives during those dark 100 days. In a subsequent interview, years later, Gaillard stated,

> The International Committee of the Red Cross, which is [a] 140-year-old organization, was not active during the Armenian genocide, it shut up during the holocaust – everybody knew what was happening with the Jews; in such circumstances, if you don't at least speak out clearly – you are participating in the genocide. If you just shut up when you see what you see – I mean morally, ethically, you cannot shut up; it's your responsibility to talk, to speak.[1]

In Rwanda, ironically, the ICRC was – four decades later – saving en masse exactly the category of people who, back in 1947–8, it did not designate as within reach of its protective coverage as proposed by its new Civilian Convention's draft. Unlike during the Second World War, in 1994, the International Committee had full legal right to intervene on behalf of Rwanda's defenceless Tutsis thanks to the legal cover and grounding that it had been granted under GC-IV's provisions. As Gaillard noted, his decision to remain in Rwanda was intimately related to the ICRC's historical record during previous genocides where it had not been active in defence of civilians. From 12 August 1949 onwards, the ICRC would have the law 'on its side' so to speak. In Rwanda, Gaillard would ardently argue for his

---

1. Greg Barker, *Ghosts of Rwanda: PBS Frontline documentary* (Canada: Frontline, 2004), minutes 1:05:00–1:07:00. Available at www.youtube.com/watch?v=VJAuyIRfYIM &t=116s (accessed 24 April 2018).

international legal right to intervene on behalf of murdered civilians – before the *génocidaire* Hutu government. History had come full circle.

Beyond the ICRC, it is to the credit of four other central actors – France, Denmark, the Soviet bloc and the WJC – that between 1946 and 1949, GC-IV, in its pervasive and unequivocal humanitarian character, came into being. At the outset of its drafting process, none of these four actors seems to have harboured the desire to extend a basic set of protections to all civilians and all combatants under all circumstances. Rather, each of them advocated an extension of GC-IV's protective purview to a specific category of persons previously not protected, whose rights they now wished to secure following the traumas of the Second World War. For France, this was first and foremost resistance combatants fighting an evil occupier. For the Soviets, it was communist combatants fighting against what they saw as non-legitimate regimes – either in-country or cross-border – and who, in their eyes, deserved POW status. For the WJC, it was civilians who were being targeted by their own legally constituted government. For the ICRC, finally, it was all of the above – yet without the category advocated for by the WJC.

As the drafting process progressed, the interests of all five actors began to converge. The first seeds of the Civilian Convention had most certainly been sown by the ICRC back in the early 1930s. Yet truth be told, the events of the Second World War simply exceeded the worst that the ICRC could have ever imagined back in days of its Tokyo draft of 1934. The text that served as the central blueprint for the Civilian Convention as we know it today was elaborated by France at the Quai d'Orsay, between the summer of 1946 and the spring of 1947, under Georges Cahen-Salvador's watchful eyes. After the experiences of the Second World War, it could not help but be radically different from the Tokyo draft. Albert Lamarle brought this text to the 1947 Governments Experts' Conference in Geneva in 1947. There it was adopted by both the government and the ICRC as the designated textual basis for the future elaboration of the Civilian Convention in Stockholm a year later.

As the documents from both the French archives and the Bulgarian former Soviet archives unequivocally prove, by February/March 1948 the entire Soviet bloc was wholeheartedly 'on board' with GC-IV's humanitarian efforts – in no small part thanks to French diplomatic efforts. The idea that the Soviet bloc delegates opted to abruptly 'show up' at the very last stage of GC-IV's drafting, at the 1949 Geneva Conference of Plenipotentiaries, is a historically baseless reading, propagated mainly by diplomats from the United Kingdom and the United States. The reason this myth has persisted up until now is simple: writers about GC-IV's drafting history have not examined the records in non-English-speaking archives, and have based their historical accounts solely upon materials from archives in English-speaking countries. Had they taken the effort to examine the historical archival material of all parties, rather than merely footnoting Geoffrey Best's 1994 account of GC-IV's drafting, they would have been exposed to a completely different historical reality. The fundamentally humanitarian approach adopted by the Soviets in Geneva in 1949 – which led the ICRC's Claude Pilloud, to conclude that he 'dare not think what would have happened to the civilian convention had it not been for the Russian delegation' – ought to have been taken face value, especially given the nature of its speaker – the ICRC´s non-biased legal-division head writing confidentially to his presidential superiors.

Such a historical misreading ought to serve as a methodological warning to authors who opt to write one-sided histories based upon a limited and immediately palatable one-sided choice of archives to be consulted. In Best's full defence, one should stress that in 1994 former Soviet archives were completely closed to him. Nevertheless, all subsequent authors have had access to the French Archive in Paris – the examination of which would have confirmed the Soviets' early support for GC-IV.

However, one should attribute the Soviet bloc's decision to participate in GC-IV's making neither to pure humanitarian motives nor to naked Machiavellian realpolitik interests alone. To be sure, in 1949, all the Great Powers – Soviet and 'Western' alike – were perpetrating their fair share of atrocities against civilians. Be it the UK in Malaya in 1948, France in Algerian Sétif in 1945, Belgium in the Congo, the Dutch in Indonesia, the Soviet Union in its gulags or the United States and its CIA-supported United Fruit Company in Latin America – all the permanent members of the UN Security Council were, in one way or another, involved in atrocious attitudes towards civilians somewhere on the planet. In this regard, the Soviets were most certainly no different to their Western counterparts.

That said, no one in 'the West' suffered anything remotely close to what the Soviet world had endured under the Nazis, between the occupation of Poland in 1939 and the fall of Berlin in 1945. The answer to the conundrum as to why, of all people, it was the Soviets who were more humanitarianly supportive towards GC-IV does not lie in some pseudo-romantic false image of humanitarianism that the Soviet bloc might have been trying to project for Western diplomats. Rather, it lies in the dovetailing of Soviet experiences under the Nazis with the more immediate developments that accompanied GC-IV's drafting from 1946 to 1949. These were the Western–communist battle fronts across the globe – from Greece, through Malaya, to Indonesia and China. Without exception, all these confrontations were being fought by communist guerrillas against 'Western'-controlled sovereign states and their regular armies. One of the most acute of these confrontations was in Greece between royalists, who were actively supported by British regular armed forces, and communist guerrillas.

In the run-up to Geneva, between 1947 and 1949, the humanitarian objectives of GC-IV's drafters conflicted in the starkest possible manner with base realities on the ground. While the Red Cross was bringing forth new humanitarian ideas, civilians were being indiscriminately murdered alongside guerrillas in the very same places where the Nazis had killed merely two years previously. The communists who had fought the Nazis in Greece were now being killed by the British. The communists in Malaya, who had fought the Japanese occupation forces there, were now being killed by yet another occupier – the disintegrating British Empire.

Within this world of sovereign states fighting irregular armed forces, and with the former being the sole subjects of international law at the time, states could pound civilians and their guerrillas to dust and get away with it. This was basically what the Nazis had done in Belarus: they annihilated a third of that country's 9.6 million people without breaking a single tenet of the 1929 Geneva Conventions. After all, no civilian or guerrilla fighter was officially legally protected before 1949. It is under these preconditions that one must understand the positions adopted by the Soviet bloc at the Geneva Conventions' drafting table. It is through this prism that one must see the Soviets' relentless push at the Conference of Plenipotentiaries in favour of the widest possible application for Common Article 3. If all-out war was now to be fought all-against-all – civilians against states, occupiers against guerrillas, foreign-deployed militaries against domestic forces – then the world needs some sort of fundamental humanitarian coverage for everyone.

Much the same is true of the failed Soviet attempt to call for a ban on the use of nuclear weapons. The fact that no historian to date has made the connection between this attempt by the Soviets, on 9 July 1949, and their detonation of their first nuclear bomb exactly six weeks later (and a fortnight after 12 August signing of the Geneva Conventions), on 27 August 1949, should call for some self-reflection. If in 2018, Iran has still not managed to acquire full nuclear capabilities, after fifteen years of trying, then there is clearly no chance that back in 1949 the Soviets could have acquired 'the bomb' in six weeks. Rather, in all probability, the Soviets came to Geneva in April 1949 with 'the bomb already in their pocket'. Should the United States, the sole nuclear power at that point, have agreed to call for a ban on such weapons, the Soviets might have refrained from detonating their own. Yet faced with US reticence and arrogance, there was very little sense in the Soviets avoiding demonstrating their nuclear capabilities. In hindsight, then, it seems as if the credit for the escalation of the nuclear arms post 1949 ought to rightfully belong to the United States and the United Kingdom. Had these Western powers opted to consider the Soviet request for a nuclear ban *ad rem*, things might have been very different today. Instead, US foreign policy experts opted to treat this Soviet request ad hominem. Correspondingly, the United States blocked any possibility of even discussing the matter concretely at the Conference of Plenipotentiaries – on the evasive technical ground of legal inadmissibility according to the conference's rules of procedure. Little wonder then, that the ICRC's own Claude Pilloud referred to this action by the United States as one of the lowest forms of 'abuse' of the legal procedure during the 1949 Conference.

At the heart of American reticence towards further extensions of GC-IV's humanitarian principles lay a rather deep sense of paranoia, which seems to have influenced US foreign policy strongly back in 1949. This sentiment was explicitly communicated to Geneva by the US secretary of state Dean Acheson, who telegrammed Ambassador Leyland Harrison and told him that 'the department is *apprehensive* lest the Soviets use the discussion on the convention for the protection of civilians as an occasion for a propaganda campaign against the US and its atomic energy policy'.[2] Be it with regard to the proposed Soviet call for

2. US-National Archives and Records Authority, College Park Maryland (hereinafter US-NARA), RG 43, Records of International Conferences, Commissions, and Expositions,

a ban on nuclear weapons or the seemingly endless deliberations on the rights of guerrilla combatants under Common Article 3 during GC-IV's drafting, the United States seems to have been largely motivated by a paranoid conception of the Soviet bloc. While this is certainly understandable given the signs of those times, one nevertheless gets the impression that US policy makers were 'failing to see the wood for the trees'. Had US policy analysts put two and two together, they could have posited that the Soviets *really did* intend to come to Stockholm in 1948. After all, one of the chief architects of the entire Soviet involvement with GC-IV's drafting since February 1948 was Nissim Mevorah, who during those very years served as the accredited Bulgarian ambassador to the United States – based in Washington, DC.

Much the same goes for the détente following the lifting of the Berlin Blockade, merely three weeks prior to the ceremonial opening of the 1949 Geneva Conference of Plenipotentiaries. The Americans should have said to themselves, if the Soviets imposed the blockade just before the opening of the Stockholm Conference in the summer of 1948 and if they lifted it three weeks before GC-IV's next and most vital drafting stage in Geneva in 1949, then maybe – just maybe – they genuinely saw a promulgation of their true interests in promoting GC-IV's humanitarian objectives. Instead, the only message that the US delegation in Geneva could send back to Washington a week after the Plenipotentiaries' Conference opened was that 'thus far, Soviet behaviour has been most surprising' and that the Soviets 'plan to assume the role of great humanitarians and possibly *endeavour to embarrass* those who oppose the Stockholm texts'.[3] God forbid that the Soviets, after all the pain that they had suffered during the Second World War – a pain never so harshly experienced by any Western country – should simply (and truly) care for civilians in war. It would take the United States's own state department historians half a century to conclude that Stalin indeed kept to his side of the Yalta bargain, and did not aid communist guerrillas in Greece.[4] In the meantime, all through the Greek Civil War, between 1947 and 1949, regular British armed forces would invariably apply a policy of 'no quarter given' towards all Greek communist guerrillas that they came across.

US Del. Diplomatic Conference/Conventions/War Victims, Lot File 77 D 127, program records 4/21/1949 – 8/12/1949, Diplomatic Conference – Geneva Box 2, Adrc ID: 2601554, DU-WX, Entry 48 B, 6 May 1949, telegram 468, Acheson for Harrison – URGENT/SECRET. Italics added.

3. US-NARA, RG 43, Records of International Conferences, Commissions, and Expositions, US Del. Diplomatic Conference/Conventions/War Victims, Lot File 77 D 127, program records 4/21/1949 – 8/12/1949, Diplomatic Conference – Geneva Box 2, Adrc ID: 2601554, DU-WX, Entry 48 B, 2 May 1949, Confidential Telegram from Troutman to the secretary of state, subject: Diplomatic Conference for protection of war Victims , summary report, United States delegation (through 29 April 1949), p. 2. Italics added.

4. See below p. 106, n. 214.

Nowhere was this obstructionism more painful to the Holocaust-surviving drafters of GC-IV than in the deliberations concerning today's Article 32 (then, still known as Article 29–A). In a lecture delivered in December 1951 to the International Diplomatic Academy in Paris, the college of accredited ambassadors to the Quai d'Orsay, Georges Cahen-Salvador noted,

> Two years ago, on 15 October 1949, I had the honour of presenting to this assembly the result of the diplomatic conference in Geneva convened so as to prepare the new international conventions applicable to the sick and wounded, to prisoners of war, and civilians during times of war … .
>
> A: The Principles – modern war, far from sparing civilian populations of its consequences, has hit them the hardest. No international instrument could have spared civilians the atrocities of collective executions, racial persecutions, tortures and assassinations. Civilians could also not avoid aerial bombardments that indiscriminately harm them and combatants alike; yet it was solely for civilians that we reserved the painful privilege of gas chambers! ('*mais on leur avez reserve le douleureux privilege des chambres à gaz!*')[5]

Cahen-Salvador's above-stated sarcasm ('privilege' of gas chambers) should be understood for what it was: a directed criticism of all those who, through legalist obstructionism, had attempted to short-circuit the Civilian Convention that he chaired. The ICRC's rigid legalistic reading of its responsibilities during the Second World War or American objections to Article 32's wording when it spoke of 'exterminations', which the United States immediately associated with Soviet attempts to insinuate the issue of nuclear weapons – these were exactly the type of legalist actions in drafting that had most strongly threatened to harm the convention.[6] To Cahen-Salvador, these international legal failures came about once delegates ceased regarding the conventions as a tool to be applied to the practical realities of warfare in the real world, which existed outside the *Genevois* halls of diplomatic and legal power.

It is one thing to note that warfare had developed to the point at which it now treated civilians as a primary target. However, the absurdity of the whole affair lay in the fact that people who took no part in hostilities (civilians) paradoxically enjoyed fewer privileges than those who actively did – and who, as combatants, could enjoy protections accorded to POWs. That the ICRC could condone a

---

5. Archive du Conseil d'Etat de France, Fonds Cahen Salvador, Ref. # 9952/4, Conference de M. Cahen Salvador Académie Diplomatique 6 Décembre 1951, pp. 1, 4 (exclamation mark on p. 4 after the words 'gas chambers' in the original).

6. US-NARA, RG 43, Records of International Conferences, Commissions, and Expositions, US Del. Diplomatic Conference/Conventions/War Victims, Lot File 77 D 127, program records 4/21/1949 – 8/12/1949, Diplomatic Conference – Geneva Box 2, Adrc ID: 2601554, DU-WX, Entry 48 B, 19 June 1949, Secret (via Bern), Telegram from Troutman/ Harrison to the secretary of state (# 610 – in red pen), subject: Diplomatic Conference p. 1.

legal position that would have resulted in the exclusion of civilians targeted for extermination by their own government from GC-IV's prospective protective purview seemed to Cahen-Salvador outright wrong. That this could still be the ICRC's position three years *after* the liberations of Auschwitz, Bergen-Belsen and Dachau cast serious doubt on that organization's sound international legal judgement. Under these circumstances, it was up to Cahen-Salvador, as the Civilian Convention's chairman, to word Common Article 3's protections in the most inclusive manner possible, and then bring this inclusivity 'top down' on the International Committee's head.

It was obvious to its drafters that Common Article 3 would become a thorn in the side of nation states, just as this was obvious to the ICRC between 1947 and the convention's signing in August 1949. From 1986 onwards, however, the 'thorn' that is Common Article 3 has become both larger and more painful to nation states. For it was in that year that the ICJ, in its judgement in *Nicaragua vs. United States*, first came to recognize Common Article 3 as constituting an integral part of customary international law – thus irrevocably binding all states to its provisions. At the ontological heart of Common Article 3 lies one simple and absolutely fundamental characteristic: *there simply cannot be any exceptions to it.* No human being – evil as they may be – is beyond its pale. It is, in this sense, truly universal.

From its outset in 1946 until its successful conclusion in August 1949, Common Article 3's drafting, as with that of so many of GC-IV's Articles, was intrinsically linked to the notion of 'treaties after trauma'. The psychological scars that had been suffered by its drafters ultimately drove each of them to chaperone the cause of a certain personally cherished human group hitherto not covered by the previous Geneva Conventions. Gradually and cumulatively, this brought about the recognition that, in fact, the only way to guarantee the convention's effectiveness was to *exclude any exclusions*. This result, however, was certainly not envisaged as such by the drafters at the outset back in 1946–7.

Something similar could be said about the positions of the United States concerning Article 32's prohibition of 'extermination'. To anybody who lived through what Cahen-Salvador had, his family forced on board Eichmann's Transport No. 62 from Drancy to Auschwitz in 1943, the word 'extermination' meant one thing – gas chambers and crematoriums. According to the US delegation at Geneva, however, 'it is abundantly clear from the debate on Article 29 A that the Soviets are seeking to outlaw aerial bombardment by characterizing it as a serious crime quote – all other means of exterminating the civilian population'.[7] Faced with such a morally repugnant reading of his own drafting intentions, one should not be too surprised

---

7. US-NARA, RG 43, Records of International Conferences, Commissions, and Expositions, US Del. Diplomatic Conference/Conventions/War Victims, Lot File 77 D 127, program records 4/21/1949 – 8/12/1949, Diplomatic Conference – Geneva Box 2, Adrc ID: 2601554, DU-WX, Entry 48 B, 19 June 1949, Secret (via Bern), Telegram from Troutman/ Harrison to the secretary of state (# 610 – in red pen), subject: Diplomatic Conference p. 1 at the very bottom.

at how Cahen-Salvador steered this Article's textual development so as to finally cover *all civilians* – including those targeted by their own governments.

History certainly has its diachronic ironies. Back in 1949, it was 'protection for all', as in Common Article 3's true meaning, and the ICJ's adjudication role that were seen as GC-IV's most heavily contested issues. In stark contrast to the endless debates devoted to these two issues by the Plenipotentiaries' Conference, Georg Cohn's prohibition on settlements and the transfer of a conqueror's own population into newly occupied territories was not even discussed at Geneva in 1949. The international unanimity on these issues was so great that Cohn's text for Article 49 paragraph 6, which he had formulated back in Stockholm in 1948, was swiftly adopted in Geneva without a single word of discussion.

In 1922, it had been Cohn who first formulated the principle of international non-recognition of territorial acquisition by force. During the 1930s, the Danish rabbi confronted Carl Schmitt – and, later, Werner Best – who advocated, and even argued for the necessity of, the right of conquest in international affairs. Following the experiences of the Second World War, delegates required very little persuasion to grasp the horrors of aggressive conquest, which was now internationally condemned. The UN Charter's Article 2 paragraph 4 merely confirmed this point. Fast-forward seven decades, however, and conquest is back on the international agenda: in Palestine, Northern Cyprus, Western Sahara, Abkhazia and Ossetia – and, more recently, in Eastern Ukraine and Crimea. The legitimizing of territorial acquisition by force is once again on the rise, and occupation – the intellectual progeny of non-recognition – is back on the defensive vis-à-vis its aggressive ontological nemesis.

Yet what is no longer being debated is the fundamental issue of the basic human rights of civilians under whichever of these alternatives might befall them: occupation or annexation. Nowadays, no self-respecting Supreme Court would dare to question Common Article 3's customary international legal status – less still, its outright *jus cogens* stature. Moreover, no country – not even genocidal Rwanda back in 1994 or war-torn Yemen today – would seriously question the ICRC's *a priori* legal right to intervene on civilians' humanitarian behalf there.[8]

The answer to the question quoted in this book's Introduction, 'Do the Geneva Conventions matter?' is not just some abstract intellectual exercise, to be answered perhaps by people who might seldom (if ever) personally experience the gruesome realties of armed conflict. It is a question that should be posed first of all to armed conflict's affected civilians themselves. When posed before Yemeni mothers whose children are saved from starvation due to the ICRC's existential food distribution, the answer to this question becomes abundantly clear. Ask Yemeni wives whether the visitation rights that Aden's ICRC delegate succeeded to secure for their jailed

---

8. International Committee of the Red Cross, *Yemen: In major breakthrough, ICRC visits conflict-related detainees in Aden*, News release, 11 February 2018. Available at: https://www.icrc.org/en/document/yemen-major-breakthrough-icrc-visits-conflict-related-detainees-aden (accessed 24 January 2019).

civilian spouses – at the deadly cost for that ICRC staffer's own lost life, and then let us discuss whether or not 'the Geneva Conventions matter'.[9]

When attempting to assess the Geneva Convention for Civilians' impact, we must first recall that without it we would have had no ICRC to intervene on war victims' behalf in the first place, since this organization would not have enjoyed any *legal* basis from which to draw. This is exactly the situation that a third of Belorussia's population found themselves in during the Second World War when exposed to the horrors of Germany's Operation Barbarossa. De Facto and de jura today, few people – members of rebel groups and insurgents included – would reject outright the ICRC's right to intervene. This is the very opposite of the insidious advantageous position in which the Nazis found themselves during the Second World War. When we ask whether the Geneva Conventions matter, we must understand that we are questioning the ICRC's entire corpus of work, and arguably even its very raison d'être. Seen in this light, such questioning seems intellectually somewhat prejudiced.

Beyond the impact implied in the ICRC's work, there remains the impact that GC-IV has had on Supreme Courts the world over, irrespective of the recognized problem of states' application of this treaty. Pundits who question its relevance should consider the alternative reality of a world devoid of GC-IV. What would the US Supreme Court's decision in *Hamdan vs. Rumsfeld*, over a plea by a tortured detainee in Guantanamo Bay, have been without Common Article 3? What would the Israeli Supreme Court's decision concerning Israel's 1982 occupation of Lebanon have looked like absent GC-IV? What would the world's judicial opinion have been had ICJ judge Platon Morosov not inserted his reference to GC-IV and Common Article 3's customary nature in that International Court's verdict on *Nicaragua vs. United States*? Upon what would the UNGA base its request to ponder the illegality of Israel's separation barrier in the midst of occupied Palestinian? On what would the statutes of the ICTY and ICTR (the International Criminal Tribunals for the former Yugoslavia and Rwanda, respectively), and the International Criminal Court itself, rest as these bodies came to define what war crimes really are? Pursuant to the basic tenet of any criminal legal system of *Nulla poena sine lege scripta* ('no penalty without written law'), the Geneva Conventions do indeed matter, since they serve as the basic legal bedrock upon which the world's entire system of international humanitarian law and international criminal law is founded.

With all that said, we would all probably be somewhat better off were we to pose more pertinent questions. In this regard, *How do we better effectuate the Geneva Convention for Civilians*? seems a far more important question to answer – and

---

9. See the obituary to Hanna Lahoud, the ICRC's detention programme manager in Yemen, who was shot and killed in April 2018. International Committee of the Red Cross, Yemen: *ICRC staff member shot and killed in Taiz,* New release 21 April 2018. Available at: https://www.icrc.org/en/document/yemen-icrc-staff-member-shot-and-killed-taiz (accessed 24 January 2019).

one which certainly merits further research and enquiry. In all probability, it is also much harder to answer since it transgresses the strict academic disciplinary boundaries of international law and demands the co-option of other fields of research, such as political science, sociology and the study of societal mobilization, all geared towards trying to understand how to exert sufficient public pressure on politicians and publics alike so as to strengthen GC-IV's application.

In this broader effort in favour of the Geneva Conventions' effectuation, historians have plenty of work before them. Much of GC-IV's historical evolution has yet to be uncovered. Where and how exactly were the words 'conflict not of an international character' first formulated, and by whom within the ICRC? Who was ultimately responsible for their insertion into the Stockholm draft of the Geneva Convention texts of May 1948? Ample signs point to the possibility that the key person behind all this was the well-respected and much-loved Jean Pictet.[10] Yet this riddle, and many others, still awaits historians. Platon Morosov's files at the Russian State Archives in Moscow still await intellectually committed researchers. They most probably hold within them much historical potential.

A week before the conclusion of the Plenipotentiaries Conference, and after three years of drafting, Georges Cahen-Salvador spoke on record for posterity's sake:

> Future readers of the Convention will have to peruse it in its entirety in order to discover, here and there, *those essential Articles* to which our efforts have been directed. Article 29 A is one of them. (Italics added)[11]

To GC-IV's long-standing drafter and chairman, both in Stockholm and in Geneva, its most *essential* tenets could be summed up in its Article 32, which

> prohibited from taking any measure of such a character as to cause the physical suffering or extermination of protected persons. ... This prohibition applies not only to murder, torture, corporal punishment, mutilation and medical or scientific experiments not necessitated by the medical treatment of a protected person, but also to any *other measures of brutality* whether applied by civilian or military agents.[12]

Avoiding brutality towards fellow humans – that, in the end, was what it was all about. Many of the people responsible for GC-IV's birth – Chairman Cahen-Salvador, Rabbi Dr George Cohn and Dr Nissim Mevorah among them – had experienced these brutalities first-hand. It was in the light of these experiences they now came to legislate. For them, history truly was intertwined with international law – both generally and personally.

10. McBride, 'The Legality of Weapons for Societal Destruction', pp. 401–9 at 403.

11. Statement by Cahen-Salvador, 3 August 1949, 26th plenary session of the Convention for the Protection of Civilians, *Final Record*, vol. 2-B, p. 409.

12. Ibid.

APPENDIX GC-IV'S FRENCH FIRST DRAFT
ADOPTED IN GENEVA – APRIL 1947

The French draft of the Fourth Geneva Convention for Civilians, which was adopted at the ICRC Governments Experts' Conference in Geneva in April 1947 as the basis for the Geneva Convention for Civilians, that was finally adopted by states in August 1949. © French Foreign Ministry Archives. Photo copyright of the author.

PROJET DE CONVENTION INTERNATIONALE

POUR LA PROTECTION DES POPULATIONS CIVILES

EN TEMPS DE GUERRE

─────

TITRE PRELIMINAIRE

DEFINITION DES PERSONNES PROTEGEES PAR LA CONVENTION

─────

ARTICLE Ier.-   Les civils protégés par la présente Convention
sont les personnes qui réunissent les conditions suivantes :

I°) Etre ressortissant d'un pays occupé à l'occasion d'un conflit armé et se trouver sur le territoire
d'un belligérant.

2°) Ne pas appartenir aux forces armées terrestres,
maritimes ou aériennes des belligérants, telles qu'elles
sont définies par le Droit International, notamment
par les articles I, 2 et 3 du réglement annexé à la
Convention N° IV de La Haye, du 18 octobre 1907, concer-
nant les lois et coutumes de la guerre. (I)

───

(I) Réglement annexé: Article Ier.- Les droits, les lois et les devoirs
de la guerre ne s'appliquent pas seulement à l'armée, mais encore
aux militaires et aux corps de volontaires réunissant les conditions suivantes :
    I°) Avoir à leur tête une personne responsable pour ses subor-
        donnés.
    2°) Avoir un signe distinctif fixe et reconnaissable à distance.
    3°) Porter les armes ouvertement.
    4°) Se conformer dans leurs opérations aux lois et aux coutumes
        de la guerre.

Dans les pays où les milices ou des corps de volontaires
constituent l'armée ou en font partie, ils sont compris sous la
dénomination d'armée.

Article 2.- La population d'un territoire non occupé qui, à l'ap-
proche de l'ennemi, prend spontanément les armes pour combat-
tre les troupes d'invasion, sans avoir eu le temps de s'organiser
conformément à l'article Ier, sera considérée, comme belligérante
si elle porte les armes ouvertement et si elle respecte les lois et
coutumes de la guerre.

../..

- 2 -

TITRE Ier.

PROTECTION DE LA POPULATION CIVILE ENNEMIE SE TROUVANT

SUR LE TERRITOIRE D'UN BELLIGÉRANT.

ARTICLE 2.-　　　　Sous réserve des dispositions de l'article 4 ci-après, les belligérants donneront, dans le plus bref délai possible, aux civils ennemis qui désireraient quitter leur territoire au début des hostilités, les autorisations nécessaires ainsi que toutes les facilités compatibles avec les opérations militaires.

Ils auront le droit de se munir de l'argent nécessaire à leur voyage et d'emporter, au moins, leurs effets personnels.

ARTICLE 3.-　　　　Dans le cas où le départ des civils serait organisé administrativement, ceux-ci devront être conduits à la frontière de leur pays ou du pays neutre le plus proche.

Il sera procédé à ces rapatriement sous la surveillance d'une Puissance protectrice, choisie d'accord entre les deux belligérants, ou d'un organisme international compétent.

Les modalités de ces rapatriements pourront donner lieu à des accords spéciaux entre belligérants.

ARTICLE 4.-　　　　Seuls, pourront être retenus, les civils ennemis appartenant aux catégories suivantes :

a) Ceux qui sont aptes à être mobilisés immédiatement.

b) Ceux au départ desquels pourront raisonnablement être opposées des considérations tirées de la sécurité des opérations militaires de la Puissance détentrice, sous réserve de l'accord de la Puissance protectrice ou

---

(I) suite.. Article 3.- Les Forces armées des Parties belligérantes peuvent se composer de combattants et de non combattants. En cas de capture par l'ennemi, les uns et les autres ont droit au traitement des prisonniers de guerre.

../..

- 3 -

de l'organisme international compétent,qui pourront être saisis soit par la Puissance belligérante en cause, soit par les Sociétés de Secours, soit par l'intéressé lui-même.

La Puissance protectrice ou l'organisme international auront toujours le droit d'exiger qu'une enquête soit ouverte et que le résultat leur en soit communiqué dans les trois mois qui suivront leur demande.

ARTICLE 5.-   Les civils ennemis se trouvant en détention préventive ou condamnés à une peine privative de liberté seront, dès leur libération, mis au bénéfice des dispositions de la présente Convention.

Le fait de ressortissir à une Puissance ennemie ne devra pas entraîner une aggravation du régime auquel ils sont soumis.

ARTICLE 6.-   Les civils ennemis restés sur le territoire, ainsi que ceux qui auront été retenus en application de l'article 4 ci-dessus, seront soumis au traitement dont jouissent les étrangers en temps ordinaire, sous réserve des mesures de contrôle ou de sûreté qui pourraient être édictées et des dispositions des articles I2, I3 et I4 ci-après.

ARTICLE 7.-   Dans le cas où le pays belligérant estimerait nécessaires des mesures de contrôle supplémentaires, il pourra recourir exceptionnellement à la mise en résidence surveillée ou à l'internement, sous réserve de l'accord de la Puissance protectrice ou de l'organisme international prévu ci-dessus, et conformément aux dispositions des articles I2, I3 et I4 ci-après.

ARTICLE 8.-   Sous réserve des mesures appliquées à la population dans son ensemble, les civils ennemis auront la possibilité de donner aux membres de leur famille des nouvelles de caractère strictement privé et d'en recevoir.

Lorsqu'un membre de leur famille (ascendants, descendants et collatéraux) se trouvera en territoire ennemi, la correspondance sera assurée par l'intermédiaire des Sociétés de Secours.

Sous la même réserve, ils auront également la possibilité de recevoir des secours.

ARTICLE 9.-   Les civils ennemis seront protégés contre les actes de violence, les insultes et la curiosité publique.

..J...

- i -

ARTICLE IO.-   Les mesures de représailles à leur égard seront interdites.

ARTICLE II.-   La désignation d'otages sera interdite.

ARTICLE I2.-   En général, seule la mise en résidence surveillée des civils ennemis sera admise.

ARTICLE I3.-   Seront notamment mis en résidence surveillée et non internés, sous réservice de la sécurité de la Puissance détentrice, les civils ennemis dont la résidence habituelle était située sur son territoire.

Cependant, lorsque la sécurité des opérations militaires l'exigera, les civils ennemis visés à l'article 4 ci-dessus et ceux dont la résidence habituelle se trouve sur le territoire de la Puissance belligérante ennemie, pourront être internés.

ARTICLE I4.-   Toute déportation des civils ennemis hors du territoire de la Puissance détentrice sera interdite, sauf accord de la Puissance protectrice ou de l'organisme international compétent.

ARTICLE I5.-   Les camps d'internement des civils ennemis seront distincts de ceux des prisonniers de guerre.

Ces camps ne pourront être installés dans des régions malsaines ou dont le climat serait nuisible à la santé des internés.

ARTICLE I6.-   Les règles en vigueur relatives au traitement des prisonniers de guerre ainsi que celles qui ont trait à l'installation de leurs camps et à leur organisation telles qu'elles résultent de la Convention de......... du...... pour la protection des prisonniers de guerre seront appliquées aux internés civils.

ARTICLE I7.-   Les civils ennemis et apatrides qui se trouveront amenés en territoire ennemi ou occupé par l'ennemi par la suite d'opérations militaires devront également être mis au bénéfice des garanties résultant du présent titre.

../..

TITRE II.

PROTECTION DES CIVILS QUI SE TROUVENT SUR LE
TERRITOIRE OCCUPE PAR UN BELLIGERANT.

ARTICLE 18.- En ce qui concerne la condition et la protection des civils qui se trouveront sur le territoire occupé par un belligérant, les Hautes Parties Contractantes s'engageront à observer les dispositions de la Section III du réglement annexé à la Convention N° IV de La Haye du 18 octobre 1907, dispositions qui demeurent inchangées à l'exception de l'article 52 modifié par l'article 19 ci-après.

ARTICLE 19.- Les Hautes Parties Contractantes s'interdiront de prendre en pays occupé toutes mesures de nature à porter atteinte à la structure et à la substance de l'économie du pays ou à y assurer leur domination économique. Les réquisitions en nature ou prestations de services autres que celles justifiées par les besoins des troupes d'occupation seront notamment interdites. Ces mesures seront en rapport avec les ressources du pays et de telle nature qu'elles n'impliquent pas pour la population l'obligation de prendre part aux opérations de guerre. Elles ne devront pas rendre nécessaire le transfert des habitants hors du lieu habituel de leur résidence.

ARTICLE 20.- Les civils habitant le territoire occupé, auront toujours la possibilité de donner aux membres de leurs familles se trouvant à l'intérieur de ce territoire des nouvelles de caractère strictement privé et d'en recevoir.

La même possibilité leur sera accordée pour la correspondance de caractère professionnel ou pour toute autre correspondance avec l'étranger, sous réserve des mesures appliquées à la population de la Puissance occupante dans son ensemble.

Ils auront également la possibilité de recevoir des secours.

ARTICLE 21.- Les Hautes Parties Contractantes s'engagent à ne prendre à l'encontre des habitants des pays occupés aucune mesure d'ordre collectif ou individuel, qui soit contraire à la dignité de la personne humaine.

Toute mesure de discrimination dictée par des motifs d'ordre national, racial, confessionnel, culturel ou

../..

- 6 -

politique sera rigoureusement exclue. La condamnation d'une
personne dont la responsabilité individuelle n'aurait pas
été établie judiciairement sera prohibée. Les mesures
telles que la désignation et l'exécution d'otages, les
déportations, les amendes collectives, la destruction des
villes et villages seront interdites.

ARTICLE 22.-
Les habitants du pays occupé qui auraient transgressé
les ordres ou réglements édictés en conformité des règles
du Droit des gens par les autorités d'occupation, ne pourront être traduits que devant un tribunal qui jugera sui-
vent les principes généraux du Droit.

Les prévenus devront être assistés d'un défenseur
librement choisi.

La pleine liberté de la défense sera assurée.

Toute violence pendant l'interrogatoire ou à quelque
occasion que ce soit demeurera interdite.

ARTICLE 23.-
Les Hautes Parties Contractantes s'interdisent toute
mesure de représailles à l'égard à l'égard de leurs ex-res-
sortissants réfugiés sur le territoire d'un pays occupé.

ARTICLE 24.-
Tout civil qui aura été capturé au cours de combats
ayant forme d'opérations militaires sera considéré comme
militaire et traité comme tel, s'il répond aux conditions
posées :

1°) par les dispositions de l'article Ier de la Convention de...... du ...... relative au traitement
des prisonniers de guerre;

2°) par le réglement annexé à la Convention N° IV de
La Haye du 18 octobre 1907;

3°) par les clauses qui viendraient ultérieurement à
modifier ce texte;

TITRE III.

DE L'EXECUTION DE LA CONVENTION.

ARTICLE 25.-
Les dispositions de la présente Convention devront
être respectées en toutes circonstances et, notamment,
lorsque les personnes à protéger ne relèvent pas d'une
autorité gouvernementale reconnue comme telle par la par-

../..

- 9 -

tie adverse.

Au cas où, en temps de guerre, un des belligérants ne serait pas partie à la Convention, les dispositions de celle-ci demeureront obligatoires.

ARTICLE 26.-

Le texte de la présente Convention et des Conventions spéciales auxquelles elle se réfère sera affiché dans tous les lieux d'internement des civils et communiqué, sur leur demande, à ceux qui se trouveraient dans l'impossibilité d'en prendre connaissance.

Ce texte sera rédigé sans la langue des intérnésés

ARTICLE 27.-

Les Hautes Parties Contractantes se communiqueront, par l'intermédiaire de la Puissance protectrice et de l'organisme international compétent, les traductions officielles de la présente Convention, ainsi que les lois et réglements qu'elles pourront être amenées à adopter pour assurer l'application de celle-ci.

ARTICLE 28.-

Les Hautes Parties Contractantes prendront l'engagement de respecter les termes de la présente Convention qui comportera la collaboration d'un organisme international et se déclareront prêtes à en accepter les bons offices

ARTICLE 29.-

L'organisme international pourra, en dehors du personnel diplomatique de la Puissance protectrice désigner ses délégués parmi les ressortissants des Puissances neutres. Cette désignation devra être soumise à l'agrément du belligérant auprès duquel les délégués exerceront leur mission.

où seront internés

Les représentants de la Puissance protectrice de l'organisme international ou ses délégués agréés, seront autorisés à se rendre dans toutes les localités les civils, ou dans celles où ceux-ci seront mis en résidence surveillée, sans aucune exception. Ils auront accès dans tous les locaux occupés par eux et pourront s'entretenir avec eux sans temoin, personnellement ou par l'intermédiaire d'interprètes.

Les belligérants seront tenus de faciliter dans la plus large mesure possible, la tâche des représentants ou des délégués agréés de la Puissance protectrice ou de l'organisme international.

Les autorités intéressées seront informées de la visite de ces représentants.

Les belligérants pourront s'entendre pour que des per-

../..

- 8 -

...sonnes de la propre nationalité des internés seront admises à participer aux voyages d'inspection.

ARTICLE 30.- En cas de désaccord entre les belligérants sur l'application des dispositions de la présente Convention, l'organisme international sera de droit saisi aux fins de règlement du différend.

Les Hautes Parties Contractantes s'engageront à exécuter les décisions du Tribunal International compétent pour se prononcer sur le caractère licite de toute mesure prise par la Puissance occupante.

Ce Tribunal pourra être saisi soit par la Puissance en cause, soit par l'intéressé lui-même, soit par les Sociétés de Secours.

ARTICLE 31.- Les dispositions qui précèdent ne sauraient faire obstacle à l'activité humanitaire que les sociétés de secours régulièrement constituées pourront déployer pour la protection des civils ennemis, sous réserve de l'agrément des belligérants intéressés.

DISPOSITIONS FINALES.

ARTICLE 32.- La présente Convention qui portera la date du....... pourra, jusqu'au............, être signée au nom de tous les pays représentés à la Conférence.

ARTICLE 33.- Les textes........... feront foi.

ARTICLE 34.- La présente Convention sera ratifiée aussitôt que possible.

Les ratifications seront déposées à.......

Un premier procès-verbal de dépôt des ratifications sera dressé dès que la présente Convention aura été ratifiée par quatre Puissances.

Dès la date de ce premier procès-verbal, elle entrera en vigueur entre les Hautes Parties Contractantes qui l'auront ratifiée.

En ce qui concerne les autres Puissances, la Convention entrera en vigueur à la date du dépôt de leur ratification.

../..

- 9 -

ARTICLE 35.-   A partir de la date de sa mise en vigueur, la présente
Convention sera ouverte à l'adhésion des Puissances non
signataires.

                      Elle entrera en vigueur à leur égard du jour de la
notification de leur adhésion.

                      Les adhésions seront déposées à........

                      Communication de ces adhésions sera donnée par......
à l'organisme international et à toutes les Puissances
parties à la Convention.

ARTICLE 36.-   L'état de guerre donnera effet immédiat aux signatu-
res données par une Puissance belligérante avant ou après
le début des hostilités.

ARTICLE 37.-   Chacune des Hautes Parties Contractantes aura la
faculté de dénoncer la présente Convention. La dénoncia-
tion ne produira effet qu'un an après notification faite
par écrit à........ et à l'organisme international.

                      La dénonciation ne vaudra qu'à l'égard de la Haute
Partie Contractante qui l'aura notifiée.

                      En outre, cette dénonciation ne produira pas effet
au cours d'une guerre à laquelle participerait la Puissance dénonçante. En ce cas, la présente Convention conti-
nuera à produire effet jusqu'à l'entrée en vigueur des
traités de paix./.

—:::—

BIBLIOGRAPHY AND SOURCES

Archives

Archives of the International Committee of the Red Cross – Geneva (AICRC)
Archives of the World Jewish Congress at the American Jewish Archives, Cincinnati: Ohio (AWJC)
Bulgarian State Archives (BSA)
Danish National Archives – Copenhagen (DNA)
French Archives of the Council of State – *Conseil d'État* – Paris
French National Foreign Ministry Archives – Paris La Courneuve (FFMA)
German Federal Foreign Ministry Archives ('*Auswärtiges Amt-Archiv*') Berlin, located at the central offices of German Foreign Ministry – Gendarmenmarkt
Israel State Archives (ISA)
Private Archive of Paul Mohn – Carolina Rediviva Library – Uppsala University – Manuscript Section.
Swedish National Archives ('Riksarkivet') – Stockholm (SNA)
UK Royal National Archives – Kew Gardens (UNA)
US National Authority for Archives and Records – NARA – College Park MD. (US-NARA)

Primary Sources

Final Record of the Diplomatic Conference of Geneva of 1949, Berne: Federal Political Department, 1950.

Bibliography

Aderet, O. (2017) 'The Quite Swedish Zionist Who Partitioned Palestine Has Become a Bit Less Mysterious', in *Haaretz*, 24 November.
Aldrich, G. (1984) 'Some Reflections on the Origins of the 1977 Geneva Protocols', in Christophe Swinarski (ed.), *Studies and Essays on International Humanitarian Law and Red Cross Principles in Honour of Jean Pictet*, The Hague: Martinus Nijhoff, pp. 129–37.
Arai-Takahashi, Y. (2016) 'Law making and Judicial Guarantees in Occupied Territories', in A. Clapham, P. Gaeta and M. Sassoli (eds.), *The Fourth Geneva Convention of 1949: A Commentary*, Oxford: Oxford University Press, pp. 1515–34.
Aronson, R. (2004) *Camus and Sartre: The Story of a Friendship and the Quarrel That Ended It*, Chicago: Chicago University Press.
Azoulay, M. (2018) 'With a Narrow Majority, the Knesset Approved the Law for the Death Penalty for Terrorists', in *YNET*, 3 January [in Hebrew].

Badian, E. (1968) *Roman Imperialism in the Late Republic* (2nd ed.), Ithaca: Cornell University Press.

Badian, E. (1958) Foreign *Clientelae: 264–70 B.C*, Oxford: Clarendon Press.

Bamberg, J. H. (1994) *The History of the British Petroleum Company: Vol. 2 – The Anglo-Iranian Years 1928–1954*, Cambridge: Cambridge University Press.

Baudendistel, R. (2006) *Between Bombs and Good Intentions: The International Committee of the Red Cross (ICRC) and the Italo-Ethiopian War, 1935–1936*, New York: Berghahn Books.

Beer, H. (1984) 'Jean Pictet and the National Societies', in Christophe Swinarski (ed.), *Studies and Essays on International Humanitarian Law and Red Cross Principles in Honour of Jean Pictet*, The Hague: Martinus Nijhoff, pp. 855–9.

Ben-Dror, E. (2015) *Ralph Bunche and the Arab-Israeli Conflict: Mediation and the UN 1947–1949*, New York: Routledge.

Ben-Nun, G. (2019) 'The Victor's Justice Dilemma: Public Imagery and Cultural Transfer from Nuremberg to The Hague', *POLEMOS*, Vol. 13 (1) (Spring), pp. 7–24.

Ben-Nun, G. (2017) 'Non-Refoulement as a Qualifier of Nation-State Sovereignty: The Case of Mass Population Flows', *Comparativ. Zeitschrift für Globalgeschichte und Vergleichende Gesellschaftsforschung*, Vol. 26 (3), pp. 111–14.

Ben-Nun, G. (2017) *Seeking Asylum in Israel: Refugees and the History of Migration Law*, London: I. B. Tauris.

Ben-Tov, A. (1990) *Das Rote Kreuz kam zu spät – Die Auseinandersetzung zwischen dem jüdischen Volk und dem internationalen Komitee vom Roten Kreuz im Zweiten Weltkrieg – Die Ereignisse in Ungarn*, Zurich: Amman Verlag. Geoffrey.

Bendersky, J. J. (1983) *Carl Schmitt: Theorist for the Reich*, Princeton: Princeton University Press.

Bendikatè, E. and Haupt, D. R. (eds.) (2015) *The Life, Times and Work of Jokūbas Robinzonas – Jacob Robinson*, Sankt Augustin: Academia Verlag.

Benvenisti, E. (2012) *The International Law of Occupation* (2nd ed.), Oxford: Oxford University Press.

Best, G. (1994) *War and Law since 1945*, Oxford: Oxford University Press.

Best, G. (1984) 'The Making of the 4th Geneva Conventions: The View from Whitehall', in Christophe Swinarski (ed.), *Studies and Essays on International Humanitarian Law and Red Cross Principles in Honour of Jean Pictet*, The Hague: Martinus Nijhoff Publishers, pp. 5–15.

Best, G. (1983) *Humanity in Warfare: Modern History of the International Law of Armed Conflicts*, London: Routledge.

Blasius, R. A. (1999) 'Die wahre Erfindung ist so wahr wie der Traum: Der schweizerische Diplomat Carl Jacob Burckhardt als historische Quelle / Die Kontroverse um die Forschungsergebnisse Paul Stauffers', *Frankfurter Allgemeine Zeitung*, 2 June.

Blau, U. (2017) 'Documents Reveal how Israel Made Amnesty's Local Branch a Front for the Foreign Ministry in the 70s', *Haaretz*, March 18.

Bothe, M. (2016) 'The Administration of Occupied Territory', in Andrew Clapham, Paola Gaeta and Marco Sassoli (eds.), *The 1949 Geneva Conventions: A Commentary*, Oxford: Oxford University Press, pp. 1455–84.

Boyd, S. M. (1971) 'The Applicability of International Law to the Occupied Territories', *Israel Yearbook on Human Rights*, Vol. 1, pp. 258–82.

Branche, R. (2017) 'The French Army and the Geneva Conventions during the Algerian War of Independence and After', Matthew Evangelista and Nina Tannenwald (eds.), *Do the Geneva Conventions Matter?* Oxford: Oxford University Press, 2017, pp. 161–74.

Branche, R. (2014) *Prisonniers du FLN*, Paris: Payot.

Browning, C. (1992) *Ordinary Men: Reserve Police Battalion 101 and the Final Solution in Poland*, New York: Harper Perennial.

Browning, C. (1983) 'Wehrmacht Reprisal Policy and the Mass Murder of Jews in Serbia', *Militärgeschichtliche Mitteilungen*, Vol. 33 (1), pp. 31–47.

Bugnion, F. (2012) 'Le Comité international de la Croix-Rouge et les Nations Unies de 1945 à nos jours: oppositions, complémentarités et partenariats', *Relations internationales*, Vol. 152 (4), pp. 3–16.

Burr, W. (2014) 'U.S. Intelligence and the Detection of the First Soviet Nuclear Test, September 1949', in George Washington University *National Security Archive*. Available at: nsarchive.gwu.edu/nukevault/ebb286/#4 (accessed 24 April 2017).

Camus, A. (1957) 'Réflexions sur la guillotine' dans Albert Camus and Arthur Kœstler, *Reflexions sur la peine Capitale*, Paris: Calmann-Levy. English edition and translation by Justin O'Brian (ed.), *Albert Camus: Resistance, Rebellion, and Death*, New York: The Modern Library, 1963, pp. 131–79.

Carr, E. H. (1939) *The Twenty Years' Crisis 1919–1939: An Introduction to the Study of International Relations*, London: Harper & Row.

Chang, I. (1997) *The Rape of Nanking: The Forgotten Holocaust of World War II*, New York: Basic Books.

Chatriot, A. (2014) 'Georges Cahen-Salvador, un réformateur social dans la haute administration française 1875–1963', *Revue d'histoire de la protection sociale*, Vol. 7 (1), pp. 103–28.

Chetail, V. (2016) 'Is there any Blood on My Hands? Deportation as a Crime of International Law', *Leiden Journal of International Law*, Vol. 29 (3), pp. 917–43.

Cohn, G. (1939a) 'La théorie de la responsabilité internationale' dans *Recueil des Cours de l'Académie de Droit International de la Haye*, Vol. 68 (1939), pp. 207–312 [*Collected Courses of The Hague Academy of International Law*].

Cohn, G. (1939b) *Neo-Neutrality*, New York: Colombia University Press.

Cohn, G. (1929) 'Kellogg-Vertrag und Völkerrecht', *Zeitschrift Für Völkerrecht*, Vol. 15 (Breslau).

Cohn-Roi, A. (2003) Courtyards of Copenhagen: Georg Cohn in Quest of War Prevention – Seven Generations in Denmark Jerusalem: Rubin Mass Publishers [in Hebrew: Hazerot Copenhagen: Georg Cohn Bemamaz Limnoa Milchama – Sheva Dorot Bedenemark]. (2003 – ד"תשס מס ראובן :ירושלים), בדנמרק דורות שבעה מלחמה למנוע במאמץ אמיליה כהן רואי. חצרות קופנהגן : גאורג כהן,

Cullen, A. (2010) *The Concept of Non-International Armed Conflict in International Humanitarian Law*, Cambridge: Cambridge University Press.

Dörmann, K. (2003) 'The Legal Situation of "Unlawful/Unprivileged Combatants"', *International Review of the Red Cross*, Vol. 85 (849) (March), pp. 45–74.

Draper, G. I. A. D. (1958) *The Red Cross Conventions*, London: Stevens & Sons.

Durand, A. (1984) *From Sarajevo to Hiroshima: History of the International Committee of the Red Cross*, Vol. 2, Geneva: ICRC & Henry Dunant Institute.

Duranti, M. (2017) *The Conservative Human Rights Revolution: European Identity, Transnational Politics, and the Origins of the European Convention*, Oxford: Oxford University Press.

Elkins, C. (2005) *Imperial Reckoning: The Untold Story of Britain's Gulag in Kenya*, New York: Henry Holt Publishers.

Evangelista, M. and Tannenwald, N. (eds.) (2017) *Do the Geneva Conventions Matter?* Oxford: Oxford University Press.

Favez, J. C. (1988) *Une Mission Impossible? Le CICR, les deportations et les camps de concentration nazis*, Lausanne: Editions Payot. English translation: *The Red Cross and the Holocaust*, Cambridge: Cambridge University Press.

Ferencz, B. B. (2016) 'A Nuremberg Legacy: The Crime of Aggression', *Washington University Global studies Law Review*, Vol. 15 (4), pp. 555–60.

Fisk, R. (2006) *The Great War for Civilization: The Conquest of the Middle East*, New York: Harper Perennial.

Forsythe, D. (2005) *The Humanitarians: The International Committee of the Red Cross*, Cambridge: Cambridge University Press.

Fraenkel, E. (1944) *Military Occupation and the Rule of Law: Occupation Government in the Rhineland 1918–1923*, Oxford: Oxford University Press.

Frank, M. (2008) *Expelling the Germans: British Opinion and Post-1945 Population Transfer in Context*, Oxford: Oxford University Press.

Friedman, D. (2002) 'In Memoria- Chaim Cohn', *Hamishpat* ['The Trial' – Hebrew], Vol. 14 (July), pp. 4–8.

Gaeta, P. (2016) 'Grave Breaches of the Geneva Conventions', in Andrew Clapham, Paola Gaeta and Marco Sassoli (eds.), *The Geneva Convention of 1949: A Commentary*, Oxford: Oxford University Press, pp. 615–46.

Gazit, S. (1999) *Trapped*, Tel-Aviv: Zmora Bitan Publishers [in Hebrew].
שלמה גזית, פתאים במלכודת, תל אביב: זמורה ביתן 1999

Gerolymatos, A. (2016) *The International Civil War: Greece, 1943–1949*, New Haven: Yale University Press.

Gillers, S. (2008) 'The Torture Memo: How Could Two Really Smart Government Lawyers Authorize Torture in Arguments That Have No Foundation in Law?' *The Nation*, 9 April.

Goldberger, L. (ed.) (1987) *The Rescue of the Danish Jews: Moral Courage under Stress*, New York: New York University Press.

Gorali, M. (2003) 'Legality Is in the Eye of the Beholder: The International Community Believes the Settlements Violate the Fourth Geneva Convention and May Even Be a War Crime Under the Terms of the International Criminal Court. Israel Disagrees', *Haaretz*, 25 September.

Gorenberg, G. (2007) *The Accidental Empire: Israel and the Birth of the Settlements 1967–1977*, New York: Henry Holt Publishers.

Gorenberg, G. (2006) 'Israel's Tragedy Foretold', *The New York Times*, 10 March.

Greayer, A. and Sjöstrand, S. (2000) *The White Buses: The Swedish Red Cross rescue action in Germany during the Second World War*, Publication of the Swedish Red Cross, Stockholm 2000, p. 8. Also published in David Cesarani and Paul A. Levine (eds.), *Bystanders to the Holocaust: A Re-evaluation*, London: Frank Cass, pp. 237–68.

Grey, Viscount Edward (1919) *The League of Nations*, Oxford: Oxford University Press.

Hartman, J. F. (1981) 'Derogations from Human Rights Treaties in Public Emergencies', *Harvard International Law Journal*, Vol. 22 (1), pp. 1–52.

Hassan, S. D. (2008) 'Never-Ending Occupations', *The New Centennial Review*, Vol. 8 (1), pp. 1–17.

Hathaway, O. and Shapiro, S. (2017) *The Internationalists: How a Radical Plan to Outlaw War Remade the World*, New York: Simon and Schuster.

Hathaway, O. A. (2002) 'Do Human Rights Treaties Make a Difference?' *Yale Law Journal*, Vol. 111, pp. 1935–2042.

Herbert, U. (1996) *Best. Biographische Studien über Radikalismus, Weltanschauung und Vernunft. 1903–1989* (3rd ed.), Bonn: J. H. Dietz Verlag.

Hershey, A. (1926) 'Judicial Settlement and the Permanent Court of International Justice', *Indiana Law Journal*, Vol. 1 (2), Article 2.

Hershey, A. S. (1911) 'The Succession of States', *The American Journal of International Law*, Vol. 5 (2), pp. 285–97.

Hirschfeld-Davis, J. (2016) 'Saying 'We all are Jews' Obama Honours American's Life-Saving Efforts during the Holocaust', *The New York Times*, 27 January.

Hitchcock, W. (2012) 'Human Rights and the Laws of War: The Geneva Conventions of 1949', in Akira Iriye, Petra Goedde and William Hitchcock (eds.), *The Human Rights Revolution: An International History*, Oxford: Oxford University Press, 93–112.

Hofnung, M. (1991) *Israel- Security Needs vs. The Rule of Law*, Jerusalem: Nevo Legal Publishers. מנחם הופנונג, ישראל- בטחון המדינה מול שלטון החוק: 1948-1991, ירושלים: נבו הוצאה לאור 1991

Horne, H. (2006) *A Savage War of Peace: Algeria 1954–1962* (3rd ed.), New York: New York Review of Books Classics.

Housden, M. (2012) *The League of Nations and the Organization of Peace*, Abingdon: Routledge.

Huber, M. (1898) *Die Staatensuccession: Volkerrechtliche und Staatsrechtliche Praxis Im XIX Jahrhundert*, Leipzig.

Ilan, A. (1989) *Bernadotte in Palestine, 1948: A Study in Contemporary Humanitarian Knight-Errantry*, London: Macmillan & St. Antony's College Oxford.

Jessup, P. (1939) 'Harvard Research in International Law – Draft Convention on the Rights and Duties of States in case of Aggression', *American Journal of International Law*, Vol. 33 (Special Supplement).

Jo, H. (2015) *Compliant Rebels: Rebel Groups and International Law in World Politics*, Cambridge: Cambridge University Press.

Junod, D. D. (1997) *La Croix-Rouge en péril, 1945–1952: La stratégie du CICRde la Seconde Guerre mondiale au conflit de Palestine – Eretz-Israël*, Lausanne: Payot. English translation: The Imperilled Red Cross and the Palestine-Eretz Yisrael Conflict 1945–1952, London: Paul Kegan and The Geneva Graduate Institute for International Studies, 2001.

Kearney, M. G. (2017) 'On the Situation in Palestine and the War Crime of Transfer of Civilians into Occupied Territory', *Criminal Law Forum*, Vol. 28, pp. 1–34.

Kelsen, H. (1945) 'The Legal Status of Germany according to the Declaration of Berlin', *American Journal of International Law*, Vol. 39 (3), pp. 518–26.

Kelsen, H. (1944) 'The International Legal Status of Germany to Be Established Immediately upon Termination of the War', *American Journal of International Law*, Vol. 38 (4), pp. 689–94.

Klabbers, J. (2003) 'International Legal Histories: The Declining Importance of Travaux Préparatoires in Treaty Interpretation?' *Netherlands International Law Review*, Vol. 50 (3), pp. 267–88.

Klarsfeld, S. (2001) *La Shoah en France. Volume 3, Le calendrier de la persécution des Juifs de France. Tome 3, septembre 1942-août 1944*, Paris: Fayard.

Klose, F. (2013) *Human Rights in the Shadow of Colonial Violence: The Wars of Independence in Kenya and Algeria*, Philadelphia: University of Pennsylvania Press.

Klose, F. (2011) 'The Colonial Testing Ground. The ICRC and the Violent End of Empire', *Humanity*, Vol. 2 (1) (Spring), pp. 107–26.

Konskenniemi, M. (2016) 'Carl Schmitt and International Law', in Jens Meierhenrich and Oliver Simons (eds.), *The Oxford Handbook of Carl Schmitt*, Oxford: Oxford University Press, 592–611.

Korman, S. (1996) *The Right of Conquest: The Acquisition of Territory by Force in International Law and Practice*, Oxford: Oxford University Press.

Kramer, M. (2017) 'Russia, Chechnya, and the Geneva Conventions, 1994–2006: Norms and the Problem of Internalization', in Matthew Evangelista and Nina Tannenwald (eds.), *Do the Geneva Conventions Matter?* Oxford: Oxford University Press, pp. 161–74.

Langer, R. (1947) *Seizure of Territory: The Stimson Doctrine and Related principles in Legal Theory and Diplomatic Practice*, Princeton: Princeton University Press.

Lauterpacht, H. (ed.) (1955) *Oppenheim's International Law*, Vol. I *Peace* (8th ed.), Vol. II *Disputes War and Neutrality* (7th ed.), London: Longman Green & Co.

Lauterpacht, H. (1933) *The Function of Law in the International Community*, Oxford: Oxford University Press.

Lema, L. (2005) 'Torture en Algérie: le rapport qui allait tout changer', *Le Temps*, 19 Aôut

Levene, M. (2013) *The Crisis of Genocide: Vol 2: Annihilation – The European Rimlands 1939-1953*, Oxford: Oxford University Press.

Lewis, M. (2014) *The Birth of the New Justice: The Internationalization of Crime and Punishment, 1919-1950*, Oxford: Oxford University Press.

Lidegaard, B. (2013) *Countrymen: The Untold Story of How Denmark's Jews Escaped the Nazis, of the Courage of Their Fellow Danes--and of the Extraordinary Role of the SS*, New York: Alfred Knopf.

Logevall, F. (2014) *Embers of War: The Fall of an Empire and the Making of America's Vietnam*, New York: Random House.

Malone, L. A. (1985) 'The Kahan Report, Ariel Sharon and the Sabra-Shatilla Massacres in Lebanon: Responsibility Under International Law for Massacres of Civilian Populations', *Utah Law Review*, Vol. 373 (2), pp. 373–433.

Malye, F. and Stora, B. (2010) *François Mitterrand et la guerre d'Algérie*, Paris: Calmann-Lévy.

Manela, E. (2007) *The Wilsonian Moment: Self-Determination and the International Origins of Anticolonial Nationalism*, Oxford: Oxford University Press.

Mantilla, G. (2018) 'Forum Isolation: Social Opprobrium and the Origins of the International Law of Internal Conflict', *International Organization*, Vol. 72 (2), pp. 317–49.

Mantilla, G. (2017a) 'Conforming Instrumentalists: Why the United States and the United Kingdom Joined the 1949 Geneva Conventions', *European Journal of International Law*, Vol. 28 (2), pp. 483–511.

Mantilla, G. (2017b) 'The Origins and Evolution of the 1949 Geneva Conventions and the 1977 Additional Protocols', in Matthew Evangelista and Nina Tannenwald (eds.), *Do the Geneva Conventions Matter?* Oxford: Oxford University Press, pp. 35–68.

Mazower, M. (2006) *Hitler's Empire*, New York: Allen Lane.

McBride, S. (1984) 'The Legality of Weapons for Societal Destruction', in Christophe Swinarski (ed.), *Studies and Essays on International Humanitarian Law and Red Cross Principles in Honour of Jean Pictet*, The Hague: Martinus Nijhoff Publishers, pp. 401–9.

Mégret, F. (2016) 'The Universality of the Geneva Conventions', in Andrew Clapham, Paola Gaeta and Marco Sassoli (eds.), *The 1949 Geneva Conventions: A Commentary*, Oxford: Oxford University Press, pp. 669–88.

Meron, T. (2017) 'The West Bank and International Law on the Eve of the Fiftieth Anniversary of the Six-Day War', *American Journal of International Law*, Vol. 111 (2) (April), pp. 357–75.

Meron, T. (2014) 'Customary International Law Today: From the Academy to the Courtroom', in Andrew Clapham and Paula Gaeta (eds.), *The Oxford Handbook of International Law in Armed Conflict*, Oxford: Oxford University Press, pp. 37–49.

Mevorah, B. (1985) 'Proffessor Nissim Mevorah's Bulgarian-Jewish Way of Life', *East-European Quarterly*, Vol. 19 (1), pp. 75–80.

Meyer, M. A. and McCoubrey, H. (1998) *Reflections on Law and Armed Conflicts: The Selected Works on the Laws of War by the late Professor Colonel G.I.A.D. Draper OBE*, The Hague: Kluwer Law.

Meyssonnier, F. (2002) *Paroles de bourreau: Témoignage unique d'un Exécuteur des Arrêts criminels*, Paris: Imago.

Mortenson, J. D. (2013) 'The Travaux of Travaux: Is the Vienna Convention Hostile to Drafting History?' *American Journal of International Law*, Vol. 107 (4), pp. 780–822.

Munch, P. (1967) *Erindringer: 1870-1947*, Copenhagen: Nyt Nordisk Forlag.

Nachmani, A. (1990) 'Civil War and Foreign Intervention in Greece: 1946–49', *Journal of Contemporary History*, Vol. 25 (4), pp. 489–522.

Nahlik, S. (1984) 'Le Problème des Sanctions en Droit International Humanitaire', in Christophe Swinarski (ed.), *Studies and Essays on International Humanitarian Law and Red Cross Principles in Honour of Jean Pictet*, The Hague: Martinus Nijhoff, pp. 469–81.

Nye, J. S. (1990) 'Soft Power', *Foreign Policy*, Vol. 80, pp. 153–71.

Olechowski, T. (2013) 'Kelsens Debellatio-These. Rechtshistorische und rechtstheoretische Überlegungen zur Kontinuität von Staaten', in Clemens Jabloner (ed.), *Gedenkschrift Robert Walter*, Wien: Manz Verlag, pp. 531–52.

Pedersen, S. (2015) *The Guardians: The League of Nations and the Crisis of Empire*, Oxford: Oxford University Press.

Penkower, M. N. (1979) 'The World Jewish Congress Confronts the International Red Cross during the Holocaust', *Jewish Social Studies*, Vol. 41 (3/4) (Summer–Autumn), pp. 229–56.

Perrson, S. (2000) 'Folke Bernadotte and the White Buses', *Journal of Holocaust Education*, Vol. 9 (2–3), pp. 237–68.

Peslyak, A. (2009) 'Building a Nuclear Deterrent for the Sake of Peace: On the 60th Anniversary of the First Soviet Atomic Test', *Russian International News Agency (RIA Novosti)*, 31 August. Available at: web.archive.org/web/20120310141609/http://en.rian.ru/analysis/20090831/155977682.html (accessed 24 April 2017).

Pictet, J. (1985) 'La formation du droit international humanitaire', *Revue International de la Croix Rouge*, Vol. 751 (January–February), pp. 2–23.

Pictet, J. (1958) *Commentary on the Geneva Convention Relative to the Protection of Civilian Persons in Time of War 12 August 1949*, Vol. IV Geneva: ICRC.

Posner, E. (2014) 'The Case against Human Rights', *The Guardian*, 4 December.

Posner, E. (2014) *The Twilight of Human Rights Law*, Oxford: Oxford University Press.

Pradelle, Paul de la (1951) *La Conférence diplomatique et les nouvelles conventions de Genéve du 12 août 1949*, Paris: Editions Internationals.

Rasch, W. (2008) 'Anger Management: Carl Schmitt in 1925 and the Occupation of the Rhineland', *The new Centennial Review*, Vol. 8 (1), pp. 57–79.

Rey-Schyrr, C. (2007) *De Yalta à Dien Bien Phu: Histoire du Comité International de la Croix Rouge 1945-1955*, Genève: CICR 2007. Translated into English as: *From Yalta to Dien Bien Phu: History of the International Committee of the Red Cross 1945-1955*, Geneva: ICRC.

Riebsamen, H. (2012) 'Saul Friedländer: Einer der großen Gelehrten', *Frankfurter Allgemeine Zeitung*, 2 Dezember.

Riegner, G. (2006) *Never Despair: Sixty Years in the Service of the Jewish People and of Human Rights*, Chicago: Ivan Dee Publishers & The US Holocaust Memorial.

Robinson, D. (1970) 'The Treaty of Tlatelolco and the United States: A Latin American Nuclear Free Zone', *American Journal of International Law*, Vol. 64 (2), pp. 282–309.

Robinson, J. (1958) 'The Metamorphosis of the United Nations', in *Collected Courses of The Hague Academy of International Law* ('Extract of the Recueil des Cours'), Vol. 94, Leiden: A.W. Sijthoff, pp. 493–592.

Rodinson, M. (1973) *Israel: A Colonial-Settler State?* New York: Pathfinder Press.

Rubin, G. (2012) 'The End of Minority Rights: Jacob Robinson and the Jewish Question in World War II', in *Simon Dubnow Institute Yearbook 2012*, Göttingen: Vandenhoeck & Ruprecht Verlage, pp. 55–72.

Sands, P. (2016) *East West Street: On the Origins of Genocide and Crimes against Humanity*, New York: Weidenfeld and Nicolson.

Sands, P. (2008) *Torture Team: Rumsfeld's Memo and the Betrayal of American Values*, New York: Palgrave Macmillan.

Schechtman, J. B. (1946) *European Population Transfers: 1939–1945*, New York: Oxford University Press.

Schindler, D. (2007) 'Max Huber', *European Journal of International Law*, Vol. 18 (1), pp. 81–95.

Schmitt, C. (2006) *The Nomos of the Earth in the International Law of the Jus Publicum Europaeum*, New York: Telos Press (originally published in 1950).

Schmoeckel, M. (1994) *Die Großraumtheorie: Ein Beitrag zur Geschichte der Volkerrechtswissenschaft im Dritten Reich, insbesondere der Kriegszeit*, Berlin: Duncker & Humblot, 1994.

Schuessler, J. (2014) 'Book Portrays Eichmann as Evil, But Not Banal', *The New York Times*, Book Section 2 September.

Schwarzenberger, G. (1968) *International Law as Applied by International Courts and Tribunals Vol. 2*, London: Stevens & Sons.

Segev, T. (2007) *1967: Israel, the War, and the Year that Transformed the Middle East*, New York: Macmillan & Henry Holt Books.

Servan-Schreiber, J. J. (1957) *Lieutenant en Algérie*, Paris: Julliard.

Sfard, M. (2017) *The Wall and the Gate: Israel, Palestine, and the Legal Battle for Human Rights*, New York: Macmillan & Henry Holt Publishers.

Shepherd, B. (2016) *Hitler's Soldiers: The German Army in the Third Reich*, New Haven, CT: Yale University Press.

Sibert, M. (1951) *Traité de Droit International Public: La Droit de la Paix*, Paris: Éditions Dalloz, 1951.

Simons, O. (2016) 'Carl Schmitt's Spatial Rhetoric', in Jens Meierhenrich and Oliver Simons (eds.), *The Oxford Handbook of Carl Schmitt*, Oxford: Oxford University Press, pp. 776–802.

Skordos, A. T. (2020) *Interdependenzen regionaler und globaler Prozesse: Die Prägung des modernen Völkerrechts durch die Konfliktgeschichte Südosteuropas*, Wien & Köln: Böhlau Verlag.

Snyder, T. (2010) *Blood Lands: Europe Between Hitler and Stalin*, London: Penguin.

Stangneth, B. (2014) *Eichmann before Jerusalem: The Unexamined Life of a Mass Murderer*, New York: Alfred Knopf.

Steinacher, G. (2017) *Humanitarians at War: The Red Cross in the Shadow of the Holocaust*, Oxford: Oxford University Press.

Steinacher, G. (2013) *Hakenkreuz und Rotes Kreuz: Eine humanitäre Organisation zwischen Holocaust und Flüchtlingsproblematik*, Innsbruck: Studien Verlag.

Steinacher, G. (2011) *Nazis on the Run: How Hitler's Henchmen Fled Justice*, Oxford: Oxford University Press.

Suny, R. G. (2006) *The Cambridge History of Russia Vol. III - the 20th Century*, Cambridge: Cambridge University Press.

Tomuschat, C. (2016) 'Prohibition on Settlements', in Andrew Clapham, Paola Gaeta and Marco Sassoli (eds.), *The 1949 Geneva Conventions: A Commentary*, Oxford: Oxford University Press, pp. 1551–74.

Troebst, S. (2017) 'Macedonian Historiography on the Holocaust in Macedonia under Bulgarian Occupation', in Stefan Troebst (ed.), *Zwischen Arktis, Adria und Armenien: Das östliche Europa und seine Ränder Aufsätze, Essays und Vorträge 1983-2016*, Köln & Wien: Böhlau Verlag, pp. 407–13.

Tuchman, B. (1985) *The Zimmermann Telegram: America Enters the War 1917–1918*, London: Penguin.

Ulmen, G. L. (2006) Translator's introduction to Carl Schmitt, *The Nomos of the Earth in the International Law of the Jus Publicum Europaeum*, New York: Telos Press.

van Dijk, B. (2018) 'Human Rights in War: On the Entangled Foundations of the 1949 Geneva Conventions', *American Journal of International Law*, Vol. 112 (4), pp. 553–82.

Verancini, L. (2006) *Israel and Settler Society*, London: Pluto press.

Vichniac, I. (1988) *Croix-Rouge, les stratèges de la bonne conscience: Enquete*, Paris: Alain Moreau.

Voigt, R. (ed.) (2008) *Großraum-Denken Carl Schmitts Kategorie der Großraum-ordnung*, Stuttgart: Steiner Verlag.

Wehberg, H. (1951) 'L'interdiction du recours à la force: le principe et les problèmes qui se posent' in *Collected Courses of The Hague Academy of International Law ('Recueil des Cours')*, The Hague Academy of International Law, Vol. 78 (1), pp. 6–120.

Wehberg, H. (1931) *The Outlawry of War*, Washington, DC: Carnegie Endowment for International Peace.

Weill, S. (2007) 'The Judicial Arm of the Occupation: The Israeli Military Courts in the Occupied Territories', *International Review of the Red Cross*, Vol. 89 (866), pp. 395–419.

Wells, H. G. (1919) *The Idea of a League of Nations*, Boston: The Atlantic Monthly Press.

Wells, H. G. (1914) *The War that Will End War*, London: Palmer.

Yahil, L. (1966) *Test of Democracy, The Rescue of Danish Jewry in World War II*, Jerusalem: The Magness Press of the Hebrew University [in Hebrew].

Zimuki, T. (2017) 'Attorney General Mandelblit Is Opposed to the Proposed Legislation Allowing for the Imposition of the Death Penalty for Terrorists', *YNET*, 19 December [in Hebrew].

INDEX